HORIZONS IN COMPUTER SCIENCE RESEARCH

VOLUME 9

HORIZONS IN COMPUTER SCIENCE

Additional books in this series can be found on Nova's website under the Series tab.

Additional e-books in this series can be found on Nova's website under the e-book tab.

HORIZONS IN COMPUTER SCIENCE

HORIZONS IN COMPUTER SCIENCE RESEARCH

VOLUME 9

THOMAS S. CLARY
EDITOR

nova publishers
New York

For permission to use material from this book please contact us:
Telephone 631-231-7269; Fax 631-231-8175
Web Site: http://www.novapublishers.com

LIBRARY OF CONGRESS CATALOGING-IN-PUBLICATION DATA

ISBN 978-1-63321-522-1

ISSN: 2159-2012

Published by Nova Science Publishers, Inc. † New York

CONTENTS

Preface **vii**

Chapter 1 Coverage and Intrusion Detection in Wireless Sensor Networks **1**
Yanping Zhang, Yun Wang, Zhifeng Xiao, Jing Liu and Patrick Mosca

Chapter 2 Computer Networks, the Internet and Green IT: Effectively Managing Computer Network Resources **11**
Chetan Kumar

Chapter 3 Security in Wireless Sensor Networks: State-of-the-art, Challenges and Opportunities **19**
Zhifeng Xiao, Yun Wang and Yanping Zhang

Chapter 4 Performance of a Tree Routing Topology for Wireless Sensor Networks Using Different Platforms **45**
S. Aparicio, J. Ranz, M. Molero, M. G. Hernández and J. J. Anaya

Chapter 5 Location Estimation in Modern Mobile Computing Environments **73**
Mohamed Maher Atia

Chapter 6 Towards a Gender-Focused Programming Performance Model
Wilfred W. F. Lau and Allan H. K. Yuen **141**

Chapter 7 A Methodologies and Processes Language for the Software Industry
Sandro J. Bolaños, Rubén A. González, Carlos A. Arismendi and Edwin J. Castañeda **153**

Chapter 8 Design of Luria Memory Test for Older Adults on Mobile Devices **183**
Amilcar Meneses Viveros, Erika Hernández Rubio and J. A. Hijar Miranda

Chapter 9	Synchronizing Nods of a Computer-Generated Character and a Speaker Using Thermal Image Processing *Yasunari Yoshitomi, Ryota Kato, Taro Asada and Masayoshi Tabuse*	**199**
Chapter 10	Evaluation of Effective Parameters of Energy Consumption in Wireless Sensor Networks *Ali Norouzi, Ahmet Sertbas and A. Halim Zaim*	**225**
Chapter 11	Computer Aided-Thermal Module Design *Jung-Chang Wang*	**251**
Chapter 12	hFAT: A High Performance Hybrid FAT32 File System *Wasim Ahmad Bhat and S. M. K. Quadri*	**285**
Index		**301**

PREFACE

This book presents original results on the leading edge of computer science research. Each article has been carefully selected in an attempt to present substantial research results across a broad spectrum. Topics discussed include coverage and intrusion detection in wireless sensor networks; computer networks, the internet, and green IT; security in wireless sensor networks; performance of a tree routing topology for wireless sensor networks using different platforms; location estimation in modern mobile computing environments; towards a gender-focused programming performance model; methodologies and processes language for the software industry; design of Luria memory test for older adults on mobile devices; synchronizing nods of a computer-generated character and a speaker using thermal image processing; evaluation of effective parameters of energy consumption in wireless sensor networks; computer aided-thermal module design; and a high performance hybrid FAT32 file system.

A Wireless Sensor Networks (WSN) has been a premier research topic due to the rapid decreasing of sensor equipment costs and the increasing number of WSN applications in both civil and military fields in the past decades. For example, forest fires take millions of acres around the world every year and a WSN can be deployed to provide surveillance service for fire detection. In a WSN application, an intuitive question is that how well the field of interest is monitored by the deployed sensors and what is the possibility that an event such as a fire happened at a specific location can be detected by the WSN. Chapter 1 answers the question by introducing two fundamental performance issues including sensing coverage and intrusion detection and surveys the problem definitions, assumptions, contributions, and primary conclusions in the state-of-the-art literature. Next, the network lifetime as a crucial performance issue in a WSN is explored under the constraints of fulfilling application-specified sensing coverage and intrusion detection requirements, and a review of sleep-scheduling algorithms in which redundant sensors are configured in sleep mode for energy conservation is provided. Then, the authors discuss the benefits of introducing a few mobile sensors (i.e., actuators) that can move around the field of interest to help improving sensing coverage, connectivity, intrusion detection capability, and lifetime enhancement. Then another question comes: how to efficiently schedule robots patrol? To address this research issues, biological inspired ideas have been introduced, which has become a hot topic in wireless sensor network. In this chapter, the authors also study bio-inspired strategies in WSNs.

Computer networks have come a long way since their introduction in the 1960s. The Internet is the largest computer network in history and it continues to grow rapidly. There has been a tremendous growth in the amount and range of information available on the Internet. At the same time, there is huge potential for improving the performance of the Internet. In Chapter 2 the authors review some studies that propose mechanisms to effectively allocate resources in multi-server computer networks. The popularity of the Internet has also resulted in a significant impact on energy consumption. The Environmental Protection Agency (EPA) and other agencies have suggested useful measures to improve efficiency of vast data centers that power the Internet. This, and other environmentally sustainable computing practices, may collectively be described as green Information Technology (IT). Computer networks have a significant energy resource impact in the form Internet usage and its data centers. Therefore managing computer networks effectively is key to greening IT. In this article the authors review different methods for managing computer networks and green IT strategies. Adopting these computer network management and green IT practices is likely to benefit all Internet players as well as the environment.

Recent advances have witnessed the popularity and success of Wireless Sensor Networks (WSNs) in the past decade. The increase of the public presence and cyber footprint of WSNs opens up avenues for compromise to hackers and individuals with malicious intent. Securing WSNs becomes one of the highest priorities for the deployment of real world sensing applications. Chapter 3 presents the state-of-the-art security studies in WSNs. The authors identify four security objectives including confidentiality, integrity, availability, and privacy, and survey how each of them can be exploited in the sensor network environment. Our main goal is to deliver a systematic study on the WSN security issues by summarizing the existing attacks and countermeasures, comparing their features, and proposing a taxonomy of attacks using an attack-defense-tree-based approach. Based on the investigation results and their analysis, the authors identify the current research challenges and opportunities towards building a securer sensor network environment.

A performance evaluation of the Collection Tree Protocol (CTP) topology of wireless sensor networks (WSNs) using different platforms is presented in Chapter 4. Three different WSNs composed of Cricket, Mica2 and Iris motes, respectively, were tested at the historical building "Leonardo Torres Quevedo". This deployment is representative of a typical building interior with numerous walls and no direct line of sight between the WSN elements. Cricket and Mica2 platforms have the same microcontroller (ATMega128L) and radio chip (Chipcon CC1000) but using different frequencies, 433 MHz and 900 MHz, respectively. Iris motes utilize the Atmega1281 microcontroller and the Atmel RF230 radio transceiver with a frequency of 2.4 GHz. A methodology to evaluate which platform using the CTP protocol is more appropriate for this particular scenario has been used. This methodology is mainly based on the analysis of two parameters, the percentage of received messages and the lifetime of the wireless sensor network. To analyze in more detail which platform gave the best performance, other communication parameters were measured, such as the number of hops required for every message to reach the base station and the father identifier for each message.

Chapter 5 includes the findings and results of dedicated research and development in the area of location determination in mobile computing environments using wireless infrastructures and other aiding sensors such as inertial sensors and dead reckoning. The theoretical formulation of the location determination problem is explained followed by a background and state of the art in location technology and current limitations and challenges. Different wireless localization technologies are analyzed theatrically using Cramer-Rao Lower Bound (CRLB) Variance analysis and practically using real experiments. The problem of wireless propagation modeling and radio maps construction and maintenance are addressed using wide range of deterministic and probabilistic estimation approaches. The theoretical justification is verified by extensive experimental demonstration. Integration of the wireless infrastructures with onboard sensors associated with current modern mobile devices are studied using Kalman Filtering (KF) and Particle Filtering (PF) supported by a comparison between these two common filtering techniques. The chapter concludes with a section about future trends and new research tracks that are expected to shape the localization and tracking landscape of the next few decades.

In the science, technology, engineering, and mathematics (STEM) fields, gender imbalance has been commonplace. There are models that examined gender differences in programming performance and yet rarely have these models included the variables learning styles and programming environment as mediators between gender and programming performance. Drawing on the pertinent literature about gender, learning styles, programming environment, and programming performance, Chapter 6 argues the importance of gender, learning styles, and programming environment in modelling programming performance. It further proposes and discusses a gender-focused performance model based on the three variables. The authors encourage further research effort to test this parsimonious model empirically in an authentic learning context.

Chapter 7 presents a Software Methodology-and-Process Modeling Language, also referred to as −SMPML−. A brief description of the vocabulary is provided, followed by a set of perspectives that are applied directly to a case study. Some of the most relevant results, obtained from an actual project, are discussed and analyzed. The modeling language presented in this document is suggested to be used as a wrap for the modeling and computational languages that are utilized within the current software industry.

This language appears as a powerful alternative proposal even for parallel-process modelling such as that involving BPMN (for industrial processes) or SPEM (for software processes).

Due to increasing life expectancy of the population, it is necessary to have tools that help provide various services to the elderly. In Chapter 8 is explained that some of these tools are related to health services. In particular, in the area of mental health, specialists use various memory tests, such as Luria, to assess the degree of mental impairment or to prevent it. The use of mobile technology could be of great help to both the specialists and the elderly in the application of Luria tests. However, such solutions involve many details in the implementation for the system to be usable and functional, because older adults may have visual, hearing or motor impairments, among others. Furthermore, the application of some tests requires contextual plasticity, because the memory depends on the user experience, so that the elements of the tests should be tailored to each user use.

In Chapter 9, the authors introduce their system for communication between a speaker and a computer-generated (CG) character for making the speaker feel more comfortable. Nonverbal communication, such as a facial expression, a nod, and a hand gesture is very important for reciprocal communication between humans. The authors used an image registered by infrared rays, which displays the thermal distribution of the face and neck, for communication between a speaker and a CG character.

In their system, the CG character can synchronize its nodding with the speaker's nodding by predicting the speaker's nod angle. The CG character starts predicting the angle just after the human begins to speak and nod, and the CG character stops nodding while maintaining a front-view face when the human maintains a front-view face and is silent. The CG character starts predicting the angle again when the human begins to speak again.

The measured feature parameter is the input to a fuzzy algorithm system to obtain the nod angle of the speaker in front of an infrared ray camera, and then a moving-average model is used to predict the nod angle of the speaker. The average error of the nod angle obtained by their system was estimated as approximately 5 degrees. In addition, the CG character nods its head, not only when a human nods his or her head, but also when a human shakes his or her head left or right.

The development of wireless sensor networks (WSNs) has never been free of challenges and many researchers have been interested in overcoming these challenges. The energy consumption, longevity, and performance of the networks are among the main challenges and have drawn a great deal of attention from researchers. Delving deeper into the issues the authors encounter more detailed parameters that are the cause of these challenges. To put it another way, there are trivial but at the same time effective parameters whose improvement can enhance the network and overcome the challenges. Chapter 10 tries to introduce and survey all the parameters from a technical viewpoint and presents a general report on the previous works. In addition, advantages and weaknesses of the factors and approaches to improving WSNs are discussed. The study proposes a classification of the parameters and processes that affect different layers of the networks. Furthermore, a comparison of the common methods and further recommendations are represented. Each comparison is concluded by a proposal of the best method to deal with the challenges and improve the networks.

The aims of Chapter 11 is to depict how a thermal module comprised with high heat transfer efficiency device design effectively to reduce the temperature of Personal Computer (PC), Note Book (NB), and Server including central processing unit (CPU) and graphic processing unit (GPU), and LED lighting lamp of smaller area and higher heat flux utilizing related computer-aided design tools. The research approach focuses on various thermal modules. For traditional cooling techniques, the extended surface, such as fin is usually added to increase the rate of heat removal. Significant advances in the design theory of heat sinks have been made over the past some decades. The heat capacity from heat source conducted and transferred through heat sink to the surroundings by convection. Thus, the point of adding fin is to help dissipate heat flow from heat source. The extended heat transfer fins are made from several materials including metals, plastics or special substance. The proper CAD/CAE tools employed in thermal modules are important. The computer-aided thermal design of heat sink with high heat transfer device such heat pipe and vapor chamber developed a composite approach ensuring the thermal conditions to provide a high-quality development. There are several theoretical models of thermal modules developed to predict their thermal performance respectively with Software and algorithms in the computer-aided design system. The programs and methods for computer-aided thermal module design are being introduced in the chapter. The developed complex provides for high quality and short time of development owing to the lesser number of iterations of the design procedures. Based on the theoretical models with empirical formula, the author had developed a computer program coded by Virtual Basic version 6.0 to develop window programs and convenience for industrials.

Magnetic disk drives are mechanical at heart and hence have performance limitations. However, a hybrid storage system that combines the advantages of the inexpensive random seek of solid state storage device with the inexpensive sequential access of the magnetic disk drive, can significantly improve the performance of a file system in a variety of situations. In Chapter 12, based on this idea, the authors propose a *high-performance hybrid FAT file system*, namely hFAT, which stores the most frequently accessed metadata of files in a FAT file system on a flash drive while as actual contents on the magnetic drive in order to eliminate the head positioning latency incurred by file system operations in FAT file systems. The empirical evaluation of hFAT using Sprite LFS small-file benchmark indicates that hFAT file system can reduce the latency incurred by FAT32 file system operations by a minimum of 25%, 10% and 90% during writing, reading and deleting a large number of small files respectively, if a solid state storage device having latency lesser or equal to 10% of that of magnetic disk is used in addition.

In: Horizons in Computer Science Research. Volume 9 ISBN: 978-1-63321-522-1
Editor: Thomas S. Clary

Chapter 1

COVERAGE AND INTRUSION DETECTION IN WIRELESS SENSOR NETWORKS

Yanping Zhang[1,*], Yun Wang[2,†], Zhifeng Xiao[3,‡], Jing Liu[4,§] and Patrick Mosca[1,‖]

[1]Department of Computer Science, Gonzaga University, Spokane, WA, US
[2]Department of Computer Science and Information Systems, Bradley University, Peoria, IL, US
[3]Department of Computer Science & Software Engineering, Penn State Erie, The Behrend College, Erie, PA, US
[4]Software Engineer at CipherCloud, San Francisco Bay Area, CA, US

Abstract

A Wireless Sensor Networks (WSN) has been a premier research topic due to the rapid decreasing of sensor equipment costs and the increasing number of WSN applications in both civil and military fields in the past decades. For example, forest fires take millions of acres around the world every year and a WSN can be deployed to provide surveillance service for fire detection. In a WSN application, an intuitive question is that how well the field of interest is monitored by the deployed sensors and what is the possibility that an event such as a fire happened at a specific location can be detected by the WSN. This chapter answers the question by introducing two fundamental performance issues including sensing coverage and intrusion detection and surveys the problem definitions, assumptions, contributions, and primary conclusions in the state-of-the-art literature. Next, the network lifetime as a crucial performance issue in a WSN is explored under the constraints of fulfilling application-specified sensing coverage and intrusion detection requirements, and a review of sleep-scheduling algorithms in which redundant sensors are configured in sleep mode for energy conservation is provided. Then, we discuss the benefits of introducing a few mobile sensors (i.e., actuators) that can move around the field of interest to help improving sensing coverage, connectivity, intrusion detection capability, and lifetime enhancement. Then another question

* E-mail address: zhangy@gonzaga.edu
† E-mail address: ywang2@fsmail.bradley.edu
‡ E-mail address: zxiao@psu.edu
§ E-mail address: jliu39@crimson.ua.edu
‖ E-mail address: pmosca@zagmail.gonzaga.edu

comes: how to efficiently schedule robots patrol? To address this research issues, biological inspired ideas have been introduced, which has become a hot topic in wireless sensor network. In this chapter, we also study bio-inspired strategies in WSNs.

1. Introduction to Wireless Sensor Network

With the advances of wireless communications and miniaturization of hardware components, it has become a reality to develop intelligent sensor nodes with low cost and low power, which are capable of data processing and wireless communication. Composed of a large number of multifunctional sensor nodes, wireless sensor networks (WSNs) have become an important technology combining sensor technology, embedded computing, distributed information processing, and wireless communication technology all together [25][26]. Originally motivated by military applications such as battle field surveillance, WSNs are now used in many commercial and industrial applications including: environment and habitat monitoring, healthcare applications, and target tracking.

As long as WSNs have been a premier research topic, there are a number of conceptual and optimization problems. In this chapter, we will study one of the fundamental problems, coverage. In fact, sensing coverage is the surveillance performance that a sensor network can provide. For example, forest fires take millions of acres around the world every year. WSNs can provide surveillance service for fire detection [6].

2. Coverage and Intrusion Detection

Coverage is a hotspot research problem which involves lots of efforts. In WSNs, sensor nodes are randomly distributed in the monitored field. Random distribution model can be uniform, Gaussian, and so on, usually based on applications.

2.1. Geometric Method

Geometric method is a common method in random coverage. It determines coverage based on the geometrical locations of sensor nodes [7]. Since geometric method is based on geographical information, knowledge of sensor nodes' locations is critical. However, the ad hoc nature of WSNs makes it impossible to have the locations of sensor nodes before deployment. Localization is then necessary to achieve the location information of each sensor node. Global Positioning System (GPS) is an elegant method for localizations. With appropriate devices, sensor nodes can receive signal from GPS to achieve their location information. However, due to several limits, like cost of hardware components, extra power for GPS components, and high requirements of monitored environment (GPS signals may be not available), GPS is not applicable in WSNs. Consequently, other techniques are employed to dynamically calculate the locations of sensor nodes. For example, the received signal strength indicator (RSSI) [1][2] of radio frequency (RF) communication, which can be used to calculate the distance between two sensor nodes. Acoustic signal [3][4] can also be used to estimate the distance between two nodes. With distance information from several neighbors, a sensor node can localize itself. Usually, at least three neighbors with the knowledge of their locations are necessary. More discussions on localization techniques and algorithm are available in [5].

With geographical location information, choosing proper geometric algorithm, network coverage can be evaluated. In [6] an algorithmic approach based on Voronoi diagram is adopted for coverage problems. Voronoi diagram [6] is a fundamental construct formed by a discrete set of points, which has been used in many domains. In [8][9], a coverage problem of an originally unknown field for mobile robots is studied using generalized Voronoi diagrams[10][11]. In [13], generalized Voronoi diagrams are also used for solving coverage problems. However, with geometric information of the monitored field in advance, the coverage problem turns to be a path planning problem [13]. In [14] and [15], both coverage and connectivity are considered, which aim to calculate the optimal number of required base stations for service objectives. However, due to the ad hoc feature of WSNs connectivity coverage becomes much more complex. Haas [12] studies how to improve and optimize network coverage in multihop ad hoc networks.

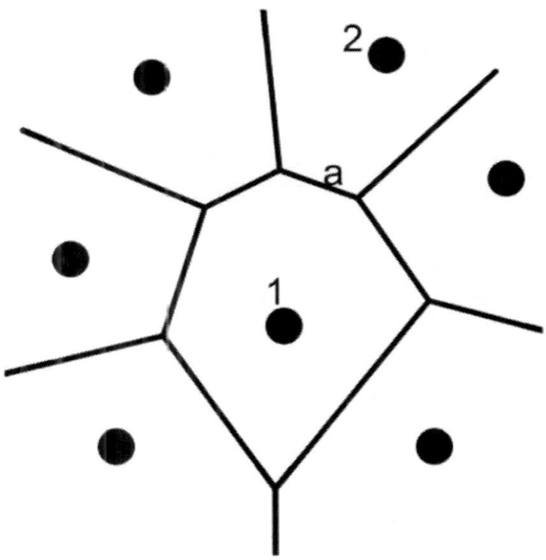

Figure 1. An Example of Voronoi diagram [13].

Figure 1 is an example of 2-dimentional (2D) Voronoi diagram. In 2D Voronoi diagram [10], a set of discrete points divide the monitored field into a set of convex polygons. Only one point in the set of discrete points will be included in each convex polygon. Compare to all other discrete points, it has the shortest distance to any other position inside the convex polygon. Based on this construction, neighboring points (ex. point 1 and 2) have the same distance to the sharing edge (edge a).

The points in the diagram are a set of randomly deployed sensors. Another structure, Delaunay triangulation [10], is directly related to Voronoi diagram, which is also adopted in coverage problems [6]. Delaunay triangulation can be achieved through connecting two points sharing an edge. Figure 2 shows an example of Delaunay triangulation. More details about Delaunay triangulation can be found in [10] [11].

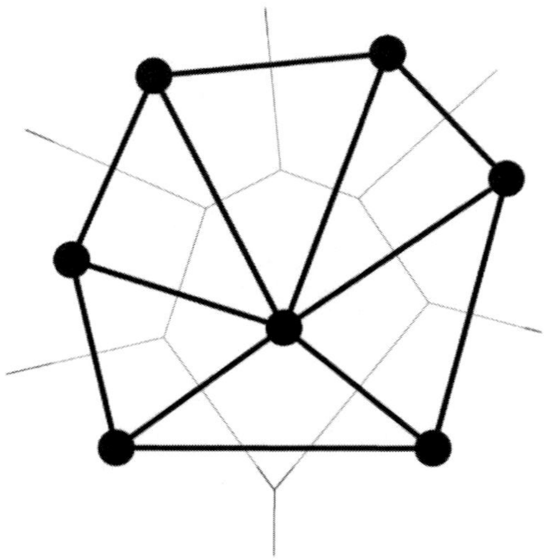

Figure 2. An example of Voronoi diagram and Delaunay triangulation. Thick lines form the Delaunay triangulation. [16].

Sensors are usually deployed to detect events, e.g., forest fire, enemy's troop, etc. In [6][7] 'agent' is used to describe events/activities. The moving feature of an agent reflects the randomness of locations where an event could happen. Voronoi diagram and Delaunay triangulation are used to search for 'path' for agents in a monitored filed [6][7]. Based on these paths authors try to solve the worst, best, and average-case coverage that sensor networks can provide. To evaluate the coverage performance of WSNs, worst and best coverage problems are formulated as follows [6][7]. In the worst case coverage, the problem is to search for the closest distance to sensors that an agent has to encounter during traveling on any path in the field. The closest distance is considered as a metric to evaluate the sensor coverage of the field. It is formulated as 'worst case' because agents may try to avoid sensors and the closest distance reflects all possible paths.

Similarly, in best case coverage, the problem is to search for the farthest distance to sensors that an agent must have during its traveling on any path in the field. The farthest distance covers the case that an agent tries to be as close to a sensor as possible although intuitively agents will try to keep far away from sensors. Best coverage problem is also studied in [16]. A justification for the correctness of using the Delaunay triangulation to solve the best coverage problem is also provided.

These two coverage problems look similar but solving different problems. Best coverage problem is to find a path which maximizes the detection probability of all points on this path. Worst-case coverage problem is to find the path which maximizes the distance from the path to all sensor nodes.

2.2. Certainty Coverage

Certainty coverage [24] usually requires a coverage threshold to guarantee the reliability of coverage. Based on the size of the monitored field, guarantee a minimum number of sensor nodes by optimizing the placement of sensor nodes.

In a typical certainty network sensor nodes are symmetrically and maybe periodically deployed in the monitored region.

There are also studies [17-19] that try to guarantee a statistical coverage in a monitored field. Sensor nodes are randomly distributed in the monitored field. Different distributions could be adopted based on applications, e.g., Gaussian distribution, uniform distribution, etc. The research problem becomes how many sensor nodes are necessary for a sensor network to provide a guaranteed statistical coverage. For example, for a given coverage requirement what is the minimum number of sensors needed to achieve the coverage requirement. This coverage requirement guarantees a probability p that a point or an object can be detected in the monitored field no matter where it is.

2.3. Sensor Scheduling Strategy

Although WSNs have so many applications, several constraints of WSNs must be considered, such as limited energy, memory space, and computation capability. Energy is vital [17-19] since after deployment sensor nodes will not be recharged. A common solution is to put some sensor nodes into sleep mode while others are still active. With proper wake up schemes, only a portion of sensor nodes are active at any time.

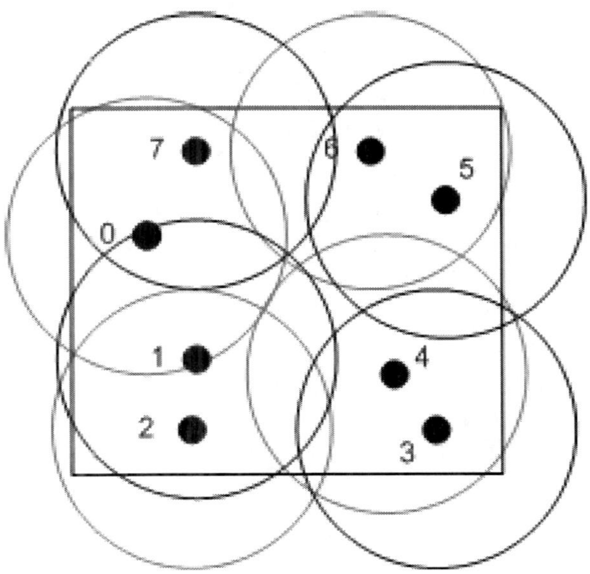

Figure 3. An example of the randomized coverage-based algorithm [20].

Even energy efficiency is critically important for WSNs, it should not be achieved with sacrificing coverage. Usually sensor nodes are densely deployed in the monitored field. The high spatial redundancy in the network makes it possible to achieve both energy efficiency and quality coverage simultaneously.Figure3 shows an example of sensor scheduling [20]. With eight sensor nodes (0-7) deployed in the square area, we can achieve a perfect coverage with high spatial redundancy. Every circle area represents the sensing coverage of a corresponding sensor node. After adopting scheduling algorithm (nodes 1,3,5,7 as a group and 0, 2, 4, 6 as the other group), we still get a good enough coverage as well as extended network lifetime.

In [20-22] and [23], a randomized coverage algorithm, k-set randomized scheduling algorithm is studied. In this algorithm, each sensor node is randomly assigned to one of k disjoint subsets, which are alternatively active. At any time, only one set of sensor nodes is working while all other sensor nodes are put into sleep mode. Network coverage intensity [20] is defined as the ratio of the time when a point in the monitored field is covered by at least one active sensor node to the total time. In these work an object is considered as a point while in reality intrusion an object is far larger than a point. In [17-19], authors continue to study the coverage problem while considering objects' size and shape in both 2 dimensional and 3 dimensional spaces.

3. Bio-Inspired Strategies in WSN

A big challenge for the surveillance and monitoring applications of WSNs focuses on event detection and handling efficiency of WSN. To address this research issues, a lot of research efforts are attracted to biological inspired research, which has become a hot topic in wireless sensor network. In this section, we will study novel biological inspired ideas that can be applied for surveillance strategies and methodologies.

Foraging behavior [28-30] has traditionally been a main concern of ecology. Foraging originally refers to the activity of searching for food, which is an integral part of the daily life of most living creatures. As a branch of behavioral ecology, foraging theory [28] studies the foraging behavior of animals in response to the animals' living environment. Foraging theory considers the foraging behavior of animals in reference to the payoff that an animal obtains from different foraging options. The natural way for organisms forage is to maximize energy intake per unit time [1], which is also the idea of optimal foraging theory (OFT), the most basic form of foraging. That is, they try their best to search for, seize, and consume those foods with the most calories while spending the least possible time to do so. Therefore, the optimal foraging is a consideration based on the constraints such as sensing and cognitive capabilities, environment (e.g., density of prey, risks from predators, and physical characteristics of the search space) etc.

There are mainly two different kinds of assumptions of optimal foraging theory (OFT) [28-30]: energy maximizers or time minimizers. The first type – Energy maximizers – refers to organisms that try to achieve the most amount of energy out of a specific environment [28-30]. The second type – Time minimizers – refers to organisms that try to get the specific amount of energy they need in the least possible time [28-30]. There are also some variations of this, i.e., Optimal diet problem, Optimal patch use problem, and Optimal load size problem.

The optimal diet model [34-35] describes when there are multiple choices of prey a forager has to decide which one of them to attack. Patch selection theory [34-35] describes a forager has all its prey concentrated in a small area with a significant travel time between them. Central place foraging theory [34-35] describes the situation that a forager has to go back to a particular place to consume its food, or perhaps to feed it to a mate or offspring.

A typical example of foraging theory is birds [28-30], since birds have nests and will go out to forage. They may forage nearby or a little far away. The point here is they will find more or larger prey far away from their nest than close to their nests [28-30].

A simple example related to bird foraging is that the crows drop welks on the ground to crack so that the shells can be open [28-30]. For cracking to open the shells, the crow has to make several decisions to take its action. A significant decision is how high should it fly before it drops the welk [28-30]. If it flies high, it is easier for the shells of welks to be open. Then crows need to drop fewer times to crack the welks [28-30]. Meanwhile, in order to fly higher, the crow has to spend more energy. It would be possible to theoretically calculate which height is the most optimum to drop the welk based on the least energy expenditure. Researchers can go out in the wild to estimate which height is the theoretical estimate for a crow to drop a welk [28-30]. It turns out that the height seen in the wild is the same as the theoretical best value [28-30].

When an organism is searching for food/prey among widely scattered patches [31], a basic and important decision to make is to choose when, where, and how long to settle or stop for a feeding bout [31]. Marginal value theorem (MVT) is an example of the simplest solutions in foraging ecology [31], which is easy to derive from a graphical analysis. In behavioral ecology, the marginal value theorem (MVT) considers an optimally foraging animal exploiting resources distributed in patches and that must decide when to leave a patch to start searching for a fresh one [32-33]. The marginal value theorem aims to find the "giving up time", that is, the time that an organism should leave a patch that it is exploiting [31]. The theorem is based on the consideration that after an animal begins feeding its energy gain gradually begins to slow down as food becomes scarcer in the patch [31]. The animal is considered to have already evolved to be able to optimize a cost/benefit ratio: the cost part is searching for and manipulating food while the benefit is food items [32-33]. Animals appear to make decisions based on an expected travel time among different patches and an observed intake rate within each patch [32-33]. Examples include bees visiting flowers, birds eating berries, or even mobile phone shop owners (in which case the "resource" being exploited is paying customers)[32-33].

Inspired by optimal foraging theory (OFT) problem or sometimes by their wide generalizations [28-30], a handful of algorithms have been developed in these years to solve engineering related optimization problems. Most prominent among them are the Ant Systems (AS) and Ant Colony Optimization (ACO), Bacterial Foraging Optimization (BFO), and the algorithms based on bees social foraging. These problems have lead to superior results in various applications in real-world problems. In some problems, the concept of foraging in much more general sense are used, e.g., human beings forage for information, musician forage for a perfect state of harmony of the notes being played (e.g., the Harmony Search Algorithm), and robots forage for events.

Collaboration strategies among static sensor nodes and mobile sensor nodes are studied in [27], which is critical for surveillance performance of WSNs. Inspired by ants' pheromone-based communication strategy, the idea of digital pheromone is introduced and a digital pheromone-based patrolling algorithm for robots is designed in [27]. According to the design, different events have different priorities. Digital pheromones are used to model events' priorities, which evaporate over time. Robots are correspondingly modeled as ants, trying to patrol the route with strongest digital pheromone.

Scent-marking, which is an important behavior among many different mammals, especially primates, is deeply studied in [25][26] and a primate-inspired method for event/target detection, pursuing, and tracking problem is proposed in [27]. Similar with the scent-marking activity of primates, pheromones play a critical role in ants' communication.

4. Conclusion

Wireless sensor networks have lots of applications no matter in military or in industry. The main purpose of deploying WSNs is for monitoring or data collection. Then coverage becomes a common issue in most applications of WSNs. Geometric approaches are direct methods to calculate how well a monitored field is covered. Localization algorithms are also needed, as location information of each sensor node is required for geometric approaches. However, due to the ad hoc feature of WSNs, a big overhead will be introduced especially when a network becomes bigger. Certainty coverage is suitable for a smaller scale of WSNs, in which sensors could be manually and periodically deployed. Usually the deployment of sensors in such applications is regular or even distribution. Other researchers try to find solutions through statistical study. Based on the limits of WSNs, like lifetime, power, size, a better performance will also require a longer lifetime of WSNs, which means a longer service.

Actuators are also introduced into a lot of applications based on WSNs, since they will enhance the surveillance performance of WSNs by improving coverage and connectivity. Actuators are active components in a network. They are moving around to collect information. Then biological inspired research becomes hot topic to study how to schedule these actuators. Sent marking, digital pheromone, and optimized foraging theory are all examples in this category of research.

Coverage is such an important metric of performance in wireless sensor networks. This field will be studied more strenuously as more and more area will introduce WSNs.

References

[1] J. Zhao, W. Xi, Y. He, Y. Liu, X. Li, L. Mo, and Z. Yang, "Localization of Wireless Sensor Networks in the Wild: Pursuit of Ranging Quality", *IEEE/ACM Transactions on Networking,* 2003, vol. 2, issue 1, pp. 311-323.

[2] B.N. Hood, and P. Barooah, "Estimating DoA From Radio- Frequency RSSI Measurements Using an Actuated Reflector", *IEEE Sensors Journal,* Volume: 11, Issue: 2, 2011, Page(s): 413 – 417.

[3] K.W. Lo, and B.G. Ferguson, "Sensor Localization Using Acoustic Transient Signal Sources with Known Positions", *3rd International Conference on Intelligent Sensors, Sensor Networks and Information*, 2007. ISSNIP 2007. Page(s): 197 - 202.

[4] J. Chen, Y. Zhang, X. Cao, X. Shen, and Y. Sun, "Acoustic Energy Based Scheme for Target Tracking in Wireless Sensor Networks*," Journal of Electronics & Information Technology*, Vol. 31, No. 11, Nov. 2009.

[5] A. Savvides, C.C. Han, and M.B. Srivastava, "Dynamic Fine-Grained Localization in Ad Hoc Networks of Sensors," *Proc. Seventh Ann. Int'l Conf. Mobile Computing and Networking (Mobi-COM 2001),* July 2001.

[6] S. Megerian, F. Koushanfar, M. Potkonjak, and M. B. Srivastava, "Worst and Best-Case Coverage in Sensor Networks", *IEEE Transactions On Mobile Computing,* VOL. 4, NO. 1, JANUARY/FEBRUARY 2005, pp. 84-92.

[7] S. Megerian, F. Koushanfar, M. Potkonjak, and M. B. Srivastava, "Coverage Problems in Wireless Ad-hoc Sensor Networks", *IEEE INFOCOM* 2001, Page(s): 1380 - 1387 vol.3.

[8] G.S. Sukhatme and M.J. Mataric, "Embedding Robots into the Internet," *Comm. ACM*, vol. 43, pp. 67-73, May 2000.

[9] Z.J. Butler, A.A. Rizzi, and R.L. Hollis, "Contact Sensor-Based Coverage of Rectilinear Environments," *Proc. IEEE Int'l Symp. Intelligent Control Intelligent Systems and Semiotics*, pp. 266-271, Sept. 1999.

[10] F. Aurenhammer, "Voronoi Diagrams—A Survey of a Fundamental Geometric Data Structure," *ACM Computing Surveys* 23, pp. 345-405, 1991.

[11] O. Setter, M. Sharir, and D. Halperin, "Constructing Two-Dimensional Voronoi Diagrams via Divide-and-Conquer of Envelopes in Space", *Sixth International Symposium on Voronoi Diagrams,* 2009. Page(s): 43 – 52.

[12] Z.J. Haas, "On The Relaying Capability of the Reconfigurable Wireless Networks," *Proc. IEEE 47th Vehicular Technology Conf.,* vol. 2, pp. 1148-1152, May 1997.

[13] C. Hofner and G. Schmidt, "Path Planning and Guidance Techniques for an Autonomous Mobile Cleaning Robot," *Robotics and Autonomous Systems*, vol. 14, pp. 199-212, May 1998.

[14] A. Molina, G.E. Athanasiadou, and A.R. Nix, "The Automatic Location of Base-Stations for Optimised Cellular Coverage: A New Combinatorial Approach," *Proc. IEEE 49th Vehicular Technology Conf.,* vol. 1, pp. 606-610, May 1999.

[15] K. Lieska, E. Laitinen, and J. Lahteenmaki, "Radio Coverage Optimization with Genetic Algorithms," *Proc. IEEE Int'l Symp. Personal, Indoor and Mobile Radio Comm.*, vol. 1, pp. 318-322, Sept. 1998.

[16] X. Li, P. Wan, and O. Frieder, "Coverage in Wireless Ad Hoc Sensor Networks," *IEEE Transactions On Computers*, VOL. 52, NO. 6, JUNE 2003.

[17] Y. Xiao, Y. Zhang, M. Peng, H. Chen, X. Du, B. Sun, and K. Wu, "Two and Three-Dimensional Intrusion Object Detection under Randomized Scheduling Algorithms in Sensor Networks," *Computer Networks*, Vol. 53, No. 14, Sept. 2009, pp. 2458–2475.

[18] Y. Zhang, Y. Xiao, K. Wu, X. Du, and B. Sun, "Three Dimensional Intrusion Objects Detection under Randomized Scheduling Algorithm in Sensor Networks," *Proceedings of The 4th International Conference on Mobile Ad-hoc and Sensor Networks (MSN 2008)*, pp. 16-22.

[19] Y. Xiao, H. Chen, Y. Zhang, X. Du, B. Sun, and K. Wu, "Intrusion Objects with Shapes under Randomized Scheduling Algorithm in Sensor Networks," *Proceedings of The 28th International Conference on Distributed Computing Systems (ICDCS 2008) Workshops*, pp. 315-320. DOI 10.1109/ICDCS.Workshops.2008.39.

[20] C. Liu, K. Wu, Y. Xiao, and B. Sun, "Random Coverage with Guaranteed Connectivity: Joint Scheduling for Wireless Sensor Networks," *IEEE Transactions On Parallel And Distributed Systems*, VOL. 17, NO. 6, JUNE 2006.

[21] Y. Xiao, H. Chen, K. Wu, C. Liu, and B. Sun, "Maximizing Network Life Time under QoS constraints in WSNs," *Proc. of GLOBECOM 2006.*

[22] Y. Xiao, H. Chen, K. Wu, and B. Sun, "Modeling Detection Metrics in Randomized Scheduling Algorithm in Wireless Sensor Networks" *Proc. of IEEE WCNC 2007.*

[23] Y. Xiao, Y. Zhang, X. Sun, and H. Chen, "Asymptotic Coverage and Detection in Randomized Scheduling Algorithm in Wireless Sensor Networks," *Proc. of IEEE ICC 2007.*

[24] Y. Lei; Y. Zhang; Y. Zhao, "The Research of Coverage Problems in Wireless Sensor Network," International Conference on Wireless Networks and Information Systems, 2009. *WNIS* '09.

[25] Y. Xiao, Y. Zhang, and X. Liang, "Primate-inspired Communication Methods for Mobile and Static Sensors and RFID Tags," *ACM Transactions on Autonomous and Adaptive Systems (TAAS) TAAS Homepage archive* Volume 6 Issue 4, October 2011, Article No. 26.

[26] Y. Zhang, Y. Xiao, and K. L. Bales, "Primate Social Systems, Scent-marking, and Their Applications in Mobile and Static Sensor Networks," *International Journal of Sensor Networks*, Vol. 5, No. 4, 2009, pp. 210-222.

[27] Y. Zhang and Y. Xiao, "Primate-inspired Scent Marking for Mobile and Static Sensors and RFID Tags," *Proceedings of 18th International Conference on Computer Communications and Networks, 2009* (ICCCN 2009). DOI: 10.1109/ICCCN.2009.5235294.

[28] R. H. MacArthur, and E. R. Pianka, On the optimal use of a patchy environment, *American Naturalist*, 100, 1966.

[29] A. C. Kamil, J.R. Krebs and H.R. Pulliam, *"Foraging Behavior"*, Plenum Press, New York and London, 1987.

[30] R. McDermott, J. H. Fowler, and O. Smirnov, "On the Evolutionary Origin of Prospect Theory Preferences," *Journal of Politics*, April 2008, Vol. 70, No. 2, pp. 335–350

[31] A. T. Pietrewicz, and A. C. Kamil, "Search image formation in the blue jay Cyanocittatacristata", *Science* 1979, 204: 1332-1333.

[32] G.A. Parker, "Marginal Value Theorem with Exploitation Time Costs: Diet, Sperm Reserves, and Optimal Copula Duration in Dung Flies", *The American Naturalist,* 1992, 139(6):1237-1256.

[33] E. L. Charnov, "Optimal foraging: the marginal value theorem", *Theoretical Population Biology,* 1976, 9:129–136.

[34] C. Rutz1, L. A. Bluff1, N. Reed, J. Troscianko, J. Newton4, R. Inger2, A. Kacelnik1, S. Bearhop2 "The ecological significance of tool use in New Caledonian Crows", *Science* 2010, 329 (5998): 1523. doi:10.1126/science.1192053.

[35] J. Goodall, "Tool-using and aimed throwing in a community of free-living chimpanzees", *Nature* 1964, 201 (4926): 1264–6.

In: Horizons in Computer Science Research. Volume 9
Editor: Thomas S. Clary
ISBN: 978-1-63321-522-1

Chapter 2

COMPUTER NETWORKS, THE INTERNET AND GREEN IT: EFFECTIVELY MANAGING COMPUTER NETWORK RESOURCES

Chetan Kumar*
Department of Management Information Systems, College of Business Administration,
California State University, San Marcos, CA, US

Abstract

Computer networks have come a long way since their introduction in the 1960s. The Internet is the largest computer network in history and it continues to grow rapidly. There has been a tremendous growth in the amount and range of information available on the Internet. At the same time, there is huge potential for improving the performance of the Internet. In this article we review some studies that propose mechanisms to effectively allocate resources in multi-server computer networks. The popularity of the Internet has also resulted in a significant impact on energy consumption. The Environmental Protection Agency (EPA) and other agencies have suggested useful measures to improve efficiency of vast data centers that power the Internet. This, and other environmentally sustainable computing practices, may collectively be described as green Information Technology (IT). Computer networks have a significant energy resource impact in the form Internet usage and its data centers. Therefore managing computer networks effectively is key to greening IT. In this article we review different methods for managing computer networks and green IT strategies. Adopting these computer network management and green IT practices is likely to benefit all Internet players as well as the environment.

Introduction

Computer networks have come a long way since their introduction in the 1960s. Kleinrock [11] first discussed communication networks by linking multiple computers that

* E-mail address: ckumar@csusm.edu; Tel: (760) 477-3976; Fax: (760) 750-3107; 333 South Twin Oaks Valley Road, San Marcos, CA 92096, US.

could transfer data and "talk" to one another. This eventually led to the architecture of the present day Internet [13]. There has been a tremendous growth in the amount and range of information available on the Internet [18, 15]. Cisco Systems report [3] forecasts a huge increase in global Internet Protocol (IP) traffic, driven by Web 2.0 technologies such as video and social networking and collaboration. Some excerpts from the Cisco report [3] are as follows.

- "Global IP traffic will increase six fold from 2007 to 2012, reaching 44 exabytes per month in 2012, compared to less than 7 exabytes per month in 2007.
- Total IP traffic for 2012 will amount to greater than half a zettabyte (or 522 exabytes). A zettabyte equals a trillion gigabytes.
- Global IP traffic in the month of December 2012 will be 11 exabytes higher than in December 2011, a single-year increase that will exceed the amount by which traffic increased in the eight years since 2000." [3]

The increase in Internet traffic is aided because making information available online is becoming relatively inexpensive, and as more people have Internet access demand for information increases. In addition, new format and contents of Web 2.0 technologies such as video, social networking and collaboration applications prompted more interest in online deliveries. The trend of increasing Internet traffic is likely to continue [4, 3, 18, 15].

Networked computer resources are now ubiquitous in the form of the Internet. However, while the Internet is the largest computer network in history, and it continues to grow exponentially, there is a huge potential for improving its performance. How do we reduce user delays? How do we achieve desired performance goals? How do we provide Quality of Service (QoS) guarantees to end users? How do we develop a market based resource allocation mechanism for computer networks? The answer to these questions will determine the future directions of computer networks. This article discusses these and related issues.

The popularity of the Internet has a significant impact on energy consumption. All Internet services such as email, social networking, web searches, web hosting, among others, require energy. These services are provided by huge data centers run by the big Internet players such as Microsoft, Google, Yahoo, and Facebook. The Environmental Protection Agency (EPA) reports [7] that data centers consumed 1.5% of national electricity usage in 2006 and this may double by 2011. EPAs ENERGY STAR partnership, a joint program of the U.S. Environmental Protection Agency and the U.S. Department of Energy, presents the following extract from the EPA report [6].

> "In its 2007 Report to Congress on Server and Data Center Energy Efficiency Opportunities, EPA estimated that the nation's servers and data centers consumed about 61 billion kilowatt-hours (kWh) in 2006 (1.5 percent of total U.S. electricity consumption) for a total electricity cost of about $4.5 billion. As one of the fastest growing sectors, national energy consumption by servers and data centers could nearly double by 2011 to more than 100 billion kWh, representing a $7.4 billion annual electricity cost. However, there is significant potential for energy efficiency improvements in data centers." [6]

Therefore, while Internet usage has a big impact on energy consumption, there are many opportunities to improve energy conservation. This may collectively be described under the umbrella of green Information Technology (IT). Green IT means environmentally sustainable computing [23]. San Murugesan [21] describes green computing, or green IT, as follows. "Green computing is the study and practice of designing, manufacturing, using, and disposing of computers, servers, and associated subsystems—such as monitors, printers, storage devices, and networking and communications systems—efficiently and effectively with minimal or no impact on the environment. " Computer networks have a significant energy resource impact in the form Internet usage and its data centers. Therefore managing computer networks effectively is key to greening IT. In this article we also discuss various methods for managing computer networks and green IT strategies.

Related Literature and Discussion

There is substantial literature on computer networks since their introduction in the 1960s. Kleinrock [11] first reported on communication networks where multiple linked computers could transfer data. This Defense Advanced Research Project Agency (DARPA) network grew to the present day Internet [13]. Most technical studies on computer networks focus on performance analysis issues, such as network architecture and topology design, for achieving system performance goals [13, 22]. Tanenbaum [22] provides a comprehensive discussion on computer networks. Mendelson [19] was one of the first to examine the control and management issues related to a computer system. He developed a transfer pricing model for equal-sized jobs arriving at a single-server environment. Mendelson and Whang [20] then extend the model to include multiple priorities and heterogeneous job sizes. The Kumar et al. [17] study examines the pricing issue for congestible resources from a broader perspective of a multi-server peer-to-peer (P2P) system. This entails investigating a multiple-server computer system in a firm that may have servers located at different coordinates. The servers or nodes behave as peers that can share their computing resources [16]. The original Mendelson [18] model thus becomes a special single-server case of the multi-server Kumar et al. [17] model. Other studies have also expanded the scope of analysis to consider multiple servers [14, 8, 9, 2, 17]. The goal is to manage computer networks effectively. The Kumar et al. [17] and related models are discussed in more detail in the next section.

In addition, there is increasing focus on effectively managing energy consumption of computer networks. The U.S. Environmental Protection Agency [7] and Depart of Energy [5] are leading efforts on this behalf. This is important as data centers account for ever greater proportion of national energy consumption. These efforts tie in to the broader discussion of green IT or environmentally sustainable computing [21, 23]. While the term green IT has been around for a while, we believe it is now critical to address it as computer networks and Internet dominates more of our lives and energy consumption. Strategies for energy saving for computer networks [5, 7] and green IT [21] are also discussed in more detail in subsequent sections below.

A Mechanism for Resource Allocation in a Multi-Server Peer-to-Peer Network

Kumar et al. [17] design a pricing and allocation mechanism for a multiple server peer-to-peer (P2P) network where the users in a firm may share their computing resources. This mechanism allows tasks (incoming jobs) to be allocated to resources (participating peers) in an organization in a decentralized manner. The base case of the Kumar et al. [17] model derives the optimal transfer price that maximizes the net value for the peers in the network. The authors consider a P2P network of queues where every location observes a fixed exogenous arrival rate of jobs. They develop a pricing scheme where every individual user makes a decision whether or not to join the system on the basis of a posted price. A job may be executed at either the location where it first arrived, or it may be allocated to a neighbor location connected by a direct link. The peers have a net value maximization objective. In this scheme the optimal price p_j^* for executing a job at location j is given by $p_j^* = v\Gamma_j^* \left(\partial W_j / \partial \Gamma_j^*\right)$, where $\partial W_j / \partial \Gamma_j^*$, the incremental delay added to waiting time W_j at j as a result of an incremental arrival Γ_j^*, is evaluated at the optimal arrival rate of Γ_j^*. The optimal price p_j^* is equal to the externality cost, which is the expected delay cost per unit time accrued on the rest of the system by an infinitesimal increase in job flow. Consequently, the optimal price for executing any job at a peer location is essentially equal to the marginal delay cost it imposes on all current jobs at that node [16]. With this pricing scheme no individual user has an incentive to overutilize shared resources. Therefore, we avoid the 'Tragedy of the Commons' for the multi-server P2P network as pooled resources are shared responsibly by users [17]. The authors then extend their basic model to incorporate situations where the peers have queue length constraints. This may be used for providing Quality of Service (QoS) guarantees to computer network users. Other studies also aim to improve efficiency of resource allocation in multi-server computer networks. Ernst et al. [9] solve a task allocation problem for minimizing cost of assigning tasks to a set of processors. The study focuses on a centralized decision making environment and does not consider a pricing mechanism. Bapna et al. [2] develop a market-based resource allocation model using a combinatorial call auction approach. Ercetin and Tassiulas [8] design a market based mechanism for minimizing user delays in a network where content delivery network (CDN) proxy caches and content providers are behaving selfishly. These are examples of some studies that attempt to effectively manage networked computer resources. Interested readers are referred to Kumar et al. [17] for a detailed discussion on multi-server peer-to-peer networks. Research along these lines contributes towards making computer networks more efficient and thereby less energy intensive.

Energy Saving for Computer Networks

Improving energy consumption efficiency of the vast data centers that power the Internet should also be an important focus area. Some studies on data center usage and efficiency provide useful directions in this regard. ArsTechnica [1] summarizes EPA's recommendations for reducing infrastructure energy usage as follows: "The EPA makes a host of recommendations for cutting down infrastructure energy use and claims that if all of them are put into place, data centers can see up to an 80 percent improvement in energy efficiency. Suggested changes include improving transformers and uninterruptible power supplies, installing higher-efficiency chillers, fans, and pumps, and installing direct liquid cooling systems. On the server side, the report recommends enabling power management on all servers, aggressively consolidating servers and storage, and eliminating unused servers." [1]. The U.S. Depart of Energy's Industrial Technologies Program (DOE ITP) [5] lists the following benefits of improving data center efficiency.

- "Constrain increased electricity demand and associated carbon emissions.
- Protect data and computing functions vital to our economy.
- Reduce risk of power outages and increase regional electricity reliability.
- Postpone need to build new electricity generation capacity.
- Support replication of energy-efficient practices across the sector.
- Free up power and cooling." [5]

It is important to highlight that the Internet does not just incur energy costs but also produces many savings. For example, shopping at online retailers such as Amazon and eBay saves gas and reduces traffic gridlock [1]. The same can be said of online banking or videoconferencing. The EPA report [7] describes this as follows: "The data processing and communications services provided by data centers can also lead to indirect reductions in energy use in the broader economy, which can exceed the incremental data center energy expenditures in some cases." While Internet usage does produce related energy savings, we should continue striving to improve data center efficiency along lines suggested by EPA and others [7, 5]. This could result in cost reductions for everyone involved and also benefit the environment.

Green Information Technology

Energy saving initiatives for computer networks may be collectively addressed under the broader discussion of green IT. Green IT is environmentally sustainable computing [23]. San Murugesan [21], who authored one of the first studies on green IT, discusses four areas for addressing environmental effects of computing. They include green use (reduced energy consumption), green disposal (refurbish, reuse and recycle old computers), green design (design energy efficient IT equipment), and green manufacturing (manufacture IT products with minimal environmental impact). Murugesan [21] contends that these four complementary paths most be adopted for a holistic approach to green IT. Since data centers that power the Internet are expected to account for 3% of national energy consumption by 2011 according to EPA, they are an important area for greening IT. Server virtualization, where one physical server is converted to multiple virtual machines using software, is another area that is fast becoming popular with organizations and data centers alike [10]. Murugesan[21] lists the following focus areas for green IT, which include managing data centers and server virtualization:

- "Design for environmental sustainability;
- Energy-efficient computing;
- Power management;
- Data center design, layout, and location;
- Server virtualization;
- Responsible disposal and recycling;
- Regulatory compliance;
- Green metrics, assessment tools, and methodology;
- Environment-related risk mitigation;
- Use of renewable energy sources; and
- Eco-labeling of IT products." [21]

Of these data center management and server virtualization directly address Internet usage. The other factors also assume greater importance due to accelerated IT use courtesy the Internet. In all cases adopting these green IT practices will be beneficial for the environment as well as frequently reduce costs.

Conclusion

Since computer networks were introduced in the 1960s, they have expanded considerably in size and scope. The Internet is the largest computer network in history and it continues to grow rapidly. There is huge potential for improving the performance of the Internet. For example, mechanisms proposed by Kumar et al. [17], Ernst et al. [9], and Bapna et al. [2], may be used to effectively allocate resources in multi-server networks. This could improve the efficiency of the computer network. The popularity of the Internet has also resulted in a significant impact on energy consumption. The EPA and other agencies have suggested useful measures to improve efficiency of vast data centers that power the Internet [7, 5]. This, and other environmentally sustainable computing practices discussed by Murugesan [21], may collectively be described as green IT. Computer networks have a significant energy resource impact in the form Internet usage and its data centers. Therefore managing computer networks effectively is key to greening IT. Adopting the recommended computer network management and green IT practices is likely to benefit all Internet players as well as the environment.

Acknowledgments

This article includes a review of the discussion of Kumar, C., Altinkemer, A., and De, P. "A Mechanism for Pricing and Resource Allocation in Peer-to-Peer Networks," *Electronic Commerce Research and Applications*, 10, 26-37, 2011; among other sources. Interested readers are referred to Kumar et al. [17], EPA report [7], and Murugesan [21] for a detailed discussion on managing computer networks, Internet energy consumption, and green IT.

References

[1] ArsTechnica, EPA: *Power usage in data centers could double by 2011*, 2007. http://arstechnica.com/old/content/2007/08/epa-power-usage-in-data-centers-could-double-by-2011.ars.

[2] Bapna, R., Das, S., Garfinkel, R., Stallaert, J. "A Market Design for Grid Computing," *Informs Journal On Computing*, 20, 1, 100-111, 2008.

[3] Cisco Systems Visual Networking Index Forecast Report 2008. http://www.cisco.com/en/us/netsol/ns827/networking_solutions_sub_solution.html#.

[4] Datta, A., Dutta, K., Thomas, H., and VanderMeer, D. "World Wide Wait: A Study of Internet Scalability and Cache-Based Approaches to Alleviate It," *Management Science*, 49, 10, 1425–1444, 2003.

[5] Depart of Energy's Industrial Technologies Program (DOE ITP) 2011. http://www1.eere.energy.gov/industry/datacenters/about.html.

[6] Energy Star Data Center Energy Efficiency Initiatives 2011. http://www.energystar.gov/index.cfm?c=prod_development.server_efficiency.

[7] Environmental Protection Agency (EPA) Report to Congress on Server and Data Center Energy Efficiency Opportunities 2007. http://www.energystar.gov/ ia/partners/prod_development/downloads/epa_datacenter_report_congress_final1.pdf.

[8] Ercetin, O. and Tassiulas, L. "Market-based Resource Allocation for Content Delivery in the Internet," *IEEE Transactions on Computers*, 52, 12, 1573–1585, 2003.

[9] Ernst, A., Jiang, H., Krishnamoorthy, M. "Exact Solutions to Task Allocation Problems," *Management Science*, 52, 10, 1634–1646, 2006.

[10] How Stuffs Work (HSW) Discovery Communication, How Server Virtualization Works, 2011. http://communication.howstuffworks.com/server-virtualization.htm

[11] Kleinrock, L., *Communication Nets*, Dover, New York, 1964.

[12] Kleinrock, L., *Queuing Systems*, Vols. I and II, John Wiley, New York, 1976.

[13] Kleinrock, L., "Creating a Mathematical Theory of Computer Networks," *Operations Research*, 50, 1, 125-131, 2002.

[14] Krishnan, R., Smith, M.D., and Telang, R., "The Economics of Peer-to-Peer Networks," *JITTA: Journal of Information Technology Theory and Application,* 5, 3, 2003.

[15] Kumar, C. "The Effect of User Location and Time of Access on Ecommerce: A Long Tail Study of Website Requests," In: *Encyclopedia of E-Business Development and Management in the Global Economy*, Lee, I. (Ed.), IGI Global, PA, 2010.

[16] Kumar, C. "Leveraging Peer-to-Peer Networks for Effectively Managing Computing Resources," In: Peer to Peer Networks and Internet Policies, Vergos, D. and Saenz, J. (Eds.), Nova Science Publishers, NY, 2010.

[17] Kumar, C., Altinkemer, A., and De, P. "A Mechanism for Pricing and Resource Allocation in Peer-to-Peer Networks," *Electronic Commerce Research and Applications*, 10, 26-37, 2011.

[18] Kumar, C., Norris, J.B. and Sun, Y. "Location and Time Do Matter: A Long Tail Analysis of Website Requests," *Decision Support Systems*, 47, 500-507, 2009.

[19] Mendelson, H., "Pricing Computer Services: Queuing Effects," *Communications of the ACM*, 28, 3, 312-321, 1985.

[20] Mendelson, H. and Wang, S., "Optimal Incentive Compatible Priority Pricing for the M/M/1 Queue," *Operations Research*, 38, 5, 870-883, 1990.
[21] Murugesan, S. "Harnessing Green IT: Principles and Practices," *IEEE IT Professional*, 24-33, 2008.
[22] Tanenbaum, A.S., *Computer Networks*, Fourth Edition, Prentice-Hall, Englewood Cliffs, NJ, 2003.
[23] Wikipedia, Green Computing, 2011. http://en.wikipedia.org/wiki/ green _computing.

In: Horizons in Computer Science Research. Volume 9 ISBN: 978-1-63321-522-1
Editor: Thomas S. Clary

Chapter 3

SECURITY IN WIRELESS SENSOR NETWORKS: STATE-OF-THE-ART, CHALLENGES AND OPPORTUNITIES

Zhifeng Xiao[1,*], Yun Wang[2,†] and Yanping Zhang[3,‡]
[1]Department of Computer Science and Software Engineering
Penn State Erie, the Behrend College, Erie, PA, US
[2]Department of Computer Science and Information Systems
Bradley University, Peoria, IL, US
[3]Department of Computer Science
Gonzaga University, Spokane, WA, US

Abstract

Recent advances have witnessed the popularity and success of Wireless Sensor Networks (WSNs) in the past decade. The increase of the public presence and cyber footprint of WSNs opens up avenues for compromise to hackers and individuals with malicious intent. Securing WSNs becomes one of the highest priorities for the deployment of real world sensing applications. This chapter presents the state-of-the-art security studies in WSNs. We identify four security objectives including confidentiality, integrity, availability, and privacy, and survey how each of them can be exploited in the sensor network environment. Our main goal is to deliver a systematic study on the WSN security issues by summarizing the existing attacks and countermeasures, comparing their features, and proposing a taxonomy of attacks using an attack-defense-tree-based approach. Based on the investigation results and our analysis, we identify the current research challenges and opportunities towards building a securer sensor network environment.

Keywords: wireless sensor network, security, attack, defense

*E-mail address: zux2@psu.edu
†E-mail address: ywang2@fsmail.bradley.edu
‡E-mail address: zhangy@gonzaga.edu

1. Introduction

Recent advances in micro-electromechanical systems (MEMS) and wireless communication have enabled the practice of wireless sensor networks. A low-cost sensor node is capable of sensing, data processing, and communicating with other sensors or computers. Sensory data is collected by multiple sensors in distributed locations. These data becomes the first hand material for a particular application. The features of WSN have greatly addressed the requirements of smart environments: detection of various environment parameters, data monitoring and collection, information assessment, data display in user interface, and alarm functions. In addition, due to the variety of sensors such as seismic, thermal, visual, infrared, acoustic, and radar, a wide range of applications have emerged. Back in 2002, Akyildiz, et al. [1] classify the WSN applications as military applications, environment applications, health applications, home applications, and other commercial applications. In the past decade, WSN has achieved great success in each category.

Despite the success of WSNs, the increase of the public presence and cyber footprint of ESNs opens up avenues for compromise to hackers and malicious individuals. Securing WSNs has become one of the highest priorities when deploying a real world sensing application. To better address the security issues for WSNs, we first discuss several constraints [2] that distinguish it from other computing systems:

- Energy - Sensor nodes are powered by batteries; hence, energy is always a priority. For a sensor node, there are three components contributing the most to energy consumption: 1) the sensor transducer which monitors and collect sensory data, 2) the communication module which deals with data exchange, and 3) the microprocessor which does computation. It has been shown that communication is more energy-consuming than computation, because transmitting one bit consumes as much as power as executing 800 - 1000 instructions [3].

- Computation - For cost reduction, a sensor node is generally equipped with a low cost microprocessor that is not as powerful as those in nodes of other distributed environments. Hence, it is not practical to perform complex cryptographic functions.

- Memory - Flash memory and RAM are the two major memory types. The former stores downloaded application code, and the latter stores application program, sensor data, etc. A sensor node is space limited, since after OS module and application code is loaded, there is not enough space for complex computation.

- Transmission range - There is always a trade-off between communication range and energy consumption for WSN. In addition, the actual transmission range depends on external factors such as weather and terrain.

Due to the above constraints, WSN security poses its own difficulties and challenges that cannot be well addressed by just copying existing security mechanisms for traditional computing systems. In addition, During our study, we find that it is a good practice to follow a security-objective-driven methodology to investigate the security issues in WSN. It turns out that each attack type is targeting at least one security objectives; meanwhile, each security objective can suffer from various attack types. Therefore, it is natural to classify attacks based on the security objective it is attempting to violate. The security objectives in WSNs can be summarized as follows:

- Confidentiality ensures that any data can only be accessed and understood by authorized entities in the system.
- Integrity ensures that any data cannot be modified by malicious entities without being detected.
- Availability ensures that the service delivered by a WSN is persistent and available tall the time in spite of a DOS/DDOS attack.
- Privacy ensures that private or sensitive information will not be leaked to any third party or attackers.

There are various ways to attack a WSN. Wang et al. [2] categorize the attack patterns as follows:

- Outsider Vs. insider attacks: outside attacks are launched from external devices that do not belong to the target network, while insider attacks require to first compromise internal components of the victim, and then perform malicious behavior.
- Passive Vs. active attacks: passive attacks aim to intercept messages in the air and recover secrecy as much as possible, while active attacks intend to tamper with messages or inject false data into packets.
- Mote-based Vs. PC-based attacks: mote-based attacks use sensor nodes as attack entities, while PC-based attacks use a laptop or more powerful devices to attack a WSN.

In this chapter, we identify four security objectives including confidentiality, integrity, availability, and privacy, and survey how each of them can be exploited in the sensor network environment. Our main goal is to deliver a systematic study on the WSN security issues by summarizing the existing attacks and countermeasures, comparing their features, and proposing a taxonomy of attacks for a deeper understanding of the state-of-the-art. Based on the investigation results and our analysis, we identify the current research challenges and opportunities towards building a securer sensor network environment.

The rest of this chapter is organized as follows. We will study four security objectives, i.e., WSN confidentiality, WSN integrity, WSN availability, and WSN privacy, in section 2, section 3, section 4, and section 5 respectively. For each security objective, we will present corresponding attacks and related countermeasures. At last, we give a summary for the entire survey and provide some open issues to shape future research in this field.

2. WSN Confidentiality

In general, the main task of a WSN is to collect data for real-time or periodic surveillance. Moreover, the feature of wireless communication enables attackers to listen to the channel and intercept messages. Therefore, protection of data transmission is of significant importance. Figure 1 highlights the main topics for WSN Confidentiality.

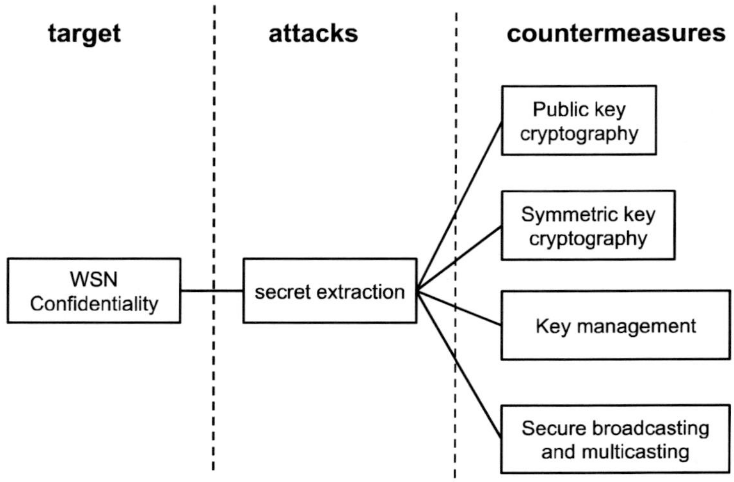

Figure 1. A summary of WSN confidentiality.

2.1. Attacks

Traditional attacks on confidentiality in wireless networks also apply to WSN. For example, an adversary may place some nodes in a deployed sensor network to intercept data exchanged between legitimate nodes. Some sensitive data may be disclosed. Also, an attacker can even physically control a legitimate node, reprogramming it and then placing it back to the field. Later, the compromised node may forward a copy of every message it has to the attacker. Tampering is one such attack, which can help an attacker to extract sensitive information such as cryptographic keys.

2.2. Countermeasures

The main tool for WSN confidentiality is encryption. However, encryption/decryption in WSN is not an easy task due to the resource constraints of a sensor node. The following subsections discuss applying cryptography to WSNs, and key management issues.

2.2.1. Applying Cryptography to WSNs

Cryptography is the fundamental method for data protection. However, in WSNs, cryptographic methods are limited by node's energy, computation capability, data size, memory capacity. Therefore, traditional practice of cryptography may not applicable. In this subsection, we discuss how to apply public key cryptography and symmetric key cryptography to WSNs with the known constraints.

- Public key cryptography - For a long time, public key algorithms are considered unrealistic for WSNs due to its high expense, which is not affordable for a sensor node. For instance, to perform a single security function, the RSA algorithm needs to execute the basic multiplication instructions thousands or even millions times, which is computationally expensive. Although public key encryption may not be an ideal solution, it does not mean it is unfeasible at all, especially when hardware upgrade also applies to the sensor node industry. Due to the excellent security properties, recent efforts [8] [6] [7] have found ways to use public key cryptography in WSNs along with the correct choice of algorithms and parameters, and other optimization techniques. A set of popular public key algorithms have been studied, including RSA [9], Rabin's Scheme [10], NtruEncrypt [11], and Elliptic Curve Cryptography (ECC) [12], in which RSA and ECC are the two of main interest. The strength of ECC is that it offers high security with less cost in terms of processing and communication overhead. Although public key schemes are applicable, compared to symmetric key schemes, they are still very expensive.

- Symmetric key cryptography - Researchers have tested different symmetric key algorithms in including RC4 [13], RC5 [14], IDEA [13], SHA-1 [16], and MD5 [15] on multiple platforms from 8 bit (Atmel AVR) to 16 bit (Mitsubishi M16C) to 32 bit widths (StrongARM, XScale) [17]. For each scheme, the code memory size and execution time are used as metrics. In addition, hashing algorithms such as MD5 and SHA leads to higher overhead compared to encryption algorithms such as RC4 and IDEA. Law et al. tested six block ciphers in [18], including Camellia[21], KASUMI [20], Rijndael [23], MISTY1 [19], RC5, and RC6 [22]. The testing results show that Rijndael is a better choice for providing high-security level and energy-efficiency. Besides Law's work, other similar studies show different results, though. [25] suggests RC5, and a study in [24] recommends RC6. In all, Law's work offers a general plan to help people decide which symmetric algorithm should be adopted in WSNs.

Cryptography Selection is fundamental to providing security services in WSNs. Most security approaches adopt symmetric key cryptography, thus introducing complex key management. Although some recent studies show public key cryptography is available for WSNs, private key operations in asymmetric cryptography schemes are still too expensive in terms of computation and energy cost for sensor nodes, and still need further studies [5].

2.2.2. Key Management

Key management is an essential scheme for building a complete security framework. The purpose of key management in WSNs is to deliver valid keys among sensor nodes for data exchange. One challenge of WSN key management is the topology dynamics, meaning that nodes may be added or removed from the sensing environment since each node has limited power. Therefore, a key management protocol should take this dynamic feature into consideration.

As we mentioned that public key schemes are limited by WSNs, researchers tend to study key management mechanisms under symmetric key cryptography. In addition, it has been pointed out that a pairwise secret key sharing scheme is not practical for large scale WSNs, because it requires each node to store $n - 1$ secret keys for every other node in the WSN, in which n is the total number of nodes. If there are thousands of nodes, then it requires a large amount of memory for the pairwise secret key sharing scheme; not to mention that most keys will never be used due to the limited communication range for a sensor node. A comprehensive investigation on WSN key management can be found in [26]. Also, Wang et al. [2] suggest a a taxonomy of key management protocols in WSNs. In this paper, we will follow Wang's taxonomy. Based on the network structure, there are centralized key schemes and distributed key schemes; based on probability of key sharing between a pair of sensor nodes, there are probabilistic key schemes and deterministic key schemes.

Network-structure-based Key Management Protocols

Based on the network structure, the key management protocols can be divided into two categories: centralized key schemes and distributed key schemes.

- Centralized key schemes - In this scheme, there is a key distribution center (KDC) playing the role of coordinator that is responsible for key generation and distribution. There is a limited number of studies about centralized key schemes for WSNs. One example is the LKHW scheme [27], which employs the base station as a KDC and the entire network forms a tree rooted at the base station through which all keys are distributed along with the key hierarchy.
- Distributed key schemes - This scheme sets up multiple controllers for key generation and distribution. This is a more robust scheme since the risk of failure is minimized. In addition, the number of controllers is proportional to the size of the WSN. Hence the scheme is more scalable. Most existing studies fall in to this category.

Key Management Protocols Based on the Probability of Key Sharing

For the rest of this section, we discuss the key management schemes based on the probability of key sharing. There are two categories: deterministic approaches and probabilistic approaches.

- Deterministic approaches - In [28], Zhu et al. have proposed a key management protocol, Localized Encryption and Authentication Protocol (LEAP) for WSNs. There are different types of keys supported by LEAP for each node: 1) An individual key shared with the base station, 2) a group key shared by all nodes in the network, 3) pairwise keys shared with immediate neighbors for the protection of P2P communication, and 4) a cluster key shared within a cluster for local broadcast. In another work, Cametepe and Yener [29] propose to use Combinatorial Design Theory for the design of a deterministic key distribution scheme in WSNs. The idea is based on block design techniques in combinatorial design theory. In particular, The scheme adopts a finite projective plane of order n in order to generate a symmetric design using parameters $n^2 + n + 1$, $n + 1$, and 1. The system supports up to $n^2 + n + 1$ nodes with a key-pool size of $n^2 + n + 1$. Also, multiple key chains of size $n + 1$ are generated such that there is only one key in common for each pair of key chains. Following this setup, every pair of nodes can only have one common key, meaning that the probability of key sharing between a pair of nodes is 1. The weakness of this scheme is that n has to be chosen from prime numbers, hence only a network whose size is a prime number can be supported. lee and Stinson [30] expand the use of combinatorial design theory and propose two more schemes: the ID-based one-way function scheme (IOS) and the deterministic multiple space Bloms scheme (DMBS). In [31], they also adopt combinatorial set systems in the design of deterministic key management mechanisms for WSNs.

- Probabilistic approaches - In work [32], Eschenauer and Gligor propose a probabilistic key sharing scheme based on a random graph consisting of senor nodes. The scheme includes three steps: key predistribution, shared key discovery, and path key establishment. In this first step, each node holds a key ring consisting of k keys that are randomly taken from a pool of P keys. Also, the scheme assumes that a pairwise key is shared between each node and the base station. In the second step, each node looks for its immediate neighbors who has a shared key. The authors suggest two methods to accomplish this goal: 1) each node broadcasts a set of key identifiers in the key ring so neighbors can check whether there is a shared key. The problem for this method is that an attacker may observe the key-sharing patterns. 2) Another method is to use the challenge-response-based hand shaking process to hide the key-sharing patterns. For the third step, a path-key will be created for nodes that are neighbors but do not share a key. If a node is attacked or compromised, the base station will send a revocation message to all other nodes to remove the key from a node's key ring. Following Eschenauer and Gligor's work, other studies have been conducted in [33]-[38]. Chan et al. [33] argue that increasing the amount of key overlap in the key ring can increase the resilience of the network against node capture. They develop a q-composite keying approach, which requires to setup at least q common keys to create a secure link for any two adjacent nodes. In work [36], Du et al. propose another pairwise key predistribution approach based on Bloms method [39]. Du's work differs from Liu's work [34] in that the latter is based on a set of bivariate t-degree polynomials while Dus scheme is based on Bloms method. Both Liu's and Du's methods enable any pair of nodes (not necessarily being neighbors) to find a shared key. Another following study is conducted by Hwang et al. They propose a cluster key grouping scheme in [38] to give further analysis on the tradeoff among energy, memory, and security robustness. Recent efforts [37] and [40] also consider location information as a key part for performance improvement (e.g., network connectivity, network resilience, memory usage) during key management, since the usage of location can help to avoid unnecessary key assignments. Although the network performance benefits from the location information, using this information during system deployment requires extra efforts.

Key management is the linchpin of cryptograph mechanism especially for symmetric key cryptography. After reviewing current approaches, we give our suggestions: adopting symmetric cryptography and one-way hash functions and using a distributed mechanism instead of a centralized mechanism; combining deployment knowledge, location information, and key predistribution; integrating node identity and key produce; adopting an adaptive re-key mechanism to defend against cryptography attacks; integrating secure resilience and a system application environment; considering network structure, etc [5].

2.2.3. Secure Broadcasting and Multicasting

Multicasting and broadcasting techniques are motivated by the need of reducing communication overhead when a node is requested to send a message to multiple users. It is important to protect data security through encryption. Traditional studies of secure multicasting and broadcasting rely on cryptography, and this is also the case for WSNs. Since the transmitted message can only be accessed by a group of nodes, it is natural to set up a group key that is shared within the group. Therefore, the technique challenge is reduced to a group key management problem, which has been well addressed in the previous section. Notice that both centralized and distributed key management schemes can be applied to build a secure multicasting/broadcasting protocol. For example, Kaya et al. present the multicast group management problem [41]. In their work, they build a security tree whose nodes can be grouped according to the locality degree. Lazos and Poovendran propose a greedy routing-aware scheme for key distribution in work [42]. They build a tree in which each leaf node keeps a key for all ancestors along the path up to the root. Also, the tree is routing-ware. The proposed scheme makes use of the routing information, making the method a more energy efficient one than the routing schemes put nodes into the tree in an arbitrary way. A follow-up work is conducted in [43]. Instead of using routing information, the authors employ geographic location information to form a cluster in which nodes can share encryption keys.

3. WSN Integrity

WSN integrity is another security objective. As discussed above, WSN confidentiality aims to provide data access only to authorized entities. Speaking of integrity for a WSN, it means the data collected or tasks performed by a WSN is accurate, not being maliciously tampered with or accidentally corrupted. To address WSN integrity, we need answer a question: how one can trust the accuracy of information provided by a WSN? In this section, we will discuss the possible attacks on WSN integrity and provide corresponding countermeasures. Figure 2 highlights the attacks and defense strategies.

3.1. Attacks

We first discuss the possible attacks on WSN integrity. We consider node or system failure as a kind of attack as well.

- A compromised node can behavior arbitrarily. For example, the node can stop sending sensory data to the base station; or even worse, it can send forged data back.
- Data aggregation is an essential part for WSNs since each node is normally responsible for a small portion of data collection. Therefore, it is beneficial to have raw data processed or fused before it is sent back to the base station. A node who deals with data aggregation is called an aggregator. However, this makes the aggregator vulnerable to external attacks due to its important function. Thus, secure data aggregation is necessary for WSNs. The main issue with regular fusion techniques is that they assume all nodes can be trusted. But the reality is a node may be compromised and the

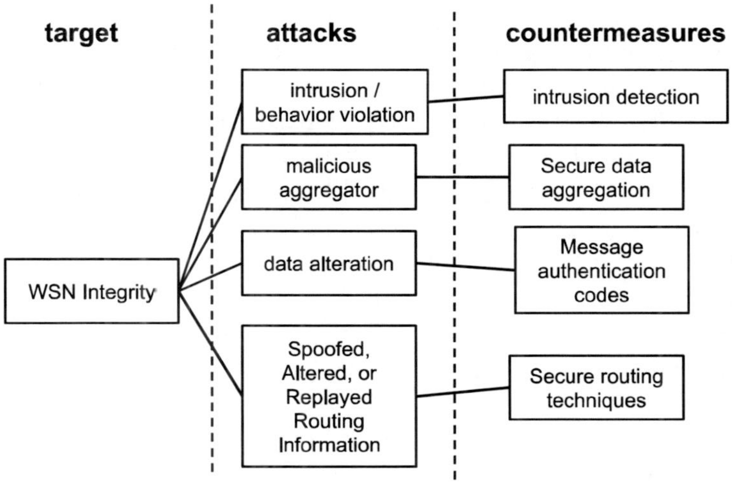

Figure 2. A summary of WSN integrity.

secure data aggregation needs to address this issue. For example, in a stealthy attack [68], the attacker seeks to provide incorrect aggregation results to the user without the user knowing that the results are incorrect.

- Data integrity is violated by both node and system failure. This could happen when 1) a node is misconfigured, 2) the embedded program has errors or faults which lead to misbehavior, and 3) data is corrupted or lost during transmission. For data collection application, the consequence of failure is more severe.
- Spoofed, Altered, or Replayed Routing Information - A routing protocol may be attacked by manipulating the routing information itself during data exchange between sensor nodes. These routing information may be spoofed, altered, or replayed by an attacker to disrupt traffic [54]. The consequences of routing attack include the creation of routing loops, attracting or repelling network traffic from select nodes, extending and shortening source routes, generating fake error messages, partitioning the network, and increasing end-to-end latency [2].

3.2. Countermeasures

3.2.1. Intrusion Detection

Intrusion detection is a common technique used to monitor network behavior for malicious activities or policy violations. Once anomaly is identified, the intrusion detection system shall report to the management station shortly. Normally, WSNs employ cryptography to protect system recourses from being accessed by external attackers. However, if a node is already compromised and controlled by an adversary, cryptographic methods is unable to detect them. Therefore, intrusion detection systems can well complement cryptography toward a solid security framework.

There are two categories for intrusion detection systems (IDS): host-based IDS and network-based IDS. A host-based IDS system works on various system trials and logs for the purpose of host auditing. If anomaly appears on a host, auditing system trials may help identify it. A network-based IDS monitors and examines the incoming and outgoing traffic. Brutch and Ko further classify IDSs into those that are signature based, anomaly based, and specification based [44]. A signature-based IDS relies on a set of signatures that are constantly updated. If the system detects a pattern match between the signature and the traffic, an alert will trigger. For an anomaly-based scheme, the system defines what correct behavior is and any deviation from that behavior will trigger the IDS. A specification-based IDS specifies a protocol's standard operation, and any violation will be regarded as abnormal operation. In addition, Brutch and Ko also present three architectures for WSN IDS.

Albers et al. propose to deploy a local IDS at each node in [45]. To obtain a bigger picture of the network, the authors suggest each local IDS to collaborate with other local IDSs. Two kinds of data, i.e., security data and intrusion alerts, are exchanged within the network. The former simply carries any message specified in the security protocol, while the latter is used to help other nodes for a local intrusion detection.

3.2.2. Secure Data Aggregation

Przydatek et al. propose a secure information aggregation technique (SIA) in [46]. SIA is designed to defend against stealthy attack. Thus the goal of SIA is to ensure that there is a high probability that any aggregated value accepted by a user is close to the true aggregation value [46]. If, however, the aggregation value is tampered with, the chance that this value is denied will be very high. To accomplish the goal, the authors develop an aggregate-commit-prove technique, which consists of three steps, as the name suggests. First, the aggregator follows an aggregating function to fuse the raw data collected from other nodes. Naturally, the aggregator will share a key with each sensor within the same group for basic authentication purpose. However, it is possible that a compromised sensor node also owns the key, or the sensor node is malfunctioning. The aggregate phase can not address such problems. In the second step (i.e., the commit phase), the aggregator needs to commit to the collected data, meaning that the aggregator shall prove that it actually uses the data from other sensors. The authors employs a Merkle hash-tree [47] to achieve this goal. By doing so, the aggregator computes a hash value for each input, which is a piece of collected data, and then assign the value to a leaf in the hash-tree. The hash value for an internal node is a concatenated value of the hash values of its children. The root node's value is used as commitment. This scheme ensures that the aggregator can not alter any inputs after hashing them. Finally, the aggregator needs to prove to the user the results are intact. The aggregator sends both the fusion results and the commitment to the user who will check whether the committed data is actually generated using data collected from the network.

Hu and Evans employ the TESLA protocol for a secure aggregation solution [48]. In their work, sensor nodes form a tree-like hierarchy in which each internal node plays the role of an aggregator. Since the TESLA protocol is asymmetry by delaying the reveal of symmetric keys, a internal node is unable to verify the authenticity for its child immediately. It is pointed out that TESLA protocol can not ensure the correctness of data provided by sensors and aggregators. To this end, the authors suggest to let the base station distribute temporary keys and the base station's current TESLA key for MAC verification. Using this TESLA key, an aggregator can verify their children's MACs.

3.2.3. Secure Routing Techniques

Routing is another important function for a WSN since sensory data needs to be eventually sent to the base station over multiple hops. In addition, the base station may exchange control messages with sensor nodes. Due to the constraints of WSNs, efficient routing algorithms are desired to make the most use of node's battery to extend the system operation time. Due the diversity of existing routing protocols, it is impossible to design a uniform solution for secure routing.

Deng et al. propose an intrusion tolerant routing protocol called INSENS [49]. The design goal of INSENS is that the system should tolerate intrusions such that the network as a whole remains functioning. They find that an intruder can simply be a malfunctioning node, while detect such a node is very difficult. Deng et al. employs redundancy to mitigate the possible damage made by an intruder. Therefore, to make sure that a message is correctly delivered to the destination, multiple copies are sent along several different paths. They also take advantage of the asymmetry property between the base station and sensor nodes. The asymmetry exists since the base station is more powerful than a sensor. Thus the authors suggest to offload the task of routing table computation to the base station. This can be done as follows: the base station first broadcast a message, which is spread to the entire network; then the base station obtains the local connectivity information from each sensor; at last, the base station generates a set of routing tables which contain the redundancy information for redundant message transmission for each node.

Tanachaiwiwat et al. describe Trust Routing for Location Aware Sensor Networks (TRANS) [51] for data centric networks. In their design, TESLA is employed to implement message authentication and confidentiality. With the support of TESLA, TRANS ensures that a message can use a route of trustworthy nodes. The process can be described as follows: first, the base station broadcasts an encrypted message to all its neighbors, but only trusted neighbors who own the shared key can read the message; the trusted neighbors can then insert their current locations into the message, encrypt it, and then spread it; once the message reaches the destination, the receiver can then follow the path information included in the message to determine a secure route.

One challenge for secure routing in WSNs is that if a malicious or malfunctioning node disrupts the route discovery process, then the entire routing protocol will be disrupted. To address this problem, Papadimitratos and Haas present a secure route discovery protocol that ensures the correctness of topological information under certain conditions [50]. The scheme employs MACs and an accumulation of the node identities when a message traverses a route. Thus, a source node can always obtain the correct topology information since each node along the path adds its identity to the message.

In summary, many sensor network routing protocols are quite simple and offer little to no security features, and there are some types of attacks that disable routing. Though there are some secure routing protocols for ad hoc networks, figuring out how to adapt them to sensor networks still needs more works. After reviewing current approaches, we give our suggestions: Authentication is required for broadcast; A system should prevent adversaries from knowing the network topology; Multi-path can tolerate routing attacks to some extent; Routing information should be encrypted; Identifying malicious nodes and isolating them from routing path will improve system security performance; Integrating location information can help a routing path immune spoof; Using localized algorithms instead of centralized ones will improve system performance; Using the special structure of cluster or hierarchical sensor networks can provide more efficient secure routing algorithm; Base station protection needs more considerations; Reduce overhead when possible; etc [5].

4. WSN Availability

Availability in WSNs means that the desired services delivered by the a sensor network should be kept available all the time. Availability is essential since most WSN applications require continuous environment surveillance. The main approaches to compromise availability are DoS attacks, which aim to disrupt, subvert, or even destroy the entire system. For WSNs, there are various ways to launch a DoS attack. In this section, we will summarize the existing DoS attack types and discuss the corresponding countermeasures. In this section, we classify DoS attacks against WSNs by the target network layer since a DoS attack can occur in any layer of a networked sensing system. Figure 3 highlights the existing DoS attacks and countermeasures.

4.1. Physical Layer

The main attack on physical layer is jamming.

4.1.1. Jamming

Since a WSN is built on a shared medium, it is easy to conduct jamming attack to interfere with the radio frequency that the system is currently using. Xu et al. [52] delivers a comprehensive study of jamming attacks against WSNs.

- Intent - Jamming attempts to cause DoS of either data transmission or reception.
- Approach - There are different attack strategies for an adversary to launch a Jamming attack.
  - A Constant jammer continuously emits a radio signal by either using a wave generator or a normal wireless device that transmits random bits to the channel without following any MAC layer protocols [52].
  - A Deceptive jammer constantly injects regular packets to the channel without any gap between subsequent packet transmissions. As a result, a normal communicator will be deceived into believing there is a legitimate packet and be duped to remain in the receive state.
  - A random jammer alternates between sleeping and jamming. Specifically, after jamming for a while, it turns off its radio and enters a "sleeping" mode to save energy.

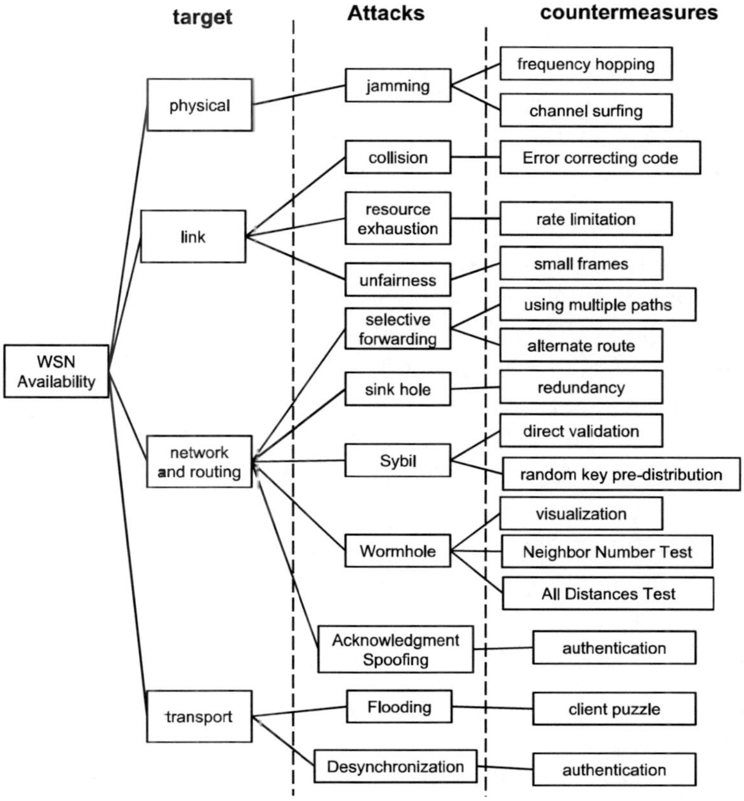

Figure 3. A summary of WSN availability.

- A reactive jammer stays quiet when the channel is idle, but starts transmitting a radio signal as soon as it senses activity on the channel. One advantage of a reactive jammer is that it is harder to detect.

• Countermeasures - Typical defense strategies include frequency hopping and Channel surfing.

  - Frequency-hopping spread spectrum (FHSS) requires both sender and receiver know a pseudo random sequence based on which the frequency channels are switched from one to another. Thus, an attacker is unable to follow the next frequency channel used by the system, which prevents the channel being jammed. However, attacker can choose to jam a wide section of the frequency band and increase the their chance.
  - Channel surfing is another method to defend against jamming. Xu et al. [53] propose two strategies for channel surfing in WSNs: coordinated channel switching, where the entire sensor network adjusts its channel; and spectral multiplexing, where nodes in a jammed region switch channels while nodes on the boundary of a jammed region act as radio relays between different spectral zones.

4.2. Link Layer

The data link layer deal with data stream multiplexing, data frame detection, medium access, and error control [1]. There are three kinds of attacks on data link layer: collisions, resource exhaustion, and unfairness.

4.2.1. Collision

A collision happens when two nodes attempt to send messages at the same time. In that case, a packet may be corrupted, leading to a mismatch of checksum at the recipient end. As a result, the packet will be discarded. Using this method, an attacker may cause collisions on purpose by sending ACK control messages strategically. One consequence is that the back-off times will be increased for certain MAC protocols.

Error-correcting codes can be used to defend against collisions. For low level collisions caused by environment errors, most codes are effective. However, error-correcting codes also add overhead for data processing and communication. Also, it always possible that an attacker can corrupt more than that can be corrected. Therefore, although malicious collision attacks can be detected, there is no perfect defense techniques existing now.

4.2.2. Resource Exhaustion

Resource exhaustion can be launched by repeated collisions. For instance, some link layer implementation may re-transmit the corrupted packets continuously, leading to energy waste. One solution is to set a rate limit so that the system can ignore excessive traffic that attempts to drain energy. Another method relies on time-division multiplexing which assign each node with a time slot. In doing so, each node can only transmit in its own slot and thus can prevent a node from re-transmitting the same package. But the time-division multiplexing technique still suffers from collisions.

4.2.3. Unfairness

Unfairness can be caused by intermittently conducting other link layer attacks. Unfairness is thus regarded as a weak DoS attack, since an attacker's purpose is to impair the network performance rather than shut down a service completely. The use of small frames lessens the effect of such attacks by reducing the amount of time an attacker can capture the communication channel [2]. However, this technique often reduces efficiency and is susceptible to further unfairness, for example, when an attacker is trying to retransmit quickly instead of randomly delaying.

4.3. Network and Routing Layer

Attacks on network and routing layer are as follows.

4.3.1. Selective Forwarding

Selective forwarding is an attack that attempts to disrupt accurate message forwarding in the network. An attacker can employ malicious nodes to drop some messages and only forward certain messages [54]. The black hole attack is a specific form of this attack in which a node drops all messages it receives. One defense against selective forwarding attacks is using multiple paths to send data [54]. A another defense is to detect the malicious node or find an alternative route to bypass it.

4.3.2. Sinkhole

A sinkhole attack attempts to forge routing information for a compromised node so that it looks more attractive to its neighbors [54]. The consequence is that the compromised node will be selected as the node for the next hop by its neighbors. This kind of attack facilitates selective forwarding, because all traffic from a large area in the network will flow through the compromised node.

4.3.3. Sybil

An attacker can conduct the Sybil attack by having a node to present multiple identities in a WSN [54] [55]. The sybil attack can affect fault-tolerant schemes, distributed storage, and network-topology maintenance. For example, if a malicious node pretends to be other nodes, then a replica-based fault-tolerance distributed system may fail since a it is possible that multiple replicas turn out to be one node.

4.3.4. Wormholes

A wormhole is a low-latency link between two portions of the network over which an attacker replays network messages [54]. Such a link may be created either by a pair of nodes in different parts of the network communicating with each other or by a single node forwarding messages between two adjacent but otherwise non-neighboring nodes [2]. The former case is closely related to the sinkhole attack, as an attacking node near the base station can provide a one-hop link to that base station via the other attacking node in a distant part of the network. Hu et al. developed a general mechanism called packet leashes to detect wormhole attacks [56]. They introduced two types of leashes: geographic leashes and temporal leashes. The proposed mechanisms can also be applied to WSNs.

Wang and Bhargava use a visualization approach MDS-VOW to detect wormholes [57]. MDS-VOW first reconstructs the layout of the sensors using multi-dimensional scaling. To compensate the distortions caused by distance measurement errors, a surface smoothing scheme is adopted. MDS-VOW then detects the wormhole by visualizing the anomalies introduced by the attack. The anomalies, which are caused by the fake connections through the wormhole, bend the reconstructed surface to pull the sensors that are faraway to each other. Through detecting the bending feature, the wormhole is located and the fake connections are identified [57].

Two more mechanisms for wormhole detection are proposed in wireless sensor networks in [58]. The first mechanism, called the Neighbor Number Test (NNT), detects the increase in the number of the neighbors of the sensors, which is introduced by the new links created by the wormhole. The second mechanism, i.e., the All Distances Test (ADT), detects the decrease of the lengths of the shortest paths between all pairs of sensors, which is because of the shortcut links created by the wormhole. Both mechanisms assume that the sensors send their neighbor list to the base station, and it is the base station that runs the algorithms on the network graph that is reconstructed from the received neighborhood information [58].

4.3.5. Hello Flood Attacks

A naive assumption is made by many protocols using HELLO messages that if such as message is received then the sender lies in the radio range. As an attacker, he/she can use a high-powered transmitter to trick a large area of nodes to believe they are neighbors of that transmitting node [54]. If the attacker falsely broadcasts a superior route to the base station, all of these nodes will attempt transmission to the attacking node, despite many being out of radio range in reality.

4.3.6. Acknowledgment Spoofing

Routing algorithms used in sensor networks sometimes require Acknowledgments. An attacking node can spoof the Acknowledgments of overheard packets destined for neighboring nodes in order to provide false information to those neighboring nodes [54]. An example of such false information is claiming a dead node as an alive one.

4.4. Transport Layer

The transport layer is responsible for managing end-to-end connections [1]. Two possible attacks in this layer, flooding and desynchronization, are discussed as follows.

4.4.1. Flooding

Whenever a protocol is required to maintain state at either end of a connection it becomes vulnerable to memory exhaustion through flooding. An attacker may repeatedly make new connection requests until the resources required by each connection are exhausted or reach a maximum limit. In either case, further legitimate requests will be ignored. One proposed solution to this problem is to require that each connecting client demonstrate its commitment to the connection by solving a puzzle. The idea is that a connecting client will not needlessly waste its resources creating unnecessary connections. Given that an attacker does not likely have infinite resources, it will be impossible for him/her to create new connections fast enough to cause resource starvation on the serving node. While these puzzles do include processing overhead, this technique is more desirable than excessive communication [57].

4.4.2. Desynchronization

Desynchronization refers to the disruption of an existing connection. An attacker may, for example, repeatedly spoof messages to an end host, causing that host to request the retransmission of missed frames. If timed correctly, an attacker may degrade or even prevent the ability of the end hosts to successfully exchange data, thus causing them to instead waste energy by attempting to recover from errors which never really existed [57].

A possible solution to this type of attack is to require authentication of all packets communicated between hosts. Provided that the authentication method is itself secure, an attacker will be unable to send the spoofed messages to the end hosts[57].

5. WSN Privacy

One of the security concerns in WSNs is privacy. Adversaries can use even seemingly innocuous data to derive sensitive information if they know how to correlate multiple sensor inputs. For example, in the famous "panda-hunter problem" [59], the hunter can imply the position of pandas by monitoring the traffic. Figure 4 describes the attacks and countermeasures for WSN privacy.

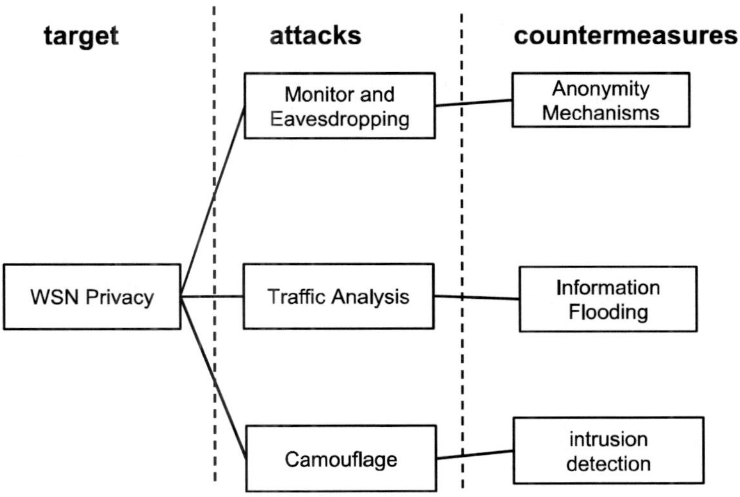

Figure 4. A summary of WSN privacy.

5.1. Attacks

Sensor networks magnify the privacy problem because they make large volumes of information easily available through remote access. Therefore, adversaries need not be physically present in the field where a WSN is deployed. This feature enables attackers to gather information in a low-risk, anonymous manner. Remote access also allows a single adversary to monitor multiple sites simultaneously [60]. Some of the more common attacks against sensor privacy are summarized in [4]:

- Monitor and Eavesdropping - This is the most obvious attack to privacy. By listening to the data, the adversary could easily discover the communication contents. When the traffic conveys the control information about the sensor network configuration, which contains potentially more detailed information than accessible through the location server, the eavesdropping can act effectively against the privacy protection [4].

- Traffic Analysis - Traffic analysis typically combines with monitoring and eavesdropping. An increase in the number of transmitted packets between certain nodes could signal that a specific sensor has registered activity. Through the analysis on the traffic, some sensors with special roles or activities can be effectively identified [4].

- Camouflage - Adversaries can insert their node or compromise the nodes to hide in the sensor network. After that these nodes can masquerade as a normal node to attract the packets, then misroute the packets, e.g. forward the packets to the nodes conducting the privacy analysis [4].

5.2. Countermeasures

There exist effective techniques to counter many of the attacks levied against a sensor. Here we describe several common techniques.

- Anonymity Mechanisms - Anonymity mechanisms depersonalize the data before the data is sent, which makes it more difficult to tell which piece of data belongs to which individual. Researchers have proposed several approaches for anonymity mechanisms, for example, Gruteser and Grunwald [61] analyze the feasibility of anonymizing location information for location-based services in an automotive telematics environment; Beresford and Stajano [62] independently evaluate anonymity techniques for an indoor location system based on the Active Bat. Total anonymity is a difficult problem given the lack of knowledge concerning a node's location. Therefore, a tradeoff is required between anonymity and the need for public information when solving the privacy problem. Three main approaches are proposed in [63][64][65][66]:

  - Decentralize Sensitive Data - The basic idea of this approach is to distribute the sensed location data through a spanning tree, so that no single node holds a complete view of the original data.
  - Secure Communication Channel - Using secure communication protocols, such as SPINS [25], the eavesdropping and active attacks can be prevented.
  - Change Data Traffic - Depatterning the data transmissions can protect against traffic analysis. For example, inserting some bogus data can intensively change the traffic pattern when needed.
  - Node Mobility - Making the sensor movable can be effective in defending privacy, especially the location. For example, the Cricket system [65] is a location-support system for in-building, mobile, location dependent applications. It allows applications running on mobile and static nodes to learn their physical location by using listeners that hear and analyze information from beacons spread throughout the building. Thus the location sensors can be placed on the mobile device as opposed to the building infrastructure, and the location information is not disclosed during the position determination process and the data subject can choose the parties to which the information should be transmitted.

- Policy-based Approaches - Policy-based approaches are currently a hot approach to address the privacy problem. The access control decisions and authentication are made based on the specifications of the privacy policies. In [67], Molnar and Wagner present the concept of private authentication, and give a general scheme for building private authentication with work logarithmic in the number of tags in (but not limited by) RFID (radio frequency identification) applications. In the automotive telematics domain, Duri and colleagues [68] propose a policy-based framework for protecting sensor information, where an in-car computer can act as a trusted agent. Snekkenes [69] presents advanced concepts for specifying policies in the context of a mobile phone network. These concepts enable access control based on criteria such as time of the request, location, speed, and identity of the located object. Myles and colleagues [70] describe an architecture for a centralized location server that controls access from client applications through a set of validator modules that check XML-encoded application privacy policies. Hengartner and Steenkiste [71] point out that access control decisions can be governed by either room or user policies. The room policy specifies who is permitted to find out about the people currently in a room, while the user policy states who is allowed to get location information about another user.

- Information Flooding - Ozturk et al. propose anti-traffic analysis mechanisms to prevent an outside attacker from tracking the location of a data source, since that information will release the location of sensed objects [59]. The randomized data routing mechanism and phantom traffic generation mechanism are used to disguise the real data traffic, so that it is difficult for an adversary to track the source of data by analyzing network traffic. Based on ?ooding-based routing protocols, Ozturk et al. have developed comparable methods for single path routing to try to solve the privacy problems in sensor network. Another strategy used to mask location information from eavesdroppers is presented in [72]. They propose a two way greedy random-walk strategy GROW (Greedy Random Walk). In this case, the random walk is taken from both the source and the sink. The sink first initiates a N-hop random walk. The source then initiates a M-hop random walk. Once the source packet reaches an intersection of these two paths, it is forwarded through the path created by the sink. Local broadcasting is used to detect when the two paths intersect. In order to minimize the chance of backtracking along the random walk, the nodes are stored in a bloom filter as the walk progresses. At each stage, the intermediate nodes are checked against the bloom filter to ensure that backtracking is minimized [72].

6. Opportunities

It is worth noting that current countermeasures can not address all security problems. In this section, some opportunities are pointed out [5].

- Inexpensive private key operations on sensor nodes: Though some studies show that asymmetric key cryptography can be used to secure WSNs, improving the efficiency of private key operations on sensor nodes is highly desirable [5].

- Key management for mobile flat WSNs: Most current key management protocols are only suitable for static WSNs. New protocols for mobile WSNs including mobile nodes and mobile base stations need to be developed [5].
- Intelligent attack/node compromise detecting mechanism: Most current detecting systems monitor all the nodes in the system without emphasis, and the system should decentralize their resources evenly in all nodes in order to monitor whether they have larger compromise probabilities or not. That makes the detecting mechanism less efficient. Due to the heavy work, the system performance may decrease largely, and may even make this work unpractical. It is highly desirable to design an efficient and effective mechanism that chooses those nodes with larger probabilities of being attacked as the main monitoring objects [5].
- Secure routing for mobile WSNs: Most current secure routing algorithms assume the sensor network is stationary. It is highly needed to study secure routing protocols for mobile WSNs [5].
- Secure routing to defend against undetected attacks: Currently, there are some protocols that let routing paths bypass the detected compromised nodes or attacks. However, most compromise activities can not be immediately detected because any detecting mechanism needs time and the fraudulent action of adversaries (adversaries dont want system to notice their attacking activities, thus they will adopt any action that one can imagine to make the detecting time longer.) makes the time even longer. Consequently, current secure routing algorithms have no effect to conquer undetected attacks. New secure routing protocols that can defend against undetected attacks or node compromise are highly desirable [5].
- Security and QoS: Most current security studies focus on individual topics of security issues. However, security overhead will degrade other performances of WSNs. The tradeoff between security and QoS needs to be evaluated [5].
- Base station protection: Most approaches assume the base station is secure and robust enough. However, in some special application environment, such as battlefield surveillance, base stations may be easy to be destroyed or attacked. Under such conditions, base station protection and the other issues that are introduced by the base station protection must be carefully investigated [5].

7. Conclusion

In this chapter, we have investigated the security attacks and countermeasures for WSNs from four aspects: WSN confidentiality, WSN integrity, WSN availability, and WSN privacy. Within each category we describe the main security issues using an attack-defense tree methodology. Our main goal of this chapter is to deliver a comprehensive review for the cutting edge security techniques for WSNs. We also expect the current and future efforts in WSN security and privacy will make WSNs a more competitive option in various applications.

References

[1] I. Akyildiz, W. Su, Y. Sankarasubramaniam, and E. Cayirci, "A survey on sensor networks," *IEEE Commun. Mag.*, vol. 40, pp. 102114, 2002.

[2] Y. Wang, G. Attebury, and B. Ramamurthy, "A survey of security issues in wireless sensor networks," *IEEE Communications Surveys Tutorials*, vol. 8, no. 2, pp. 223, 2006.

[3] J. Hill et al., "System Architecture Directions for Networked Sensors," *ASPLOSIX: Proc. 9th Int'l. Conf. Architectural Support for Programming Languages and Operating Systems*, New York: ACM Press, 2000, pp. 93104.

[4] J.P. Walters, et al. "Wireless sensor network security: A survey." *Security in distributed, grid, mobile, and pervasive computing* 1 (2007): 367.

[5] X. Chen, K. Makki, K. Yen, and N. Pissinou, "Sensor network security: a survey," *IEEE Communications Surveys Tutorials*, vol. 11, no. 2, pp. 5273, 2009.

[6] N. Gura et al., "Comparing Elliptic Curve Cryptography and RSA on 8-bit CPUs," *CHES '04: Proc. Wksp. Cryptographic Hardware and Embedded Systems*, Aug. 2004.

[7] A. S. Wander et al., "Energy Analysis of Public-Key Cryptography for Wireless Sensor Networks," *PerCom 05: Proc. 3rd IEEE Int'l. Conf. Pervasive Computing and Commun.*, Mar. 2005.

[8] G. Gaubatz, J.-P. Kaps, and B. Sunar, "Public Key Cryptography in Sensor Networks-Revisited," *ESAS 04: 1st European Wksp. Security in Ad-Hoc and Sensor Networks*, 2004.

[9] R. L. Rivest, A. Shamir, and L. Adleman, "A Method for Obtaining Digital Signatures and Public-Key Cryptosystems," *Commun. ACM*, vol. 26, no. 1, 1983, pp. 9699.

[10] M. O. Rabin, "Digitalized Signatures and Public-Key Functions as Intractable as Factorization", *Tech. Rep.*, Cambridge, MA, 1979.

[11] J. Hoffstein, J. Pipher, and J. H. Silverman, "Ntru: A Ring-Based Public Key Cryptosystem," *ANTS-III: Proc. 3rd Int'l. Symp. Algorithmic Number Theory*, London: Springer-Verlag, 1998, pp. 26788.

[12] V. S. Miller, "Use of Elliptic Curves in Cryptography," Lecture notes in computer sciences; *218 on Advcnces in Cryptology- CRYPTO 85*, New York: Springer-Verlag, 1986, pp. 41726.

[13] A. J. Menezes, S. A. Vanstone, and P. C. V. Oorschot, *Handbook of Applied Cryptography*, Boca Raton, FL: CRC Press, 1996.

[14] R. L. Rivest, "The RC5 Encryption Algorithm," *Fast Software Encryption*, B. Preneel (Ed.), Springer, 1995, pp. 8696.

[15] R. L. Rivest, *The MD5 Message-Digest Algorithm*, RFC 1321, Apr. 1992.

[16] D. Eastlake III and P. Jones, *"US Secure Hash Algorithm 1 (SHA1)"*, RFC 3174 (Informational), Sept. 2001.

[17] P. Ganesan et al., Analyzing and Modeling Encryption Overhead for Sensor Network Nodes, *WSNA '03: Proc. 2nd ACM Int'l. Conf. Wireless Sensor Networks and Applications*, New York: ACM Press, 2003, pp. 15159.

[18] Y. W. Law, J. M. Doumen, and P. H. Hartel, Benchmarking Block Ciphers for Wireless Sensor Networks (Extended Abstract), *1st IEEE Int'l. Conf. Mobile Ad-hoc and Sensor Systems*, IEEE Computer Society Press, Oct. 2004.

[19] M. Matsui, New Block Encryption Algorithm Misty, *Proc. 4th Int'l. Wksp. Fast Software Encryption*, in LNCS, E. Biham (Ed.), vol. 1267, London: Springer-Verlag, 1997, pp. 5468.

[20] ETSI/SAGE, *Specification of the 3GPP Confidentiality and Integrity Algorithms Document 2: KASUMI Specification*, Dec. 1999.

[21] K. Aoki et al., *Specification of Camellia: A 128-Bit Block Cipher, specification version 2.0*, Nippon Telegraph and Telephone Corporation and Mitsubishi Electric Corporation, 2001.

[22] R. L. Rivest et al., *The RC6 Block Cipher*, submitted to NIST as a candidate for the AES, 1998.

[23] J. Daemen and V. Rijmen, AES Proposal: Rijndael, *Proc. 1st AES Conf.*, Aug. 1998.

[24] S. Slijepcevic et al., On Communication Security in Wireless Ad-Hoc Sensor Networks, *Proc. 11th IEEE Int'l. Wksp. Enabling Technologies: Infrastructure for Collaborative Enterprises (WETICE02)*, 2002, pp. 13944.

[25] A. Perrig et al., SPINS: Security Protocols for Sensor Networks, *Wireless Networks*, vol. 8, no. 5, Sept. 2002, pp. 52134.

[26] J. Zhang and V. Varadharajan, Wireless sensor network key management survey and taxonomy, *Journal of Network and Computer Applications*, vol. 33, no. 2, pp. 6375, Mar. 2010.

[27] R. D. Pietro et al., LKHW: A Directed Diffusion-Based Secure Multicast Scheme for Wireless Sensor Networks, *ICPPW 03: Proc. 32nd Intl. Conf. Parallel Processing Wksps.*, IEEE Computer Society Press, 2003, pp. 397406.

[28] S. Zhu, S. Setia, and S. Jajodia, LEAP: Efficient Security Mechanisms for Large-Scale Distributed Sensor Networks, *CCS 03: Proc. 10th ACM Conf. Comp. and Commun. Security*, New York: ACM Press, 2003, pp. 6272.

[29] S. A. Cametepe and B. Yener, Combinatorial Design of Key Distribution Mechanisms for Wireless Sensor Networks, *Proc. 9th European Symp. Research Computer Security*, 2004.

[30] J. Lee and D. R. Stinson, Deterministic Key Predistribution Schemes for Distributed Sensor Networks, *Proc. Selected Areas Cryptography*, 2004, pp. 294307.

[31] J. Lee and D. R. Stinson, A Combinatorial Approach to Key Predistribution for Distributed Sensor Networks, *Proc. IEEE Wireless Commun. and Net. Conf.*, 2005.

[32] L. Eschenauer and V. D. Gligor, A Key-Management Scheme for Distributed Sensor Networks, *CCS 02: Proc. 9th ACM Conf. Comp. and Commun. Security*, New York: ACM Press, 2002, pp. 4147.

[33] H. Chan, A. Perrig, and D. Song, Random Key Predistribution Schemes for Sensor Networks, *Proc. IEEE Symp. Security and Privacy*, May 2003.

[34] D. Liu and P. Ning, Establishing Pairwise KeysDistributed Sensor Networks, *CCS 03: Proc. 10th ACM Conf. Comp. and Commun. Security*, New York: ACM Press, 2003, pp. 5261.

[35] R. D. Pietro, L. V. Mancini, and A. Mei, Random Key-Assignment for Secure Wireless Sensor Networks, *SASN 03: Proc. 1st ACM Wksp. Security of Ad Hoc and Sensor Networks*, New York: ACM Press, 2003, pp. 6271.

[36] W. Du et al., A Pairwise Key Predistribution Scheme for Wireless Sensor Networks, *CCS 03: Proc. 10th ACM Conf. Comp. and Communications Security*, New York: ACM Press, 2003, pp. 4251.

[37] W. Du et al., A Key Management Scheme for Wireless Sensor Networks using Deployment Knowledge, *Proc. IEEE INFOCOM*, Hong Kong, 2004, pp. 58697.

[38] D. D. Hwang, B. Lai, and I. Verbauwhede, Energy-Memory- Security Trade-OffsDistributed Sensor Networks, *Proc. 3rd Intl. Conf. Ad-Hoc Networks and Wireless*, July 2004, pp. 7081.

[39] R. Blom, An Optimal Class of Symmetric Key Generation Systems, *Proc. EUROCRYPT 84 Wksp., Advances in Cryptology*, New York: Springer-Verlag, 1985, pp. 33538.

[40] D. Liu and P. Ning, Location-Based Pairwise Key Establishments for Static Sensor Networks, *Proc. ACM Wksp. Security Ad Hoc and Sensor Networks*, Oct. 2003.

[41] T. Kaya, G. Lin, G. Noubir, and A. Yilmaz. Secure multicast groups on ad hoc networks. In *Proceedings of the 1st ACM workshop on Security of Ad hoc and Sensor Networks (SASN 03)*, pages 94102. ACM Press, 2003.

[42] L. Lazos and R. Poovendran. Secure broadcast in energy-aware wireless sensor networks. In *IEEE International Symposium on Advances in Wireless Communications (ISWC02)*, 2002.

[43] L. Lazos and R. Poovendran. Energy-aware secure multicast communication in adhoc networks using geographic location information. In *Proceedings of IEEE International Conference on Acoustics Speech and Signal Processing*, 2003.

[44] P. Brutch and C. Ko. Challenges in intrusion detection for wireless ad-hoc networks. In *2003 Symposium on Applications and the Internet Workshops (SAINT03 Workshops)*, 2003.

[45] P. Albers and O. Camp. Security in ad hoc networks: A general intrusion detection architecture enhancing trust based approaches. In *First International Workshop on Wireless Information Systems, 4th International Conference on Enterprise Information Systems*, 2002.

[46] B. Przydatek, D. Song, and A. Perrig. *Sia: Secure information aggregation in sensor networks*, 2003.

[47] R. C. Merkle. Protocols for public key cryptosystems. In *Proceedings of the IEEE Symposium on Research in Security and Privacy*, April 1980.

[48] L. Hu and D. Evans. Secure aggregation for wireless networks. In *SAINTW 03: Proceedings of the 2003 Symposium on Applications and the Internet Workshops (SAINT03 Workshops)*, page 384. IEEE Computer Society, 2003.

[49] J. Deng, R. Han, and S. Mishra. INSENS: intrusion-tolerant routing in wireless sensor networks. In Technical Report CU-CS-939-02, *Department of Computer Science*, University of Colorado, 2002.

[50] P. Papadimitratos and Z. J. Haas. Secure routing for mobile ad hoc networks. In *Proceedings of the SCS Communication Networks and Distributed System Modeling and Simulation Conference (CNDS 2002)*, 2002.

[51] S. Tanachaiwiwat, P. Dave, R. Bhindwale, and A. Helmy. Poster abstract secure locations: routing on trust and isolating compromised sensors in locationaware sensor networks. In *Proceedings of the 1st international conference on Embedded networked sensor systems*, pages 324325. ACM Press, 2003.

[52] W. Xu, K. Ma, W. Trappe, and Y. Zhang, Jamming Sensor Networks: Attack and Defense Strategies, *Netwrk. Mag. of Global Internetwkg.*, vol. 20, no. 3, pp. 4147, Sep. 2006.

[53] W. Xu, W. Trappe, and Y. Zhang, Channel Surfing: Defending Wireless Sensor Networks from Interference, in *Proceedings of the 6th International Conference on Information Processing in Sensor Networks*, New York, NY, USA, 2007, pp. 499508.

[54] C. Karlof and D. Wagner, Secure Routing in Wireless Sensor Networks: Attacks and Countermeasures, *Proc. First IEEE Int'l. Wksp. Sensor Network Protocols and Applications*, May 2003, pp. 11327.

[55] J. Newsome et al., The Sybil Attack in Sensor Networks: Analysis and Defenses, *IPSN '04: Proc. IEEE Int'l. Conf. Info. Processing in Sensor Networks*, Apr. 2004.

[56] Y.-C. Hu, A. Perrig, and D. B. Johnson, Packet Leashes: A Defense Against Wormhole Attacks in Wireless Networks, *Proc. IEEE INFOCOM* 2003, Apr. 2003.

[57] W. Wang and B. Bhargava. Visualization of wormholes in sensor networks. In *WiSe 04: Proceedings of the 2004 ACM workshop on Wireless security*, pages 5160, New York, NY, USA, 2004. ACM Press.

[58] L. Buttyn, L. Dra, and I. Vajda, statistical Wormhole Detection in Sensor Networks, in *Security and Privacy in Ad-hoc and Sensor Networks*, R. Molva, G. Tsudik, and D. Westhoff, Eds. Springer Berlin Heidelberg, 2005, pp. 128141.

[59] C. Ozturk, Y. Zhang, and W. Trappe. Source-location privacy in energyconstrained sensor network routing. In *Proceedings of the 2nd ACM workshop on Security of Ad hoc and Sensor Networks*, 2004.

[60] H. Chan and A. Perrig. Security and privacy in sensor networks. *IEEE Computer Magazine*, pages 103105, 2003.

[61] M. Gruteser and D. Grunwald. Anonymous usage of location-based services through spatial and temporal cloaking. In *Proceedings of the First International Conference on Mobile Systems, Applications, and Services (MobiSys)*. USENIX, 2003.

[62] A. R. Beresford and F. Stajano. Location Privacy in Pervasive Computing. *IEEE Pervasive Computing*, 2(1):4655, 2003.

[63] M. Gruteser and D. Grunwald. A methodological assessment of location privacy risks in wireless hotspot networks. In *First International Conference on Security in Pervasive Computing*, 2003.

[64] M. Gruteser, G. Schelle, A. Jain, R. Han, and D. Grunwald. Privacy-aware location sensor networks. In *9th USENIX Workshop on Hot Topics in Operating Systems (HotOS IX)*, 2003.

[65] N. B. Priyantha, A. Chakraborty, and H. Balakrishnan. The cricket locationsupport system. In *Proc. of the Sixth Annual ACM International Conference on Mobile Computing and Networking (MOBICOM)*, August 2000.

[66] A. Smailagic, D. P. Siewiorek, J. Anhalt, and Y. Wang D. Kogan. Location sensing and privacy in a context aware computing environment. In *Pervasive Computing*, 2001.

[67] D. Molnar and D. Wagner. Privacy and security in library rfid: Issues, practices, and architectures. In *ACM CCS*, 2004.

[68] S. Duri, M. Gruteser, X. Liu, P. Moskowitz, R. Perez, M. Singh, and J. Tang. Framework for security and privacy in automotive telematics. In *2nd ACM International Worksphop on Mobile Commerce*, 2000.

[69] E. Snekkenes. Concepts for personal location privacy policies. In *Proceedings of the 3rd ACM conference on Electronic Commerce*, pages 4857. ACM Press, 2001.

[70] G. Myles, A. Friday, and N. Davies. Preserving Privacy in Environments with Location-Based Applications. *IEEE Pervasive Computing*, 2(1):5664, 2003.

[71] U. Hengartner and P. Steenkiste. Protecting Access to People Location Information. In *Proceedings of First International Conference on Security in Pervasive Computing*, LNCS. Springer, Mar 2003.

[72] Y. Xi, L. Schwiebert, and W. Shi. Preserving privacy in monitoring-based wireless sensor networks. In *Proceedings of the 2nd International Workshop on Security in Systems and Networks* (SSN 06), IEEE Computer Society, 2006.

In: Horizons in Computer Science Research. Volume 9
Editor: Thomas S. Clary
ISBN: 978-1-63321-522-1

Chapter 4

PERFORMANCE OF A TREE ROUTING TOPOLOGY FOR WIRELESS SENSOR NETWORKS USING DIFFERENT PLATFORMS

S. Aparicio*[*]*, J. Ranz, M. Molero, M. G. Hernández and J. J. Anaya
Instituto de Tecnologías Físicas y de la Información "Leonardo Torres Quevedo",
ITEFI (CSIC), Madrid, Spain

Abstract

A performance evaluation of the Collection Tree Protocol (CTP) topology of wireless sensor networks (WSNs) using different platforms is presented. Three different WSNs composed of Cricket, Mica2 and Iris motes, respectively, were tested at the historical building "Leonardo Torres Quevedo". This deployment is representative of a typical building interior with numerous walls and no direct line of sight between the WSN elements. Cricket and Mica2 platforms have the same microcontroller (ATMega128L) and radio chip (Chipcon CC1000) but using different frequencies, 433 MHz and 900 MHz, respectively. Iris motes utilize the Atmega1281 microcontroller and the Atmel RF230 radio transceiver with a frequency of 2.4 GHz. A methodology to evaluate which platform using the CTP protocol is more appropriate for this particular scenario has been used. This methodology is mainly based on the analysis of two parameters, the percentage of received messages and the lifetime of the wireless sensor network. To analyze in more detail which platform gave the best performance, other communication parameters were measured, such as the number of hops required for every message to reach the base station and the father identifier for each message.

Keywords: Wireless Sensor Networks, collection tree protocol, architectural heritage, real applications

[*] E-mail address: sofia.aparicio@csic.es (Corresponding author).

1. Introduction

WSNs are currently being employed in a variety of real applications. Wireless sensor networks consist of distributed, wirelessly enabled embedded devices capable of employing a variety of electronic sensors. The most attractive feature of wireless sensor networks is their autonomy avoiding the need of costly and ungainly wiring between nodes, instead relying on the flexibility of routing algorithms to transport information from node to node. This allows nodes to be deployed in almost any location and for any application.

Over the last decade, there is a growing effort to protect and support the Cultural Heritage. The need to protect our heritage from the environmental degradation is widely recognized by, e.g., the European Commission. Research has focused on solutions to preserve movable and immovable cultural heritage assets using WSNs [1-5].

The design of a WSN for monitoring and conservation of heritage sites depends on the application scenario. It must consider specific requirements such as the environment, resources, cost, hardware and system constrains. One of the clues of this kind of WSNs is the routing topology that the messages follow to reach the base station. Therefore a preliminary analysis about which topology is more adequate should be carried out in this application scenario.

In this chapter a performance evaluation of the CTP topology of wireless sensor networks using different platforms is presented. Three different WSNs composed of Cricket, Mica2 and Iris motes, respectively, were tested at the historical building “Leonardo Torres Quevedo”. This deployment is representative of a typical building interior with numerous walls and no direct line of sight between the WSN elements. A methodology to evaluate which platform using the CTP protocol is more appropriate for this particular scenario has been used. This methodology has been sent for publication in [6] ant it is mainly based on the analysis of two parameters, the percentage of received messages and the lifetime of the WSN. This topology was selected because it is the most commonly used [7-10]. To analyze in more detail which platform gave the best performance, other communication parameters were measured, such as the number of hops required for every message to reach the base station and the father identifier for each message.

2. Wireless Sensor Networks

Sensor technology plays an important and growing role in todays industry and life. Many production processes rely on sensors for coordination and control. Sensors are crucial as part of security systems and also for monitoring environmental conditions or the structural integrity of buildings. Traditionally those sensors were connected by wires to some central computing device which processes and interprets the sensor signals. This wiring is expensive and severely limits the flexibility and reusability of the sensors. Therefore the use of wireless technologies is gained importance.

The design of a WSN for a real application depends on the scenario. It must consider specific requirements such as the environment, resources, cost, hardware and system constrains. The most important characteristics of this type of networks are the bandwidth, the coverage range, the routing topology and the power consumption. Depending of the number and frequency of measurements required in the application, an adequate bandwidth should be selected. The arrangement of the scenario will define the best routing topology to be deployed. Therefore a routing protocol for a wireless sensor network should ensure that data is forwarded through the network in the most efficient way avoiding unnecessary resending. The main limitation of sensor motes is energy. Being small and independent devices they have to rely on batteries as their energy supply. Several strategies or modes for saving energy are included in these platforms.

In this section a brief overview of the wireless sensor networks developed by MEMSIC Company is presented. This company was selected because it offers several types of platforms suitable for the application presented in this chapter.

2.1. Hardware Platforms

The commercial devices used in this work were purchased from MEMSIC company. MEMSIC supplies different types of motes to meet the specific needs of the application as Cricket, MICA2, MICAz, TelosB, IRIS and the latest generation of motes, LOTUS, see Table 1.

Programs for the MEMSIC motes are written in NesC (an object-oriented extension of C) and run under the TinyOS operating system [11]. This platform was selected mainly because it is an open source wireless sensor platform with open access hardware and software designs.

2.2. Routing Algorithms

The basic network topologies are shown in Figure 1 and include star, ring, bus, tree, fully connected and mesh configurations.

Table 1. Specifications of WSN platforms from MEMSIC

WSN Platform	MICA2 & z	TelosB	IRIS	LOTUS	CRICKET
Application	Educational	R & D	OEM Edition	Industrial Monitoring	Educational
Processor	Atmel ATMega 128L, 8bit	TI MSP 430 16bit RISK	Atmel ATMega 1281	Cortex M3 LPC 17xx 32bit	Atmel ATMega 128L, 8bit
Speed	8 - 16 MHz	8MHz	8 MHz	10-100MHz	8 - 16 MHz
RAM	4Kbytes	10Kbytes	8Kbytes	64Kbytes	4Kbytes
Radio Frequency Range	868-916 MHz, 2.4-2.48 GHz	2.4 - 2.48 GHz ISM	2.4GHZ ISM	2.4GHZ ISM	433 MHz
Tx/Rx	TI - CC 1000 / 2420	TI - CC 2420	RF230 Atmel	RF231 Atmel	TI - CC1000
Data Rate	38.4/250Kbit s/s	250Kbits/s	250Kbits/s	250Kbits/s	115Kbits/s

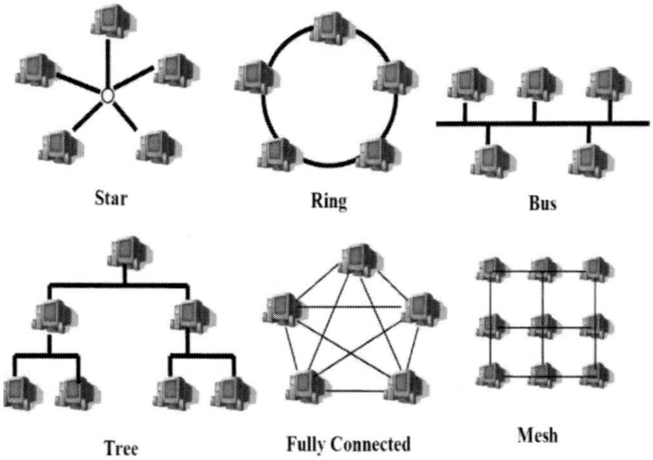

Figure 1. Network topologies [12].

Star Topology

Many home networks use the star topology. A star network features a central connection point called a "hub node" that may be a network hub, switch or router. If the hub fails, however, the entire network also fails.

Ring Topology

In a ring network, every device has exactly two neighbors for communication purposes. All messages travel through a ring in the same direction (either "clockwise" or "counterclockwise"). A failure in any cable or device breaks the loop and can take down the entire network.

Bus Topology

Bus networks (not to be confused with the system bus of a computer) use a common backbone to connect all devices. A single cable, the backbone functions as a shared communication medium that devices attach or tap into with an interface connector. A device wanting to communicate with another device on the network sends a broadcast message onto the wire that all other devices see, but only the intended recipient actually accepts and processes the message.

Tree Topology

Tree topologies integrate multiple star topologies together onto a bus. In its simplest form, only hub devices connect directly to the tree bus, and each hub functions as the root of a tree of devices. This bus/star hybrid approach supports future expandability of the network much better than a bus (limited in the number of devices due to the broadcast traffic it generates) or a star (limited by the number of hub connection points) alone.

Fully connected Topology

In a fully connected network every device is connected to every other.

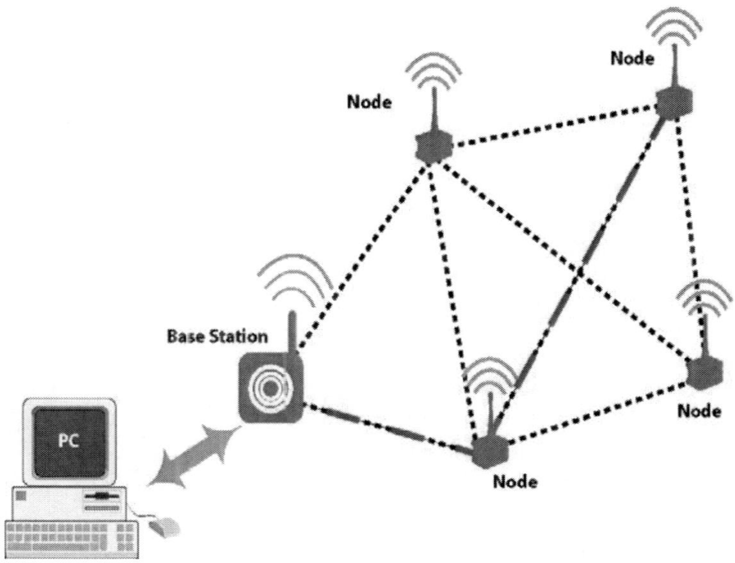

Figure 2. XMESH network diagram [14].

Mesh Topology

Mesh topologies involve the concept of routes. Unlike each of the previous topologies, messages sent on a mesh network can take any of several possible paths from source to destination.

The topologies most commonly used for this type of applications is tree or mesh.

Route and MintRoute were the "standard" routing protocols in TinyOS-1.x and make route decisions based on both link quality estimation and number of hops. Route performs link-quality estimates but bases routing decisions mainly on hop count, using link-quality estimates simply as a threshold to prune very low quality links. In MintRoute, link quality is based on how many packets are sent and overheard successfully on the link. Thus, a node computes the number of overheard packets from a neighbour, but it relies on the neighbour to compute the number of successful transmitted packets [13].

XMESH is a full-featured, multi-hop, ad-hoc, mesh networking protocol developed by MEMSIC for wireless networks [14]. Xmesh is a software library using the TinyOS operating system.

The TinyOS-2.x operating system provides a well-tested, tree-based routing protocol called collection tree protocol [15].

2.3. Power Supply

Power efficiency is a vital factor in software for systems built around battery powered wireless sensor platforms. Not only must sensor system software operate correctly, it must also be structured to conserve battery power to be able to operate on relatively small batteries (e.g., AA) from six months to a year or beyond.

Table 2. Current consumption for the Motes under Various Operations

Operating Current (mA)	IRIS	MICAz	MICA2&CRICKET
Processor, full operation	8 (7.37 MHz)	12 (7.37 MHz)	12 (7.37 MHz)
Processor, sleep	0.008	0.010	0.010
Radio, receive	16	19.7	7
Radio, transmit (1 mW power)	17	17	10
Radio, sleep	0.001	0.001	0.001
Serial flash memory, write	15		
Serial flash memory, read	4		
Serial flash memory, sleep	0.002		

Asynchronous low power listening (LPL) is a strategy provided by TinyOS-2.x used to duty cycle the radio while ensuring reliable message delivery [16]. Using this library motes consume only a few μA when they are sleeping.

3. The Wireless Sensor System

In this section the wireless sensor network systems used by the authors are described. The systems are based on commercial devices.

3.1. The Hardware Platform

Three different WSNs using the same routing topology composed of Cricket, Mica2 and Iris motes, respectively, purchased from MEMSIC were employed, see Figure 3.

The Cricket/Mica2 motes come in three models according to their RF frequency band: the MPR400 (915 MHz), MPR410 (433 MHz), and MPR420 (315 MHz). As previously mentioned, these motes use the Chipcon CC1000, FSK modulated radio and are controlled by an Atmega128L micro-controller with a frequency tunable radio with extended range. The MPR410 and MPR400 models, emitting maximum power, were used in this experiment for Cricket and Mica2 motes respectively.

The Iris motes, XM2110 (2400 MHz to 2483.5 MHz band) uses the Atmel RF230, IEEE 802.15.4 compliant, ZigBee ready radio frequency transceiver integrated with an Atmega1281 micro-controller. These enhancements provide up to three times improved radio range and twice the program memory over previous generation MICA Motes. The same MICA family, 51 pin I/O connector, and serial flash memory is used; all application software and sensor boards are compatible with the XM2110. The Iris motes used in this experiment were also configured to emit a maximum power.

Software programs for motes were written in NesC (an object-oriented extension of C) and run using the TinyOS operating system [11]. Cricket motes run under an old and unsupported version of the TinyOS-1.x operative system, therefore they had been adapted to run under TinyOS-2.x. Each WSN was composed of 7 motes and the base station. Motes were programmed to send a data package of 41 bytes every 2 minutes.

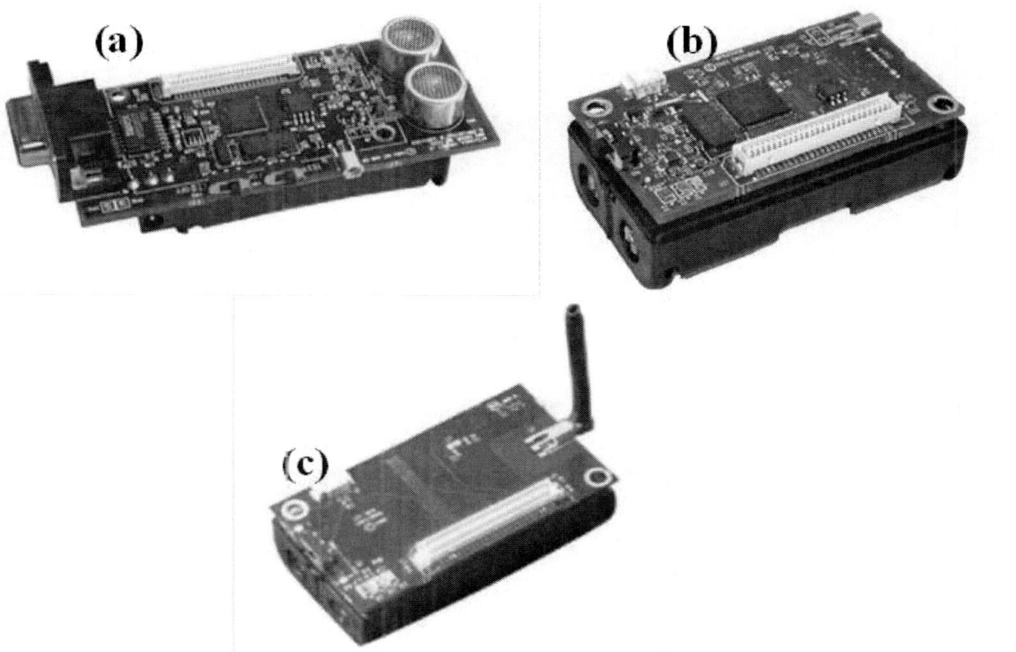

Figure 3. (a) Cricket mote(b) Mica2 mote (c) Iris mote.

3.2. The Routing Algorithm

The TinyOS-2.x operating system provides a well-tested, tree-based routing protocol called CTP. A number of nodes in a network advertise themselves as tree roots. The remaining nodes form a set of routing trees to these roots. CTP is address-free in that a node does not send a packet to a particular root; instead, it implicitly chooses a root by choosing the next hop. Nodes generate routes to roots using a routing gradient [17]. CTP uses expected transmissions (ETX) as its routing gradient, with roots having an ETX of 0. The ETX of a node is the ETX of its parent plus the ETX of its link to its parent. This additive measure assumes that nodes use link-level retransmissions. Given a choice of valid routes, CTP should choose the one with the lowest ETX value.

The main problems that emerge in a CTP network are routing loops and packet duplication. Routing loops generally occur when a node chooses a new route that has a significantly higher ETX than its old one, perhaps in response to losing connectivity with a candidate parent. If the new route includes a node which was a descendant, then a loop occurs. Packet duplication is an additional problem that can occur in CTP. This occurs when a node receives a data frame successfully and transmits an acknowledgment (ACK), but the ACK is not received. The sender retransmits the packet, and the receiver receives it a second time. This can have disastrous effects over multiple hops, as the duplication is exponential.

For example, if each hop on average produces one duplicate, then on the first hop there will be two packets, on the second there will be four, on the third there will be eight, and so on.

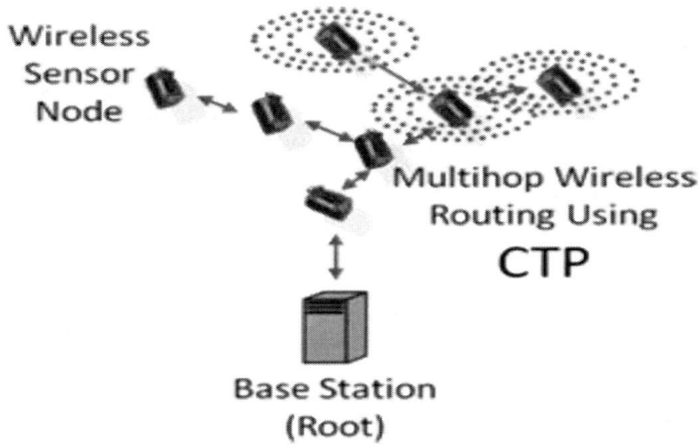

Figure 4. CTP network diagram [17].

3.3. The Power Supply

In the experiments reported here power supply was not taken into account. The main purpose of this work was to test which system is more appropiated to be use in a real environment. Therefore power supply algorithms were not taken into account.

4. Experimental

In this section, we present the scenario of the WSN deployments and the experimental results are reported.

4.1. Scenario of the WSN Deployments

Three experiments were performed at the historical building "Leonardo Torres Quevedo". This deployment is representative of a typical building interior with numerous walls and no direct line of sight between the WSN elements. Three different floors, 2nd , 3rd and 4^{th}floors, of the building were considered during the experiments. The base stations for the three WSNs were always placed at the 3rd floor with id number 0, but the motes were interchanged between floors for each experiment. In Figures 5, 6 and 7 the WSNs deployments located at each floor are presented.

As previously mentioned, each WSN was composed of 7 motes (mote ids from 1 to 7) and the base station (mote id 0). Three different experiments were performed exchanging the motes but keeping the same general spatial configuration, to check the robustness of the results obtained. The motes distribution for each experiment was the same for each WSN network and it is explained in Table 3.

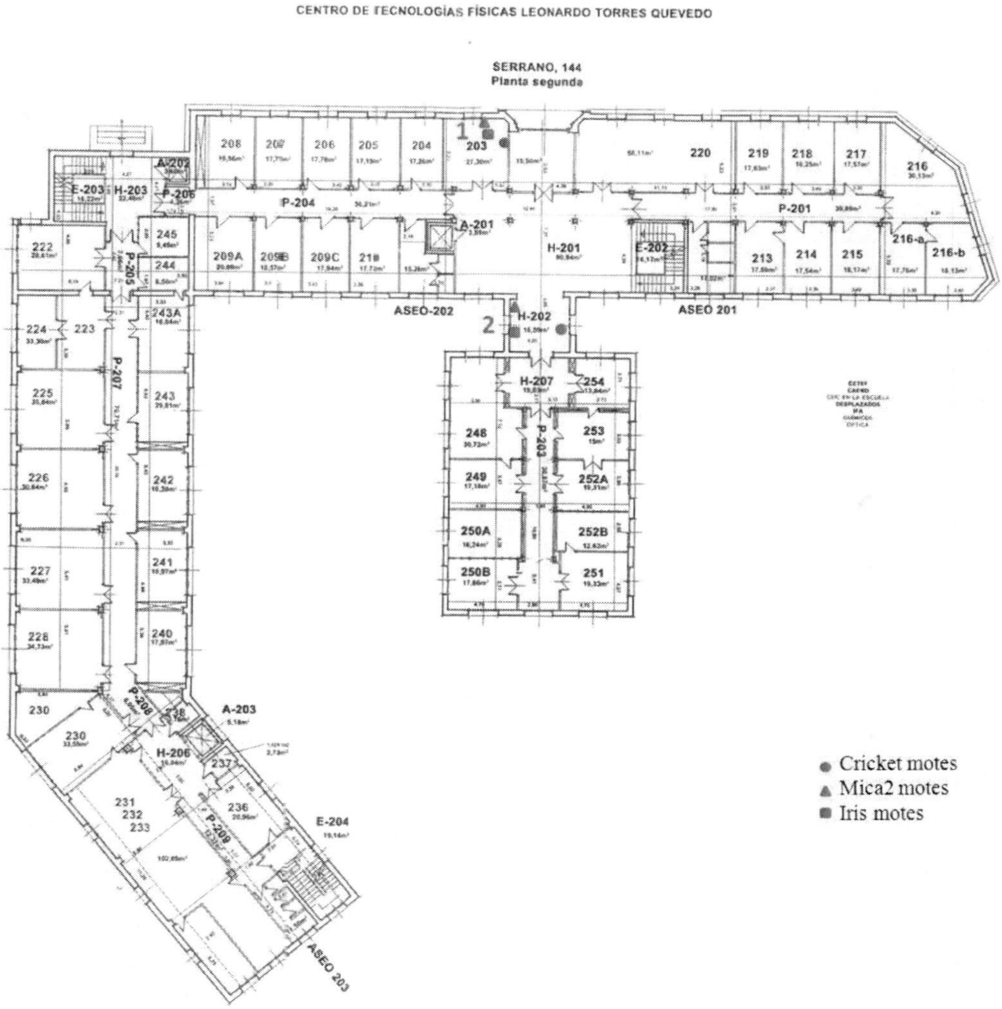

Figure 5. WSNs deployment on the second floor of the ITEFI institute.

Table 3. Motes distribution for each experiment

Room number	203	H-202	306	305	303	H-302	405	H-402
Mote Position	1	2	0	3	4	5	6	7

Experiments started and ended in the morning of different days: Experiment 1 was performed from Friday to Wednesday, Experiment 2 from Wednesday to Monday and Experiment 3 from Monday to Saturday.

Figure 6. WSNs deployment on the third floor of the ITEFI institute.

4.2. Experimental Results and Discussion

In this section, the results obtained with the WSNs during the three experiments are presented. The number of lost messages was compared with the lifetime of the network to analyze the network behavior for a particular scenario and to detect hardware failures. To prevent erroneous data due to the lack of battery power needed to compute the numbers of lost messages, only measurements up to 6930 minutes were considered for each experiment.

The total number of lost messages as a function of time during the three experiments is shown in Figures 8, 9 and 10 for Cricket, Mica2 and Iris networks, respectively.

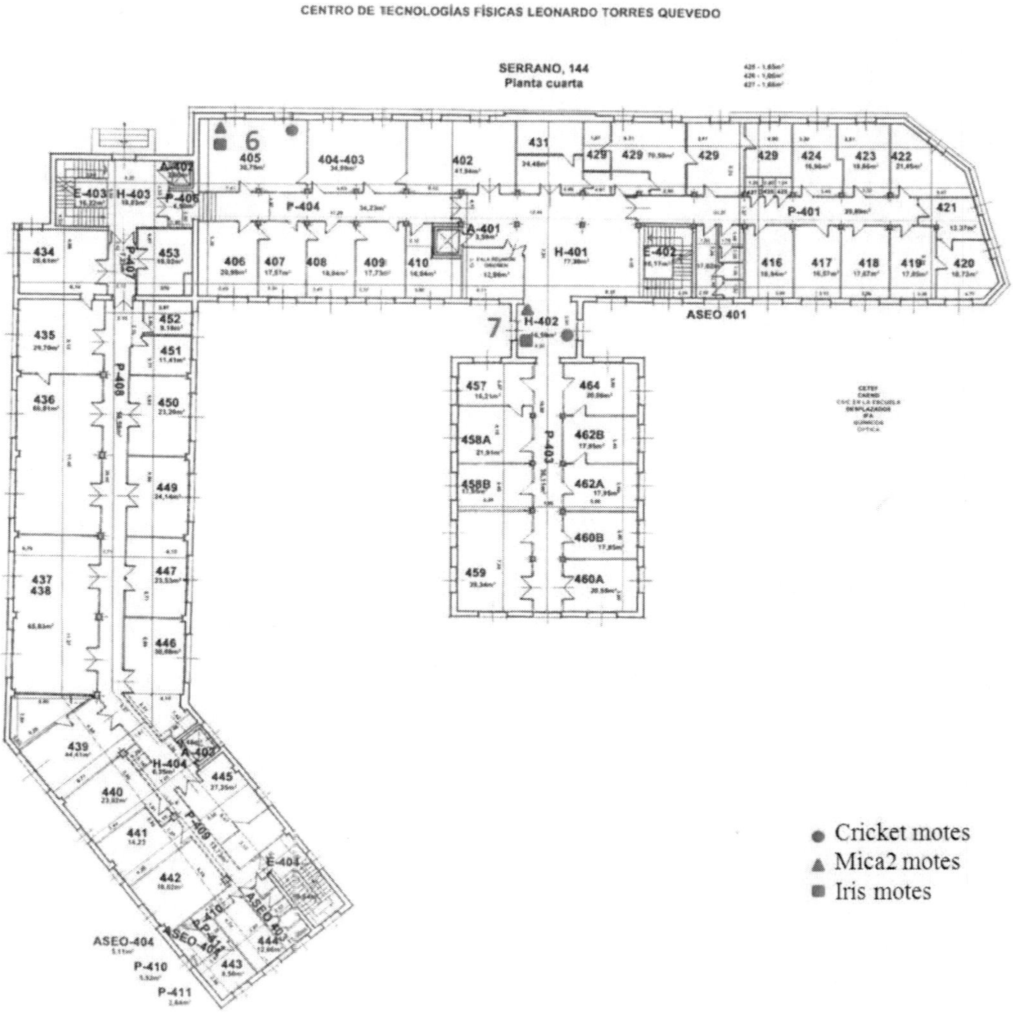

Figure 7. WSNs deployment on the fourth floor of the ITEFI institute.

In the Cricket network, the number of lost messages increased in Experiment 1 and 2 during the week days and in Experiment 3 during the whole experiment since it was performed only during working days.

In the Mica2 network, there was a problem with Mote 6 during Experiment 1. Excluding this problem, it can be noticed that Experiment 1 lost more messages during the working days. Experiments 2 and 3 were very similar during working and not working days.

In the Iris network, Experiment 1 was very similar during working and not working days but in Experiments 2 and 3 there were more lost messages during working days than during the weekend.

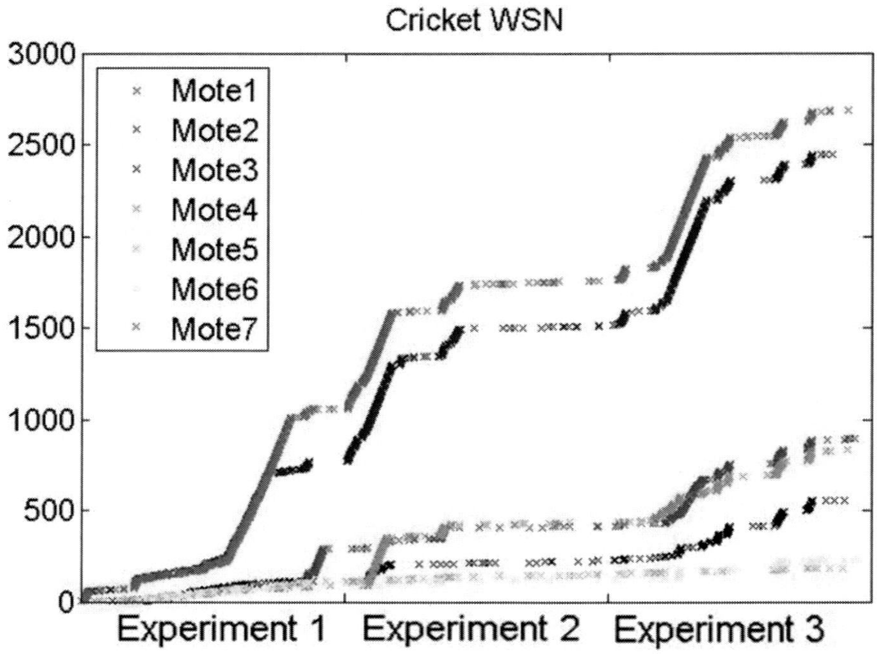

Figure 8. Total number of lost messages as a function of time using the Cricket WSN during all experiments.

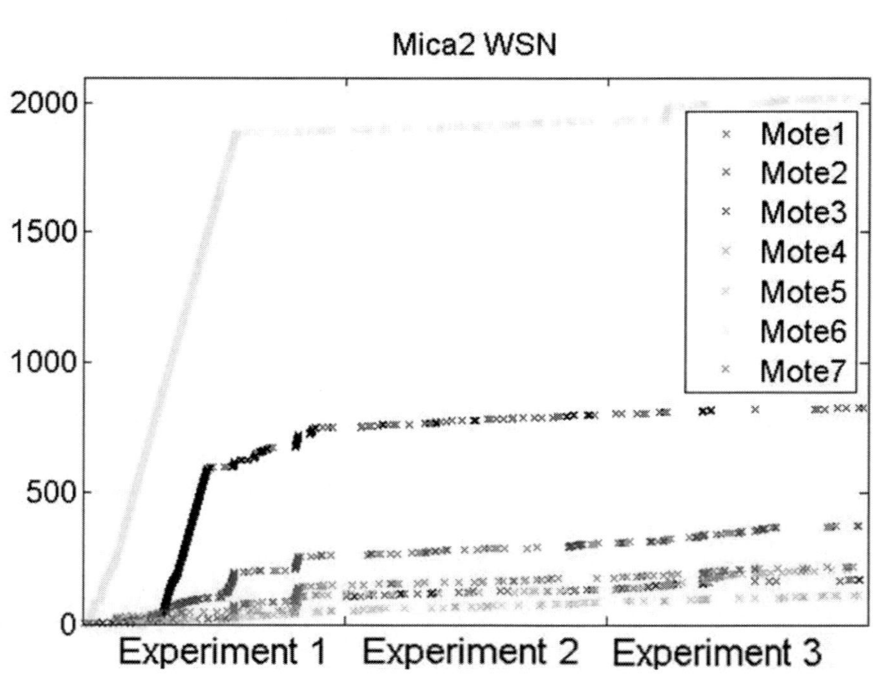

Figure 9. Total number of lost messages as a function of time using the Mica2 WSN during all experiments.

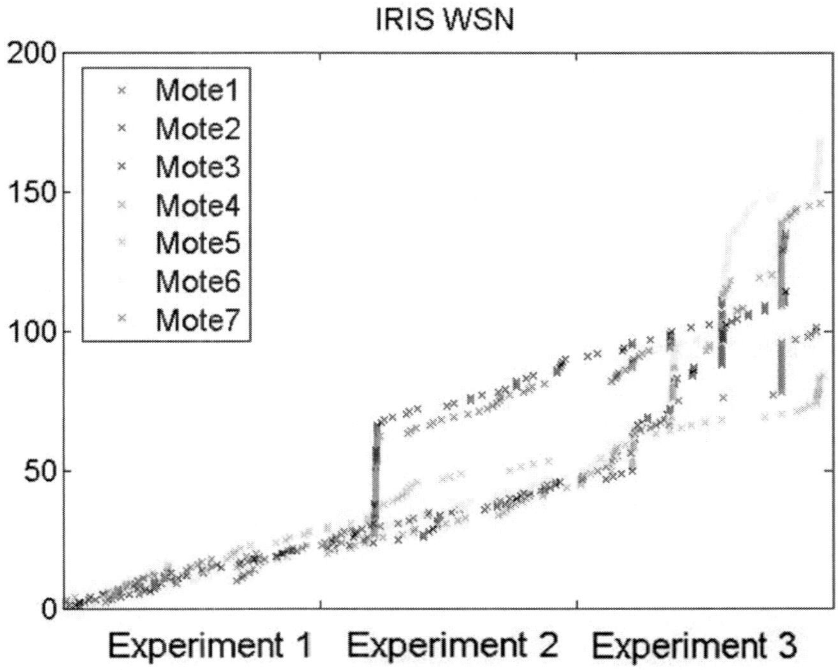

Figure 10. Total number of lost messages as a function of time using the Iris WSN during all experiments.

Table 4 presents the total percentage of received messages for each WSN during the three experiments. The percentage of received messages using the Cricket WSN was lower compared to the Mica2 and Iris WSNs. The percentage of received messages was very similar for Mica2 and Iris WSNs.

The mean and the standard deviation of the percentage of received messages for each WSN in the three experiments is shown in Figure 11. It can be seen that the standard deviation is higher for Cricket motes than for Mica2 and Iris motes. This means that in the Cricket network the number of received messages depends strongly on the relative positions of the motes.

Table 4. Percentage of received messages (R. M.) using the CTP protocol

Mote Position: Cricket/Mica2/Iris	**1**	**2**	**3**	**4**	**5**	**6**	**7**	**Avg**
Cricket R. M. (%)	91.1	75.8	94.5	91.9	76.2	97.7	73.3	81.7
Mica2 R. M. (%)	96.3	98.3	91.9	97.9	98.1	80.1*	97.8	96.7
Iris R. M. (%)	99.0	98.7	98.9	98.6	98.5	98.3	98.7	98.7

*The value of Mote 6 during Experiment 1 has not been considered to compute the average.

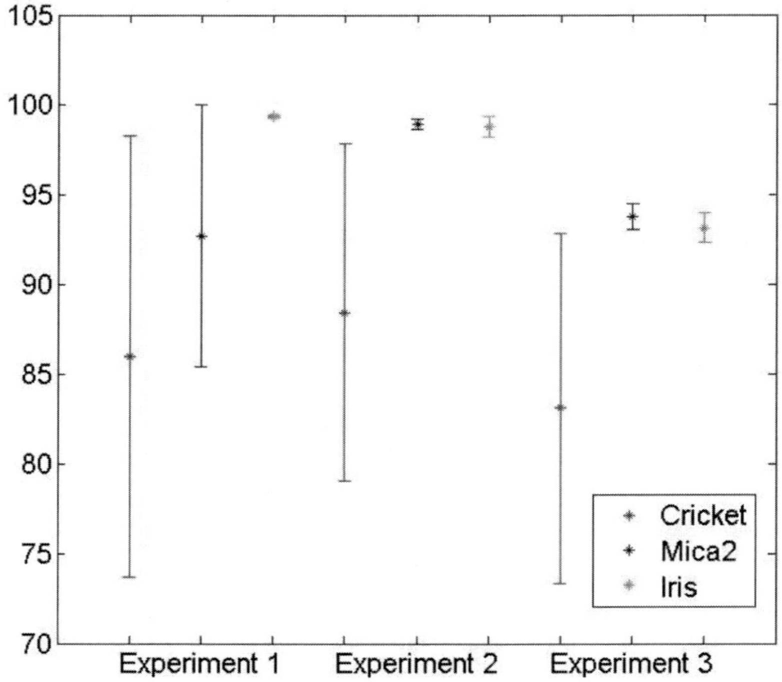

Figure 11. Mean and standard deviation percentage of received messages for each WSN in the three experiments.

The percentage of the relative lifetime of each mote using the different platforms in Experiment 3 is presented in Table 5. The relative lifetime for each experiment corresponds to the lifetime of each mote, where 100% corresponds to the lifetime of the last mote that depleted its energy. The Iris WSN depleted its energy faster than the Cricket and Mica2 WSNs. Considering that the radio was always on and the consumption values provided in Table 2, the expected lifetime of the Iris network should be around 25% lower than the other two networks, but it was only 2% lower. Therefore, if the consumption of the processor is taken into account, the Iris network is more energetically efficient than the Cricket and Mica2 networks. On average, the relative lifetime of the Cricket and Mica2 networks was very similar.

Table 5. Percentage of the relative lifetime of each mote during Experiment 3

Mote Position: Cricket/Mica2/Iris	1	2	3	4	5	6	7	Avg
EXPERIMENT 3								
Cricket Lifetime (%)	98.6	97.9	96.8	98.9	97.9	98.6	100	98.4
Mica2 Lifetime (%)	98.6	98.2	98.6	98.6	98.2	98.2	97.9	98.3
Iris Lifetime (%)	96.1	96.1	96.1	96.5	96.5	97.2	96.8	96.5

Table 6. Average number of hops (A. H.) reached by each WSN and during each experiment

Mote Position: Cricket/Mica2/Iris	1	2	3	4	5	6	7	Avg
EXPERIMENT 1								
Cricket A. H.	0.8	2	0	0.5	1.6	0.5	1.8	1
Mica2 A. H.	1.1	1.4	0.7	0	1.2	0	2.2	0.9
Iris A. H.	1.7	3	0	1	2	0.8	3	1.6
EXPERIMENT 2								
Cricket A. H.	0.9	1.9	0	0.4	1.8	0	1.5	0.9
Mica2 A. H.	0.7	1.9	0	0.9	1.9	0	1.9	1
Iris A. H.	1.1	2.7	0	1	2.2	0	2.7	1.4
EXPERIMENT 3								
Cricket A. H.	0.5	1.4	0.3	0.6	0.9	0.2	1.8	0.8
Mica2 A. H.	0.8	1.4	0.3	0.4	1.4	0	1.6	0.8
Iris A. H.	1.2	2.3	0	0.5	1.7	0	1.9	1.1

Table 6 presents the average number of hops (A.H.), made before a message reaches the base station, for each WSN and during each experiment. In all experiments the A.H. was always larger using the Iris WSN than the Cricket and Mica2 networks. The A.H. using Cricket and Mica2 network was very similar in all experiments, probably because they use the same radiofrequency chip. As expected, the nodes located closer to the base station (3, 4 and 6) presented on average the lowest number of hops for all WSNs and the nodes located farther away from the base station (2 and 7) had the largest number of hops.

The total number of times that a mote was father using the Cricket, Mica2 and Iris networks for each experiment is presented in Figures 12, 13 and 14, respectively. In the Cricket network, most of the motes had direct connection to the base station, Motes 3 and 4 were fathers for a longer time, but also the other motes acted as fathers. In the Mica2 network, usually most of the motes made a direct connection to the base, or alternatively Mote 4 was the father. In the Iris network, most of the motes made a direct connection to the base or alternatively Motes 3, 4 and 5 were the fathers. Comparing the three WSNs, it is found that the number of motes with direct connection to the base station is lower in the Iris network.

A comparison between the number of times that a mote was father and the relative lifetime (Table 5) shows that the number of transmissions does not affect the lifetime of the motes. For example, during Experiment 3 the number of times that the Mica2 Mote 4 was father is very high while Mote 7 very rarely acted as father, but their lifetimes were similar, 98.6% for the former and 98 3% for the latter.

Usually Motes 1, 3, 4 and 6 were the only nodes with direct connection to the base station and, excluding the base station, Motes 3, 4 or 5 were the fathers for a longer time depending on the WSN platform and the experiment.

The number of times that a mote was father for each node using the Cricket, Mica2 and Iris networks for the three experiments is presented in Tables 7, 8 and 9, respectively. Usually Motes 1, 3, 4 and 6 were the only nodes with direct connection to the base station.

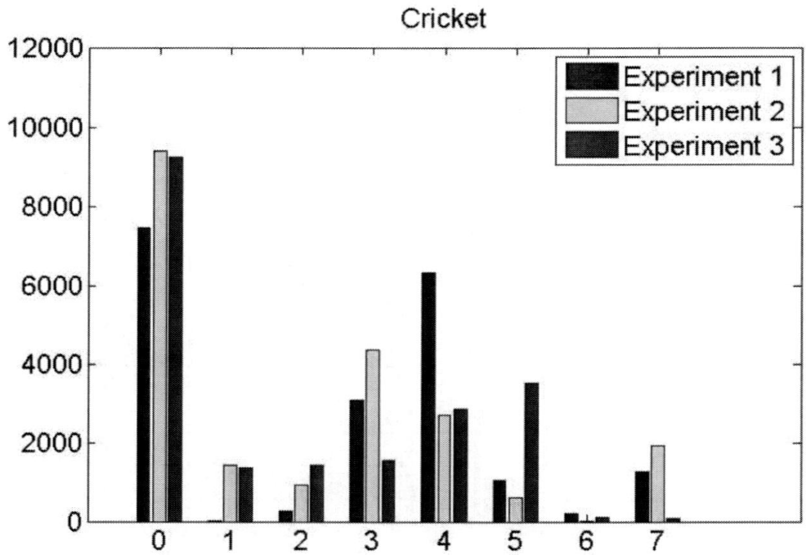

Figure 12. Total number of times that a mote was father for each node using the Cricket network for each experiment.

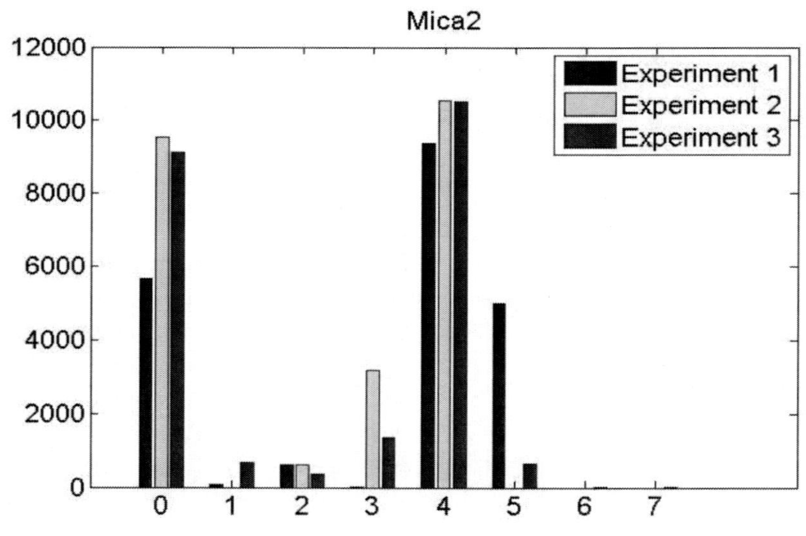

Figure 13. Total number of times that a mote was father for each node using the Mica2 network for each experiment.

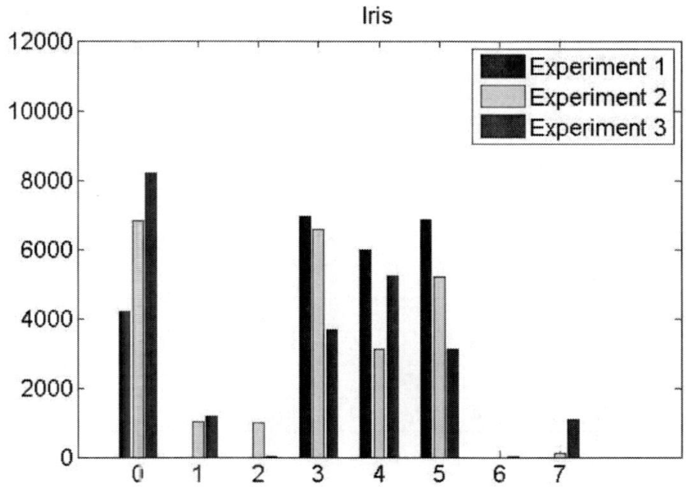

Figure 14. Total number of times that a mote was father for each node using the Iris network for each experiment.

Table 7. Number of times that a mote is father for each node using the Cricket WSN during the three experiments

Cricket	FATHER ID							
	0	1	2	3	4	5	6	7
Mote 1	3255	0	63	3294	2588	36	7	1
Mote 2	504	886	0	402	1311	2708	0	1890
Mote 3	8677	270	3	0	511	49	113	1
Mote 4	4997	1332	37	2576	0	253	79	85
Mote 5	798	247	975	1112	3298	0	30	1288
Mote 6	7823	1	0	930	1120	72	0	0
Mote 7	3	53	1548	667	3066	2069	74	0
Total	26057	2789	2626	8981	11894	5187	303	3265

Table 8. Number of times that a mote is father for each node using the Mica2 WSN during the three experiments

Mica2	FATHER ID							
	0	1	2	3	4	5	6	7
Mote 1	4120	0	991	16	4502	153	1	0
Mote 2	0	662	0	0	7797	1524	0	0
Mote 3	6577	0	0	0	2763	0	14	0
Mote 4	5428	1	4	4531	0	0	0	4
Mote 5	0	91	567	0	9320	0	0	0
Mote 6	8142	0	0	6	0	0	0	0
Mote 7	0	0	10	0	5986	3944	0	0
Total	24267	754	1572	4553	30368	5621	15	4

Table 9. Number of times that a mote is father for each node using the Iris WSN during the thre experiments

Iris	FATHER ID							
	0	1	2	3	4	5	6	7
Mote 1	72	0	2	6426	3573	0	0	0
Mote 2	0	2010	0	0	1	7626	0	412
Mote 3	10071	0	0	0	0	0	0	0
Mote 4	1849	182	0	8008	0	3	1	2
Mote 5	6	2	437	1	8809	0	0	782
Mote 6	7252	0	0	2764	3	0	0	0
Mote 7	1	0	549	1	1968	7531	0	0
Total	19251	2194	988	17200	14354	15160	1	1196

The objective of this work was to evaluate the CTP topology of WSNs using different platforms: Cricket, Mica2 and Iris. Following the methodology proposed in [6], two parameters, the percentage of received messages and the lifetime of the WSN, were proposed to analyze which WSN gives the best performance using the CTP topology in a particular deployment. According to the results reported in Tables 4 and 5, the percentage of received messages using the Cricket WSN was always lower than that using the Mica2 and Iris networks. The Iris WSN depleted its energy faster than the Cricket and Mica2 networks but, if only the consumption of the processor is taken into account, the Iris network was more energetically efficient than the Cricket and Mica2 networks. On average, the relative lifetime of the Cricket and Mica2 networks was very similar.

A more detailed analysis of the data was developed to understand why the Cricket WSN performed worse than the Mica2 and Iris networks in all the experiments. For this purpose, the communication parameters described above will be presented as a function of time during the experiment.

The route followed by each message as a function of time is shown in Figures 15, 16 and 17 during all three experiments for the Cricket, Mica2 and Iris WSN, respectively. The black dot represents the mote that created the message (source mote), a blue dot represents the father of a mote (the first father), a red dot the father of the father (the second father, i.e. a grandfather in human terms), a green dot the third father, a cyan dot the fourth father, a magenta dot the fifth father, a yellow dot the sixth father and a black cross the seventh father.

Comparing the three experiments, it can be seen that the results were indepent of the hardware, i.e. they have not been affected by the use of different motes for the same spatial positions in each experiment.

It was also observed that the Iris WSN network was more stable than the Cricket and Mica2 networks, i.e. there were fewer changes from one father to another. Once a father was selected it was kept for a longer time interval. A comparison between the Mica2 and Cricket networks shows that the former was also more stable than the latter. Considering the lifetime of the networks presented in Table 5, it can be concluded that the instability of the Cricket network does not imply a higher power consumption.

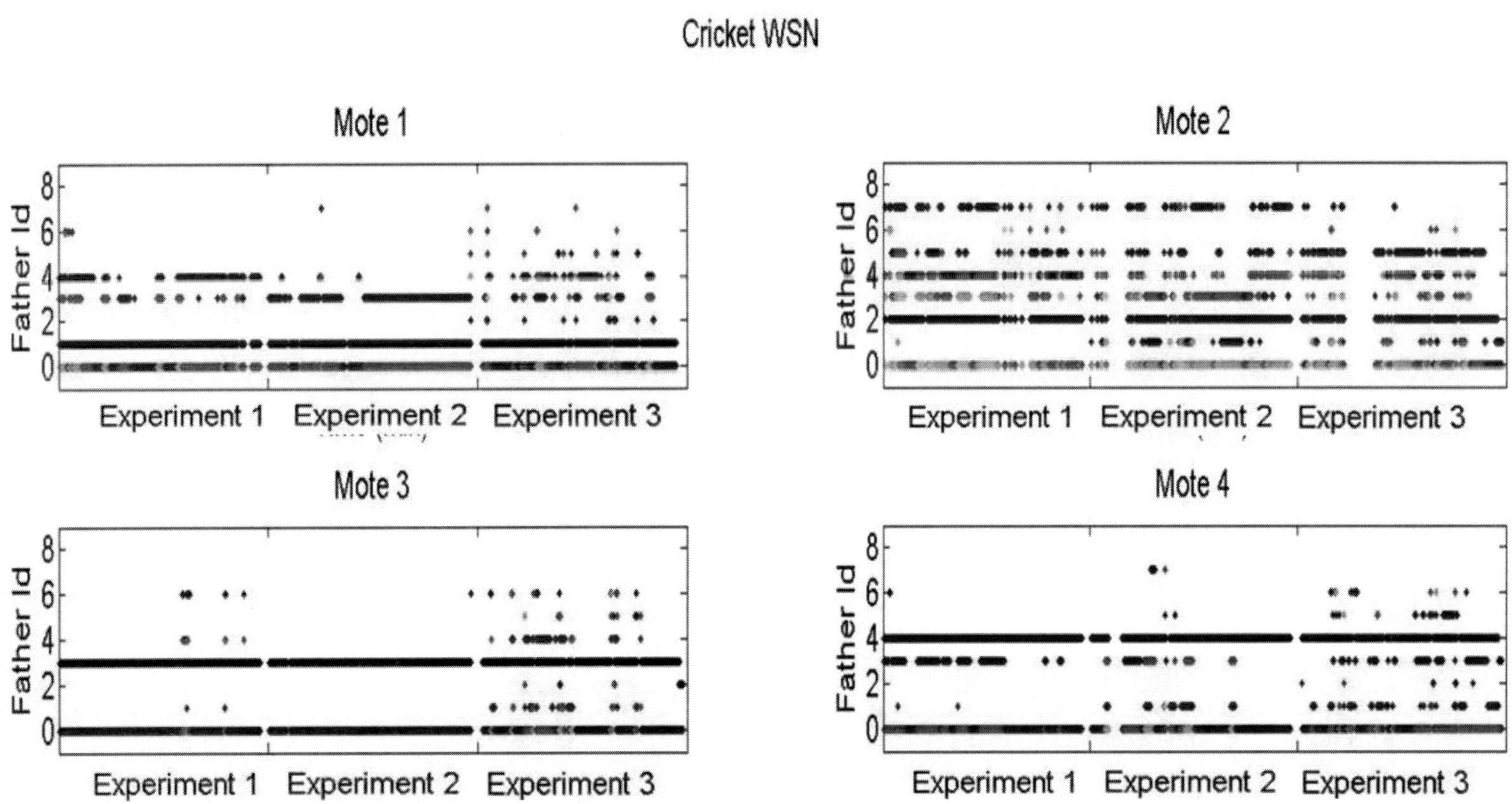

Figure 15. Continued on next page.

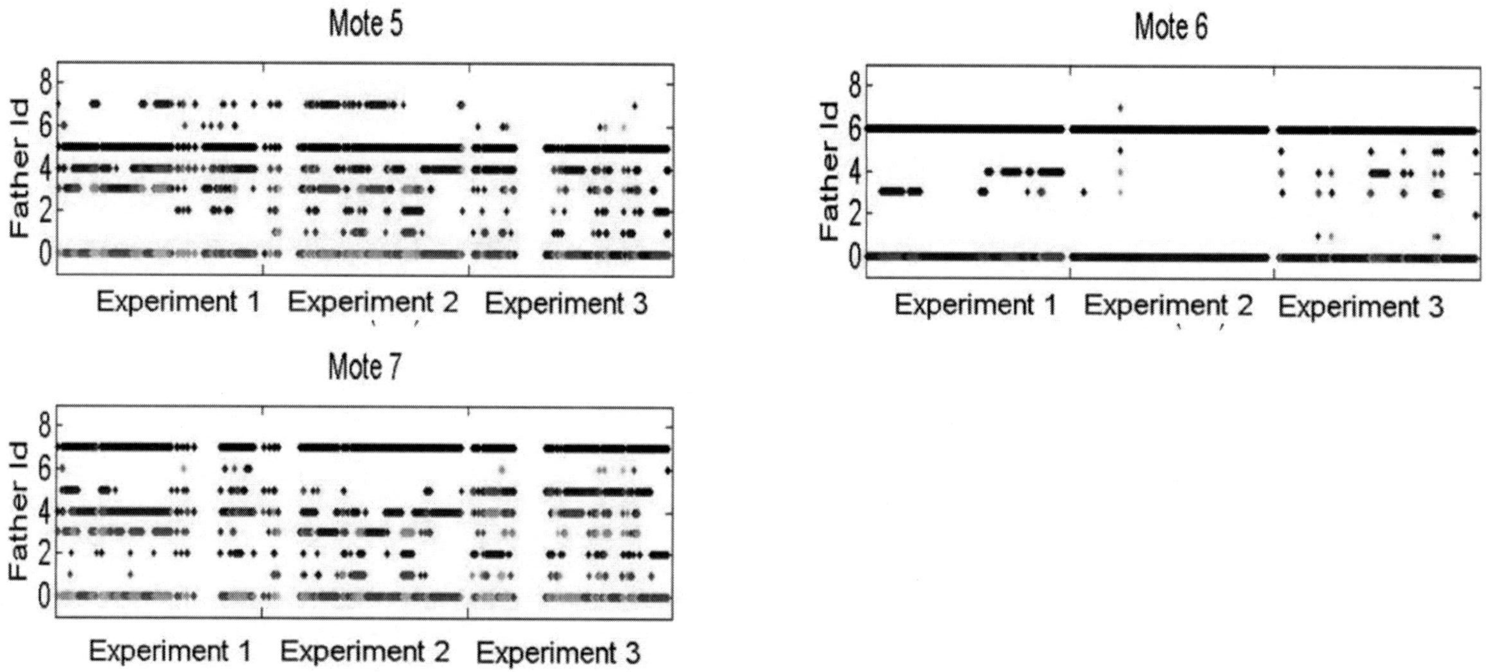

Figure 15. Route distribution for the Cricket WSN during all three experiments.

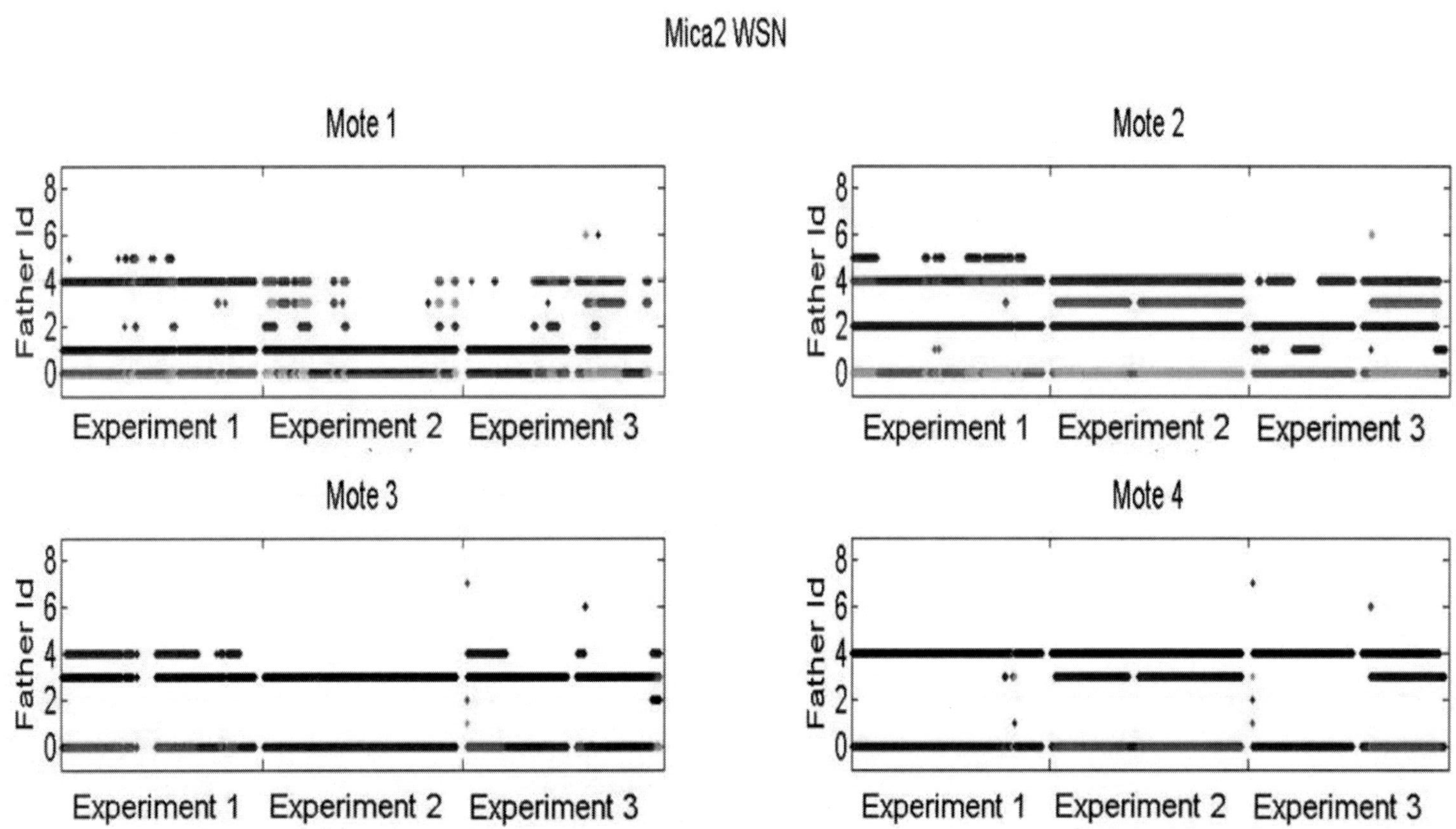

Figure 16. Continued on next page.

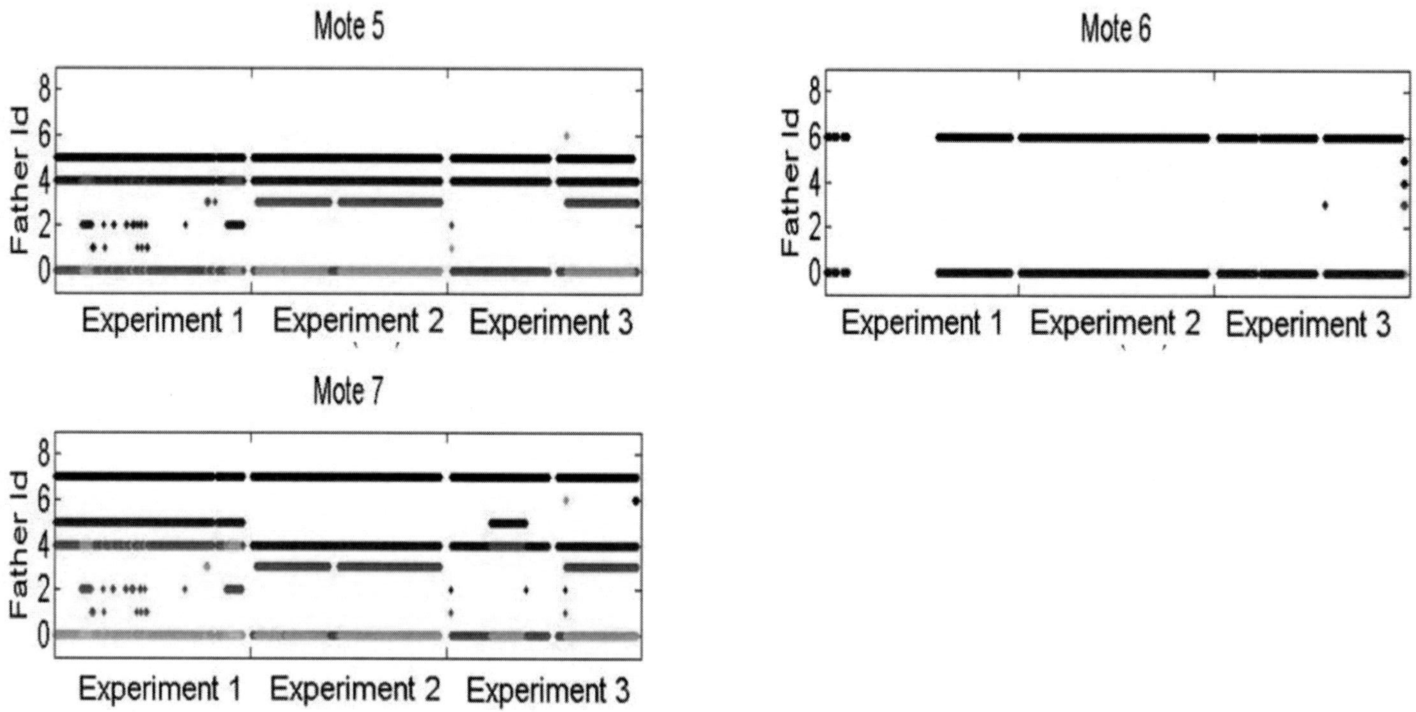

Figure 16. Route distribution for the Mica2 WSN during all three experiments.

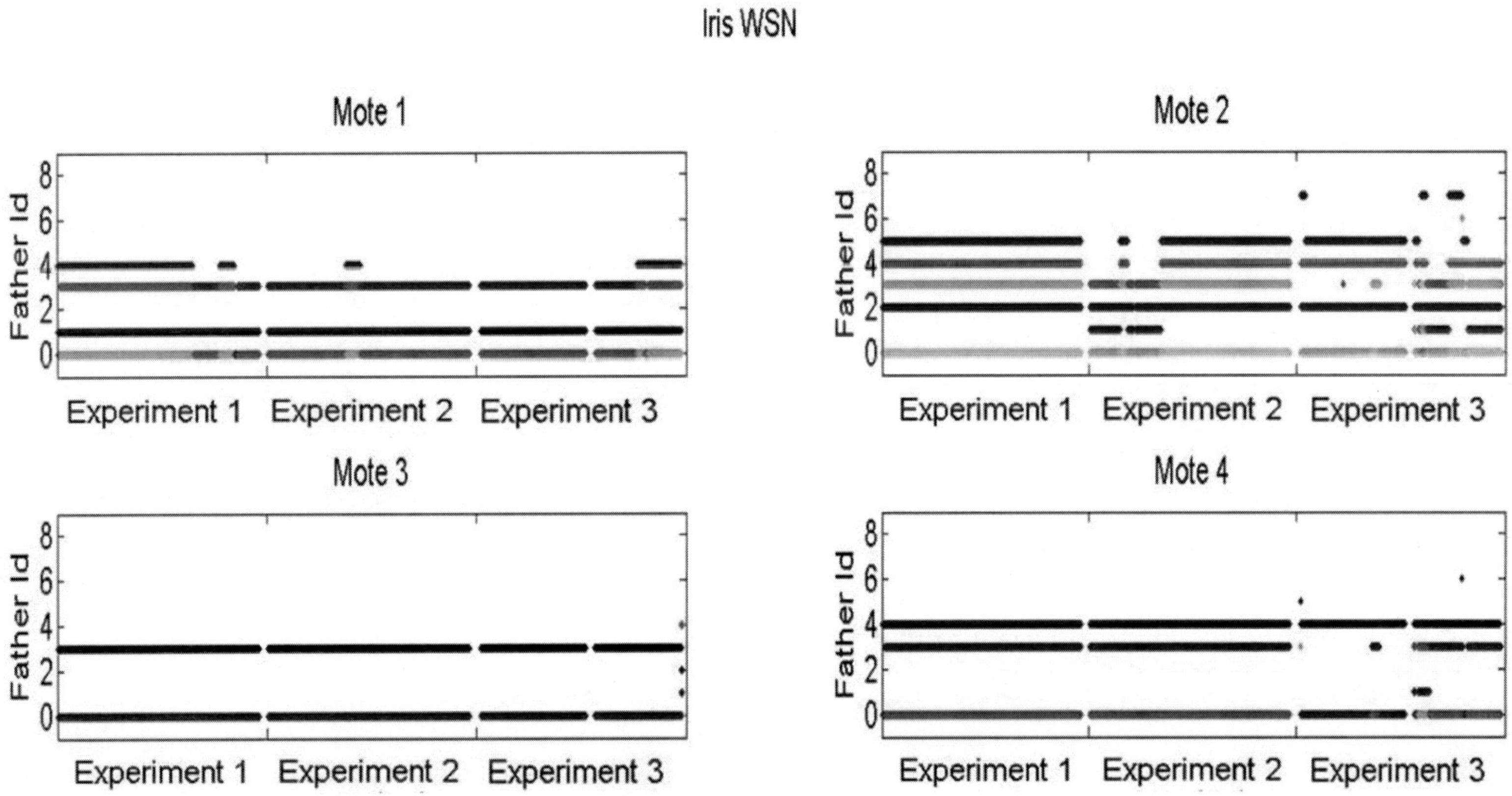

Figure 17. Continued on next page.

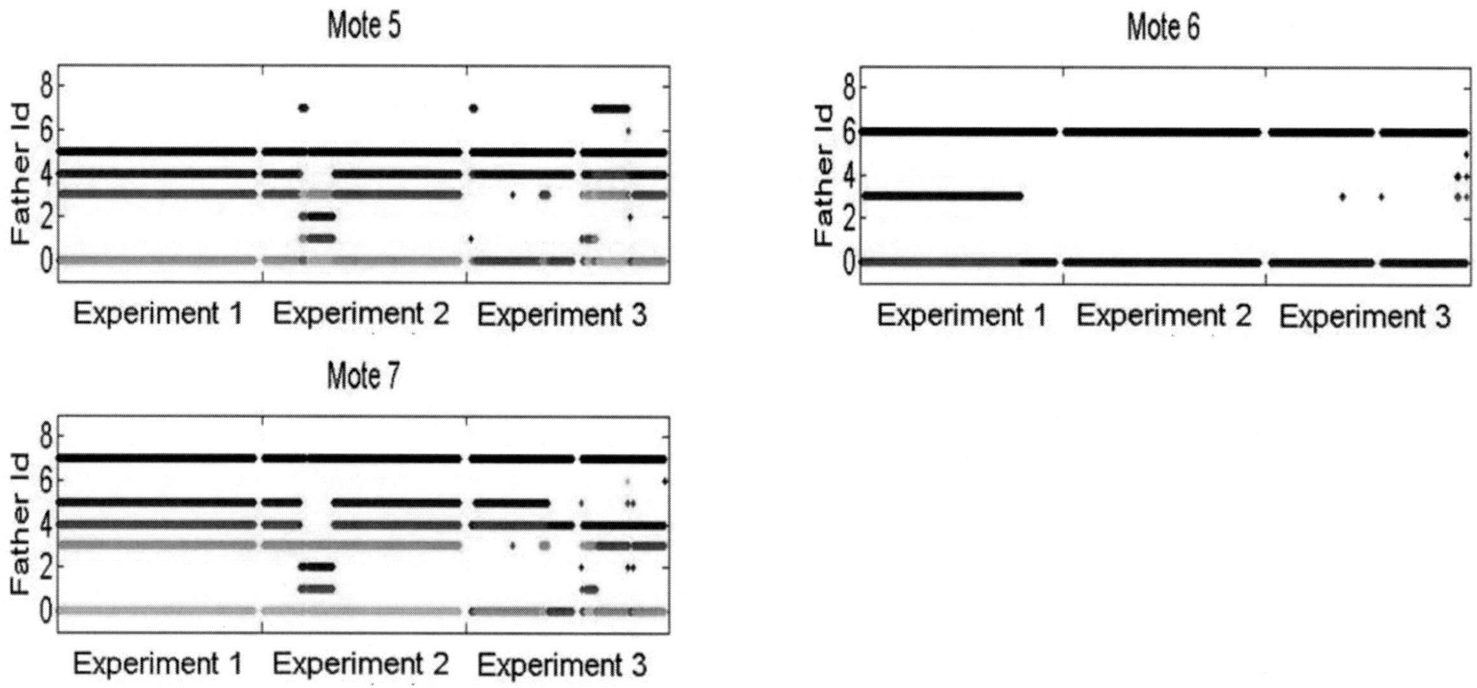

Figure 17. Route distribution for the Iris WSN during all three experiments.

5. Conclusion

In this chapter, we presented a performance evaluation of the CTP topology of WSNs using different platforms. Three different WSNs composed of Cricket, Mica2 and Iris motes, respectively, were tested at the historical building "Leonardo Torres Quevedo". This deployment is representative of a typical building interior with numerous walls and no direct line of sight between the WSN elements. A methodology presented in [6] to evaluate which platform using the CTP protocol is more appropriate for this particular scenario has been used. This methodology is mainly based on the analysis of two parameters, the percentage of received messages and the lifetime of the WSN. To analyze in more detail which platform gave the best performance, other communication parameters were measured, such as the number of hops required for every message to reach the base station and the father identifier for each message.

The Cricket and Mica2 platforms employ the same microcontroller (ATMega128L) and radio chip (Chipcon CC1000) but run at different frequencies, 433 MHz and 900 MHz, respectively. Iris motes utilize the Atmega1281 microcontroller and the Atmel RF230 radio transceiver with a frequency of 2.4 GHz.

Three different experiments were performed to check the robustness of the results obtained. During these experiments the motes were exchanged while keeping the same general spatial configuration.

The percentage of received messages using the Cricket WSN was always lower than that using the Mica2 and Iris networks. The Iris WSN depleted its energy faster than the Cricket and Mica2 networks but, if only the consumption of the processor is taken into account, the Iris network was more energetically efficient than the Cricket and Mica2 networks. On average, the relative lifetime of the Cricket and Mica2 networks was very similar. It was also found that the Iris WSN was more stable than the Cricket and Mica2 WSNs during all the experiments, i.e. there were fewer changes from one father to another, but the average hoping distance was higher. A comparison between the Mica2 and Cricket networks shows that the former was also more stable than the latter. Therefore, it was also found that the instability of the Cricket network does not imply a higher power consumption.

Using this methodology, it can be concluded that, in our experiments, the Cricket WSN performed in general worse than the Mica2 and Iris WSNs. The Iris WSN was found to be more stable than the Mica2, but, in general, the performance was very similar. Therefore, varying the radio frequency from 433 MHz (Cricket) to 900 MHz (Mica2) increases the performance of the network, but varying it from 900 MHz to 2.4 GHz no.

Acknowledgments

The Spanish Ministry of Economy and Competitiveness supported this research under grant number TEC2012-38402-C04-03.

J. Ranz was awarded by the FPI grant BES-2010-038826 from the Ministry of Education, Culture and Sports.

References

[1] Rodriguez-Sanchez, MC; Borromeo, S; Hernandez Tamames, JA."Wireless sensor networks for conservation and monitoring cultural assets", *IEEE Sensors J.*, vol. 11, 1382 -1389, 2011.

[2] European Commission 6th Framework Program—2nd Call Galileo Joint Undertaking. *Cultural Heritage Space Identification System (CUSPIS).* [Online]. Available: http://www.cuspis-project.info.

[3] EU-project, *Smart Monitoring of Historic Structures* (2008). University of Stuttgart. Stuttgart, Germany. [Online]. Available: http://www.smoohs.eu/tiki-index.php

[4] Augello, A; Santangelo, A; Sorce, S; Pilato, G; Gentile, A; Genco, R; Gaglio, S."MAGA: A mobile archaeological guide at Agrigento", *Mobile Guide*, 06,2006.

[5] La Marca, A; Chawathe, Y; Consolvo, S; Hightower, J; Smith, I; Scott, J; Sohn, T; Howard, J; Hughes, J; Potter, F; Tabert, J; Powledge, P; Borriello, G; Schilit, B. "Place lab: Device positioning using radio beacons in the wild," in *Proc. 3rd Int. Conf. Pervasive Computing*, 2005, 116–133.

[6] Aparicio, S; Martínez-Garrido, MI; Ranz, J; Fort, R; Izquierdo, MAG. A Methodology to Evaluate Experimentally the Performance of Routing Topologies of Wireless Sensor Networks. Submitted for publication in *Ad-Hoc Networks*, 2013.

[7] Koubaa, A; Cunha, A; Alves, M."A time division beacon scheduling mechanism for IEEE 802.15.4/ZigBee cluster-tree wireless sensor networks", *Proc. 19th Euromicro Conf. Real-Time Systems* (ECRTS 2007), 2007.

[8] Koubaa, A; Alves, M; Tovar, E. "Modeling and Worst-Case Dimensioning of Cluster-Tree Wireless Sensor Networks", in *27th IEEE Real-Time Systems Symposium (RTSSV6)*, Rio de Janeiro (Brazil), 2006.

[9] Colesanti, U; Santini, S. *A Performance Evaluation Of The Collection Tree Protocol Based On Its Implementation For The Castalia Wireless Sensor Networks Simulator.* Tech. Rep. 681, ETH Zurich (August 2010).

[10] Octav Chipara, Chenyang Lu, Thomas C. Bailey, Gruia-Catalin Roman, *Reliable Clinical Monitoring using Wireless Sensor Networks: Experience in a Step-down Hospital Unit*, SenSys 2010.

[11] TinyOS Community. http://www.tinyos.net/

[12] Lewis, F. Wireless Sensor Networks, In *Smart Environments: Technology, Protocols and Applications*, ISBN: 978-0-471-54448-7, 2004.

[13] Woo, A; Tony, T; Culler, D. Taming the Underlying Challenges of Reliable Multihop Routing in Sensor Networks. *ACM SenSys*, November 2003.

[14] Memsiccompany. http://www.memsic.com/

[15] Fonseca, R; Gnawali, O; Jamieson, K; Levis, P. *Collection tree protocol.* http://www.tinyos.net/tinyos-2.x/doc/html/tep119.html.

[16] Moss, D; Hui, J; Klues, K. *Low Power Listening*. http://www.tinyos.net/tinyos-2.x/doc/html/tep105.html.

[17] Gnawali, O; Fonseca, R; Jamieson, K; Moss, D; Levis, P. Collection tree protocol, *Proceedings of the 7th ACM Conference on Embedded Networked Sensor Systems*, November 04-06, 2009, Berkeley, California.

In: Horizons in Computer Science Research. Volume 9
Editor: Thomas S. Clary
ISBN: 978-1-63321-522-1

Chapter 5

LOCATION ESTIMATION IN MODERN MOBILE COMPUTING ENVIRONMENTS

Mohamed Maher Atia*
Navigation and Instrumentation Research Lab,
Royal Military College of Canada at Kingston, ON, Canada

"To my Mother, the greatest woman I have ever known in my life."

Abstract

This chapter includes the findings and results of dedicated research and development in the area of location determination in mobile computing environments using wireless infrastructures and other aiding sensors such as inertial sensors and dead reckoning. The theoretical formulation of the location determination problem is explained followed by a background and state of the art in location technology and current limitations and challenges. Different wireless localization technologies are analyzed theatrically using Cramer-Rao Lower Bound (CRLB) Variance analysis and practically using real experiments. The problem of wireless propagation modeling and radio maps construction and maintenance are addressed using wide range of deterministic and probabilistic estimation approaches. The theoretical justification is verified by extensive experimental demonstration. Integration of the wireless infrastructures with onboard sensors associated with current modern mobile devices are studied using Kalman Filtering (KF) and Particle Filtering (PF) supported by a comparison between these two common filtering techniques. The chapter concludes with a section about future trends and new research tracks that are expected to shape the localization and tracking landscape of the next few decades.

* E-mail address: Mohamed.maher.atia@gmail.com; Research Associate and Deputy Director of Navigation and Instrumentation Research Lab. Royal Military College of Canada at Kingston, ON, Canada

Introduction

With the recent revolution in computation and communication systems, mobile computing environments [1] started to grow dramatically bringing unprecedented challenges. A major aspect in any mobile computing environment is "situation awareness" [2] where systems users, operators, managers, and also hardware/software components need to be "aware" about the current "context" of any computing process. To enable efficient situation awareness in mobile computing environments, "Location" of objects and people is a core piece of information. Knowledge about location is critically important to accomplish tasks such as dynamic resource allocation, load balance, routing management, channel estimation, hand-over, data protection, and security rules enforcement. Historically, location determination developed from using starts, the moon, the sun, magnetic compass, dead reckoning (where positioning is performed using time, direction, and speed) to modern satellite-based navigation systems. Since mid-nineties, the Global Positioning System (GPS)[3][4] has been used as the dominant location determination technology in several areas including mobile computing environments. Although GPS and other Global Navigation Satellite Systems (GNSS) provide worldwide anytime localization service, unfortunately, GNSS are only reliable in open-sky environments. According to recent market research reports, 70% of cellular calls and 80% of wireless data connectivity originate from indoors where GPS and other GNSS-based systems do not work [5]. Since the backbone of the basic infrastructure of mobile computing environments is wireless communication, significant research has been focused on developing location determination techniques for wireless networks that do not depend on GPS. In this context, this chapter is dedicated for the approaches and algorithms commonly used to tackle the problem of localization determination and navigation within wireless networks.

To develop a location determination system for mobile nodes in wireless networks, three basic components have to be determined. The first component is the source of measurements and observations that will be used for location determination and this component can be called "sensors". The second component is the nature of measurements that sensors will provide. For example, a wireless interface card is a sensor that can provide different kind of measurements such as received signal strength, angle of arrival or time of arrival of a wireless signal. The third component is the "methodology" applied on the sensors measurements to calculate location. The sensors can be categorized into two categories; Proprioceptive sensors and exteroceptive sensors. Proprioceptive sensors are sensors that are attached to (part of) the moving platform such as wireless interface card, an inertial measurement unit[6] (IMU), a laser range finder [7] (LiDAR). Exteroceptive sensors are the sensors available in the environment and not attached and not part of the platform to be localized such as wireless access points, routers, digital floor maps, and landmarks existing in the environment. Since the main focus of this chapter is on location determination and navigation in wireless networks, the sensor that will be considered in this chapter is the "wireless interface" of the platform that needs to be localized. The platform to be localized within a wireless network can be a wheeled vehicle, pedestrian, an aerial vehicle, or even a network node.

This chapter was written with the objective to make it "easy to understand". To make it easy to understand for wide range of readers interested in location technology, it is important to emphasize on the aforementioned terms to build a common understanding of the different concepts that will be addressed in this chapter. The following terms have been defined: platform to be localized, sensors, measurements, location determination methodology (or simply "methodology"). Those terms will be used repeatedly to explain systems and algorithms described in this chapter. The coming section is an important preparation before studying the background and state of the art in location technology. It gives an overview about important concepts in the theory of "Estimation" [8]. In fact, as we will see in next few pages, location technology is all about "Estimation".

The Concept of Estimation

In order to model any physical phenomenon or a process, a mathematical model is commonly developed. Generally, a physical phenomenon or a process is modeled as a "system" with determined inputs and outputs. A common approach to describe a system is the differential equations [9] as follows:

$$\sum_{k=0}^{n} a_k \frac{d^k y(t)}{dt^k} = \sum_{k=0}^{m} b_k \frac{d^k x(t)}{dt^k} \tag{1}$$

where $y(t)$ is the system output and $x(t)$ is the system input $\frac{d^k}{dt^k}$ represents the kth order derivative and a_k and b_k are coefficients that can be constant or time variant. There are two limitations of this system representation. Generally, in complex systems, solving differential equations in this form is not always easy. Additionally, internal system dynamics are not sufficiently clear. Thus, systems are represented in another form called "state space"[9][10] where internal dynamics of the system is described by "states" or "parameters". The general representation of a system in the state space representation is given by the following two fundamental equations:

$$\dot{x}(t) = \mathrm{f}\left(x(t), u(t)\right) \tag{2}$$

$$y(t) = h\left(x(t)\right) \tag{3}$$

where $y(t)$ is the system "*observable*" outputs and $x(t)$ is state vector (the parameters) of the system and $u(t)$ is the control input that stimulates system state evolution over time. In estimation theory, the preferred representation if a system is the state space representation.

If the system model is linear, the fundamental state space representation of the system is given by

$$\dot{x}(t) = F(t)x(t) \tag{4}$$

$$y(t) = H(t)x(t) \tag{5}$$

where F is the transition matrix and H is the design matrix.

Estimation is the discipline of science that deals with estimating the parameters (states) of a mathematical model based on observables. The problem of estimation is simply the answer to the following question: Given some system observables $y(t)$, what is the values of the states or the parameters $x(t)$. Two common techniques for estimation exist. For simplicity, we will discuss only the linear estimation since it is the dominant technique used so far in most of current existing location technologies. In fact, even nonlinear systems can be solved by linear estimation techniques. This is achieved by linearizing the nonlinear system equations around an operating point and apply the estimation only to the "error" states $\delta x(t)$ as will be seen in sub-sequent sections.

Least-Square

The least-square is simply the optimal solution to the system measurement model $y(t) = H(t)x(t)$. In fact, this is the technique commonly used in GPS receivers [3][4]. If observations Y^* is available, Least-Square technique tries to minimize the following cost function:

$$J(x) = \sum_{i=0}^{N-1} \left[Hx - Y^* \right]^2 \tag{6}$$

If observations comes with weighting information W, the optimal estimation of x^* is given by

$$x^* = \arg\min_x \left(J(x) \right) = \arg\min_x \left(\left(Hx - Y^* \right)^T W \left(Hx - Y^* \right) \right) \tag{7}$$

The solution to this equation is calculated by simply differentiating $J(x)$ with respect to x and set the result to zero which leads to the common least-square solution given by

$$x^* = (H^T W H)^{-1} H^T Y^* \tag{8}$$

Kalman Filter

The system described in (4) and (5) is a deterministic system. However, in real life, physical systems are stochastic [11] by nature. In a stochastic system, both system states x and observables y are contaminated by noise. Estimation should consider these noise properly which is not well-addressed in the simple least-squares described above. Furthermore, in least-squares, the states evolution dynamics conveyed in the transition matrix and the dynamic model $\dot{x}(t) = F(t)x(t)$ is not used. To benefit from this extra information, optimal filtering techniques are used for estimation. The most common technique for estimation by filtering is Kalman Filter (KF)[12] and Particle Filtering (PF)[13]. The concepts of KF and PF will be introduced in the integration section of this chapter where the problem of improving wireless-based positioning techniques by integrating other sensors (mainly inertial sensors) is introduced.

The Location Determination as an Estimation Problem

The general location determination problem is commonly modeled as an estimation problem. The analogy between the location determination problem and the estimation theory is easily understood by thinking about the platform to be localized as the "system" of interest. The state vector $x(t)$ of the system is mainly the navigation state (position, velocity, and attitude). The sensors as usually seen as the control signals that stimulate the states evolving dynamics ($u(t)$) with time.

This concludes the introduction section. The following section is a background and state of the art about current navigation technology.

Background and State of the Art in Wireless Positioning Systems

This section gives the reader a background and state of the art about current location systems. Although the focus of this chapter will be non-GPS wireless positioning systems in wireless networks, it is important to have a quick look on it with some information about limitations in indoor areas.

Common Wireless Infrastructures Used for Positioning

Global Navigation Satellites System

GPS is the most popular working Global Navigation Satellite Systems (GNSS) is the one developed by United States Department of Defense in early 1970s [14][15]. GPS consists of a constellation of 24 satellites and some active spares. This constellation can be seen in Figure 1. The satellites are arranged in six orbits around the earth with at least four satellites per orbit. This geometry permits four to ten GPS satellites to be visible anywhere in the world, if an elevation angle of 10° is considered [15]. The definition of an elevation angle is shown in Figure 2. Each satellite transmits a signal that contains the necessary information to enable user receiver's position calculation. The satellites constellation is called the space segment. Two additional segments exist in GPS, the ground and the user segments. Ground segment consists of a worldwide network of tracking stations that monitor and control satellite motion, system integrity, behaviour of satellites atomic clocks and other consideration. The user segment includes all GPS users. With a GPS receiver and antenna, a user can receive GPS signals and use them to calculate his/her position anywhere in the world. GPS utilizes the concept of time of arrival ranging [16][17][18][19] to determine the receiver position. The distances of GPS receiver to the visible satellites are calculated using the time it takes the GPS radio signal to travel from each satellite to the receiver. The estimated distances are called the pseudo-ranges. The location of each satellite is known to the receiver through the navigation message sent by the satellite. With these pseudo-ranges and satellite coordinates, the position of the GPS receiver can be computed by Trilateration [18]. This is based on the intersection of the signal propagation spheres (satellite at the centre of the sphere, radius equal to the receiver-satellite distance). In theory, a minimum of 3 satellites are needed to be visible to the GPS receiver to get its location. However, a 4th satellite is needed to account for the clock offset of the receiver. In addition to the pseudo-ranges, a GPS receiver may estimate the Doppler frequency of the received GPS signals, which can be used to determine the receiver's velocity. Typically, a GPS receiver can provide position and velocity information as long as it can receive a signal from at least four satellites.

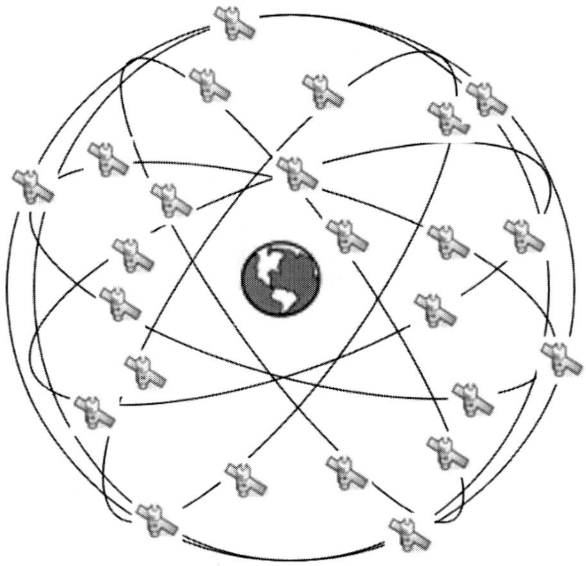

Figure 1. GPS constellation of satellites around the earth.

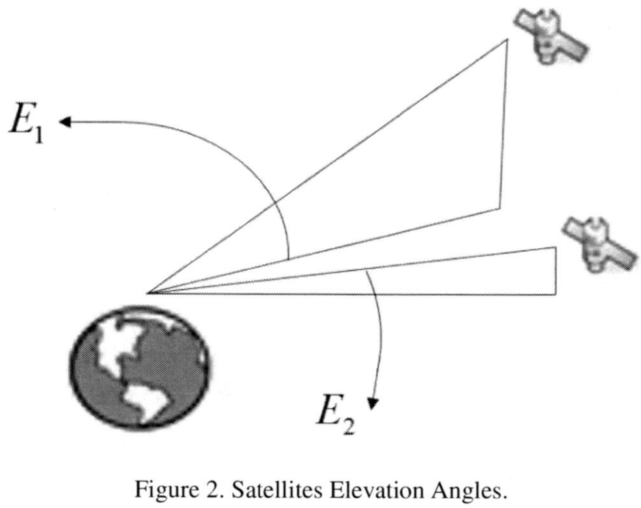

Figure 2. Satellites Elevation Angles.

Limitations of GPS and other Satellites-Based Systems

Several forms of errors in the measurement of the satellite-to-receiver range exist [20][21]. They are summarized in the following list:

1. Receiver clock bias and drifts: It is a time varying error with the receiver clock.
2. Satellite clock bias and drifts: It is a time varying error with the satellites clocks.
3. Tropospheric delay: The Troposphere is the lower part of atmosphere ranging from 8 to 40 km above the surface of the earth. This layer has changes in weather that affects the speed of light, so their changes cause errors in the range measurements.
4. Ionospheric delay: The Ionosphere is the layer of atmosphere that is above 50 km. It consists of ionized air, and changes in the ionization level influence the travel time of the GPS signals through the Ionosphere.
5. Multipath: Multipath errors are caused by the reflection of signals from surfaces near the receiver and causes errors in range measurements. This is main limiting factor of GPS that makes it unreliable for almost 80% of wireless connectivity activities over the world.

Cellular Mobile Networks

To overcome the coverage limitations of GPS, other wireless infrastructures may be used. An ideal already existing and wide-spread infrastructure is the basic cellular network architecture [22][23] (Figure 3).It consists of Base Station Controllers (BSC) and GSM controllers (GSMC). Each mobile device is covered by one or more tower (Base Station). Mobile devices receive radio frequency signals from many different towers. Cells information received by mobile devices can determine the location of the user within current cell. Clearly, this method has limited accuracy because some cells may have a coverage range of 4 km [22][23]. GSM networks can assist GPS in environments in which GPS signal is weak.

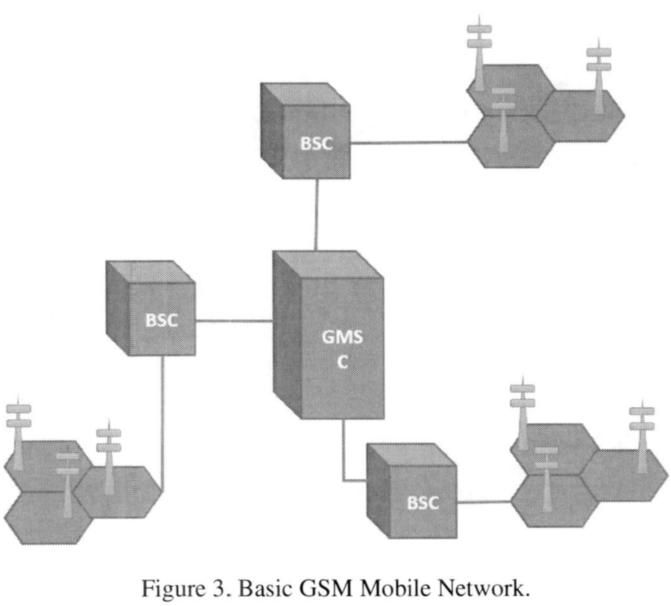

Figure 3. Basic GSM Mobile Network.

This is achieved by equipping the towers in open sky areas with GPS receivers and using each tower to transmit GPS data among with the signal it transmits to the mobile devices. Hence, the GPS receivers inside mobile devices can acquire GPS orbital and time information. In addition, and based on the accurate knowledge of towers positions, local Ionospheric conditions and other conditions affecting the GPS signal can be estimated and communicated to mobile devices.

Wireless Local Area Networks

Wireless Local Area Networks (WLAN) [23][24] has been developed since 1980s and standardized in 1994 under the IEEE Standards family devoted to defining Local and Wide Area Networks. Currently almost every enterprise have WLAN that covers the whole enterprise buildings. This makes WLAN an ideal choice to expand location capabilities in the challenging indoor area (the area that 80% of human wireless connectivity activities originate). As will be elaborated shortly, based on the received signal from different access points, many algorithms can be used to estimate the mobile device position.

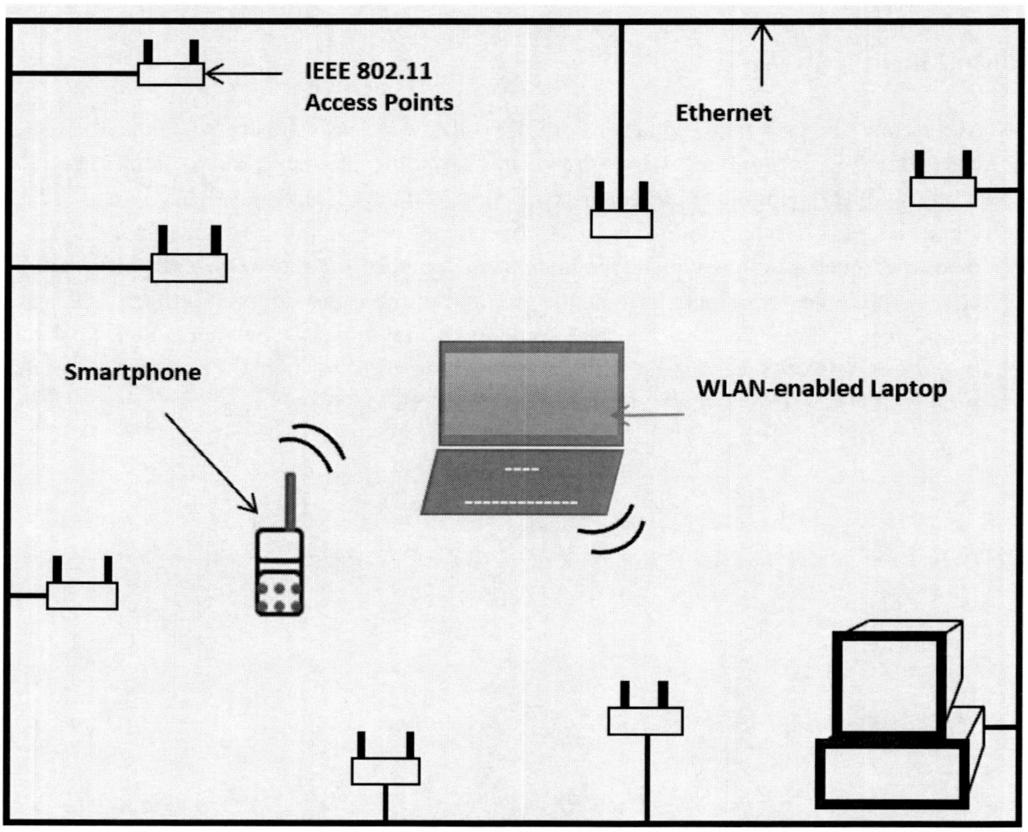

Figure 4. Basic WLAN Architecture.

Wireless Sensor Networks

A wireless sensor network (WSN) consists of spatially distributed autonomous sensors to cooperatively monitor physical or environmental conditions, such as temperature, sound, vibration, pressure, motion or pollutants [25][26]. Each node in a sensor network is typically equipped with a radio transceiver, a small microcontroller, and an energy source, usually a battery. A sensor network normally constitutes a wireless ad-hoc network, meaning that each sensor supports a multi-hop routing algorithm (several nodes may forward data packets to the base station). Sensor Networks can be used in positioning using variety of techniques [17][18] as will be elaborated shortly in the subsequent sections.

Common Wireless Positioning Techniques

This section is a brief survey about some common methods and approaches that are used to address wireless positioning problem in indoor and dense urban areas.

Time-Based Techniques

Time of Arrival (TOA)

TOA [17][18][19][16][27] is the time elapsed since the first bit in the physical layer of the transmitter is transmitted until the first bit hits the physical layer of the receiver. TOA is an indication of the range. Trilateration algorithm uses the ranges between multiple base stations (BS) and the mobile device to estimate its position. As shown inFigure 5, the mobile device is located by the intersection point of the 3 circles elaborated in the figure. Each circle has a radius corresponding to the distance between the mobile device and the considered BS. The position of the target can be computed by minimizing the sum of squares of a nonlinear cost function, i.e., least-squares algorithm [28][29]. In this case, the system parameters is mobile platform location and the observables are the measured distances between the mobile platform and the BSs. In 2D, assume the mobile device location is (x_o, y_o), the problem formulation in in the form $y(t) = h\left(x(t)\right)$ can be written as

$$R_i = \sqrt{(x_i - x_o)^2 + (y_i - y_o)^2} \tag{9}$$

where N is the number of base stations, (x_i, y_i) is the 2D location of the ith base station, and R_i is a the "observable" distance between the ith base station and the mobile platform.

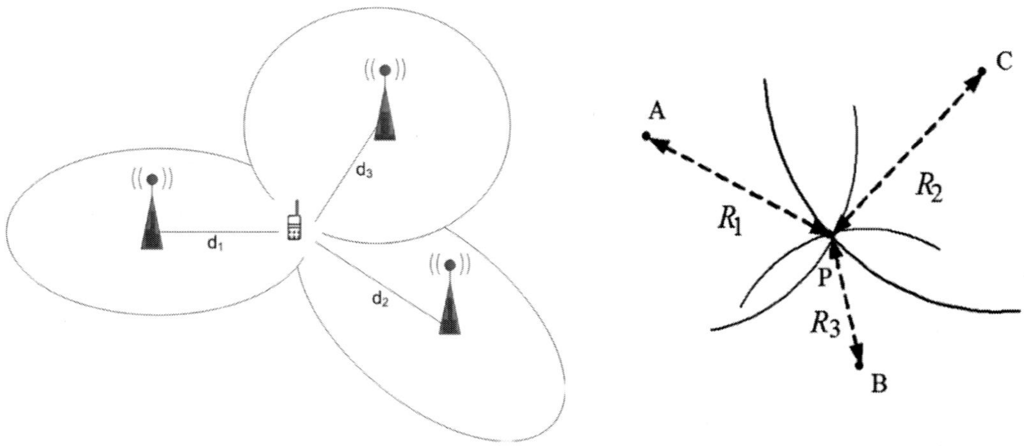

Figure 5. Trilateration Method.

Limitations of TOA Method

The accuracy of the TOA depends on the accuracy and synchronization between transmitter's clock and receiver's clock. Furthered more, TOA methods requires direct LOS between transmitter and receiver. Obviously this is a challenge in dense urban and indoor environments.

Time Difference of Arrival (TDOA)

The idea of TDOA is to determine the relative position of a mobile transmitter by examining the difference in time at which the signal arrives at multiple measuring units[17][18]. For each TDOA measurement, the transmitter must lie on a hyperboloid with a constant range difference between the two measuring units. An explanation of this method is shown in Figure 6. The range between the mobile node location (x_p, y_p, z_p) and the ith fixed measurement unit is given by:

$$R_i = \sqrt{(x_i - x_p)^2 + (y_i - y_p)^2 - (z_i - z_p)^2} \tag{10}$$

If we have three known measurement units A, B, and C, in addition to the mobile device P, the equation of the hyperboloid that the mobile node must be located in is given by

$$R_{i,j} = \sqrt{(x_i - x_p)^2 + (y_i - y_p)^2 - (z_i - z_p)^2} - \sqrt{(x_j - x_p)^2 + (y_j - y_p)^2 - (z_j - z_p)^2} \tag{11}$$

where (x_i, y_i, z_i) is the location of fixed measurements units and (x_p, y_p, z_p) is the target object location.

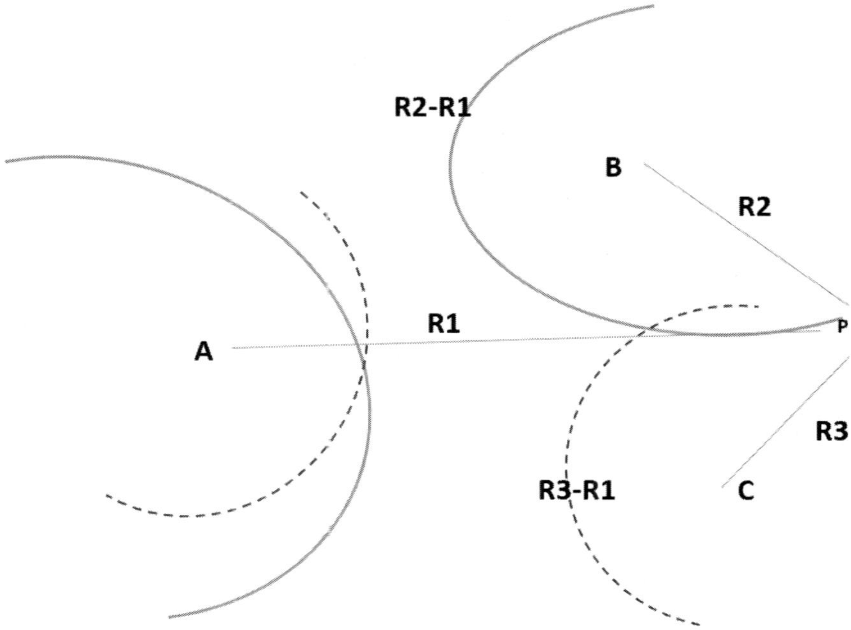

Figure 6. TDOA method.

Limitations of TDOA Method

Although the TDOA eliminated the accurate synchronized timing constraints, the non-LOS problems have the same effect on TDOA method because it will break the relationship between the measured time differences and the true distances between the receivers and the transmitters. Another problem with TDOA method is that if too many transmitters exist, the receivers will be overloaded which may degrade the scalability and performance of the entire system.

Angle-Based Techniques

Direction of Arrival (Known also as Angle of Arrival (AOA))

In AOA [17][18][30], the location of the desired target can be found by the intersection of several pairs of angle direction lines. As shown in Figure 7, AOA methods may use at least two known reference points (A, B), and two measured angles θ1, θ2 to derive the 2-D location of the target P. Estimation of AOA, commonly referred to as direction finding (DF), can be accomplished either with directional antennas or with an array of antennas [17][18]. The advantages of AOA are that no time synchronization between measuring units is required.

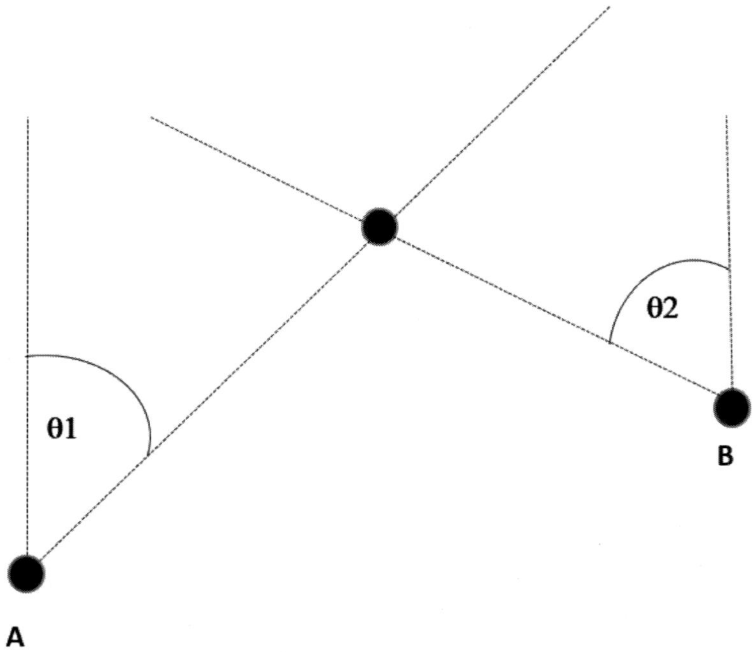

Figure 7. AoA Method.

Limitations of AOA Method

The disadvantages include relatively large and complex hardware requirements [30]. The location estimation accuracy degrades as the mobile target moves farther from the measuring units. For accurate positioning, the angle measurements need to be accurate, but the high accuracy measurements in wireless networks may be limited by shadowing, multipath reflections arriving from misleading directions, or by the directivity of the measuring aperture.

Signal-Strength-Based Techniques

Fingerprinting-Based Techniques

It is also known as scene analysis [18][31][32][33][34]. RF-based scene analysis refers to the type of algorithms that first collect features (fingerprints) of a scene and then estimate the location of an object by matching online measurements with the closest a priori location fingerprints. Location fingerprinting refers to techniques that match the fingerprint of some characteristic of a signal that is location dependent. There are several location fingerprinting-based positioning algorithms [17][18] using pattern recognition technique so far: probabilistic methods, k-nearest-neighbor (KNN), neural networks, support vector machine (SVM), and smallest M-vertex polygon (SMP).

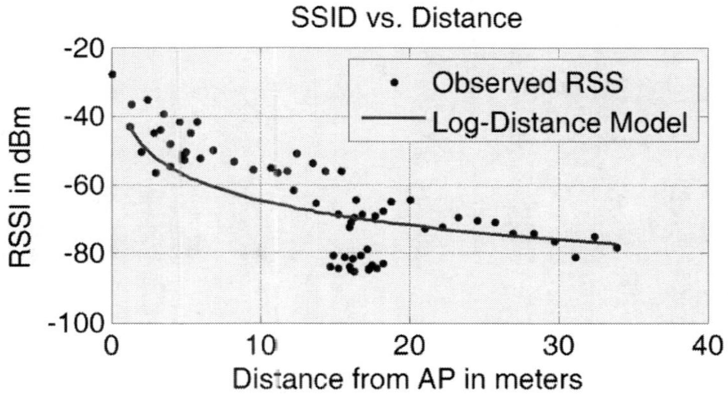

Figure 8. Path Loss Modeling for Distance Estimation.

Propagation Modeling Techniques

Path loss (or path attenuation) is the reduction in power density (attenuation) of an electromagnetic wave as it propagates through space [22][35][34]. Path loss is affected by many factors, such as free-space loss, refraction, diffraction, reflection, aperture-medium coupling loss, and absorption. Path loss is also influenced by terrain contours, environment (urban or rural, vegetation and foliage), propagation medium (dry or moist air), the distance between the transmitter and the receiver, and the height and location of antennas. If path loss model can be identified, it can be a measure of distance. The simplest form of path loss model in open air is given by [22]

$$P = P_0 - 10n\log_{10}(d/d_0) \tag{12}$$

where P is the received signal strength, n is the loss exponent, d is the distance between the transmitter and receiver and P_0 is power measured at reference distance d_0. The model parameters can be estimated using different non-linear systems identification algorithms [18][36]. Once the path loss model is accurately identified, distance between receiver and multiple transmitters can be estimated and trilateration [17][18] can be used to estimate the receiver location.

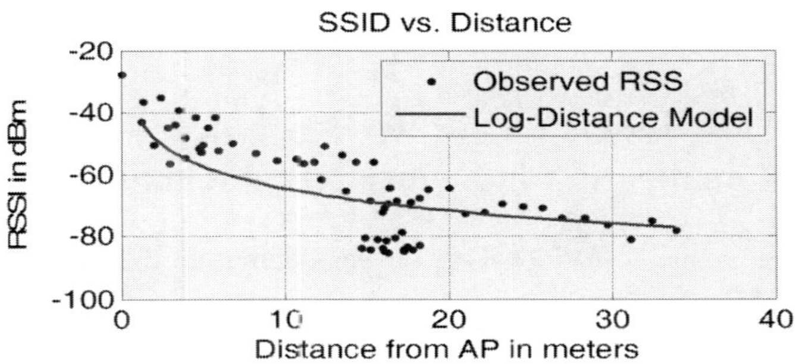

Figure 9. Path Loss Modeling for Distance Estimation.

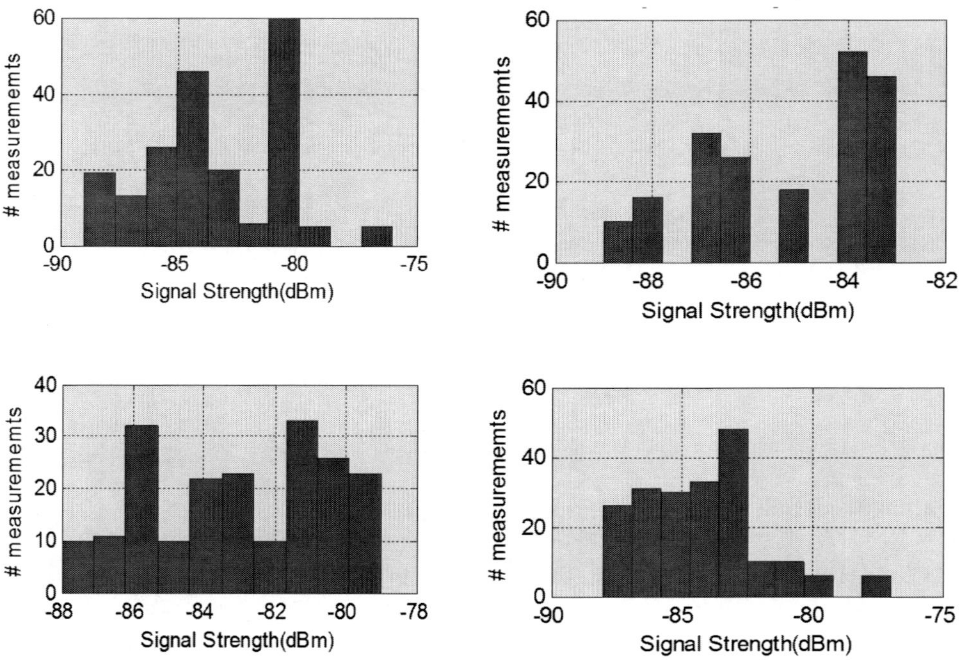

Figure 10. Signal Strength histogram at 4 locations in an indoor area.

Limitations of Propagation Modeling Techniques

NLOS conditions indoors causes odd RSS observations patterns that do not follow the logarithmic decay formulas. In addition, due to environment dynamics and changes, logarithmic decay models will be no longer valid and need to be updated. Figure 9shows real RSS measurements taken in an indoor area and modeled using logarithmic-decay formula. It is noticed in Figure 9 that some RSS are too small (-80 to -90 dBm) although the corresponding distance is short (almost 15 meters). This "odd" power pattern is due to indoor obstructions of the wireless signal and cannot be simply modeled using logarithmic decay formulas. To further demonstrate the noisy nature of RSS observations indoors, Figure 10shows histogram of 200 signal strength measurements taken at the same location in an indoor area. The figure shows how noisy RSS observations are and also shows that it does not follow the common Gaussian distribution.

Performance Evaluation for Time-Based, Angle-Based and RSS-Based Localization in Severe NLOS Conditions

The three basic radio signal features used for positioning are the Time of Flight (ToF) and Received Signal Strength (RSS) and Angle of Arrival (AoA). The NLOS conditions affect all of these measurements in different ways. In Time-Based Positioning systems, NLOS causes the receiver to receive distorted multiple copies of the radio signal which jeopardize the accuracy of calculating the ToF needed to estimate the distance [16]. In RSS-Based systems, NLOS creates odd power/distance pattern that does not follow the nice common log-distance. In Angle-based methods, a multipath signal will indicate a totally wrong AoA. In this chapter, these three basic radio signals measurements and estimation models are analyzed using Cramer-Rao Lower Bound Analysis (CRLB) [37]. The objectives of CRLB analysis to theoretically assess the effect of the NLOS conditions on the positioning accuracy if Time-Based, RSS-Based or Angle-Based Positioning Systems are used.

Cramer-Rao Lower Lower-Bound

CRLB is the lower bound on the variance of any unbiased estimator for unknown parameters [37]. If $\hat{\theta}$ is an estimate of a true parameter vector θ estimated by an unbiased estimator from on measurements Y, then the minimum achievable variance $var(\hat{\theta})$ is given by:

$$var(\hat{\theta}) = E\left\{(\hat{\theta} - \theta)(\hat{\theta} - \theta)^T\right\} \geq CRLB_{\hat{\theta}}(\theta) \tag{13}$$

$$CRLB_{\hat{\theta}}(\theta) = I^{-1}(\theta) \tag{14}$$

where $I(\theta)$ is the Fisher Information Matrix (FIM) given by [16][38][37]:

$$I(\theta) = E\left\{\left[\frac{\partial}{\partial\theta}\log P(Y|\theta)\right]\left[\frac{\partial}{\partial\theta}\log P(Y|\theta)\right]^T\right\} \tag{15}$$

Where $\log P(Y|\theta)$ is the measurement likelihood density function defined as the probability of measurement Y given the parameters θ.

CRLB under Measurement Model with Zero-Mean Gaussian Noise

In any estimation problem, a measurement model is used that maps the measurements (Y) to the parameters to estimate (θ). The general form of the measurements model is given by:

$$Y = h(\hat{\theta}) + w_k \tag{16}$$

In CRLB analysis, it is assumed that w_k is zero-mean Gaussian noise with covariance R which means the measurements Y is Gaussian centered around $h(\hat{\theta})$ with covariance R given by:

$$P(Y|\theta) = \mathcal{N}(h(\theta), R) \tag{17}$$

Based on this assumption, $\log P(Y|\theta)$ is given by:

$$\log P(Y|\theta) = -\frac{m}{2}\log(2\pi) - \frac{m}{2}\log(|R|) - \frac{1}{2}\left(Y - h(\theta)\right)^T R^{-1}\left(Y - h(\theta)\right) \tag{18}$$

and in the FIM $I(\theta)$ will be given by

$$I(\theta) = E\left\{\left[\frac{\partial}{\partial\theta}\log P(Y|\theta)\right]\left[\frac{\partial}{\partial\theta}\log P(Y|\theta)\right]^T\right\} = \left(\frac{\partial}{\partial\theta}h(\theta)\right)^T R^{-1}\left(\frac{\partial}{\partial\theta}h(\theta)\right) \quad (19)$$

The term $\frac{\partial}{\partial\theta}h(\theta)$ is the Jacobian matrix of $h(\theta)$ with respect to every element in parameter vector θ.

Time-Based Positioning Systems Measurements

In 2D Time-Based Positioning Systems, the measurements model is given by

$$d_i = \sqrt{(x - x_i)^2 + (y - y_i)^2} + \sigma \quad (20)$$

where x, y is the user location and x_i, y_i is the i^{th}network node andd_i is the measured range that is calculated by user's radio receiver by multiply signal ToF by the speed of light. It is assumed that this calculated range (d_i) is contaminated with a white zero-mean Gaussian noiseσ. Assuming K network nodes, in this case, $\frac{\partial}{\partial\theta}h(\theta)$ is given by:

$$H = \frac{\partial}{\partial\theta}h(\theta) = \begin{bmatrix} \frac{(x-x_1)}{\sqrt{(x-x_1)^2+(y-y_1)^2}} & \frac{(y-y_i)}{\sqrt{(x-x_1)^2+(y-y_1)^2}} \\ \cdot & \cdot \\ \cdot & \cdot \\ \cdot & \cdot \\ \frac{(x-x_K)}{\sqrt{(x-x_K)^2+(y-y_K)^2}} & \frac{(y-y_K)}{\sqrt{(x-x_K)^2+(y-y_K)^2}} \end{bmatrix} \quad (21)$$

and the CRLB of accuracy at location (x, y)will be given by

$$CRLB(x, y) = \sqrt{tr((H^T R^{-1} H)^{-1})} \quad (22)$$

where$R = diag(\sigma_1^2, \sigma_2^2, \ldots\ldots, \sigma_K^2)$ where σ_i^2 is the variance ofi^{th}measurement.

Angle-Based Positioning Systems Measurements

In 2D Angle-Based Positioning Systems, the measurements model is given by:

$$A_i = tan^{-1}\left(\frac{y-y_i}{x-x_i}\right) + \sigma \quad (23)$$

where x, y is the user location and x_i, y_i is the i^{th}network node andA_i is the measured angle calculated by user's radio receiver by any technique such as antenna arrays or smart antenna[39]. It is assumed that this calculated angle (A_i) is contaminated with a white zero-mean Gaussian noise σ. Assuming K network nodes, in this case, $\frac{\partial}{\partial\theta}h(\theta)$ is given by:

$$H = \frac{\partial}{\partial\theta}h(\theta) = \begin{bmatrix} \frac{-(y-y_1)}{(x-x_1)^2+(y-y_1)^2} & \frac{(x-x_1)}{(x-x_1)^2+(y-y_1)^2} \\ \cdot & \cdot \\ \cdot & \cdot \\ \cdot & \cdot \\ \frac{-(y-y_K)}{(x-x_K)^2+(y-y_K)^2} & \frac{(x-x_K)}{(x-x_K)^2+(y-y_K)^2} \end{bmatrix} \tag{24}$$

and the CRLB of accuracy at location (x, y)will be given by(22).

RSS-Based Positioning Systems Measurements

In 2D RSS-Based Positioning Systems, the measurements model is generally given by[22][36]:

$$P_i = P_o - 10n_i log_{10}(\sqrt{(x-x_i)^2 + (y-y_i)^2}/d_0) + \sigma \tag{25}$$

where x, y is the user location and x_i, y_i is the i^{th}network node, P_o is the RSS measured power at reference distance $d_0$from the i^{th}network node andP_i is the measured power (RSS) that is measured by user's radio receiver and $n_i$the path loss exponent [36]. It is assumed that this calculated RSS is contaminated with a white zero-mean Gaussian noise σ. Assuming K network nodes, in this case, $\frac{\partial}{\partial\theta}h(\theta)$ is given by:

$$H = \frac{\partial}{\partial\theta}h(\theta) = \begin{bmatrix} \frac{-10n_p(x-x_1)}{ln(10)[(x-x_1)^2+(y-y_1)^2]} & \frac{-10n_p(y-y_1)}{ln(10)[(x-x_1)^2+(y-y_1)^2]} \\ \cdot & \cdot \\ \cdot & \cdot \\ \cdot & \cdot \\ \frac{-10n_p(x-x_K)}{ln(10)[(x-x_K)^2+(y-y_K)^2]} & \frac{-10n_p(y-y_K)}{ln(10)[(x-x_K)^2+(y-y_K)^2]} \end{bmatrix} \tag{26}$$

and the CRLB of accuracy at location (x, y)will be given by (22).

Assessment of CRLB of Different Radio Positioning Methods

A quick look on equations (21), (24), and (26)one can easily realize that AoA and RSS methods are both scale-dependent which means if the area increased by scaling, the CRLB will increase. ToA methods has the advantage of not depending on area scaling where CRLB will not be affected if(21)is multiplied by a distance scale, the CRLB will be unit-less and increasing or decreasing the area will not affect it. Although this is an obvious advantage of ToA methods over AoA and RSS based methods, the severe NLOS conditions will have negative effect on the CRLB. In order to assess this effect, simulation was done in which we have 4 network nodes and the NLOS conditions are represented by different measurement noises. For example, a time error of only 0.1 microseconds will result in a 30 meter distance error. Moreover, in a network such as WiFi, the timestamp resolution is 1 microsecond which corresponds to 300m [40]. Based on the results reported in [16],[40] we put a distance error of 10m in the ToA method in our simulation as a NLOS effect. In AoA we put a noise of 20 degrees angle error. In RSS methods, based on the experiments done in this research and reported in many papers [41][18][42], a 10 dBm signal noise in NLOS was used.4 network nodes with different area and different measurement noises and different geometry were simulated to compare the expected performance of each type of systems in severe NLOS conditions.

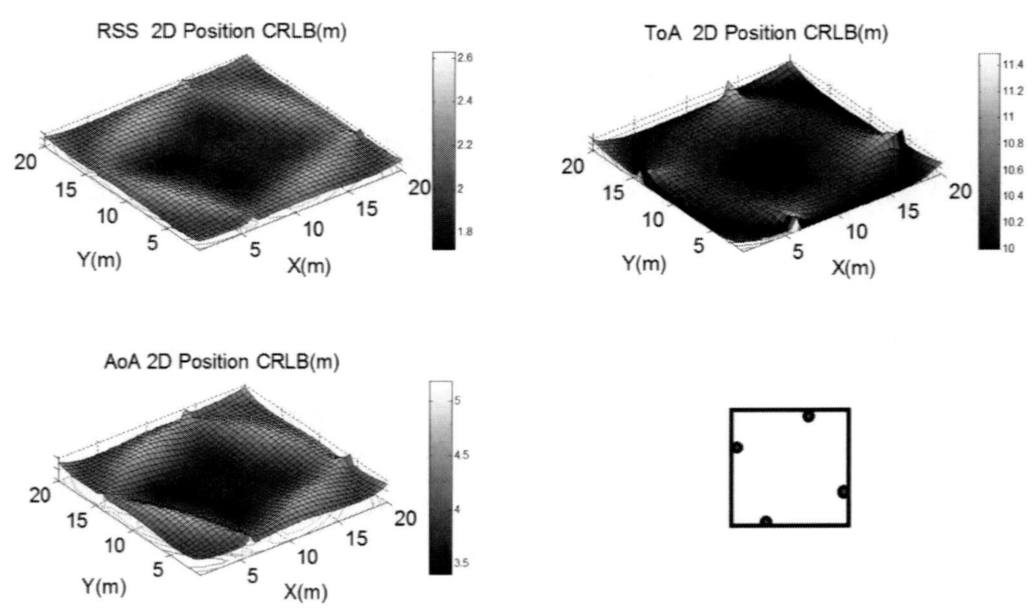

Figure 11. CRLB for the three basic radio positioning approaches. Area: 20mx20m, ToA Noise: 10m, AoA Noise: 20°, RSS Noise: 10 dBm.

Effect of Scaling the Experiment Area

The effect of scaling the environment area on the CRLB for different wireless positioning techniques is shown in Figure 11 and Figure 12. Figure 12 is scaling by two of the area in Figure 11. As mentioned earlier, both RSS and AoA methods were affected by the scaling while ToA is not. An interesting note is that RSS and AoA methods are close to each other in terms of distribution. This is expected from the mathematical formulas of RSS and AoA CRLBs.

Effect of Measurement Noise

In this simulation, a 30% increase in the measurements noise for the three methods were simulated. Figure 13 shows that RSS-based method is the least affected method and the ToA is the most affected method. This is very important since in NLOS, most probably the measurements will be contaminated with higher noises instantaneously due to dynamic changes in the environment.

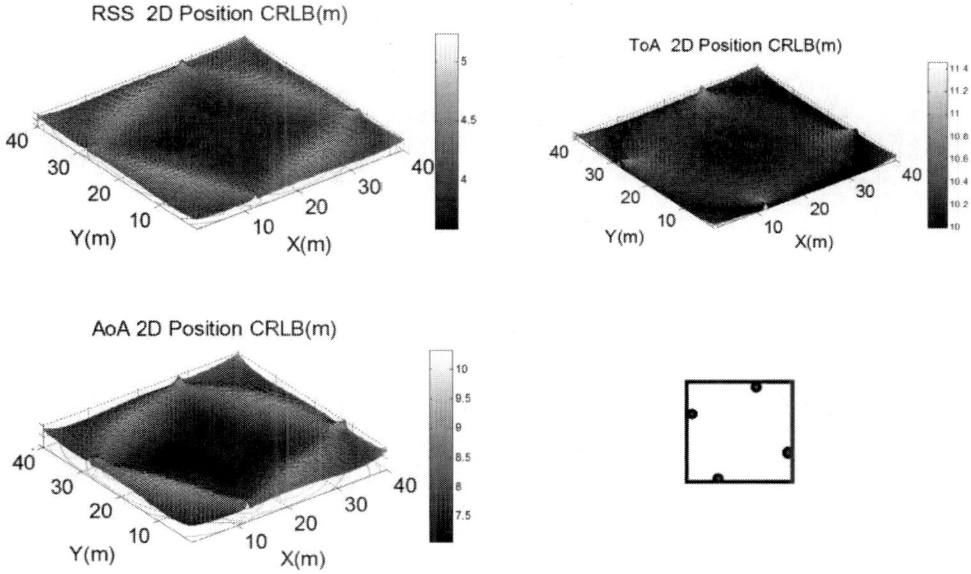

Figure 12. CRLB for the three basic radio positioning approaches after scaling the area. Area: 40mx40m, ToA Noise: 10m, AoA Noise 20°, RSS Noise: 10 dBm.

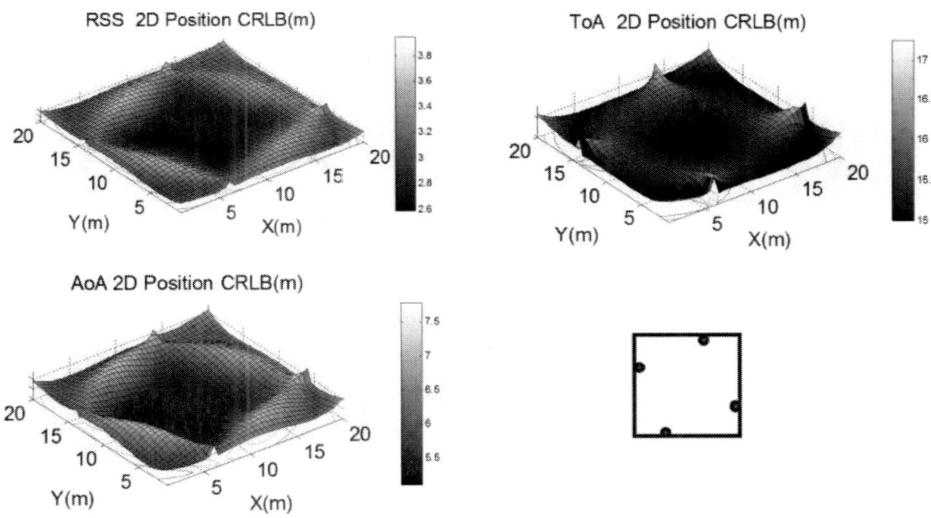

Figure 13. CRLB with 30% noise increase. Area: 20mx20m, ToA Noise: 15m, AoA Noise: 30°, RSS Noise: 15 dBm.

Effect of Network Nodes Geometry

Figure 14shows that ToA is better in coverage that RSS and AoA. Although ToA CRLB is higher than that of RSS and AoA. ToA achieves its minimum CRLB in most of the area with different geometries.

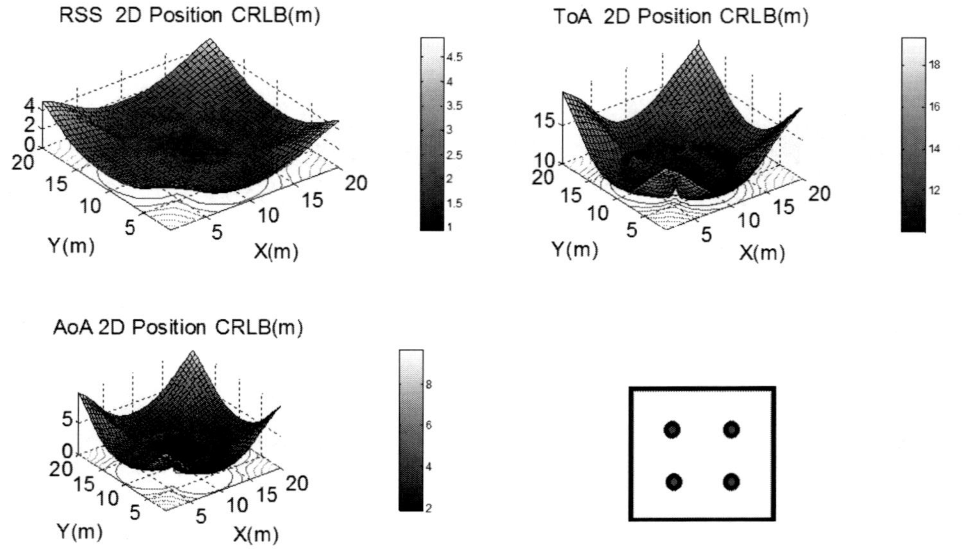

Figure 14. CRLB for ToA/RSS/AoA with different geometry. Area:20mx20m, ToA Noise: 10m, AoA Noise: 20°, RSS Noise: 10 dBm.

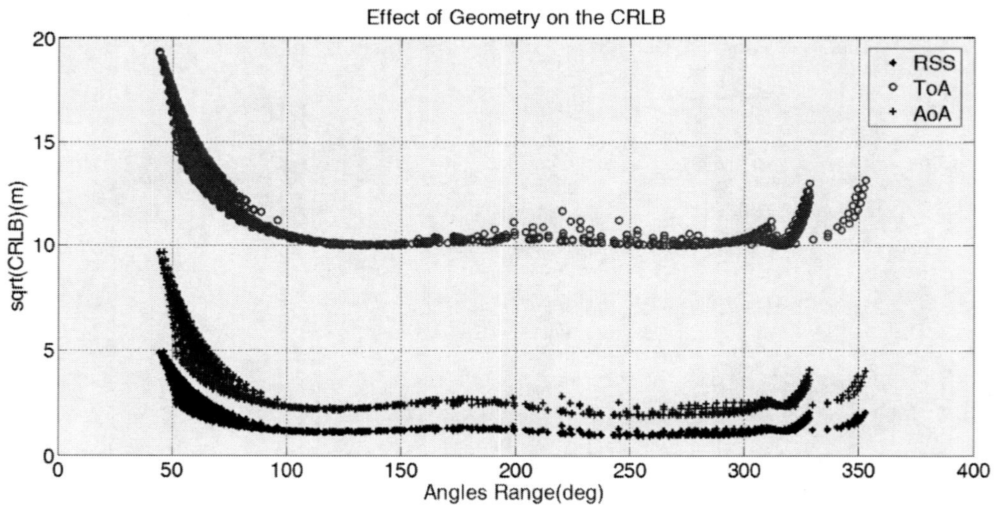

Figure 15. Effect of Geometry on CRLB.

Better Assessment

To have a better idea about the effect of different conditions on the CRLB, a simulation at different noise, scaling, and geometry were done. The geometry was measured as the absolute difference between the maximum and minimum angle of the direct LOS between the user locations and the network nodes. Figure 15shows the geometry effect. There is a similarity between RSS and AoA. An interesting note is that RSS has the lowest CRLB in all angle ranges. Figure 16 shows the effect of increasing measurement noise. Obviously, RSS-based method is the best and the ToA is more severely affected by measurement noise. Figure 17 shows the effect of scaling which shows that although ToA is not affected by scaling of the area, the CRLB of ToA is still much higher that RSS CRLB and AoA CRLB for the fifth scaling of the area. Another note is that RSS-based methods are less affected by scaling than AoA.

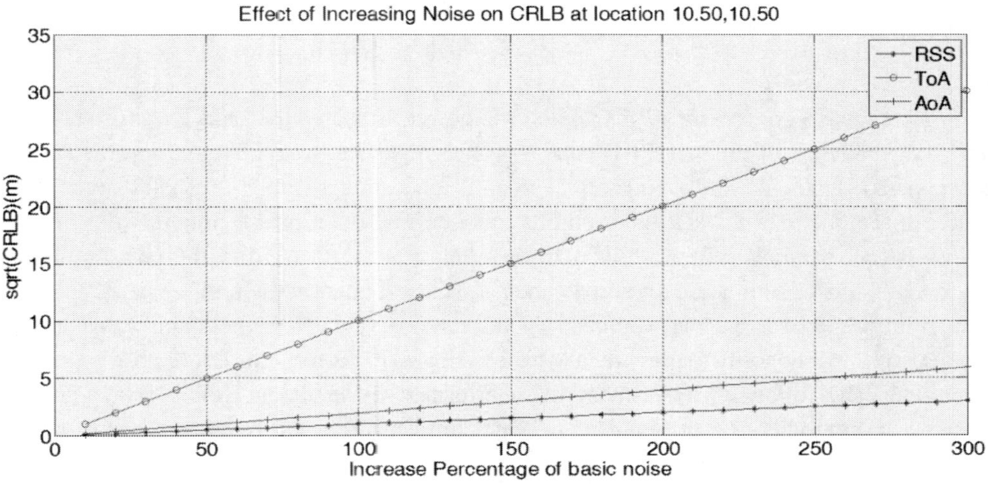

Figure 16. Effect of Measurement Noise on CRLB.

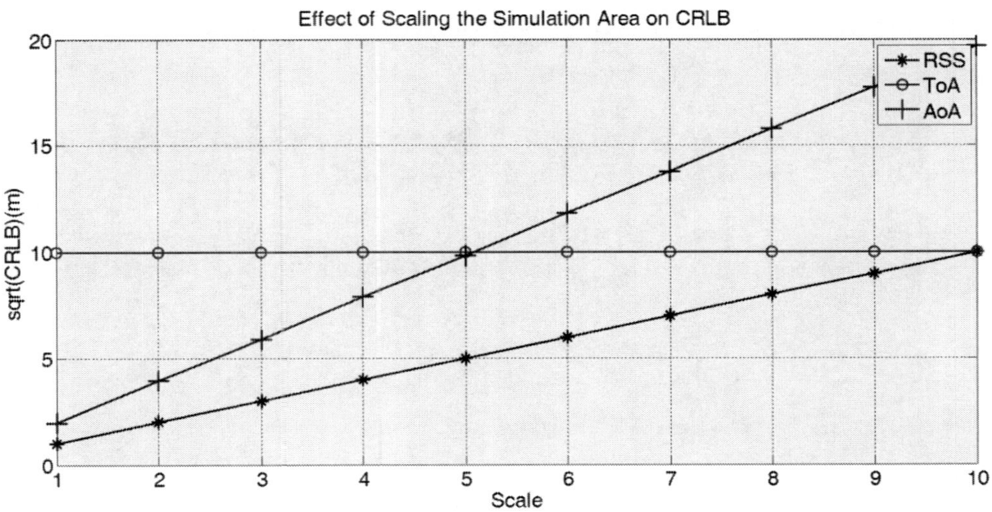

Figure 17. Effect of area scaling on CRLB.

Indoor Localization Using Wireless Propagation Modeling (PM)

In the previous section, it was shown that RSS-based methods theoretically outperforms other wireless positioning systems (AoA-Based and ToA-Based methods). Thus, this section is dedicated to experimental work on the problem of Path-Loss modeling in sever NLOS conditions indoors.

Least Squares Log-distance Wireless Propagation Modeling

Common Log-Distance Propagation Modeling (PM) techniques share the general given formula [36]:

$$P_{RX} = P_o - 10n_i log_{10}(d_{\mathrm{RX}}/d_0) \tag{27}$$

where P_{RX} is the RSS at receiver, P_o is a reference power measured at distance d_0 (usually d_0=1) and n_i is the path loss exponent [18][17] and d_{RX} is the distance from the signal source. The path-loss exponent (n) indicates the attenuation degree of signal strength and it is usually larger indoors than free-space due to walls and other objects indoors. The traditional technique to estimate the path-loss model parameters is to collect some RSS measurements from the environment and perform least-squares estimation to estimate the pass loss exponent n_i assuming that P_o and d_0 are known from pre-knowledge measurements in the environment. Now, let's apply this in a real indoor environment not only to estimate a distance but also to perform the entire positioning using Trilateration. The following experiment was performed in an indoor office area with dense obstacles and constructions (see Figure 18). The experiment was performed on the existing WiFi network. Using a WiFi-enabled laptop, a radio survey was performed and RSS observations from the wireless access points 1,2,3, and 4 shown in Figure 18 were taken and saved. In the following, a least-square log-distance propagation modeling will be performed.

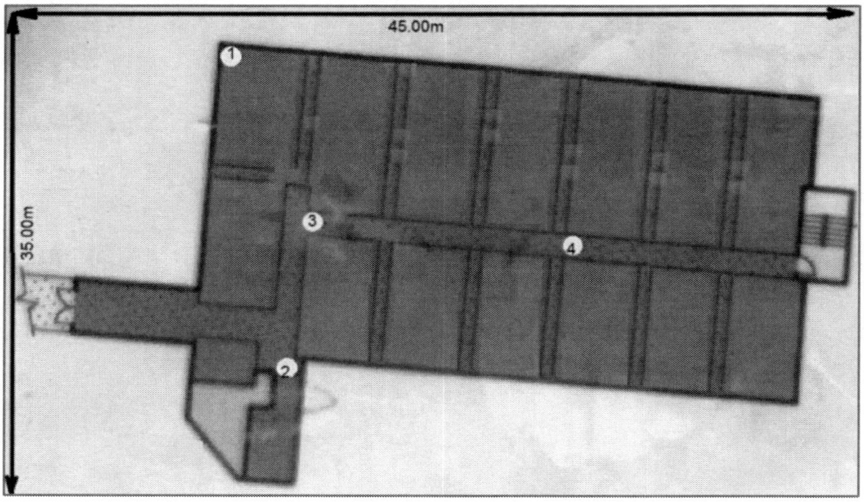

Figure 18. Indoor Experimental Area in Sixth floor, ECE Dept. at Queen's University. RSS Observations for Access Point #1.

The RSS observations of the wireless access point #1 and the Log-Distance fitted model result is shown in Figure 19. There is clear ambiguity around the distances 14-17 meters where at the same distance we have totally different RSS patterns. This is mainly due to obstacles distribution differences in different directions. Obviously, such ambiguities cannot be properly modeled using a single mathematical formula fitted to RSS observations.

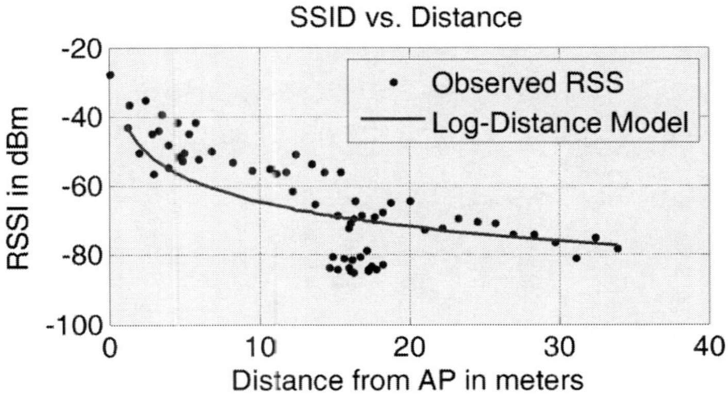

Figure 19. Log-Distance Model results for AP#1 (8.4119, 18.039): $P_o = -42.91, d_o = 1.24, n = 2.379$.

RSS Observations for Access Point #2

The RSS observations of the wireless access point #2 and the Log-Distance fitted model result is shown in Figure 20. There is a high variance at around the distance 5 meters due the multi-path effects indoors which cannot be properly modeled using a single mathematical formula fitted to some RSS observations.

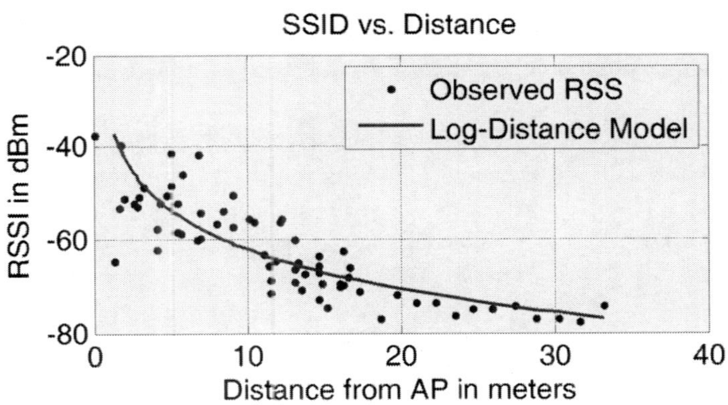

Figure 20. Log-Distance Model results for AP#2 (6.8436, 2.1046): $P_o = -37.00, d_o = 1.30, n = 2.836$.

RSS Observations for Access Point #3

The RSS observations of the wireless access point #3 and the Log-Distance fitted model result is shown in Figure 21. This is another example of "ambiguity" around the distance 10 meters.

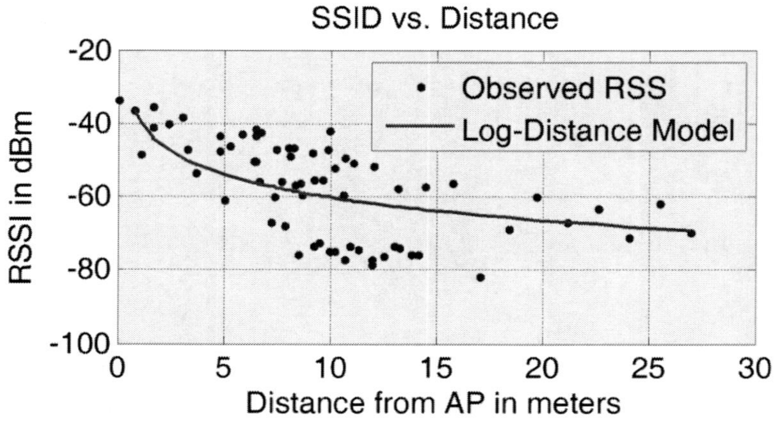

Figure 21. Log-Distance Model results for AP#3 (12.9268, 7.867): $P_o = -36.50, d_o = 0.73, n = 2.085$.

RSS Observations for Access Point #4

The RSS observations of the wireless access point #4 and the Log-Distance fitted model result is shown in Figure 22. Note here we have a different pattern. The propagation is almost partitioned into different segments. The segment from 0m to 10m, the segment from 10m to 23m and the segment from 23m to 30m. This is another pattern that results from multi-path effects with different obstacles distribution inside buildings. Similarly, this pattern cannot be modeled properly using a single mathematical formula fitted to some RSS observations.

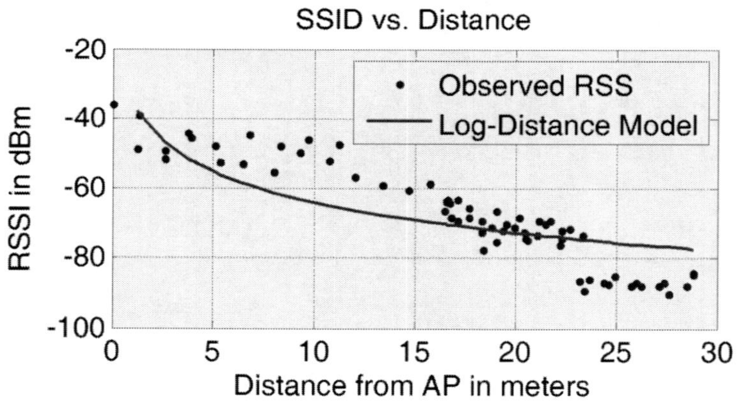

Figure 22. Log-Distance Model results for AP#4 (28.6101, 6.3638): $P_o = -38.00, d_o = 1.29, n = 2.920$.

Positioning Accuracy of Log-Distance Models Indoors

TheoreticalExpected2D Location Accuracy Using CRLB Analysis

Figure 23 shows the CRLB for the experimental area with the four access points in Figure 18. The RSS-based method has the lower CRLB. Also it can be expected an accuracy around 5 meters in most of locations and bad accuracy at the most right part of the area. These results will be verified through the experimental work results.

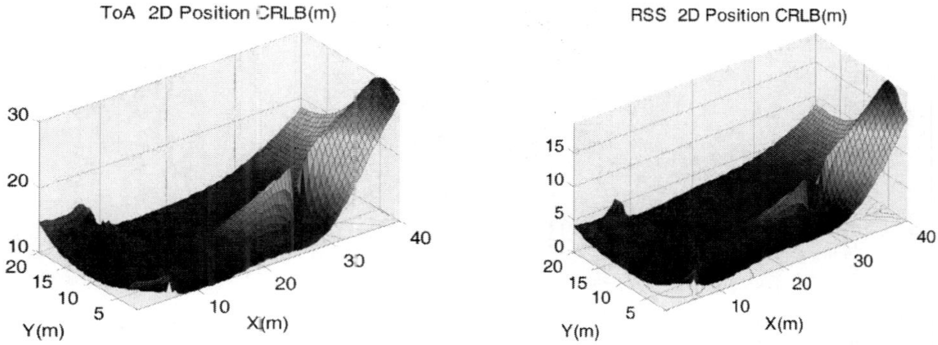

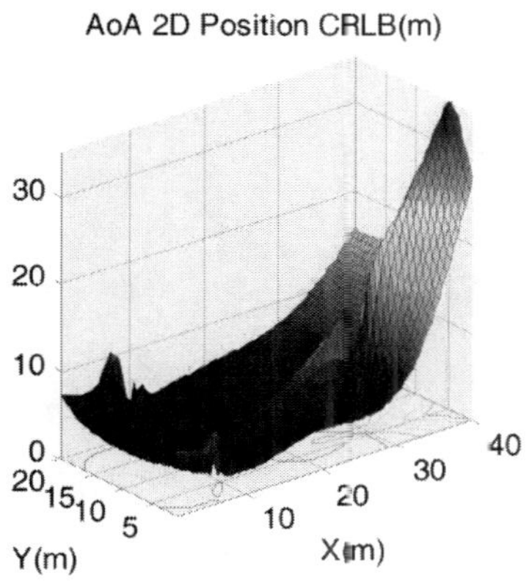

Area	20mx20m
ToA Noise	10m
AoA Noise	20°
RSS Noise	10 dBm

Geometry

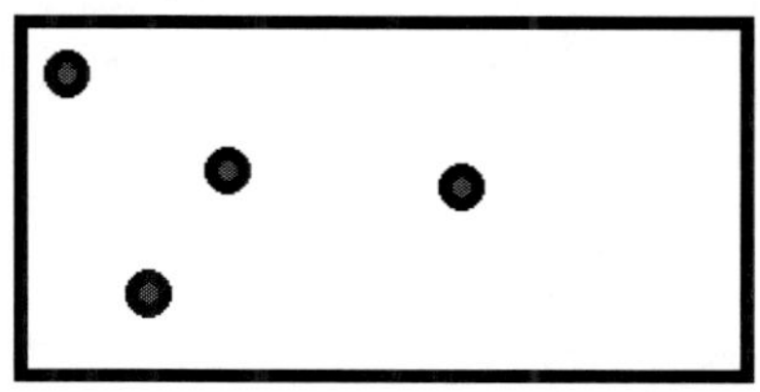

Figure 23. CRLB for the arrangement and configuration given in experimental work.

Experimental Positioning Accuracy

A testing trajectory was planned in the experimental area of Figure 18 is shown in Figure 24. In this trajectory, a collection of 20 known locations was taken as way-points for the trajectory. In those way-points, during doing the trajectory testing, the known locations were recorded so that an error can be calculated between those reference points and the solution presented.

To calculate a position, the received signal strength from the access points were used to estimate a distance based on the Log-Distance model. Trilateration was performed and solved using least-squares algorithm. Figure 25 shows the positioning solution in east component. It is noticed that the accuracy in east channel is much better than that in the North Channel shown in Figure 26. Figure 28 shows the overall accuracy over the testing points showing also the horizontal dilution of precision (HDOP)[11]. Dilution of precision is an accuracy measure calculated from the least-square algorithm. For more details about HDOP, the reader is referred to [10]. An average accuracy of 5 meters as shown in Figure 28 conforms with the CRLB which is expected since CRLB was calculated using the same Log-Distance path loss model as a measurement model.

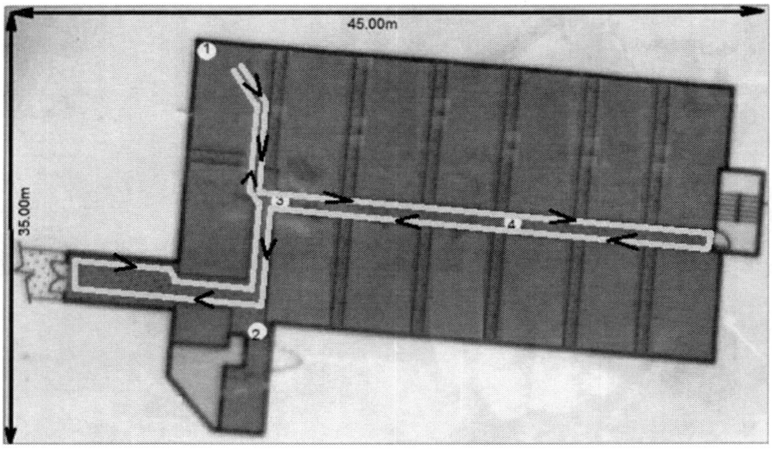

Figure 24. Testing Trajectory (yellow lines and arrows).

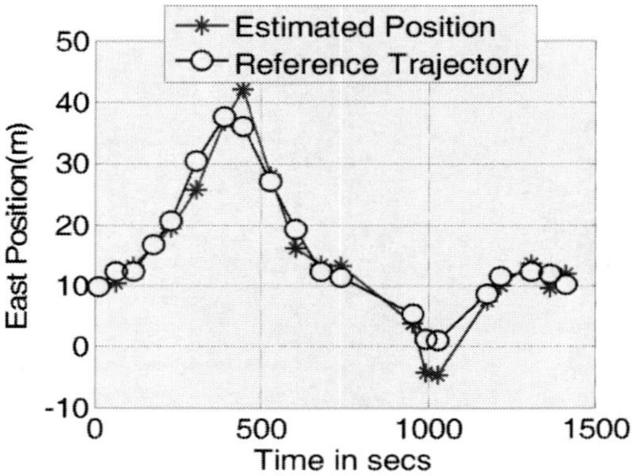

Figure 25. East Position Solution.

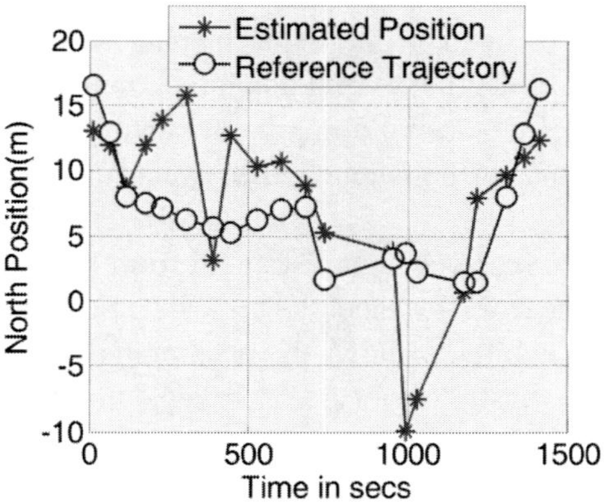

Figure 26. North Position Solution.

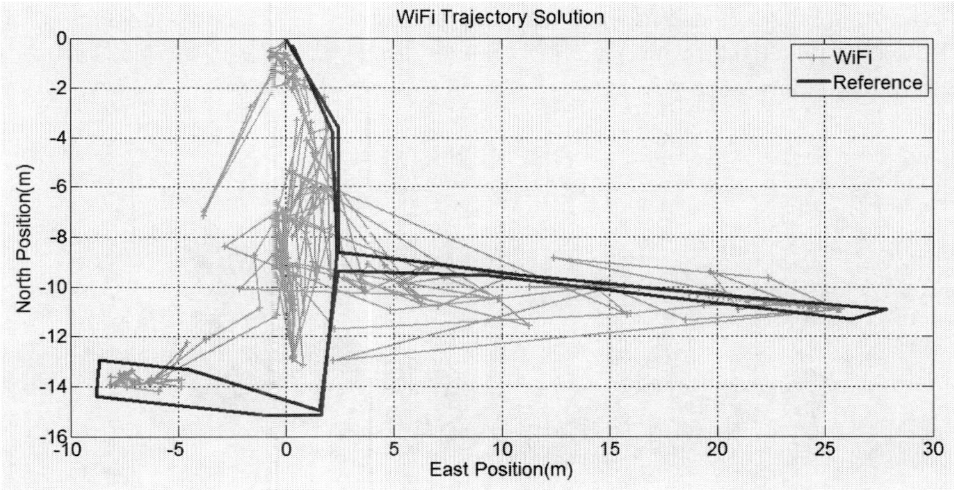

Figure 27. 2D plot for the generated WiFi solution.

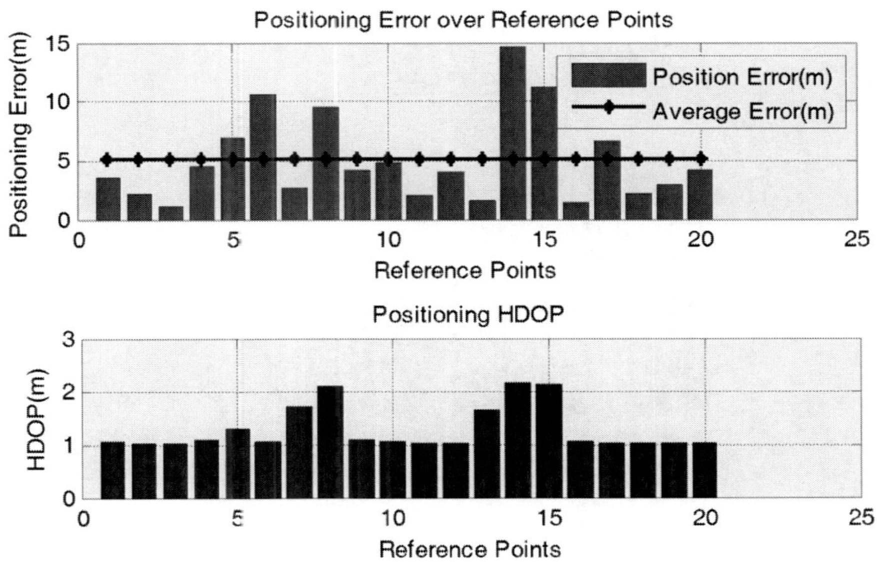

Figure 28. Positioning Accuracy of Log-Distance PM Method.

So far, the results are expected and justified but only one note is worth mentioning and analyzing which is the low accuracy along north component. In a trial to explain this, a suitable idea is to calculate the CRLB for the x and y (east and north) components separately and compare the results. This was done and the calculated CRLB for east and north components separately are shown in Figure 29 and Figure 30 respectively. Results show that the CRLB for north component is larger than that of east component which is strongly consistent with the experimental results obtained by applying the Log-Distance PM method. The 2D plot of the trajectory solution is shown in Figure 27 which shows clearly how noisy the solution is. This is a common problem in all wireless positioning systems indoors where NLOS dominates the environment and case many outliers due to multipath. Note that the results shown in Figure 25 and Figure 26 are only at the reference locations at which we have known location to compare with while the solution displayed in 2D in Figure 27 shows the entire trajectory points.

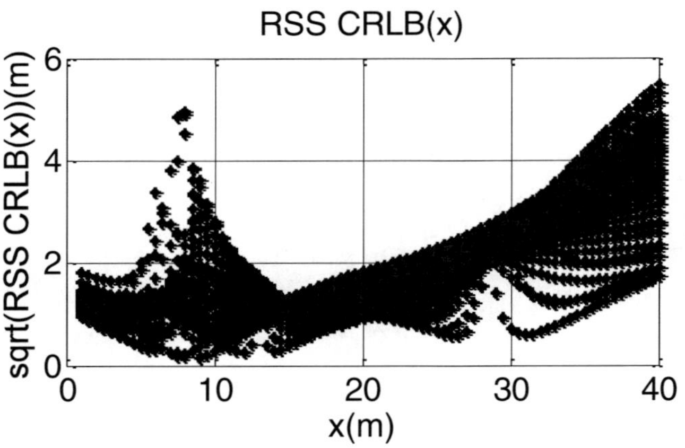

Figure 29. CRLB (East Component).

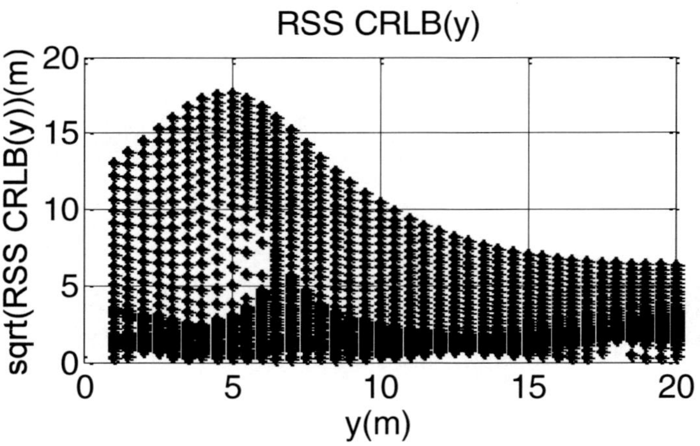

Figure 30. CRLB (North Component).

Using Radial Basis Functions Artificial Neural Networksin Wireless Propagation Modeling

The Log-Distance model approach is simple and efficient. However, it cannot effectively deal with complex RSS/Distance patterns that occur due to complex multipath signals (ambiguity, multiple-segments, and high noise variations). In this section, another approach is explored which is the Radial-Basis-Function Artificial Neural Networks (RBF ANN) [43]. Neural networks can be seen as a complex system comprising several, but not necessarily identical, subsystems—the neurons (see Figure 31). Radial Basis Functions are powerful techniques for interpolation in multidimensional space.

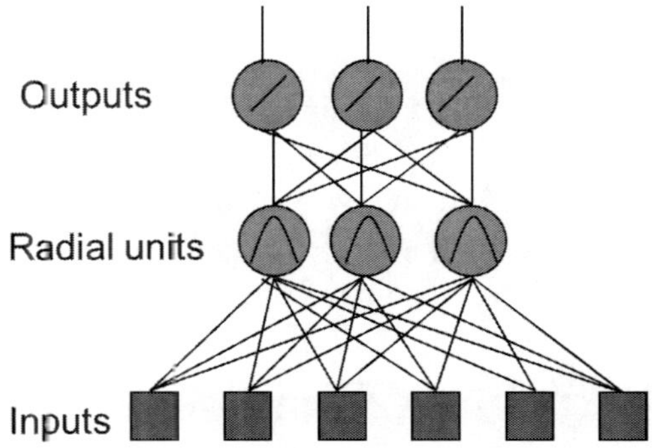

Figure 31. Radial Basis Function Neural Network Architecture.

The RBF network is a three-layer feed-forward network that uses a linear transfer function for the output units and a nonlinear transfer function (normally the Gaussian) for the hidden units (see Figure 31). The input layer simply consists of *n* units connected by weighted connections to the hidden layer. The net input to a hidden unit is a distance measure between some input presented at the input layer and the point represented by the hidden unit; The Gaussian is then applied to the net input to produce a *radial* function of the distance between each pattern vector and each hidden unit weight vector. Hence, a RBF unit carves a hyper-sphere within a pattern space.

Pattern Classification Example

In the following circle classification problem, 4 or 5 sigmoid hidden nodes are required for a good classification. Only 1 RBF node is required if the function can approximate the circle.

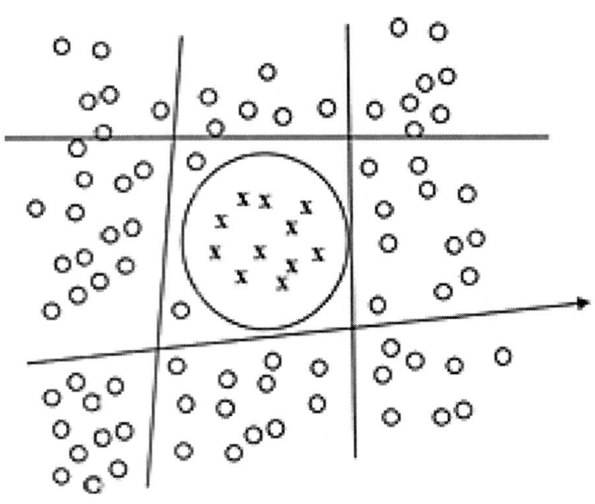

Figure 32. Pattern Classification Example using RBF NN.

RSS Observations Modeling Using RBF

The RBF ANN-based propagation modeling for the wireless access point #1 to #4 is shown in figures (Figure 33 - Figure 36). Although the general pattern is RSS decaying with distance, RBF network model tries to follow the complex RSS/Distance patterns such as ambiguity, multiple segments, and high noise variations. However, RBF networks have limited predictability of outputs corresponding to out-of-training-range inputs.

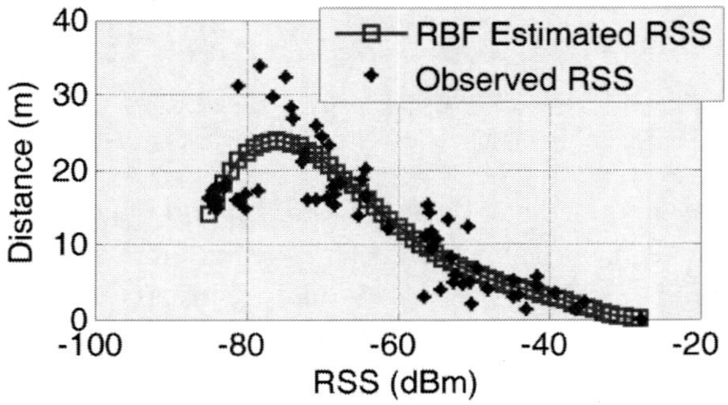

Figure 33. RBF ANN Model results for AP#1 (8.4119, 18.039).

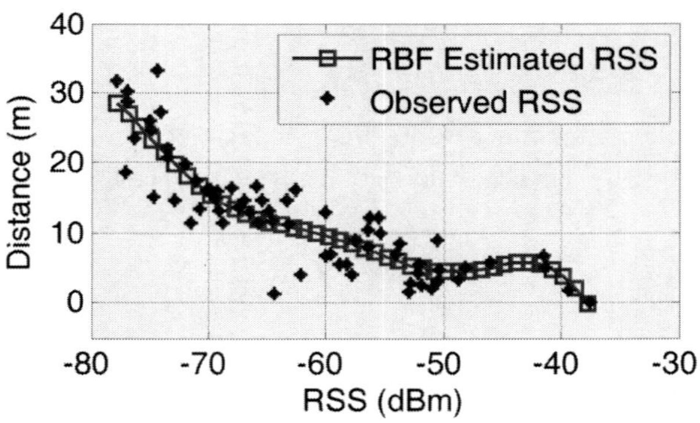

Figure 34. RBF ANN Model results for AP#2 (6.8436, 2.1046).

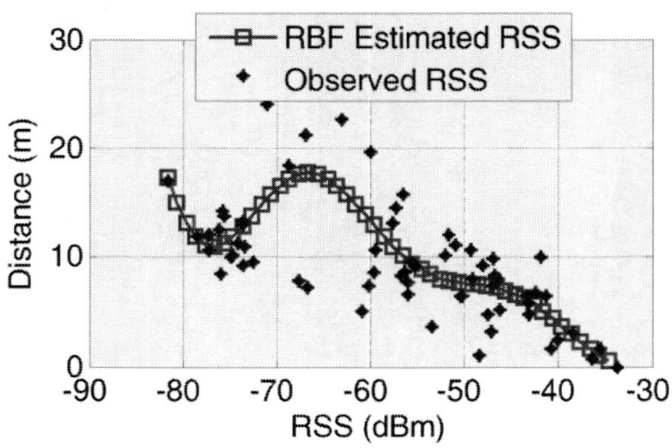

Figure 35. RBF ANN Model results for AP#3 (12.9268, 7.867).

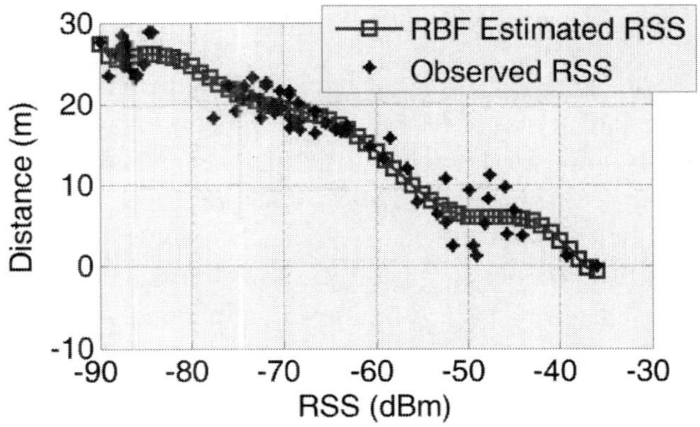

Figure 36. RBF ANN Model results for AP#4 (28.6101, 6.3638).

Positioning Accuracy of RBF ANN Models Indoors

On the same testing trajectory shown in Figure 24, the test was done using the RBF-based PM. Figure 37 shows the overall accuracy over the testing points showing also the HDOP. An average accuracy over 5 meters as shown in Figure 37 shows the best accuracy could be obtained from RBF-based PM method. These results indicates that the RBF-based PM is inherently very close to the Log-Distance PM. These results shows that we still need better approaches to provide better PM-based positioning accuracy.

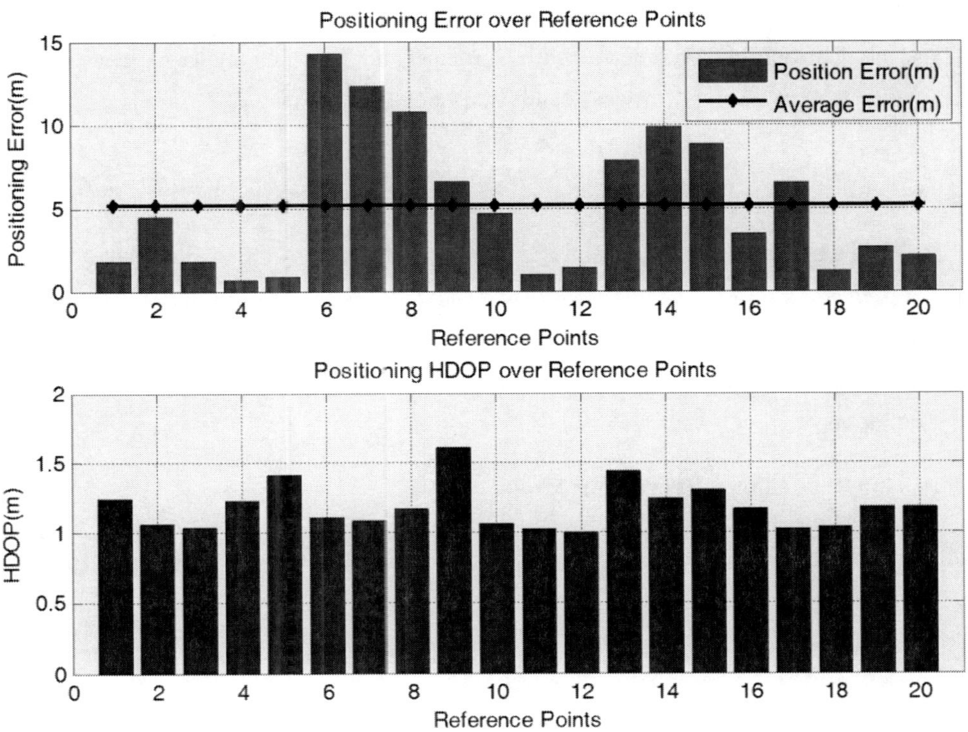

Figure 37. Positioning Accuracy of RBF PM method.

Probabilistic Wireless Propagation Modeling

The models described and tested so far are an example of parametric models [37][44]. In very noisy environments, these types of models are not flexible enough. Thus, in this section, a probabilistic approach is proposed. In probabilistic approaches, states and measurements are represented by probability distributions instead of crisp values. One advantage of the probabilistic methods is the ability to provide an accuracy measure (standard deviation) with each prediction [45]. In this section, a data driven probabilistic model is explored; that is Gaussian Process Regression (GPR) [45]. A brief over view about GPR is given first and then the technique is applied to propagation modeling problem.

Gaussian Process Regression (GPR)

Bayesian Modeling Using Gaussian Process

Gaussian Process Regression (GPR) [45] is proposed as a non-parametric probabilistic modeling approach which is suitable to handle noisy observations. GPR has been recently used to solve complex machine learning problems [45][46][47][48] such as functions approximation and patterns classification. In the following section we describe the GPR concepts and how the radio propagation problem can be modeled and solved using GPR.

Gaussian Processes (GPs)

A Gaussian process is a vector of random variables X , any finite number of which has a joint Gaussian distribution [45] determined by a mean function $m(x)$ and covariance function $k(x,x')$ where $x \in X$ .A noisy process can be expressed as

$$Y = f(X) + \varepsilon \tag{28}$$

where $\{Y, X\}$ is a training data set. Assuming ε is an additive zero-mean Gaussian noise with covariance δ_n^2 , any arbitrary function Y can be modeled as a Gaussian process. An important feature of GPs is marginalization [45] which enables to calculate the posterior probability [37] [44] at unknown inputs x^* if some observations from the noisy function are available at some given inputs x .

Standard Gaussian Linear Regression Model

The linear regression model to model the process in (28)can be written as:

$$f(X) = X^T W \tag{29}$$

where X is input vector, W is a weight vector, f is the estimated process output. In Bayesian analysis [37] [44], best weights are the weights that maximize the likelihood function which is the probability of the observations given the parameters (weights) which is given by the following formula assuming n independent observations:

$$p(Y \mid X,W) = \prod_{i=1}^{n} p(y_i \mid x_i,W) \tag{30}$$

(30)can be written as:

$$\begin{aligned} p(Y \mid X,W) &= \prod_{i=1}^{n} \frac{1}{\sqrt{2\prod \delta_n}} \exp\left(-\frac{y_i - x_i^{T} W}{2\delta_n^{2}} \right) \\ &= \frac{1}{(2\prod \delta_n^{2})^{n/2}} \exp\left(-\frac{1}{2\delta_n^{2}} \mid Y - X^{T} W \mid^{2} \right) \end{aligned} \tag{31}$$

which is a Gaussian distribution of mean $X^T W$ and a covariance $\delta_n^{2} I$. If the prior probability density functions of weights is Gaussian with zero mean and covariance $\sum_p$:

$$p(W) = N(0, \Sigma_p) \tag{32}$$

The posterior probability density function of weights is given by Bayes' rule as follows:

$$p(W \mid Y,X) = \frac{p(Y \mid X,W)\, p(W)}{p(Y \mid X)} \tag{33}$$

Substituting from (31)and (32)in (33), noting that $p(Y \mid X)$ is a normalization factor, the posterior PDF of weights is Gaussian and given by:

$$p(W \mid X,Y) \propto N(\overline{W} = \frac{1}{\delta_n^{2}} A^{-1} XY, A^{-1}) \tag{34}$$

where $A = \delta_n^{-2} XX^{T} + \Sigma_p^{-1}$.

To compute a predictive posterior probability density function for new inputs x^{*}, we average the output over all weights with their posterior probabilities as follows:

$$p(y_* \mid x_*, X, Y) = \int p(y_* | x_*, W) p(W \mid X, Y) dW$$
$$= \int x_*^T W p(W \mid X, y) dW \quad (35)$$
$$= N(\frac{1}{\delta_n^2} x_*^T A^{-1} XY, x_*^T A^{-1} x_*)$$

Non-linear Gaussian Process Regression

To overcome the limitation of linear models, inputs Xcould be projected into higher dimensional feature space in which the problem becomes linearly separable [43]. Actually this is what the hidden layer does in multilayer perception neural networks [43].Thus, the function $\phi(x)$ is used to map the D-dimensional input vectors to N-dimensional feature space. In this case, the model is given by:

$$f(X) = \phi(X)^T W \quad (36)$$

and the predictive posterior probability density function for unknown inputs x^* given the observations X, Y is given by:

$$\begin{aligned} &p(y_* \mid x_*, X, Y) = \\ &N(\phi(x_*)^T \Sigma_p \phi(X)(K + \delta_n^2 I)^{-1} Y, \phi(x_*)^T \Sigma_p \phi(x_*) \\ &- \phi(x_*)^T \Sigma_p \phi(X)(K + \delta_n^2 I)^{-1} \phi(X)^T \Sigma_p \phi(x_*)) \end{aligned} \quad (37)$$

where $K = \varphi(X)^T \Sigma_p \varphi(X)$.

Gaussian Kernel Learning

In (37), the term $\phi(x^*)^T \sum_p \phi(X)$ can be seen as a covariance function or kernel [45]. In Bayesian analysis, instead of learning the weights like the case in neural networks [43], Gaussian Regression learns the kernel (Covariance of training data). This has the advantage of having a non-parametric non-linear regression model that is robust to observations noises. The most common kernel covariance function is the exponential given by:

$$Cov(y_i, y_j) = k(x_i, x_j) + \sigma_n^2 \delta(i - j) \quad (38)$$

$$k(x_i, x_j) = \sigma_f^2 \exp\left(-\frac{1}{2}(x_i - x_j)^T M (x_i - x_j)\right) \quad (39)$$

where $x_i, x_j \in X$ and $y_i, y_j \in Y$ and δ is the Delta Dirac function. Parameters σ_n^2, σ_f^2, and M are called the hyper-parameters and they can be learned and optimized by maximizing the log likelihood function given by:

$$Log(p(Y \mid X)) = -\frac{1}{2}Y^T(K+\sigma_n^2 I)^{-1}Y - \log\left|K+\sigma_n^2 I\right| - \frac{n}{2}\log 2\pi \quad (40)$$

where $K$is the covariance matrix over all data input vectors in X.

Radio Propagation Modeling Using GPR

To model the radio propagation using GPR, the training data set will be consisting of $X = RSS, Y = Distance$. Thus, the GPR model will take unknown input $x^* = ObservedRSS$. Then the required output from GPR model (distance probability distribution at RSS input = $x^* = ObservedRSS$) will be calculated as follows:

$$\mu_{x^*} = k(x^*, X)\left(K+\sigma_n^2 I\right)^{-1} Y \quad (41)$$

$$\sigma_{x^*}^2 = k(x^*, x^*) - k(x^*, X)^T (K+\sigma_n^2 I)^{-1} k(x^*, X) \quad (42)$$

where μ_{x^*} is the predicted distance mean at this x^* given the training data points $X = RSS, Y = Distance$ and σ_{x^*} is the distance standard deviation and K is the covariance matrix over training data points.

RSS Observations Modeling Using GPR

The GPR-based propagation modeling for the wireless access point #1 to #4 is shown in the following figures. The GPR is close to RBF where it tries to follow the complex RSS/Distance patterns such as ambiguity, multiple segments, and high noise variations. However, an additional piece of information is available which is the confidence (STDV) of the prediction is. This STDV will be used to weight the observations while positioning using Trilateration.

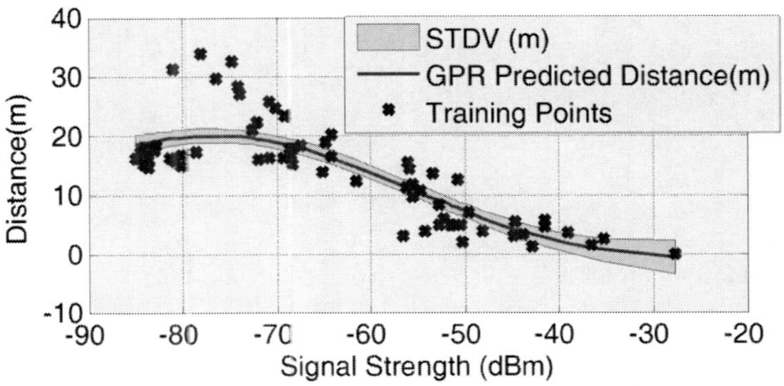

Figure 38. GPR Model results for AP#1 (8.4119, 18.039): $\sigma_n = 10dBm, \sigma_f = 10dBm, l = 5$.

Positioning Accuracy of GPR-based-Models

On the same testing trajectory shown in Figure 24, the test was done using the GPR-based Propagation Model. In the Trilateration algorithm, the standard deviation of the GPR prediction was converted from dBm (signal strength units) to a corresponding standard deviation in distance (meters). The standard deviations in meters were fed as measurements accuracy covariance matrix to be used in the least-squares algorithm. Figure 42 shows the overall accuracy over the testing points showing also the HDOP. An average accuracy below 5 meters as shown in Figure 42 shows the best accuracy could be obtained from GPR-based Propagation Model method which shows a slight improvement over previously mentioned models. This should be promising because this accuracy is very close to the theoretical CRLB. Although the GPR-based PM is close to RBF-based PM, the usage of the STDV in the Trilateration proved to be useful.

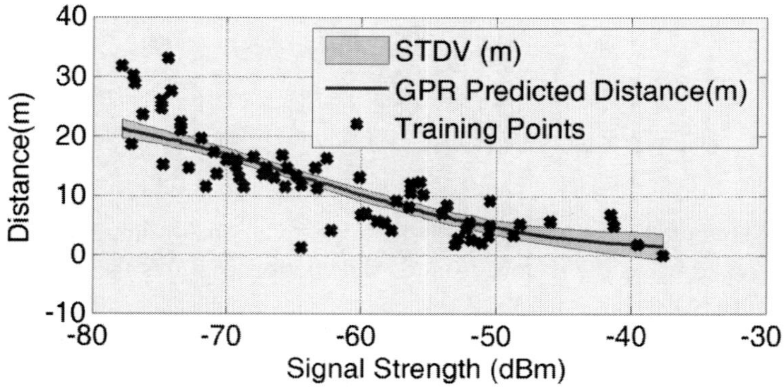

Figure 39. GPR Model results for AP#2 (6.8436, 2.1046): $\sigma_n = 10dBm, \sigma_f = 10dBm, l = 5$.

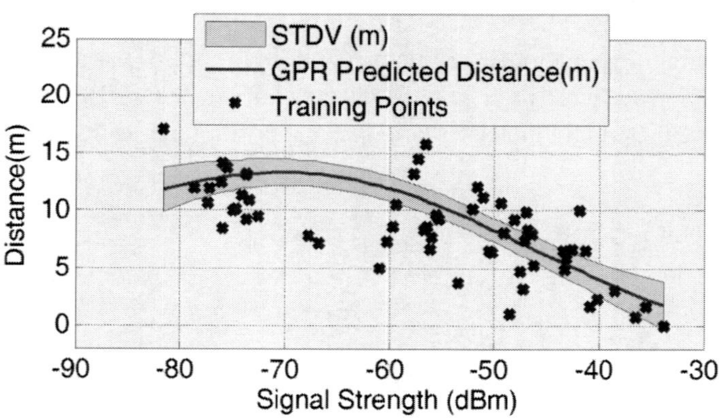

Figure 40. GPR Model results for AP#3 (12.9268, 7.867): $\sigma_n = 10dBm, \sigma_f = 10dBm, l = 5$.

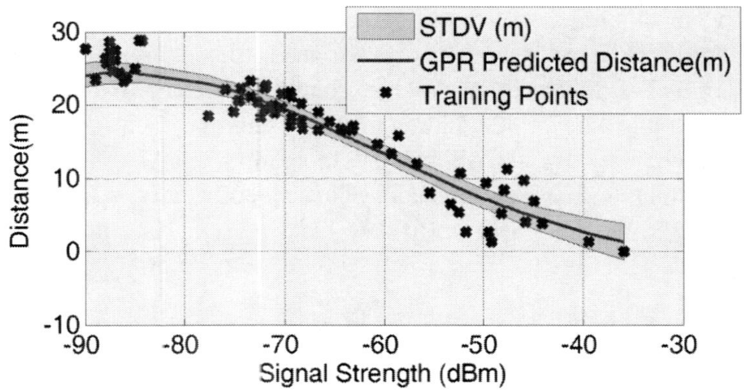

Figure 41. Log-Distance Model results for AP#4 (28.6101, 6.3638): $\sigma_n = 10dBm, \sigma_f = 10dBm, l = 5$.

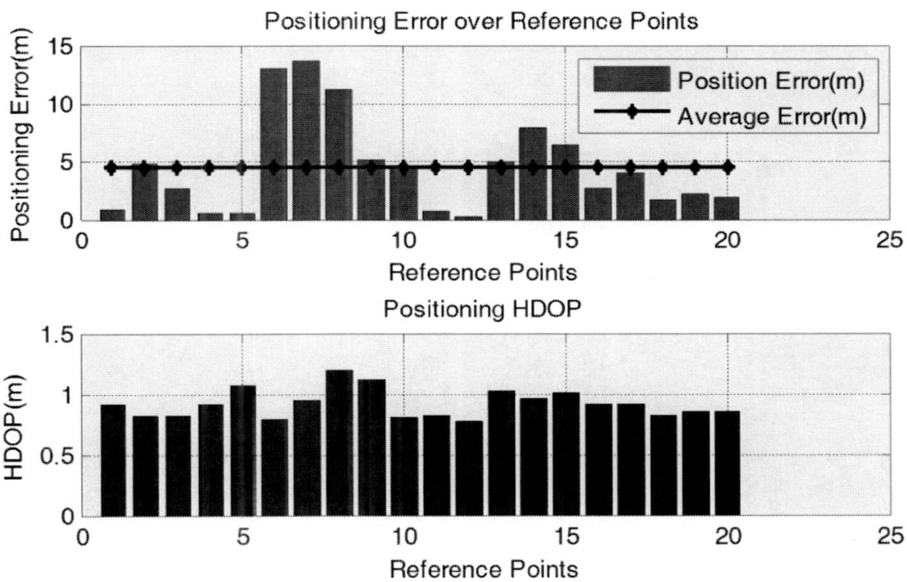

Figure 42. Overall Positioning Accuracy of GPR-based PM methods.

Adaptive Wireless Propagation Modeling

In all the presented work so far in this chapter, a training data set collected offline was needed to build the necessary models. This offline training phase is not desirable in practical applications for the following reasons:

1) It consumes a lot of time before the positioning system can start and work.
2) It usually needs manual work which is not practical.
3) It needs to be repeated if the environment is changing which is very likely in indoors.

One objective of this research is building adaptive dynamic models that does not need offline survey. The key feature of the network that needs to be there to enable such adaptive positioning system is the mutual information exchange between network nodes which was introduced by Lim et all [42]. In [42], Lim et all suggested that each AP signal includes AP Location and RSS received by the AP from its neighbouring APs. This is what we call "Access Points Mutual RSS Measurements". Consequently, any WLAN-enabled device will be able to receive the necessary up-to-date local training data in the following table (Table 1):

Table 1. Online APs' signal strength pattern measurements

	AP1 MAC	AP2 MAC	...	APN MAC
AP1 LOC1	$RSSI_{1,1}$	$RSSI_{1,2}$	...	$RSSI_{1,N}$
AP2 LOC2		$RSSI_{2,2}$	...	$RSSI_{2,N}$
....	...		...	...
APN LOC	$RSSI_{N,1}$	$RSSI_{N,2}$		$RSSI_{N,N}$
USER LOC (Unknown)	$RSSI_{user,1}$	$RSSI_{user,2}$	...	

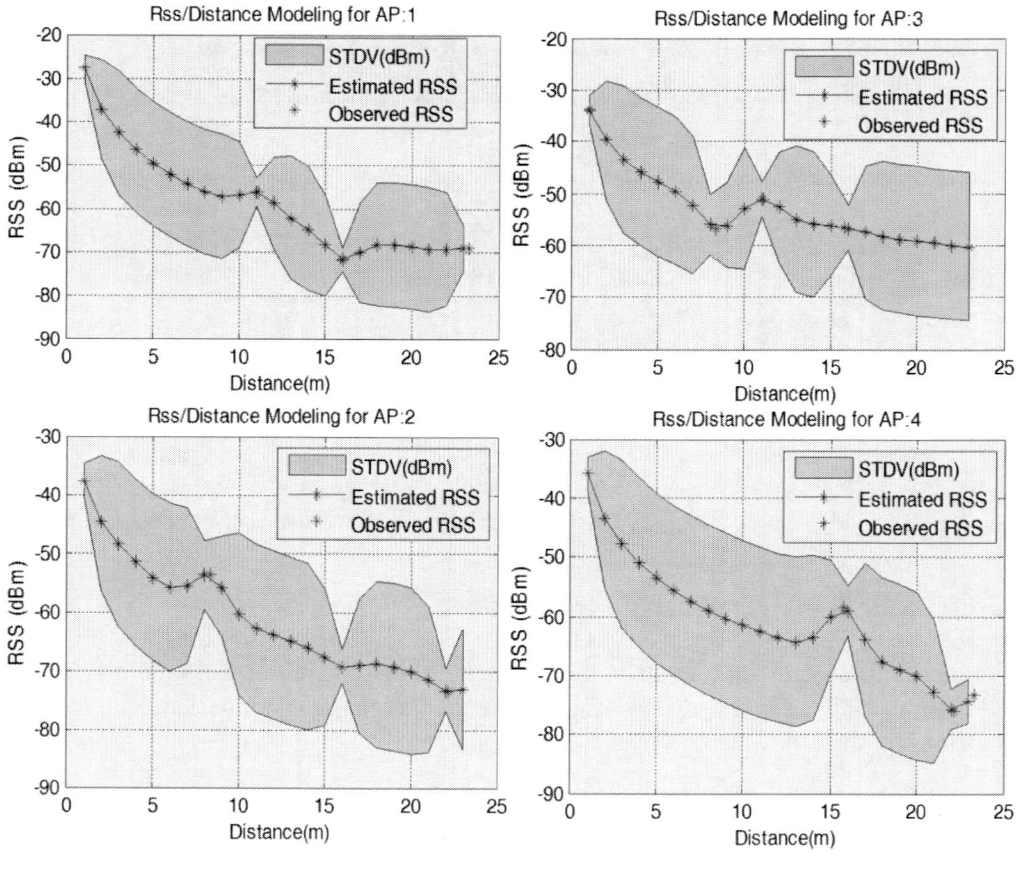

Figure 43. Online PM Building Using Hybrid PM method.

Having the APs locations known, Table 1 can be seen as a compact training set of RSS/Distance pairs for each visible AP. This compact training set can be used to perform PM online and predict distance between user (USER LOC) and each visible AP. For our experiment area shown in Figure 18 which contains 4 APs, Table 1 will contain only 4 rows. Any kind of the propagation modeling techniques described in this chapter can be used to provide distance estimation and, hence, positioning.

Experiments were performed in the same area shown in Figure 18 on the existing WiFi network where wireless monitors were added to do the job on behave of the Aps as described in [42]. A WiFi-enabled laptop was used to collect the measurement and build the propagation models. Experiments were performed using hybrid GPR-Log-Distance PM described earlier. The hybrid modeling results are shown in Figure 43 and the positioning accuracy of the obtained models are shown in Figure 44.

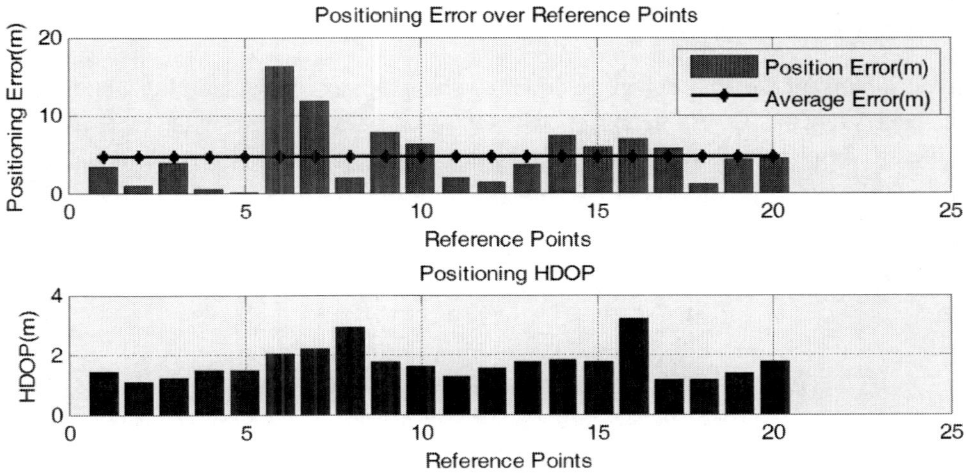

Figure 44. Over all Positioning accuracy Adaptive Hybrid GPR-Log-Distance PM Methods.

Indoor LocalizationUsing Radio Maps

Fingerprint [49][32][33][34], [41] [31] [50] [51] wireless positioning outperforms propagation modeling since the radio map database almost copies the RSS in all locations of interests in the area while propagation modeling does not take orientation into consideration. Fingerprint wireless positioning has usually two common phases; offline and online. In offline training phase, signal strength patterns are collected from known locations and saved in a database. An example of a radio map with N reference locations is shown in Table 2 where $RSS_j^{(i)}$ refers to received signal strength from j^{th} access point at i^{th} location. In online phase where a signal strength pattern is received in an unknown location, any pattern recognition/matching method such as K-Nearest Neighbor (K-NN) [52] [17] or Artificial neural networks [43] can be used to search the saved signal strength patterns and chose the best position thereof.

Table 2. An Example of a Radio Map

	AP1 RSS	AP2 RSS	AP3 RSS	AP4 RSS
Location 1	$RSS_1^{(1)}$	$RSS_2^{(1)}$	$RSS_3^{(1)}$	$RSS_4^{(1)}$
Location 2	$RSS_1^{(2)}$	$RSS_2^{(2)}$	$RSS_3^{(2)}$	$RSS_4^{(2)}$
. .	. .	. .	. .	. .
Location N	$RSS_1^{(N)}$	$RSS_2^{(N)}$	$RSS_3^{(N)}$	$RSS_4^{(N)}$

K-NN Algorithm for Wireless Fingerprinting

In the online phase (the actual positioning phase), the K-NN algorithm compares the current signal strength "power fingerprint" with the saved power patterns in the radio map using a weighted-KNN algorithm to provide a location. In a weighted-KNN algorithm, a weighted average is performed by giving the highest weight to the most nearest radio map power patterns. Thus, given current WiFi fingerprint $RSSI_c$, the current positionis estimated by:

$$P_c = w_1 P_1 + w_2 P_2 + ... + w_k P_k \tag{43}$$

$$w_i = \frac{\exp(-[RSSI_c - RSSI_i]^2)}{\sum_1^k \exp(-[RSSI_c - RSSI_j]^2)} \tag{44}$$

where is the WiFi power pattern recorded with point in the radio map.

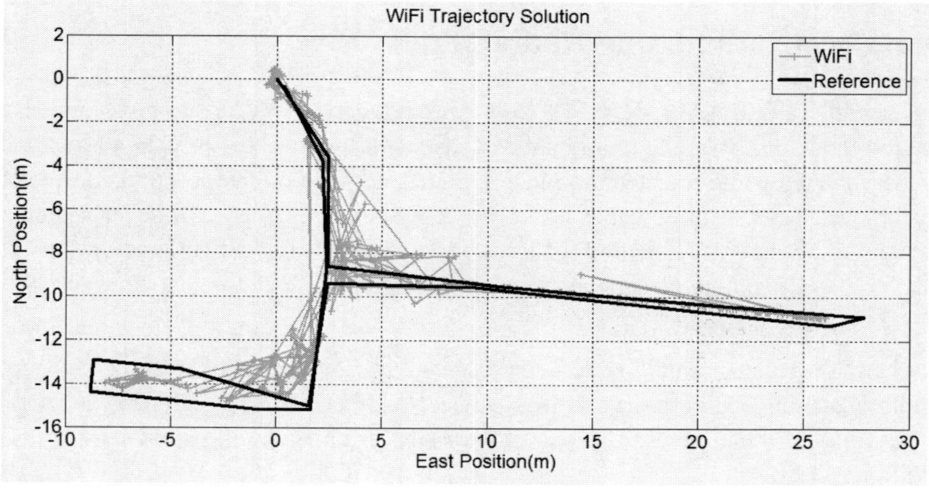

Figure 45. 2D Trajectory Solution.

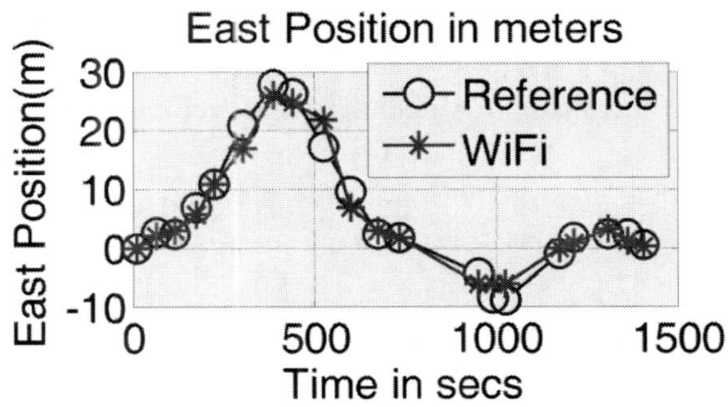

Figure 46. East Positioning Accuracy.

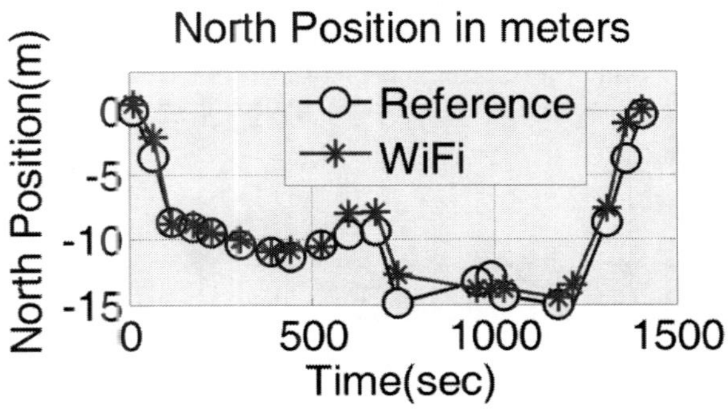

Figure 47. North Positioning Accuracy.

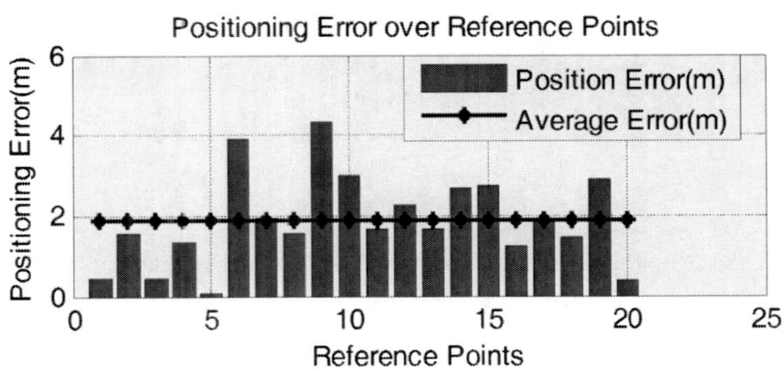

Figure 48. Overall Positioning Accuracy of the K-NN with traditional radio map.

Positioning Accuracy of K-NN Algorithm for Wireless Fingerprinting

An experiment and radio map has been collected in the same environment shown in Figure 18. The positioning results are shown in Figure 45-Figure 48. It can be noticed that the good east/bad north accuracy pattern disappeared and we have better accuracy in both east/north components. The overall accuracy touched the 3 meters for the first time which is even lower than the CRLB given earlier in previous chapters.

Positioning Accuracy of GPR Algorithm for Wireless Fingerprinting

As GPR is a powerful function approximation tool as well, it can be also used to calculate a new position based on new RSS patterns that were not exactly found in the database of the radio map. During the training, the inputs for the GPR are the signal strength patterns and the output are the corresponding locations. During positioning, user power fingerprint is input to the GPR and the output is the predicted location. The GPR has the advantage of providing an accuracy measure that gives a confidence level of the GPR-prediction. Using the GPR trained on 100% of the traditional radio map data points, we get a positioning accuracy of 3.341 which is pretty good even if it is not better than the K-NN results. However, some advantages of the GPR exist as will be explained shortly. Positioning results of the GPR is shown in Figure 49.

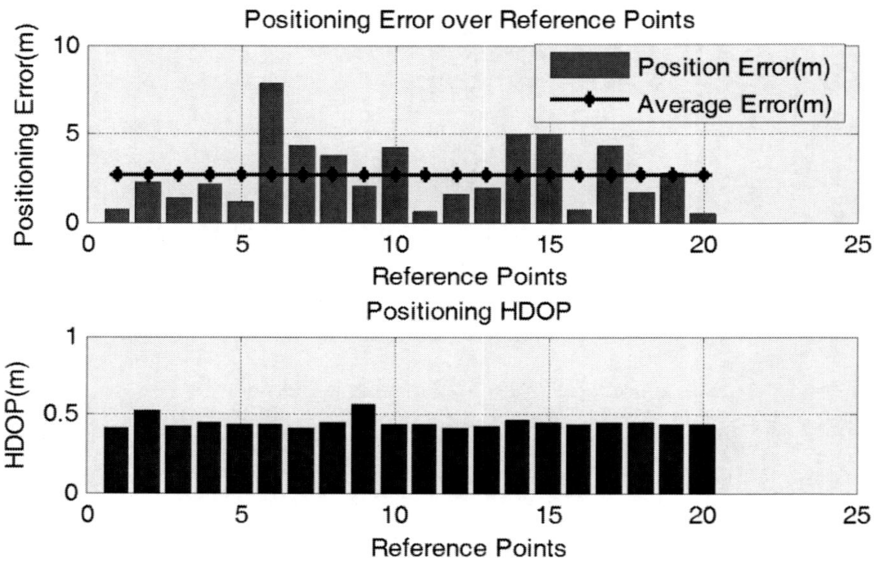

Figure 49. Overall positioning accuracy of GPR with traditional radio map.

Comparison between GPR Performance and Full Survey K-NN Algorithm

One of the merits of GPR is the ability to estimate useful information from few data points. This means it can be used to reduce the size of radio maps while keeping acceptable accuracy. To test this feature, the K-NN and GPR were used over different size ratios of radio-map points. The results show the robustness of GPR since it could achieve reasonable accuracy with only 12.5% of the radio-map points which means it is more robust than K-NN algorithms. A cumulative error percentage graph for both K-NN and GPR is shown in Figure 50.

Adaptive Radio Maps Construction

In all the presented work so far in this chapter, a training data set collected in an offline phase was needed to build the necessary radio map before positioning can be implemented. Similar to adaptive propagation modeling, adaptive dynamic radio map can be developed. In this context, a methodology is introduced by the author in[53] that does not need offline training or extra network hardware.

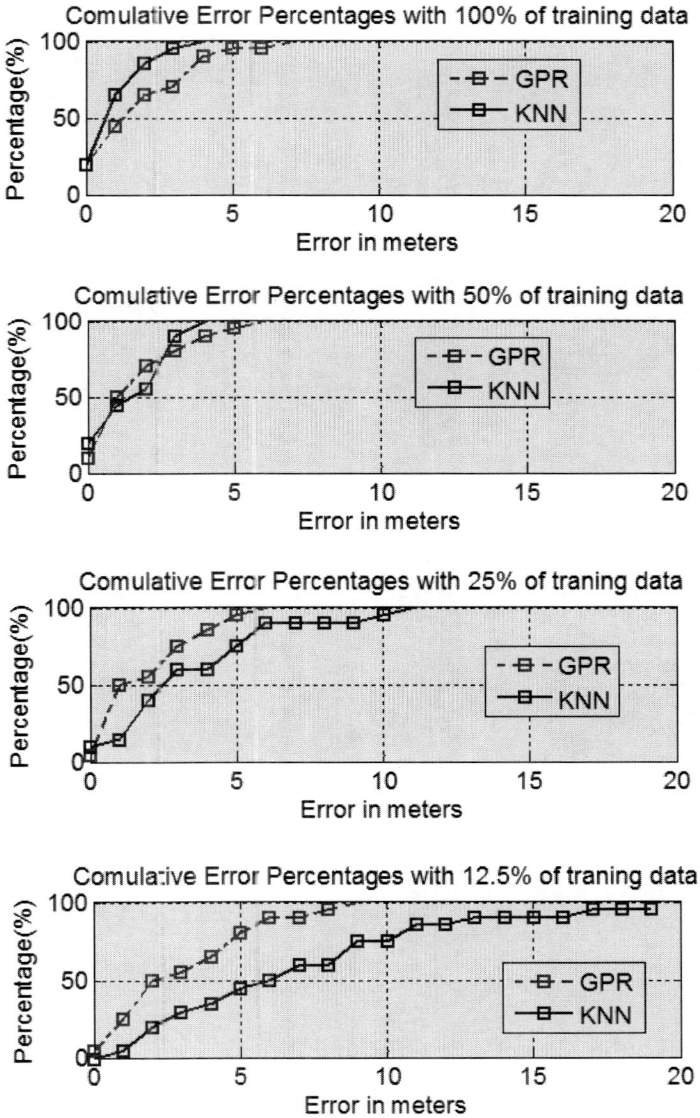

Figure 50. GPR vs. KNN Positioning under different sizes of the radio map.

Building Adaptive Radio Maps Using Log-Distance Models

The regular Log-Distance model can be fitted to the measurements of each AP as extracted from online measurement as described in [42](see Table 1). Then, to predict the received signal strength at this location, distance from that location to the access point is calculated and the fitted Log-Distance model can be used to predict the RSS at that location. A snapshot of predicted signal strength of the four access points (power profiles) using this technique in the experimental area of Figure 18 are shown in Figure 51.

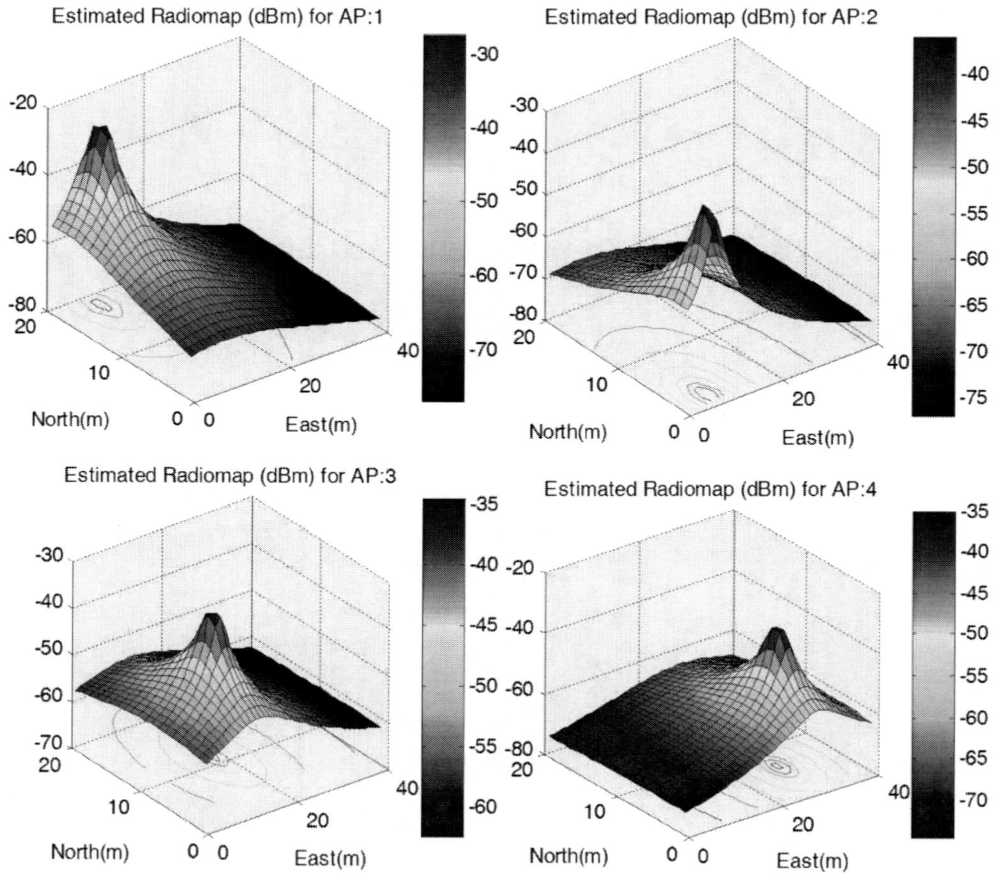

Figure 51. Log-Distance-Based Radio Maps.

Building Adaptive Radio Maps Using GPR and PM

A better modeling of received signal strength can be developed by considering the Log-Distance propagation formula as a mean and let GPR estimate the residual RSS that cannot be modeled by the Log-Distance propagation formula. In this case, the predicted residual RSS for unknown location will be given by:

$$\mu_{x^*} = m(x^*) + k(x^*, X)\left(K + \sigma_n^2 I\right)^{-1}(Y - m(X)) \tag{45}$$

$$m(x^*) = A + B.\log\left(\left\|x^* - r_{AP}\right\| / d_o\right) \tag{46}$$

where $\left\|x^* - r_{AP}\right\|$ is the distance from the AP location to the input location x^*. Note that the variance formula will be the same. This hybrid modeling is shown in Figure 52.The results of hybridized-estimated power profiles are shown in Figure 53.

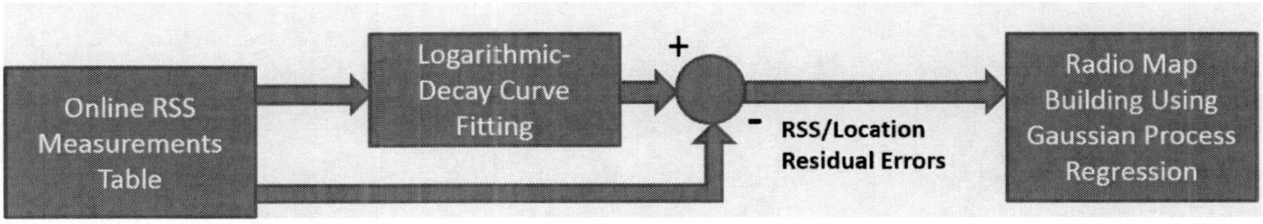

Figure 52. The proposed hybrid radio map construction technique.

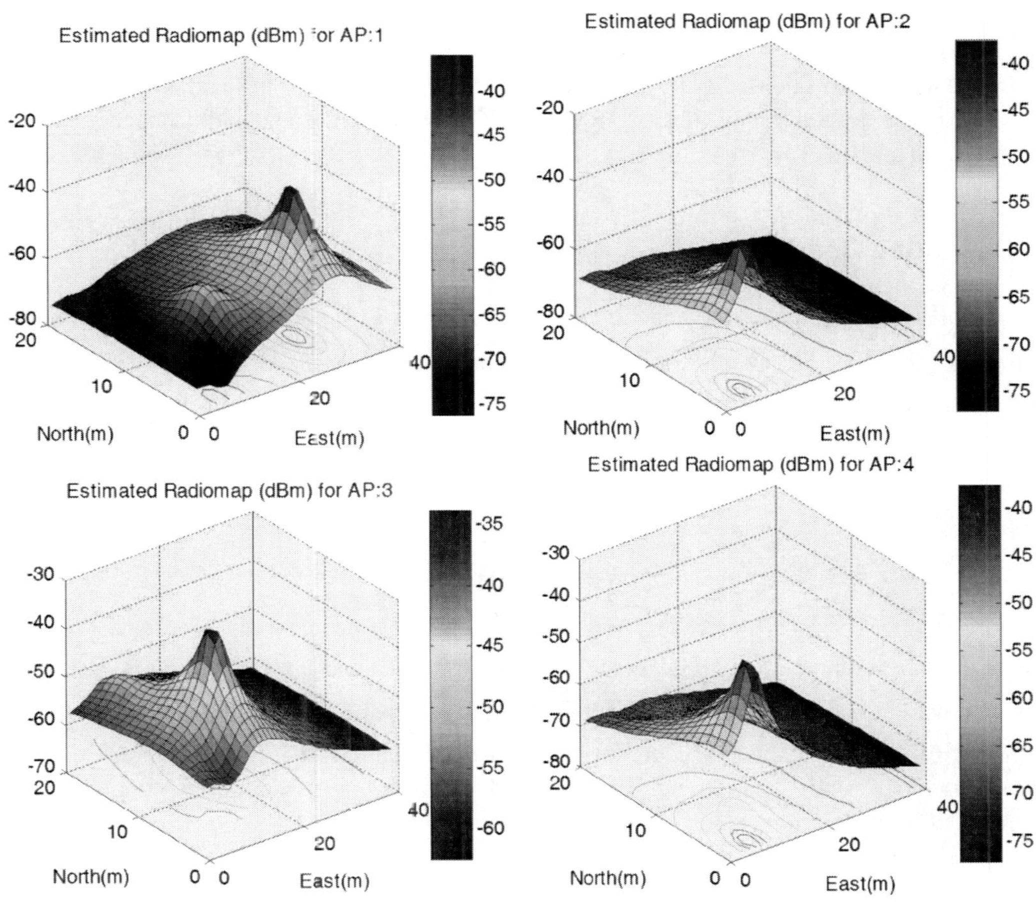

Figure 53. Hybridized-estimated Radio Maps.

Wireless-Aided MultisensorPositioning Systems Using Filtering Algorithms

Although the wireless positioning systems provide a consistent accuracy, the positioning is not accurate enough for many location based services because the positioning is very noisy with too many outliers due to multipath. Thus, integration between wireless measurements and other sensors is necessary. In this section, a theoretical overview about sensors fusion and system integration is given followed by experimental work on an indoor navigation system for a mobile robot that integrates inertial sensors and odometer readings with the received signal strength from a wireless network.

Integrated Navigation Systems

Integrating Integration algorithms aim at integrating different source of information to optimally estimate a system state [54][55].If the integration is online and recursive it is called filtering [11][21][56][57]. Two common filtering techniques exist, Kalman Filtering (KF) [11][58] and Particle Filtering (PF) [13]. While KF is characterized by it is optimality (in least square sense) and its computational efficiency [11], it impose limitations on systems characteristics such as linearity and Gaussian assumption of system states and noise components. On the other-side, PF is characterized by its flexibility to handle non-Gaussian and Non-linear systems and signals. However, it is sub-optimal and it introduces a large computation burden [13].

The Filtering Concept

Recall from (2) and (3) the general representation of a dynamic system with states $x(t)$ and observables $y(t)$. This representation is deterministic while physical systems in real life are stochastic. The general representation of a stochastic system is given as follow:

$$\dot{x}(t) = \mathrm{f}\left(x(t), u(t)\right) + G(t)w(t) \tag{47}$$

$$y(t) = h\left(x(t)\right) + v(t) \tag{48}$$

where $w(t)$ is system noise whose covariance matrix $Q(t)$ and $v(t)$ is measurement noise whose covariance matrix $R(t)$ and $G(t)$ is called noise shaping matrix. The two equations (47) and (48) are fundamental equations in filtering. Equation (47) is called prediction or transition model and equation in (48) is called observation or measurement model. To perform filtering solution in any problem, these two models have to be clearly defined. The estimation accuracy is measured by the error covariance $P(t)$. These terms ($Q(t)$,, $P(t)$) are fundamental concepts to understand the concept of filtering. Those terms are mathematically defined as follows:

$$Q(t) = \left\langle w(t)^T w(t) \right\rangle \tag{49}$$

$$R(t) = \left\langle v(t)^T v(t) \right\rangle \tag{50}$$

$$P(t) = \left\langle \left(x(t) - \hat{x}(t)\right)^T \left(x(t) - \hat{x}(t)\right) \right\rangle \tag{51}$$

where $\langle . \rangle$ is the expectation operator defined by $\langle x(t) \rangle = \int xp(x)dx$ where $p(x)$ is the probability of x.

The general concept of the filtering is explained as follows:

1. The mean of the states $x(t)$ and the error covariance matrix $P(t)$ are predicted using the transition model, the control signal $u(t)$, and the prior knowledge about the state $x^+(t)$. This will result in prior estimate of states $x^-(t)$ and $P^-(t)$. The mathematical formula to calculate these terms are intractable if the system is not linear and the noise terms are not zero-mean Gaussian. In case of a linear system with zero-mean Gaussian noise terms, the equations to calculate those terms are greatly simplified as we will see shortly.
2. When an external observations (measurements) are available, the system states $x(t)$ and the states error covariance matrix $P(t)$ are updated to obtain posterior states $x^+(t)$ and posterior states error covariance matrix $P^+(t)$. The mathematical formula to calculate these terms are intractable of the system is not linear and the noise terms are not zero-mean Gaussian. In case of a linear system with zero-mean Gaussian noise terms, the equations to calculate those terms are greatly simplified as we will see shortly.

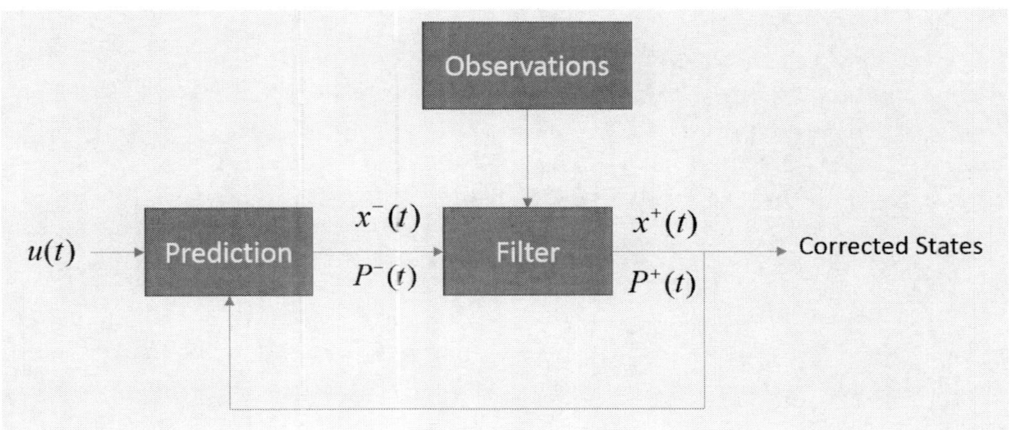

Figure 54. General Filtering Concept.

The general concept of filtering is illustrated in Figure 54. If the dynamic system is linear and the noise terms are zero-mean Gaussian noise, the filtering algorithm can be Kalman Filter or Particle Filter. However, Kalman Filter in this case would be the optimal solution while Particle Filter is sub-optimal. In case of nonlinear system and non-Gaussian noise terms, only PF can be used in this scheme.

Nonlinear Filtering

Nonlinear Filtering Using Extended Kalman Filter

In real life, most systems are not linear and noise terms are not generally Gaussian. To perform filtering in this case two options exist, the first option is to use PF since it can deal with such systems as described above. However, KF still can be used in such systems by linearization using Tylor series expansion. In this case, the filter states are not directly the main system states $x(t)$ but instead KF works on the *error states* $\delta x(t)$. In this case, a linear dynamic system for the "error states" ($\delta x(t)$) is developed by linearizing the main nonlinear system model. This linearized system relates "error states" $\delta x(t)$ to error in observations $\delta y(t)$ .In this case, the algorithm is called Extended Kalman Filter (EKF). The general concept of nonlinear systems filtering is shown in Figure 55. Although this introduction about filtering describes the general concepts, more details will be elaborated when we physically apply these filtering algorithms on a practical Wireless-Aided Integrated Navigation system.

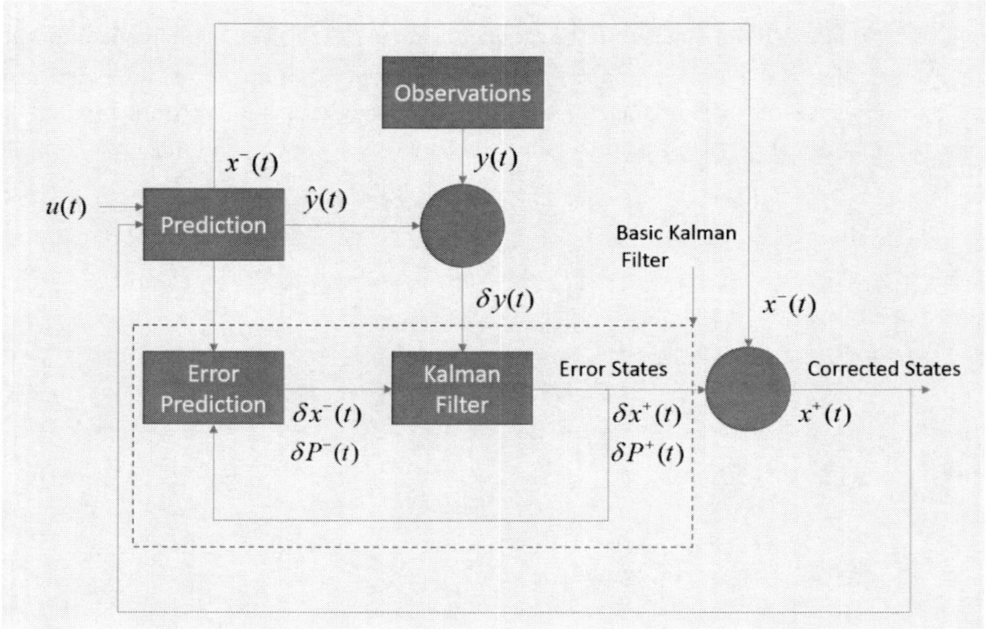

Figure 55. EKF Filtering Scheme.

Kalman Filtering

To implement KF, it is better to describe the implementation steps in the discrete domain. In discrete time domain, the prediction step is performed using the following equation:

$$x_{k+1}^{-} = \emptyset_{k,k+1} x_k^{+} \tag{52}$$

where x_k^{+} represent the current prior knowledge about the states andx_{k+1}^{-} represent the predicted states and $\emptyset_{k,k+1}$ is the transition matrix given by

$$\emptyset_{k,k+1} = I + FT \tag{53}$$

where *T* is the sampling period. In Kalman Filter, the current prior knowledge about the variance of error in the estimated states is referred to by the covariance matrix P_k^{+}. The predicted covariance matrix P_{k+1}^{-} is given by:

$$P_{k+1}^{-} = \emptyset_{k,k+1} P_k^{+} \emptyset_{k,k+1}{}^{T} + Q_d \tag{54}$$

$$Q_d \cong GQG^T T \tag{55}$$

where *T* is the sampling period and Q is the system noise matrix.

Measurements Model (Update Model)

The general linear measurement model is given by

$$z_{k+1} = Hx_{k+1} + v_{k+1} \tag{56}$$

where H is called the design matrix that relates the states to the measurements.

When observations is available (z_{k+1}), the error between the observations and the predicted output is taken as a measurement update to the Kalman Filter and a Kalman gain is calculated as follows:

$$K_{k+1} = P_{k+1}^{-} H^T [HP_{k+1}^{-} H^T + R_k]^{-1} \tag{57}$$

and the updated states is given by

$$x_{k+1}^{+} = x_{k+1}^{-} + K_{k+1}(z_{k+1} - Hx_{k+1}^{-}) \tag{58}$$

and the updated error covariance matrix is given by:

$$P_{k+1}^{+} = (I - K_{k+1})\, P_{k+1}^{-} \tag{59}$$

Particle Filtering

PF was proposed as a Monte-Carlo based solution for the Bayesian Filtering problem [59][60][61][62]. Bayesian filtering algorithms [61][62] get $p(x|Z)$; the probability density function (PDF) of a system state(x) conditioned on external measurements (Z). The estimated $p(\mathbf{x}|Z)$represents all the knowledge about the system state (x). Bayesian filtering considers the aiding sources as observations and assumes that the sates are 1st order Markov process [61][62][60].The knowledge about system state x_k (state at instant$k$) comes from two important probabilistic models; the state transition model $p(\mathbf{x}_k|\mathbf{x}_{k-1},\mathbf{u}_{k-1})$ and the observation likelihood $p(\mathbf{z}_k|\mathbf{x}_k)$ (aiding measurements). To estimate the navigation state, the new density $p(\mathbf{x}_k|Z_k)$ is computed recursively at each time step in two phases [13][59][60][61][62]: prediction phase and update phase. In the prediction phase, the transition is performed according to transition model as follows:

$$p(\mathbf{x}_k|Z_{k-1}) = \int p(\mathbf{x}_k|\mathbf{x}_{k-1},\mathbf{u}_{k-1})p(\mathbf{x}_{k-1}|Z_{k-1})d\mathbf{x}_{k-1} \tag{60}$$

In the update phase, the observation likelihood is used to obtain the posterior PDF using Bayes rule:

$$p(\mathbf{x}_k|Z_k) = \frac{p(\mathbf{z}_k|\mathbf{x}_k)p(\mathbf{x}_k|Z_{k-1})}{p(\mathbf{z}_k|Z_{k-1})} \tag{61}$$

$$p(\mathbf{z}_k|Z_{k-1}) = \int p(\mathbf{z}_k|\mathbf{x}_k)p(\mathbf{x}_k|Z_{k-1})d\mathbf{x}_k \tag{62}$$

PF is an approximate solution to Bayesian filtering problem that can handle the cases in which the system and measurement models are not linear and the states are not Gaussian. At each time step k, PDFs are approximated by a set of N random samples (particles) $S_k = \{s_k^{(1)},...,s_k^{(N)}\}$. The ith sample consists of the value of the state $\mathbf{x}_k^{(i)}$ and the associated weight $\pi_k^{(i)}$. At k=0, the sample set $S_0 = \{(\mathbf{x}_0^{(i)},\pi_0^{(i)})|i=1,...,N\}$ is initialized with equal weights based on any knowledge about the object's initial state. An iteration of PF has three important steps:

1. Prediction phase: starting from the set of samples $S_{k-1} = \{(\mathbf{x}_{k-1}^{(i)},\pi_{k-1}^{(i)})|i=1,...,N\}$ (where $\pi_{k-1}^{(i)} = \frac{1}{N}$) the state transition model

is applied to each sample $s_{k-1}^{(i)} = \left(\mathbf{x}_{k-1}^{(i)}, \frac{1}{N}\right)$ and one sample $s_k'^{(i)} = \left(\mathbf{x}_k'^{(i)}, \frac{1}{N}\right)$ is drawn from $p\left(\mathbf{x}_k \middle| \mathbf{x}_{k-1}^{(i)}, \mathbf{u}_{k-1}\right)$. Thus, a new sample set (S_k') is obtained that approximates the predictive density $p\left(\mathbf{x}_k \middle| Z_{k-1}\right)$.

2. The update phase: measurement is taken into account and each of the samples in S_k' is weighted using an observation likelihood $p\left(\mathbf{z}_k \middle| \mathbf{x}_k'^{(i)}\right)$. Then all weights are normalized. The weighted sample set $\tilde{S}_k$ approximates the density $p\left(\mathbf{x}_k \middle| Z_k\right)$.
3. Resampling step: the sample set $S_k = \left\{\left(\mathbf{x}_k^{(i)}, \pi_k^{(i)}\right) \middle| i = 1,...,N\right\}$ (where $\pi_k^{(i)} = \frac{1}{N}$) is obtained by randomly selecting from the weighted set $\tilde{S}_k = \left\{\left(\tilde{\mathbf{x}}_k^{(i)}, \tilde{\pi}_k^{(i)}\right) \middle| i = 1,...,N\right\}$ such that each sample is selected number of times proportional to its weight. Thus, the obtained S_k approximates the required $p\left(\mathbf{x}_k \middle| Z_k\right)$.

Integration between WLAN and Inertial Sensors/Odometer

To illustrate how location determination in indoor environments can be enhanced by integrating other sensors using filtering techniques described above, in this section, WiFi localization is integrated with inertial sensors and odometer on a mobile robot platform. Although the example system is a wheel-based ground vehicle mobile platform, the same integration concept and algorithms can be applied to any kind of sensors and measurements such as pedestrian portable navigation using wearable devices. In this example, the system dynamics will be used to enhance the noisy WiFi positioning. The described integrated positioning system consists of WiFi-enabled Laptop, vertically aligned gyroscope that measures rotation rate around the vertical axis of the platform, and the mobile robot speed measurements measured by odometery. This configuration is referred by RISS (Reduced Inertial Sensors System). The used gyroscope is a very low-cost MEMS-based gyroscope included in an inertial measurement unit (IMU) from Crossbow Inc.[63]. One common problem of MEMS inertial sensors is the drifts over time which is integrated to accumulate a huge heading error which consequently lead to positioning error. To prevent this drift, integration with WiFi positioning will be used using PF and KF for comparison purposes. A diagram that describe the RISS integrated localization system is shown in Figure 56.

The RISS Inertial Navigation Dynamic System Model

In the example system described here, the motion is mainly in 2D. Motion equations are implemented in local navigation frame (East, North, and Up (Vertical)). In 2D, we are concerned only about azimuth (heading), north, and east velocity and position components. The azimuth angle (A) of the vehicle is calculated using the following equation:

$$A = \int (\omega_z - \omega^e \sin\varphi - \frac{V_e \tan\varphi}{R_N + h})dt \tag{63}$$

where ω_z is the gyroscope reading, ω^e is the earth rotation rate (15°/hr), V_e is the velocity in east direction, ϕ is the latitude, R_N is the normal radius of curvature of earth, and h is the altitude.

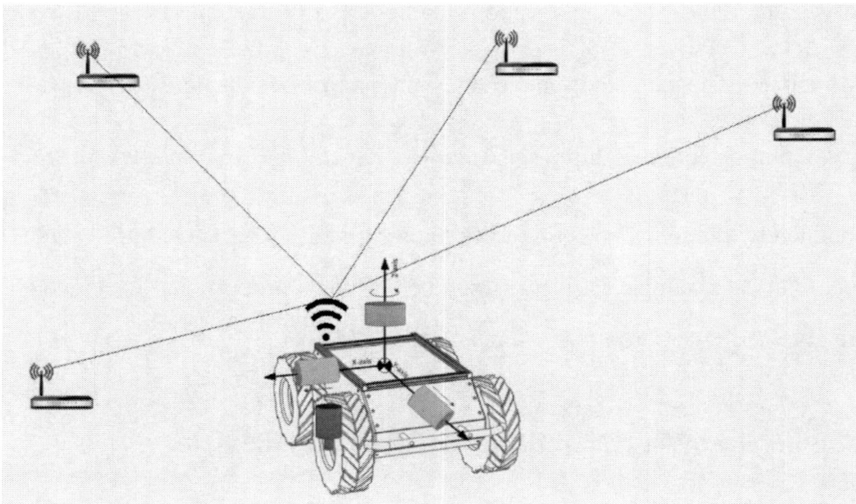

Figure 56. Wireless-Aided Integrated Positioning System for Mobile Robots.

Once the heading angle (A) of the platform is calculated, it can be used along with the vehicle odometer V_{od} to calculate east and north velocities as follows:

$$V_e = V_{od} \sin A \tag{64}$$

$$V_n = V_{od} \cos A \tag{65}$$

Position (Latitude ϕ and Longitude λ) are given by:

$$\phi = \int \frac{Vn}{R_M + h} dt \tag{66}$$

$$\lambda = \int \frac{Ve}{(R_N + h)\cos(\phi)} dt \tag{67}$$

where R_M is the meridian radius of curvature of the earth at current position.

Latitude ϕ and Longitude λ can be then converted to meters using the following equations:

$$P_{North} = (\phi - \phi_0)(R_M + h) \quad (68)$$

$$P_{East} = (\lambda - \lambda_0)(R_N + h)\cos\phi \quad (69)$$

A block diagram that describes the inertial/odometer positioning system is shown in Figure 57.

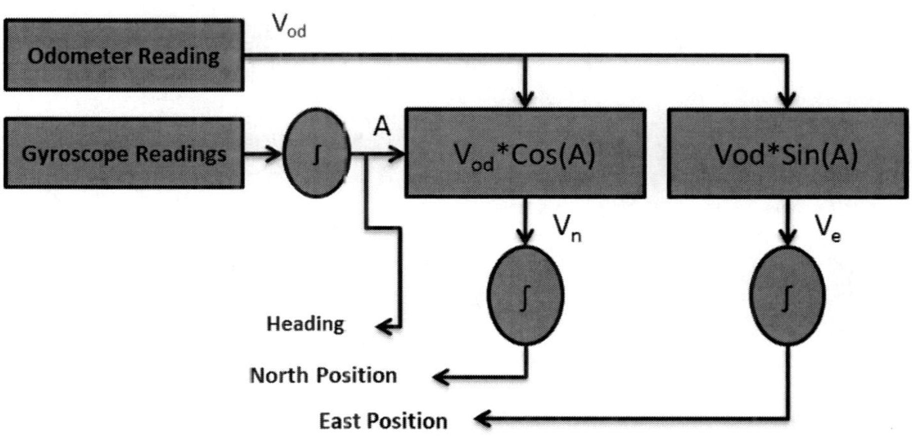

Figure 57. Inertial/Odometer Positioning System.

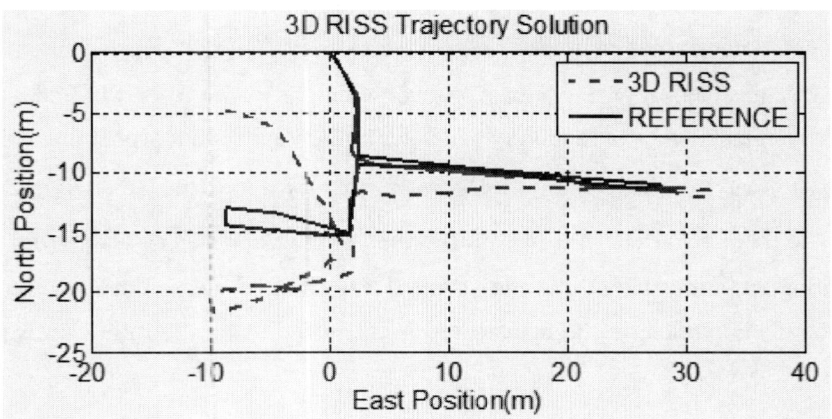

Figure 58. RISS Solution showing effects of gyroscope drifts and odometer errors.

Figure 58 shows the results of RISS system on the testing trajectory shown in Figure 24 in the same experimental area shown in Figure 18. The mobile robot was used to collect WiFi and RISS data. The collected data was then post-processed. The overall root mean square error of the RISS-alone solution is 4.4743m. The effect of the gyroscope drifts can be seen clearly from the heading errors which cause the trajectory to deviate from the reference. Also the effect of odometer error is clear from the graph where we can see stretch in the most right part of the trajectory. Odometer error is also known from calculations since the reference distance travelled is 110.5m while the odometer reading shows a distance travelled of 118.8m.

The WiFi Fingerprinting Solution

Using the radio map collected in the experimental area and the RSS data collected by the WiFi-enabled laptop, K-NN weighted average algorithm was applied and the solution obtained is shown in Figure 59. The overall accuracy of the WiFi solution in this experiment is 3.4 meters.

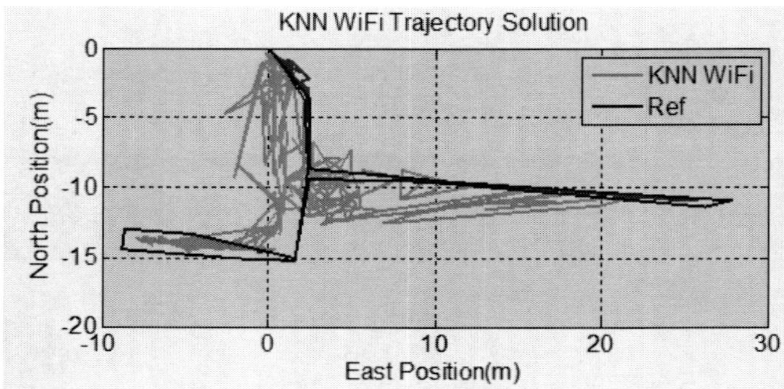

Figure 59. WiFi Trajectory Solution.

The WiFi/RISS Integrated Solution Using PF

The results of applying PF on the collected WiFi/RISS data is presented in this section. The PF algorithm is initialized with samples from a Gaussian density with mean equivalent to static WiFi positioning solution in static state. Predictive PDF $p(\mathbf{x}_k|Z_{k-1})$ is approximated by applying RISS mechanization equations on every sample in the prior PDF adding to the sensors measurements (u_{k-1}) a randomly generated noise with certain probability distribution $p(w_{k-1})$ (system noise).The posterior PDF $p(\mathbf{x}_k|Z_k)$ is approximated by weighting the samples in the predictive PDF $p(\mathbf{x}_k|Z_{k-1})$ according to the Euclidean distance from the WiFi K-Nearest fingerprinting output and the standard deviation of measurement noise $p(v_{k-1})$. The weights of the particle in the update step is calculated using the following exponential formula:

$$w_i = ae^{-b\|x_{RISS}-x_{WiFi}\|^2} \tag{70}$$

where w_i the ith particle weight, x_{RISS} is the 2D location estimated by RISS, x_{WiFi} is the 2D position estimated by WiFi KNN algorithm. The integrated RISS/WiFi system output is shown in Figure 62andFigure 63 which show that the integration between RISS and WiFi system not only improves the overall accuracy and reduces RISS drifts, but also smooth and filters out the noisy scattered output resulting from WiFi noisy signal strength effect. Figure 62 shows the 2D position components confidence intervals. The confidence intervals represent the error standard deviation of the integrated output which starts large expressing high degree of uncertainty and then convergence with measurements updates. The total root mean square error (RMSE) achieved by integrating both RISS and WiFi is 1.6 meters. Comparing to RISS only accuracy (4.4743m), and WiFi only accuracy (3.4m), the integration between WiFi and RISS systems reduced the RMSE by approximately 40%. Figure 64 reflects the cumulative error percentage which shows that the integrated WiFi/RISS navigation system achieves an accuracy of 1 meter for 70% of the time.

Figure 60 shows the initial probability density function (PDF) of the states before starting the filtering process. As shown in this figure, PDFs are initially Gaussian. Figure 61 shows the status of the PDFs after 123 epochs. As can be seen in this figure, due to position updates (North Position (NP) and East Position (EP)), the PDF width of NP and EP are decreased significantly expressing less degree of uncertainty. At the same time, because we do not have direct heading updates, the heading PDF has large width (high uncertainty). It is noted also that the PDF of NP and EP are not Gaussian. The particles weights and the weights histogram are also displayed in Figure 61.

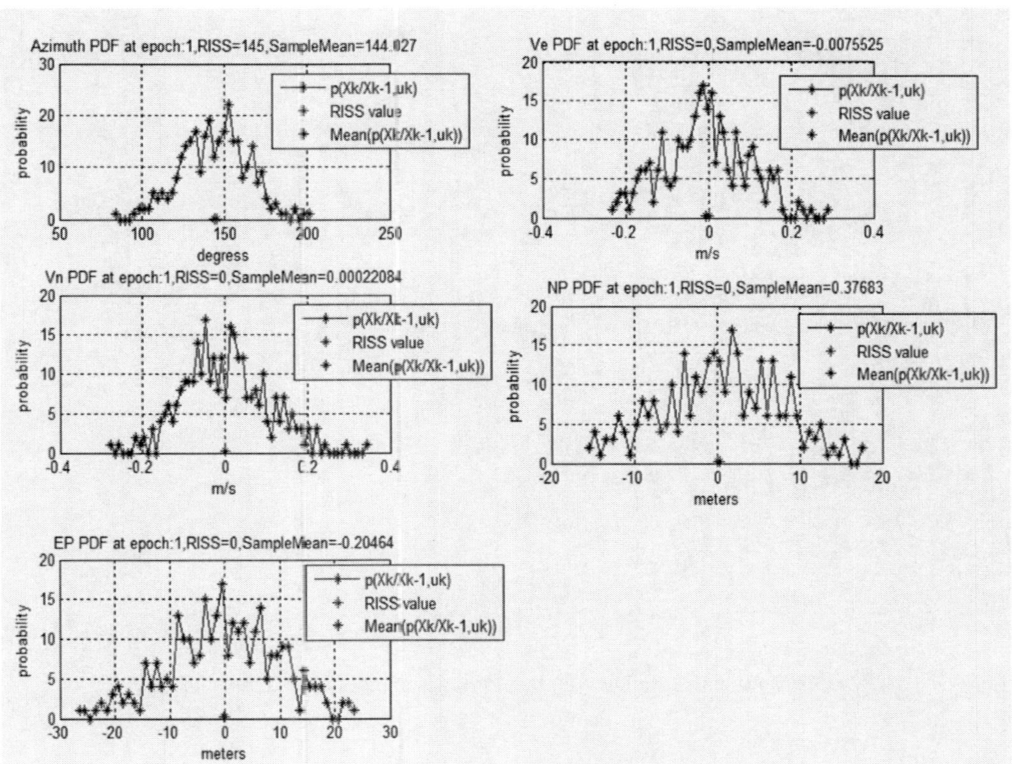

Figure 60. Initial Probability Distributions of Navigation States.

The WiFi/RISS Integrated Solution Using KF

In RISS/WiFi integrated navigation system, Kalman Filter works on errors in vehicle state instead of the vehicle states themselves. Then, Kalman Filter uses different models. The state in this case will be as follows:

$x = [\delta\varphi_k, \delta\lambda_k, \delta A_k, \delta Ve_k, \delta Vn_k, \delta a_{od}, \delta w_z]$ where $\delta a_{od}, \delta w_z$ are stochastic error of the odometer-derived acceleration, and the gyroscope respectively.

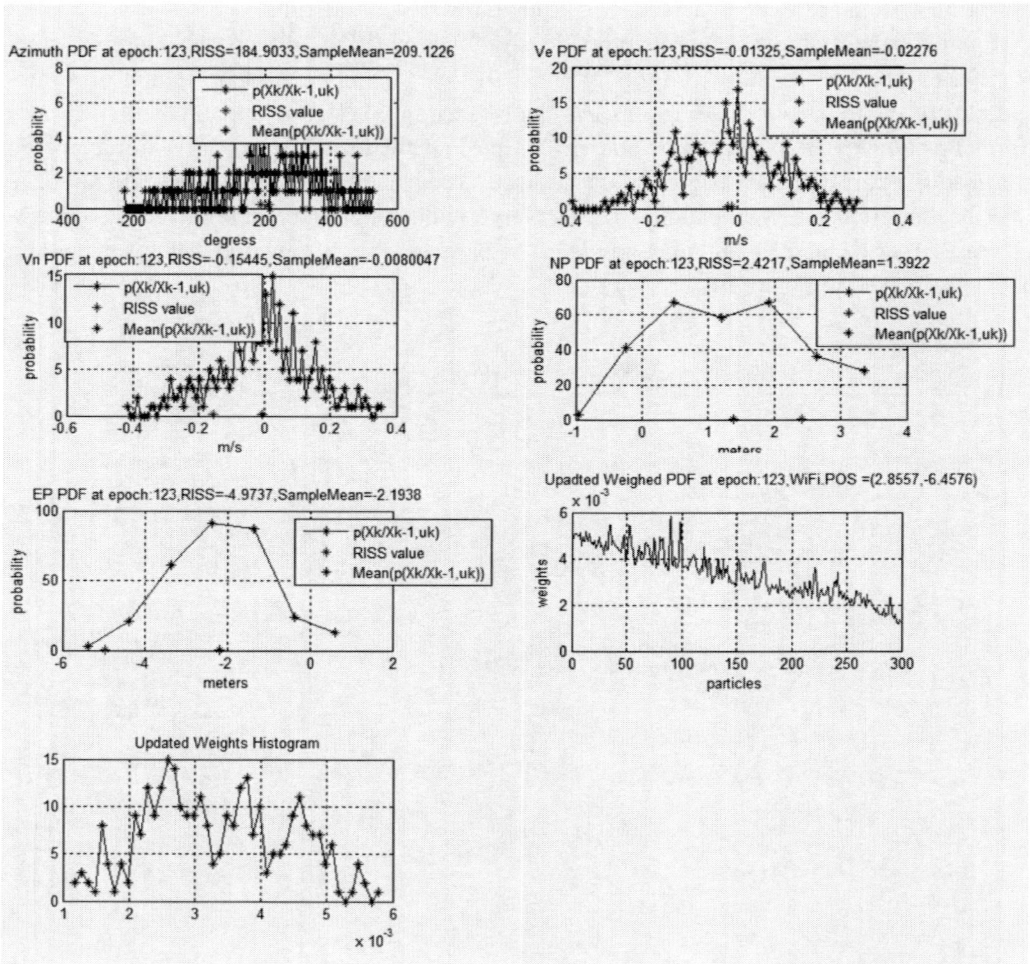

Figure 61. States Distributions, Particles Weights, Particles Weights Histograms after 123 epochs.

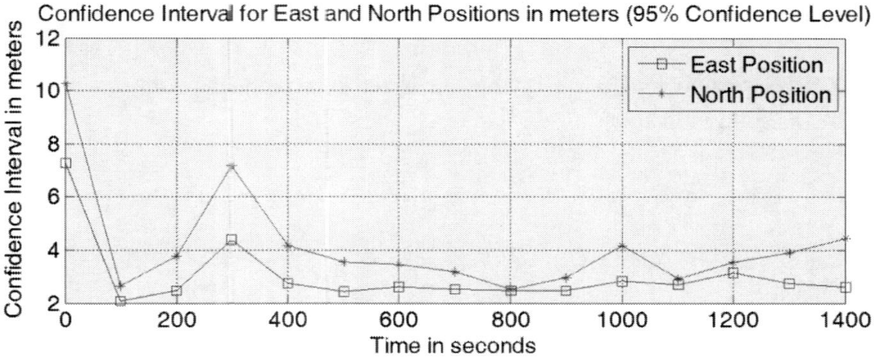

Figure 62. Confidence Intervals for Position Components (95% Confidence Level).

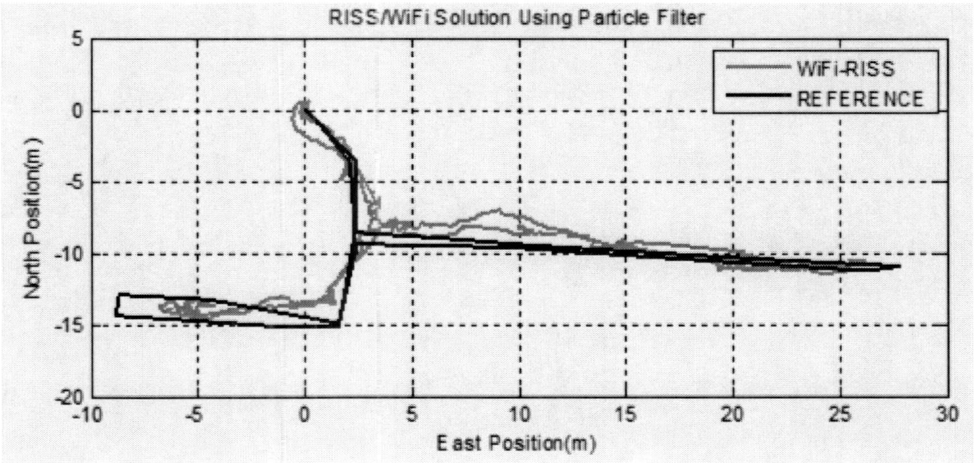

Figure 63. WiFi/RISS Integrated System Output.

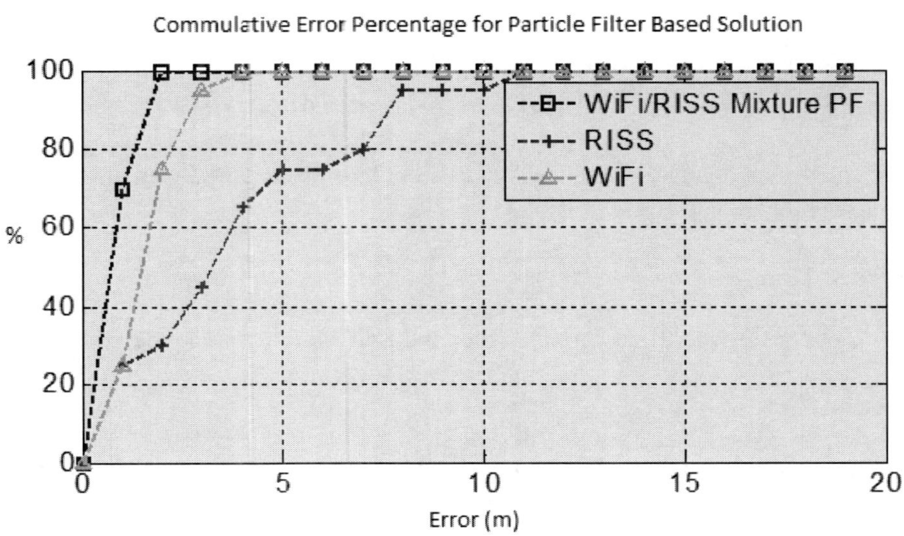

Figure 64. Cumulative Error Percentages.

System Model

In a 2D RISS system [57][57][64], the linearized error model in the form of equation (4)is given by the following equations:

$$\begin{bmatrix} \frac{d}{dt}\delta\varphi \\ \frac{d}{dt}\delta\lambda \\ \frac{d}{dt}\delta V_e \\ \frac{d}{dt}\delta V_n \\ \delta\frac{d}{dt}A \\ \frac{d}{dt}\delta a_{od} \\ \frac{d}{dt}\delta\omega_z \end{bmatrix} = \begin{bmatrix} 0 & 0 & 0 & \frac{1}{R_M+h} & 0 & 0 & 0 \\ 0 & 0 & \frac{1}{(R_N+h)\cos(\varphi)} & 0 & 0 & 0 & 0 \\ 0 & 0 & 0 & 0 & a_{od}\cos(A) & \sin(A) & 0 \\ 0 & 0 & 0 & 0 & -a_{od}\sin(A) & \cos(A) & 0 \\ 0 & 0 & 0 & 0 & -1 & 0 & 0 \\ 0 & 0 & 0 & 0 & 0 & -\beta_{od} & 0 \\ 0 & 0 & 0 & 0 & 0 & 0 & -\beta_{gyro} \end{bmatrix} \begin{bmatrix} \delta\varphi \\ \delta\lambda \\ \delta V_e \\ \delta V_n \\ \delta A \\ \delta a_{od} \\ \delta\omega_z \end{bmatrix}$$

$$+ \begin{bmatrix} 0 \\ 0 \\ 0 \\ 0 \\ 0 \\ \sqrt{2\beta_{od}\delta_{od}} \\ \sqrt{2\beta_{gyro}\delta_{gyro}} \end{bmatrix} w(\mathrm{t}) \quad (71)$$

Measurements Model (Update Model)

Since only 2D position updates are available, the design matrix $H$is given by

$$H = \begin{bmatrix} 1 & 0 & 0 & 0 & 0 & 0 & 0 \\ 0 & 1 & 0 & 0 & 0 & 0 & 0 \end{bmatrix}$$

The results of applying KF on the WiFi/RISS 2D system are shown in figures from Figure 65 to Figure 67.

Convergence Time

In terms of convergence time, Particle Filter and Kalman Filter are kind of the same.

Computation Time

In terms of execution time on Matlab on a Sony VAIO Laptop with Intel i5 processor, the execution time of KF was 0.481633 sec and for the PF was 2.682612 sec.

Positioning Accuracy

In terms of accuracy, the RMSE of KF was 2.2076m with maximum position error of 3.4837m and the RMSE of PF was 1.6404m with maximum position error of 2.9681m.

Discussion about Results

Obviously, PF is computationally expensive since the execution time of PF is almost 5 times that of KF while the positioning accuracy of PF is 23% better than KF. This indicates that in such a noisy environments like indoors, a nonlinear/non-Gaussian filter such as PF may be worth if the necessary computation power is not an issue. However, in some limited-resources CPUs or power-critical devices such as hand-held device and smart-phones, this could be an issue. If computation resources are limited in a system design, then, instead of overloading the navigation processor with unnecessary computations in such environments, a Kalman filter may be sufficient in this case.

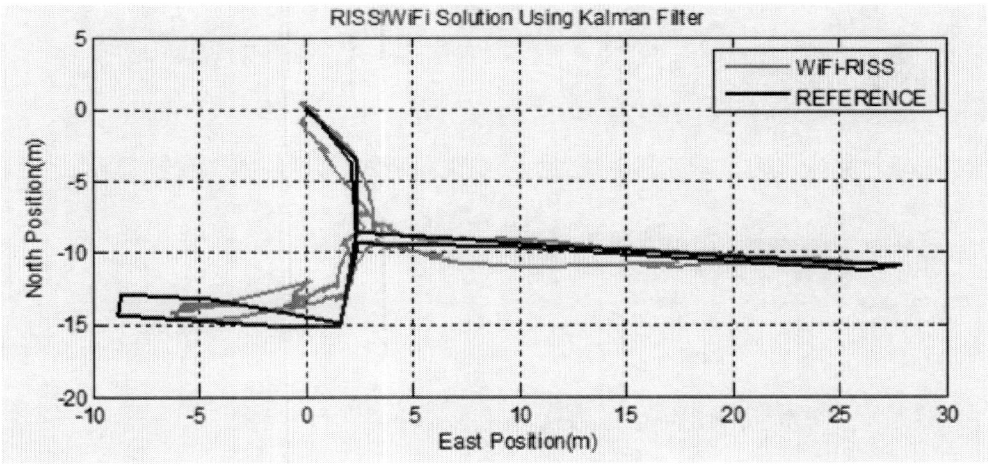

Figure 65. 2D Solution of WiFi/RISS 2D System Based on Kalman Filter.

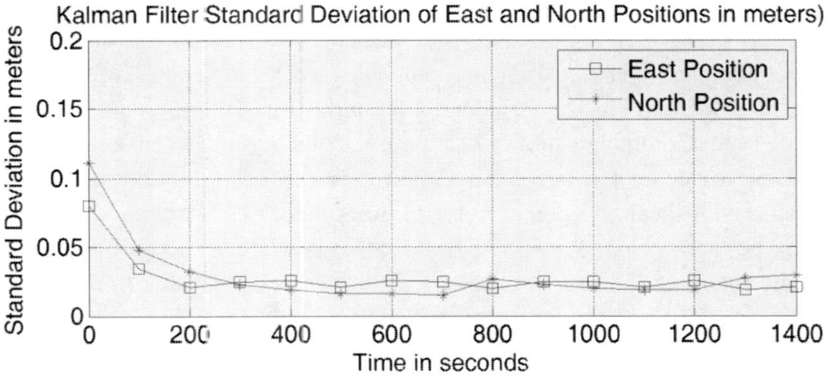

Figure 66. KF Standard Position Deviation and Convergence Time.

Future Trends in Location Technology in Mobile Computing Environments

As mentioned earlier in the introduction section of this chapter, according to recent market research reports, 70% of cellular calls and 80% of wireless data connectivity originate from indoors where GPS and other GNSS-based systems do not work[5]. This huge demand for location technology for indoor areas has created an extremely active competition for development of next generation location technology. Currently, there is a major trend in indoor location technology that depends on a heterogeneous set of sensors both proprioceptive and exteroceptive sensors [14]. Current mobile devices such as smartphones and tablets are equipped with a wide range of these sensors. The major sensors proprioceptive and exteroceptive sensors currently considered for location technology are as follows:

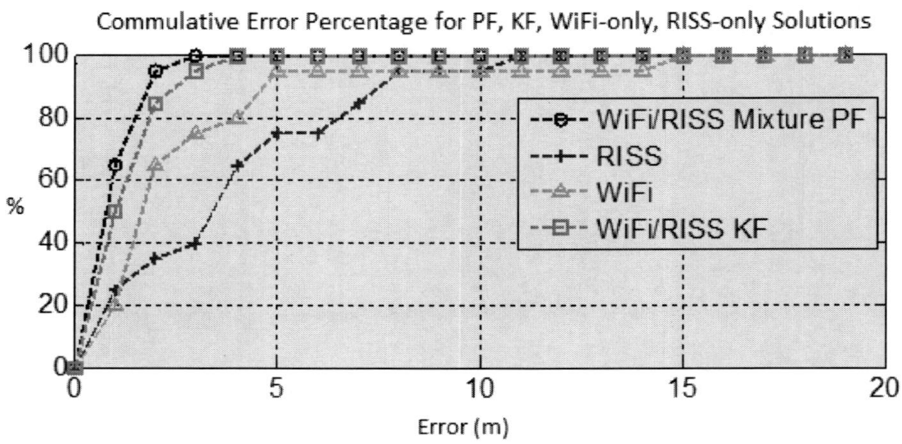

Figure 67. Performance Comparison between PF and KF.

1. Motion Sensors: There is a significant focus on motion sensors especially in smartphones industry. Motion sensors on the phone can be used to detect orientation changes and speed of the mobile platform. With the recent advance in the MEMS-based sensors which significantly reduced the cost and concurrently increased the accuracy of such systems, there is a promising potential for this research track. Some interesting work in this track can be found in [66].
2. Visible Light Communication (VLC): Since visible light devices are available indoors, they can provide an accurate estimation of locations as well in the same way any radio frequency signal can. A good example of this kind of trends can be found in [18].
3. Vision Sensors: This is a major trend as well where vision capabilities aided by visually recognized features in the area can be used for location determination. An example of this trend can be found in [30].
4. Laser Scanners: Light Detection and Ranging (LiDAR) is also a promising technology that can help in localization. Good example of using LiDAR to assist positioning systems can be found in [36].
5. 2D and 3D Maps: There is a huge technological advances in the track of word representation by 2D and 3D maps that expands to cover indoor areas. These maps

are currently developed and maintained by large companies such as Google and Apple for the purposes of location determination and other purposes as well. Coupled with other sensors such as LiDAR and Vision, these 2D and 3D maps are great source of help to provide accurate localization service in indoor. An example of this trend can be found in [32].

Finally, so far, there is no single technology that can provide stand-alone location determination system in challenging areas such as indoor environments. The future trend is the integration between these wide range of heterogeneous sensors and infrastructures.

WiFi Surveying Software Tools Used in This Work

The developed WiFi surveying tools is a tool set developed using C# and XML technology. In unknown environment equipped by WiFi network, this tool set is capable of performing WiFi surveying, constructing radio maps, calculating wireless access points locations, creating an accurate image-based floor map of the area, matching and verifying visually the created map by integrating with Google Maps and hence calculating the absolute location of any object inside the area by a simple click on the screen while the map is loaded. Furthermore, it can record the signal strength information of a walking person or a moving object with the ability to interact with the screen online to enter a reference location to be recorded as well with the user signal strength information. In conclusion, it is a C# based Indoor Radio map Manager Tool with GUI that is capable of:

- Load and display 2D floor maps with specific corners coordinates
- Software to convert screen based pixels coordinates to Latitude and Longitude coordinates for indoor localization where we do not have GPS
- Integrate with Google Maps to show current location on the real maps to verify that what is on the screen is exactly what is in reality and calibrate the corners coordinates if needed through the GUI.
- WiFi location/Signal Strength survey construction with Latitude/Longitude
- A user can build the radio map easily by clicking on the screen on the desired map location (where GPS is not available) and click scan and add to radio map file
- Scan with higher rates more than 1Hz
- radio map Saving in XML based files for portability (XML can be processed in any development environment and in databases tools also)
- Code generator that generate MATLAB code to transform the XML radio map into Matlab data structures suitable for WiFi positioning software
- MATLAB code that estimate the access points locations
- Load and display graphically already or previously gathered radio maps for review or errors correction
- WiFi online trajectory logging with the ability to inject a reference known location WiFi scan at any time so you have a via points or reference point for accuracy comparisons

- MATLAB code generator to transform the gathered WiFi trajectory into MATLAB data suitable for development and applying positioning accuracy.
- Load and graphically display any gathered WiFi trajectory with reference via points

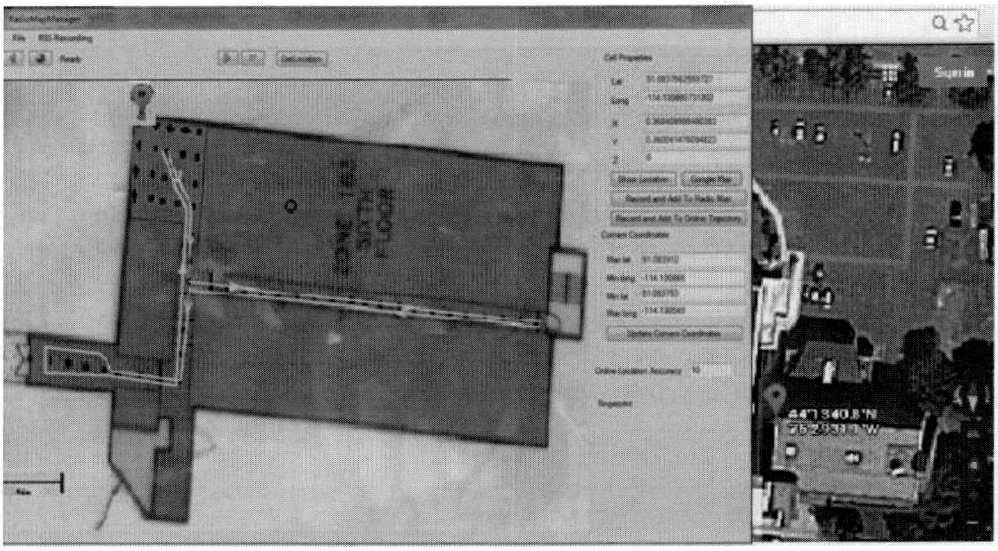

Figure 68. WiFi Surveying Tools Set. In the figure, a calculated location on the tool screen on a floor map of an indoor area is compared to the corresponding location on Google Maps.

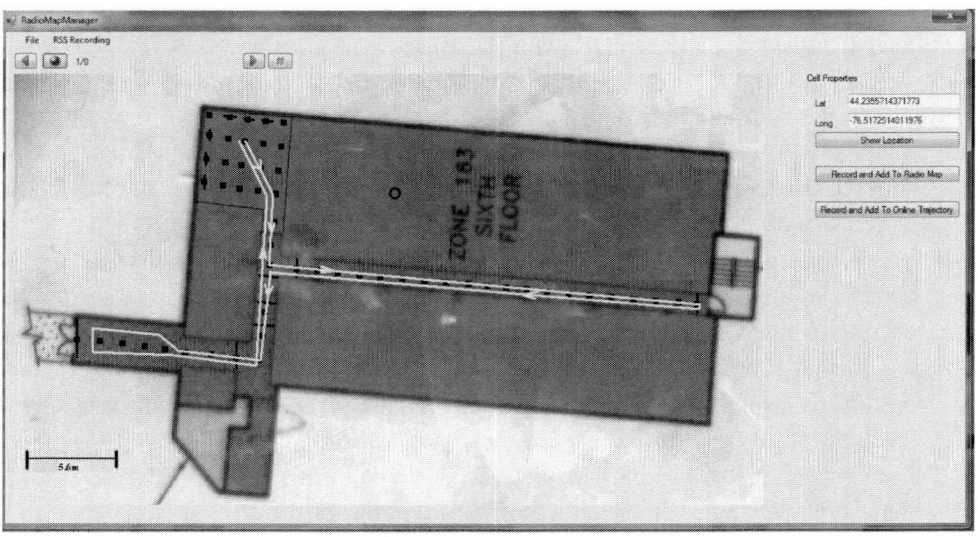

Figure 69. Snapshot of the WiFi surveying Tool set. A floor map with a reference solution is shown.

References

[1] L. Yang, *Mobile Intelligence,* Wiley-IEEE Press, 2010.

[2] "Localization Services for Online Common Operational Picture and Situation Awareness," *IEEE Access, Practical Innovations,* vol. 1, no. 2013, pp. 742-757, November 1, 2013.

[3] P. Misra and P. Enge, "Global Positioning System, Signals, Measurements, and Performance," *Ganga-Jamuna Press,* 2011.

[4] A. El-Rabbany, *Introduction to GPS: The Global Positioning System,* Artech House, 2002.

[5] I. L. Consultancy, *"Indoor Location & Mapping Services Report,"* Indoor LBS Consultancy, January 2014.

[6] D. H. T. a. J. L. Weston, *Strapdown Inertial Navigation Technology*, 2nd Ed., The Institution of Electrical Engineers, 2004.

[7] A. Soloviev, *"Tight coupling of GPS, laser scanner, and inertial measurements for navigation in urban environments,"* Monterey, CA, 5-8 May 2008.

[8] D. Simon, *Optimal State Estimation*, John Wiley, 2006.

[9] C. L.Phillips, J. M.Parr and E. A. Riskin, *Signals, Systems and Transforms,* Prentice Hall, 2007.

[10] A. Farrell, *"Aided Navigation, GPS with High-Rate Sensors,"* McGraw Hill, 2008.

[11] A. Farrell, *"Aided Navigation, GPS with High-Rate Sensors"*, McGraw Hill, 2008.

[12] H. Durrant-Whyte, *"Introduction to Estimation and the Kalman Filter,"* Australia, 2001, p. Australian Centre for Field Robotics.

[13] M. S. Arulampalam, S. Maskell, N. Gordon and T. Clapp, "A Tutorial on Particle Filters for Online Nonlinear/Non-Gaussian Bayesian Tracking," *IEEE Transactions on Signal Processing,* vol. 50, no. 2, pp. 174-88, Feb 2002.

[14] P. Misra and P. Enge, *"Global Positioning System, Signals, Measurements, and Performance",* Ganga-Jamuna Press, 2011.

[15] A. El-Rabbany, *"Introduction to GPS: The Global Positioning System",* Artec House Inc, 2006.

[16] Alcatel-Lucent, Bell Labs and Holmdel, "On the Geolocation Bounds for Round-Trip Time-of-Arrival and All Non-Line-of-Sight Channels," *EURASIP Journal on Advances in Signal Processing,* p. 584670 (10 pp.), 2008.

[17] A. Roxin, J. Gaber, M. Wack and. A. Nait-Sidi-Moh, "Survey of Wireless Geolocation Techniques," *Globecom Workshops,* pp. 1-9, Washington DC, 2007.

[18] H. Liu, H. Darabi, P. Banerjee and L. Jing, "Survey of Wireless Indoor Positioning Techniques and Systems," *IEEE Transactions on Systems, Man, and Cybernetics, Part C, Applications and Reviews,* vol. 37, no. 6, pp. 1067-1080, 2007.

[19] Y. Qi, H. Kobayashi and H. Suda, "Analysis of Wireless Geolocation in a Non-Line-of-Sight Environment," *IEEE Transactions on Wireless Communications,* vol. 5, no. 3, pp. 672-81, 2006.

[20] A. El-Rabbany, "Introduction to GPS: The Global Positioning System", Artech House Inc., 2002.

[21] M. Grewal, S. L. R. Weill and A. P. Andrews, *Global Positioning Systems, Inertial Navigation, and Integration,* Wiley & Sons Inc, 2007.

[22] U. Black, *"Mobile and Wireless Networks",* Prentice Hall Series, 1996.

[23] C. Smith and J. Meyer, *"3G Wireless with WiMAX and WiFi",* McGraw-Hill, 2005.

[24] K. Daniel, *"Wireless Internet Telecommunications",* mobile communication series, Artech House Inc, 2005.

[25] K. Sohraby, Minoli and T. Znati, *"Wireless sensor networks : technology, protocols, and applications"*, Hoboken, N.J.: Wiley, 2007.

[26] A. Alemdar and M. Ibnkahla, "Wireless sensor networks: Applications and challenges," *9th International Symposium on Signal Processing and Its Applications ISSPA,* p. 6, Sharjah, UAE, 2007.

[27] G. Ismail, uvenc, C. Chong, F. Watanabe and H. Inamura, "NLOS Identification and Weighted Least-Squares Localization for UWB Systems Using Multipath Channel Statistics," *Hindawi, EURASIP Journal on Advances in Signal Processing,* pp. 1-14, 2008.

[28] B. Fang, "Simple solution for hyperbolic and related position fixes," *IEEE Transactions on Aerospace Electronic Systems,* vol. 26, no. 5, p. 748–753, 1990.

[29] M. Kanaan and K. Pahlavan, "A comparison of wireless geolocation algorithms in the indoor environment," *Proceedings of IEEE Wireless Communication,* vol. 1, pp. 177-182, Atlanta, GA, United states, 2004.

[30] F. Athley, "Threshold Region Performance of Maximum Likelihood Direction of Arrival Estimators," *IEEE Transactions on Signal Processing,* vol. 53, no. 4, pp. 1359-73, 2005.

[31] N. Hernandez, F. Herranz, M. Ocana, L. Bergasa, J. Alonso and L. Magdalena, "WiFi localization system based on Fuzzy Logic to deal with signal variations," *IEEE Conference on Emerging Technologies & Factory Automation,* pp. 1-6, Mallorca, Spain, 2009.

[32] Q. Chen, D. Lee and W. Lee, "Rule-based WiFi Localization Methods," *IEEE/IFIP International Conference on Embedded and Ubiquitous Computing,* pp. 252-8, Shanghai 2008.

[33] M. Youssef, A. Agrawala and A. Udaya Shankar, "WLAN location determination via clustering and probability distributions," *IEEE International Conference on Pervasive Computing Communication,* p. 143–151, Fort Worth, TX, USA,2003.

[34] Y. Chiou, C. Wang, S. Yeh and M. Su, "Design of adaptive positioning system based on WiFi radio signals," *Elsevier, computer communications,* vol. 32, no. 7-10, pp. 1245-54, 2009.

[35] I. Popescu, D. Nikitopoulos, P. Constantinou and I. Nafornita, "Comparison of ANN Based Models for Path Loss Prediction in Indoor Environment," *Vehicular Technology Conference,* pp. 1-5, Montreal, QC, Canada, 2006.

[36] A. Bose and C. H. Foh, "A practical path loss model for indoor WiFi positioning enhancement," *Proceedings of International Conference in Information and Communication, Signal Processing,* pp. 1309-13, Singapore, 2007.

[37] S. Kay, "Fundamentals of Statistical Signal Processing: Estimation", Englewood Cliffs, NJ: Prentice-Hall, Jun. 1993.

[38] M. Zhang, S. Knedlik and O. Loffeld, "Performance Analysis of Data Fusion for Ground Target Tracking Using GSM Networks," *12th International Conference on Information Fusion,* pp. 1092-9, Seattle, WA, USA, July 2009.

[39] S. Lalchand, A. Ijaz, M. Manzoor, I. Awan and A. Siddique, "Error estimation in angle of arrival in smart antenna," *International Conference on Information and Communication Technologies (ICICT),* pp. 1-3, Karachi, Pakistan, 2011.

[40] W. Xinrui, L. Tien-Fu and C. Lei, "Synchronization and Time Resolution Improvement for 802.11 WLAN OWPT Measurement," *Proceedings of the International MultiConference of Engineers and Computer Scientists,* vol. 1, pp. 378-83, Hong Kong 2009.

[41] Q. Chen, D. Lee and W. Lee, "Rule-Based WiFi Localization Methods," *IEEE/IFIP International Conference on Embedded and Ubiquitous Computing,* pp. 252-8, Shanghai, 2008.

[42] H. Lim, L. Kung and J. Hou, "Zero-configuration indoor localization over IEEE 802.11 wireless infrastructure," *Wireless Networks,* vol. 16, no. 2, pp. 405-420, 2006.

[43] F. Ham and I. Kostanic, "Principles of Neurocomputing for Science and Engineering", McGraw Hill, 2011.

[44] B. Kovacevic and Z. Durovic, *"Fundamentals of Stochastic Signals, Systems and Estimation Theory With Worked Examples,* 2nd ed", Springer, 2008.

[45] C. E. Rasmussen and C. K. I. Williams, *"Gaussian Processes for Machine Learning",* The MIT Press, Cambridge, Massachusetts, London, England, 2006.

[46] N. Duy, "Local Gaussian process regression for real-time model-based robot control," *IEEE/RSJ International Conference on Intelligent Robots and Systems,* pp. 380 - 385, Nice, France, 2008.

[47] H. Asheri, H. Rabiee, N. Pourdamghani and M. Rohban, "A Gaussian Process Regression Framework for Spatial Error Concealment with Adaptive Kernels," *Proceedings of the 2010 20th International Conference on Pattern Recognition,* pp. 4541 - 4544, 2010.

[48] H. He and S. Wan-Chi, "Single image super-resolution using Gaussian process regression," *2011 IEEE Conference on Computer Vision and Pattern Recognition,* pp. 449 - 456, Providence, RI, USA, 2011.

[49] R. Farivar, D. Wiczer, A. Gutierrez and R. Campbell, "A statistical study on the impact of wireless signals' behavior on location estimation accuracy in 802.11 fingerprinting systems," *IEEE International Symposium on Parallel & Distributed Processing,* p. 1–8, July Rome, Italy, 2009.

[50] A. Tsui, Y. Chuang and H. Chu, "Unsupervised Learning for Solving RSS Hardware Variance Problem in WiFi Localization," *Springer, Mobile Netw Appl,* vol. 14, p. 677–691, January 2009.

[51] M. Ocan, L. Bergasa, M. Sotelo, R. Flores, E. Lo´pez and R. Barea, "Training Method Improvements of a WiFi Navigation System Based on POMDP," *Proceedings of the 2006 IEEE/RSJ, International Conference on Intelligent Robots and Systems Beijing, China,* pp. 5259-5264, Beijing, China,October, 2006.

[52] M. M. Atia, M. Korenberg and N. Aboelmagd, "Fast Features Reduction of Radio Maps for Real-time Fingerprint-based WirelessPositioning Systems," *Electron. Letters,* vol. 47, no. 20, pp. 1151-1153, 2011.

[53] M. M. Atia, N. Aboelmagd and M. Korenberg, "Dynamic Online-Calibrated Radio Maps for Indoor Positioning In Wireless Local Area Networks," *IEEE Transactions on Mobile Computing,* vol. PP, no 99, p. 1, 2012.

[54] R. Brown and P. Hwang, *"Introduction to random signals and applied Kalman filtering"*, John Wiley and Sons, New York, 1997.

[55] G. Borriello and J. Hightower, "Location systems for ubiquitous computing," *IEEE Computer Mag.*, vol. 34, no. 8, p. 57–66, 2001.

[56] A. Doucet, S. Godsill and C. Andrieu, "On Sequential Monte Carlo Sampling Methods for Bayesian Filtering," *Statistics and Computing*, vol. 10, no. 3, p. 197–208, July 2000.

[57] U. Iqbal and A. Noureldin, *"Integrated Reduced Inertial Sensor System/GPS for Vehicle Navigation"*, 2009.

[58] R. E. Kalman, "A New Approach to Linear Filtering and Prediction Problems," *Transactions of the ASME – Journal of Basic Engineering*, vol. 82, no. Series D, pp. 35–45, 1960.

[59] J. Georgy, A. Noureldin, M. Korenberg and M. Bayoumi, "Low Cost 3D Navigation Solution for RISS/GPS Integration Using Mixture Particle Filter," *IEEE Transactions on Vehicular Technology*, vol. 59, no. 2, pp. 599-615, 2010.

[60] H. Dyckman, S. Sloat and B. Pettus, "Particle Filtering to Improve GPS/INS Integration," *Proceedings of the ION GNSS 2004*, pp. 1619-1626, Long Beach, CA, September 2004.

[61] J. Diard, P. Bessière and E. Mazer, "A survey of probabilistic models, using the Bayesian Programming methodology as a unifying framework," in *the International Conference on Computational Intelligence, Robotics and Autonomous Systems*, Singapore, December 2003.

[62] N. J. Gordon, D. J. Salmond and A. F. Smith, "Novel Approach to Nonlinear/Nongaussian Bayesian State Estimation," *IEE proceedings-F (Radar and Signal Processing)*, vol. 140, p. 107–113, Kittila, Finland, 1993.

[63] IMU300, "Crossbow Technology Inc, IMU300—6DOF Inertial Measurement," 2011.

[64] M. M. Atia, M. Korenberg and A. Noureldin, "Particle Filter-based WiFi-Aided Reduced Inertial Sensors Navigation System for Indoor and GPS-denied Environments," *International Journal of Navigation and Observation, Hindawi, Article ID 753206*, vol. 2012, 2012.

[65] L. D. L. P. W. S. M. D. Adams, "The Estimation Theoretic Sensor Bias Correction Problem in Map Aided Localization," *The International Journal of Robotics Research*, vol. 25, no. 7, pp. 645-667, July 2006.

[66] R. Harle, "A Survey of Indoor Inertial Positioning Systems for Pedestrians," *IEEE Communications Surveys &Tutorials*, vol. Third Quarter, no. 2013, p. 1281, 2013.

[67] H.-S. Kim, D.-R. Kim, S.-H. Yang, Y.-H. Son and S.-K. Han, "An Indoor Visible Light Communication Positioning System Using a RF Carrier Allocation Technique," *Journal of Lightwave Technology*, vol. 31, no. 1, p. 134, 2013.

[68] G. N. DeSouza and A. C. Kak, "Vision for Mobile Robot Navigation: A Survey," *IEEE Transactions on Pattern Analysis and Machine Intelligence*, vol. 24, no. 2, p. 237, 2002.

[69] A. Soloviev, D. Bates and F. V. Graas, "Tight Coupling of Laser Scanner and Inertial Measurements for a Fully Autonomous Relative Navigation Solution," in *Position, Location and Navigation Symposium (PLANS)*, Monterey, CA, 2008.

[70] N. Mattern and G. Wanielik, "Camera-based Vehicle Localization at Intersections using Detailed Digital Maps," in *Position Location and Navigation Symposium (PLANS)*, Indian Wells, CA, USA, May 2010.

[71] D. Torrieri, "Statistical theory of passive location systems," *IEEE Transactions on Aerospace Electronic Systems* vol. 20, no. 2, pp. 183-197, 1984.

[72] M. M. Atia, A. Noureldin and M. Korenberg, "Dynamic Propagation Modeling For Mobile Users' Position and Heading Estimation in Wireless Local Area Networks," *IEEE Wireless Communication Letters,* vol. 1, no. 2, pp. 101-104, 2012.

[73] P. Bahl and V. Padmanabhan, "RADAR: An In-Building RF-Based User Location and Tracking System," *Proceeding of IEEE Infocom 2000,* p. 775–784, Tel Aviv, Israel, 2000.

[74] M. Ocan, L. Bergasa, M. Sotelo, R. Flores, E. Lo´pez and R. Barea, "Training Method Improvements of a WiFi Navigation System Based on POMDP," *Proceedings of the 2006 IEEE/RSJ, International Conference on Intelligent Robots and Systems,* pp. 5259-5264, Beijing, China,October, 2006.

[75] Y. Ji, S. Biaz, S. Pandey and P. Agrawal, "ARIADNE: a dynamic indoor signal map construction and localization system," *Proceeding of IEEE Mobile Systems Conference.,* vol. 2, p. 151–164, Uppsala, Sweden, 2006.

[76] "IEEE Standard for Information technology, Telecommunications and information exchange between systems, Local and metropolitan area networks, Specific requirements Part 11: Wireless LAN Medium Access Control (MAC) and Physical Layer (PHY) Specifications," 2007.

[77] F.Xia and H.Ya-lou, "Fast image indexing based on color theme," *Journal of Data Acquisition & Processing,* vol. 20, no. 2, pp. 198-202, June 2005.

[78] M.Frackiewicz and H.Palus, "Clustering with k-harmonic means applied to colour image quantization," *8th IEEE International Symposium on Signal Processing and Information Technology,* pp. 52-7, Sarajevo, Serbia, 2008.

[79] S. J. Wan, S. K. M. Wong and P. Prusinkiewicz, "An algorithm for multidimensional data clustering," *ACM Transactions on Mathematical Software (TOMS),* vol. 14, no. 2, pp. 153 - 162, June 1988.

[80] J. Georgy, U. Iqbal and A. Noureldin, "Quantitative comparison between Kalman filter and Particle filter for low cost INS/GPS integration," *Proceeding of International Symposium on Mechatronics and its Applications, 2009. ISMA '09. 6th,* Sharja, United Arab Emirates 2009.

[81] A. Noureldin, T. Karamat, M. D. Eberts and A. El-Shafie, "Performance enhancement of MEMS based INS/GPS integration for low cost navigation pplications," *IEEE Trans. Veh. Technol.,* vol. 58, no. 3, pp. 1077-1096, 2009.

In: Horizons in Computer Science Research. Volume 9 ISBN: 978-1-63321-522-1
Editor: Thomas S. Clary

Chapter 6

Towards a Gender-Focused Programming Performance Model

Wilfred W. F. Lau*[*] *and Allan H. K. Yuen
Faculty of Education, The University of Hong Kong,
Hong Kong SAR, China

Abstract

In the science, technology, engineering, and mathematics (STEM) fields, gender imbalance has been commonplace. There are models that examined gender differences in programming performance and yet rarely have these models included the variables learning styles and programming environment as mediators between gender and programming performance. Drawing on the pertinent literature about gender, learning styles, programming environment, and programming performance, this paper argues the importance of gender, learning styles, and programming environment in modeling programming performance. It further proposes and discusses a gender-focused performance model based on the three variables. We encourage further research effort to test this parsimonious model empirically in an authentic learning context.

Keywords: gender, learning styles, programming environment, performance model

Introduction

Every year, billions of apps are downloaded from the Apple Store and Android Market respectively. Apps stand for computer applications. According to the website of about.com of Google (http://google.about.com/), "Apps is an abbreviation for applications. An app is a piece of software. It can run on the Internet, on your computer, or on your phone or other electronic device". Engagement in the Information Technology (IT) industry seems to bring good prospect to graduates. However, low participation and high attrition of students in Computer Science courses at the secondary school and university levels are two existing

[*] E-mail address: wwflau@ hku.hk. Tel: 852 22415449; Fax: 852 25170075 (Corresponding author).

common threats to the development of related-industries in many countries. Mahmoud, Dobosiewicz, and Swayne (2004) reported that withdrawal, failure, and D-grade rate have approached 50% in introductory programming courses in universities in the U.S., Canada, and elsewhere. Sloan and Troy (2008) found that the annual attrition rate among freshman and sophomores who majored in Computer Science in the U.S. has been shown to average 19%, and at some schools as high as 66%. In the U.S., figures drawing from a number of sources by the National Center for Women & Information Technology (NCWIT) revealed remarkable gender differences in terms of participation and performance in the IT industry (http://www.ncwit.org/resources/ncwit-scorecard-report-status-women information-technology). Computer programming has been taught as part of the curriculum of Computer Studies in high schools since the 1980s. However, from the experiences in many countries, more failures than successes have been observed among students. Numerous endeavours have been devoted to the study of learning and teaching of computer programming. While there have been attempts to improve teaching practices, such as using animation, simulation or visualization tools, the issue of learner differences has been rarely addressed.

In the domain of computer programming, a variety of assessment methods have been used to assess students' programming ability. According to the results of a survey conducted by Computer Science educators from seven universities, it was found that practical work (74%), closed book exam (57%), and other written exercise (55%) were the top three most used types of assessment (Carter et al., 2003). Recently, other forms of assessment also received much attention in the literature, including automated assessment (Ala-Mutka, 2005) and peer assessment (Chinn, 2005).However, existing assessment methods do not seem to be able to assess students' programming ability accurately, and "traditional assessment (commonly called testing) is being challenged in many academic circles by those who favour alternative assessment approaches" (Reeves, 2000, p. 103). It was found that even first-year university students were unable to solve simple programs involving postfix and infix expressions (McCracken et al., 2001). Daly and Waldron (2004) critiqued current programming assessment practices (written examinations and programming assignments) as problematic, and said that "normal assessment of programming ability does not work" (p. 210). The main problem is that the majority of prevailing assessment methods have tended to focus on the outcomes instead of the process at a low order level. Also, there is a lack of consideration of learner differences in designing assessment tasks (Birenbaum et al., 2006).

Even with the introduction of Computer Assisted Assessment (CAA) (Carter et al., 2003), it was reported that "people use CAA more for summative assessment than formative assessment, although it is used for both" (p. 115), and "the most widely available test type in current CAA systems is the multiple-choice test, or variations on this theme" (p. 116). Relying only on these assessments results in a situation where weaker students cannot program well and stronger students are not challenged (Lister & Leaney, 2003). This calls for alternative assessment strategies that go beyond simply numbers and allow teachers to diagnose students' learning processes in order to promote high order conceptual understanding with consideration of learner characteristics.

The problem addressed in this paper is that existing pedagogical approaches, tools, and assessment methods are mostly ineffective due to their inadequate consideration of learner differences, contributing to the prevailing phenomena of low participation and high attrition in programming courses. Based on the premise of the educational benefits of adaptive instruction (Jonassen & Grabowski, 1993; Riding & Rayner, 1998), the proposition is that in order to improve learning and teaching of computer programming, there is a need to understand, accommodate, and respond to learner characteristics such as gender and learning styles.

Definition of Terms

While some researchers attempt to distinguish between sex and gender (Giddens, 1993), in this paper, the term gender refers to the biological differences between males and females. The term programming refers to "the process of understanding and solving a problem, designing its solution, coding the solution in a programming language, and testing it to completion" (Prasad & Fielden, 2002, p. 102). In spite of variations in its definition, the term learning styles refer to "characteristic modes of perceiving, remembering, thinking, problem solving, and decision making, reflective of information-processing regularities that develop in congenial ways around underlying personality trends. They are inferred from consistent individual differences in ways of organizing and processing information and experience" (Messick, 1994, p. 122). Messick (1994) uses the label cognitive styles for the above definition (cognitive styles and learning styles are occasionally used interchangeably in the literature). Nevertheless, the definition here focuses on innate individual differences in terms of perceiving and processing information. The term programming environment is defined as "the software applications that are used to create other software applications. At minimum, this would consist of a text editor and the programming language itself" (Miller, 2004, p. 64). Programming performance refers to the scores obtained in a programming performance test that assesses declarative knowledge (DK), procedural knowledge (PK), conditional knowledge (CK), and strategic knowledge (SK) (Oliver, 1993).

A Gender-Focused Programming Performance Model

The situation of gender imbalance in the science, technology, engineering, and mathematics (STEM) fields is well-documented in the literature. The term gender digital divide traditionally refers to the differential access to digital resources between the sexes. However, within the confines of computer programming, it has a further connotation of gender differences in terms of computing course participation and performance. Unfortunately, even after several decades of efforts, this digital divide still persists and there is no sign of narrowing of the gender gap. According to a research report, college-bound females, regardless of race and ethnicity, show significantly less interest than males in computing. Females are more inclined to associate computing with "typing", "math", and "boredom" while for males, they tend to associate computing with "video games", "design", "electronics", "solving problems", and "interesting" (WGBH Educational Foundation and the Association for Computing Machinery, 2009).

Over the years, a number of models have been developed to examine factors influencing programming performance such as computer attitude, computer anxiety, computer self-efficacy, and computer experience. For instance, in Charlton and Birkett's (1999) study, gender, personality, intellect and computer attitudes, ownership, and experience were investigated as the factors influencing computing behaviour and computing course performance. Ramalingam, LaBelle, and Wiedenbeck (2004) proposed a model for explaining course performance of novice programmers that comprised four variables, namely, previous experience, pre-self-efficacy, post-self-efficacy, and mental model.

Rarely have these models included the factors learning styles and programming environment as mediators between gender and programming performance. We argue that these two factors do contribute to explain gender differences in programming performance. Internally, much of the research has indicated that learning styles affect programming performance (Bishop-Clark, 1995; Bishop-Clark & Wheeler, 1994; Thomas, Ratcliffe, Woodbury, & Jarman, 2002; Wu, Dale, & Bethel, 1998). Externally, there is evidence suggesting the effects of programming environment on programming performance (Cuniff, Taylor, & Black, 1989; Satratzemi, Dagdilelis, & Evagelidis, 2001; Smith & Webb, 2000; Webber, 1996). Therefore, drawing on the pertinent literature about gender, learning styles, programming environment, and programming performance, this paper proposes and discusses a gender-focused programming performance model as shown in Figure 1. Our integrative model presented here intends to incorporate the variables learning styles and programming environment and thus extends previous work in related research.

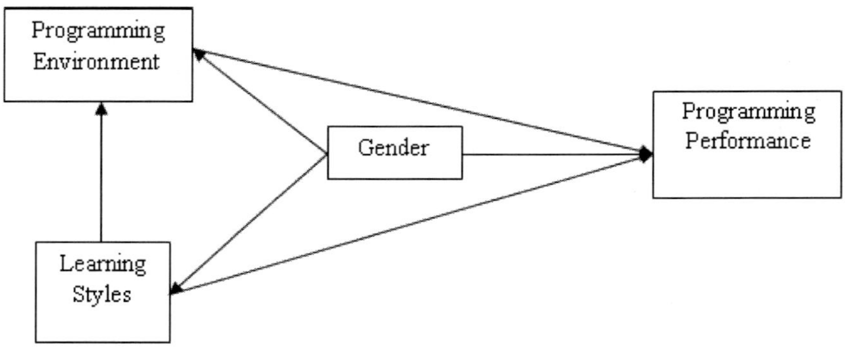

Figure 1. A gender-focused programming performance model.

Why Learning Styles and Programming Environment?

While various teaching practices have been adopted to help novice programmers to overcome learning difficulties, they are still inadequate, since many have favoured a certain style of learning due to their implicit assumption. For instance, visualization tools tend to favour visual learners while a stepwise refinement approach to programming, which is commonly practiced in a top-down design, may cause problems for bottom-up learners. These practices are not able to cater to the diversified needs of all learners. As Ford (2001) remarked, "learning outcomes were dramatically affected when individuals were presented with learning materials that were matched and mismatched with their information processing style" (p. 605). Traditional teaching methods have been critiqued for being unable to support learning styles of all students (Gomes & Mendes, 2007). In order to improve this bias in teaching, it is posited that the issues of gender and learning styles need to be incorporated in pedagogical innovations, an approach that requires further investigation of the role of gender and learning styles in learning to program.

Many programming environments have tried to reinforce uniformly a mental model of programming for novices, i.e., a mechanism for learners to understand how programs work. They mostly pay inadequate attention to learners' misconceptions brought to learning and their personal characteristics. As noted by Ma, Ferguson, Roper, and Wood (2007), visualization tools have been used for more than 20 years and yet "they have been used from a traditional, objectivist perspective, ignoring a student's pre-existing models" (p. 503). Parvez and Blank (2008) argued that "For the ITSs (Intelligent Tutoring Systems) to match the success of good human tutors, ITSs need to adapt not only to the knowledge level but also to the learning style of the student to maximize learning" (p. 291). In reality, it is observed that this uniform model approach fails to help some learners since they do not learn exactly the way they are taught. Instead, they tend to construct mental models idiosyncratically according to their gender and learning styles (Beckwith, 2007; Beckwith & Burnett, 2004). Therefore, there is a need to understand the mental models as constructed by learners of different genders and learning styles so as to make pedagogical changes. This consideration of learner differences and how it affects learning to program is the motivation of this paper.

Relationships among the Factors

The following elaborations based on the relevant literature attempt to justify the relationships in the proposed model. As shown in various studies, gender differences are found in learning styles of students. The fact that males and females differ in their preferred styles of learning is noticeable from the findings of studies using a variety of inventories (Honigsfeld & Dunn, 2003; Keri, 2002; Nuby & Oxford, 1996; Severiens & Ten Dam, 1994; Wehrwein, Lujan, & DiCarlo, 2007). As such, we posit that there is a gender effect on learning styles.

In an attempt to address the gender issue in the design of end-user programming environment, Beckwith and Burnett (2004) devised a taxonomy pertaining to gender differences in end-user programming from five domains, namely, computer science education, computer games, psychology, marketing, and education. The three issues addressed in the taxonomy were confidence, support, and motivation. Under each issue, a number of sub-issues were considered and stated as hypotheses. For example, regarding problem-solving style, as males preferred competition whereas females preferred collaboration in playing games, it was hypothesized that programming environment that supports collaboration enhances the chance of task completion for females than those that do not. Another example is about gender differences in information processing style. Theory suggests that females tend to use elaborate information processing strategies regardless of task difficulty whereas males tend to use heuristic information processing strategies for a simple task and elaborate strategies for a more complicated task. It was hypothesized that it is less likely for males to read detailed help manuals than females. Although stated as hypotheses, they were grounded on relevant literature. There is some empirical evidence to support gender differences in their preferences of programming environment. For example, females were found to have lower self-efficacy in their ability to debug than males. They were also less willing to accept new debugging features and more prone to new bugs than males (Beckwith, 2007). These differences are important when it comes to the design of programming environment that is capable to accommodate learners of different genders. As such, we posit that there is a gender effect on programming environment.

It is generally expected that males outperform females in computer science courses. McDowell, Werner, Bullock, and Fernald (2003) found that male students who worked in pairs scored significantly higher than their female counterparts in final examination but the difference was insignificant when the Scholastic Assessment Tests (SAT) mathematics scores were controlled for. A few studies reported opposite results regarding superior performance of females. Pioro (2004) showed that the average scores obtained for women were higher than for men on both programming problems and multiple-choice parts of the final examination. There was even a significant gender difference in performance of programming problems. Houston (1993) also found that female students seemed to perform better in lecture and laboratory although there was no significant difference in performance between women and men. Houston explained that the phenomenon might be due to the "dedication and hard work that may have been brought on by the anxiety of not being expected to do well" (p. 73). Nevertheless, we posit that there is a gender effect on programming performance.

Studies have consistently shown that computer-based or computer-aided instruction does not accommodate the needs of all learners equally (Ames, 2003; Ross & Schulz, 1999). There was a learning style effect on instruction using computers. Ross and Schulz (1999) showed that abstract random participants adopted the least linear navigation pattern among the four dominant learning style groups as measured by the Gregorc Style Delineator (GSD). On average, they had fewer interactions with computer program than did the other three dominant learning style groups. They were considered to be at-risk in doing computer-aided tasks. Ames (2003) also found that abstract random and concrete random learners as predicted by the GSD were "less inclined to be receptive to technology-facilitated instruction" (p. 240) and the author called for more attention in curriculum development and classroom facility design. As such, in the context of learning of computer programming, we posit that learning styles have an effect on programming environment.

Thomas et al. (2002) investigated the effect of different learning styles on performance in an introductory programming course using the Index of Learning Styles (ILS). Student performance was assessed by the course and examination marks. Results indicated that reflective learners outperformed active learners ($p <.05$) whereas verbal learners outperformed visual learners ($p <.05$). Wu et al. (1998) demonstrated that students having abstract learning styles learned better than those having concrete learning styles. Using the Myers-Briggs Type Indicator (MBTI), Bishop-Clark and Wheeler (1994) showed that sensing students outperformed intuitive students on programming assignments, and that judging students outperformed perceptive students on programming averages. However, there were no significant differences between any personality types and examination grade or final grade. In a later study, Bishop-Clark (1995) examined the possible effect of cognitive style on stages of computer programming. Cognitive style was measured by the Group Embedded Figures Test (GEFT) and performances in the design and coding stages of programming were measured by two respective tests. It was found that the correlation between GEFT and design was significantly higher than that between GEFT and coding, and the hypothesis that cognitive style affects the stages of computer programming differently was supported. As such, we posit that learning styles have an effect on programming performance.

A work by Cuniff et al. (1989) described how the graphical programming language FPL (First Programming Language) helps students to reduce missing syntax bugs and misplaced plan component bugs in programs in contrast to students learning to program in Pascal. The success of FPL is attributed to its visual nature that allows students to see how the code is organized. Smith and Webb (2000) designed a programming tool called Bradman that helps novice programmers to learn C as the first programming language. The tool allows students to dynamically see the execution of a program through providing a number of windows that show changes of the states of the variables as the statements execute. There is also an explanation window to users to explain how and why the changes occur. Satratzemi et al. (2001) created an educational programming environment, AnimPascal, that helps novice programmers to develop, verify, debug, and execute their programs. The tool provides a dynamic visualization feature during program execution. It traces the execution of program and gives messages to students when errors occur. It helps teachers to diagnose the problems encountered by students. To evaluate the tool, students were asked to implement the binary search algorithm in the environment. The tool seems to be successful in assisting students to detect bugs. Webber (1996) noted that most lecturers tend to skip too soon to advanced topics at the expense of rudimentary algorithms. To remedy this problem, Webber created a tutoring system, Pascal Trainer, to assist students to learn from simple expressions. It is essentially a drill-and-practice system in which students are presented with a menu of exercises to choose from and those completed exercises are dimmed. The Trainer also gives feedback to students and most students were able to write a simple function correctly on a test by the end of semester. In short, the efficacy of programming environment appears to be established through program visualization and algorithm animation. As such, we posit that programming environment has an effect on programming performance.

Significance of the Model

The status quo of high attrition, gender imbalance, and low interest of students in the Computer Science courses at the secondary school and university levels is pervasive. Whereas the aforementioned problems are multi-faceted, a review of current teaching and assessment practices indicated that these practices fail to cater to the individual learning needs of students. It is argued that gender and learning styles are important vehicles affecting students learning to program. Although there are previous related studies in the literature, this paper offered practical suggestions as to how gender and learning styles can be used to help improve student learning.

The model of this paper has significant implications and contributions for researchers as well as practitioners. For researchers, it can be argued that research into gender and learning styles in the context of learning to program enriches the body of knowledge of learning and teaching of computer programming. Despite the importance of the issues, researchers have not historically paid them enough attention. This paper can help to fill this missing and yet significant part of research and contribute to the development of a pedagogical theory on computer programming.

For practitioners, the model suggests that through various interventions with consideration of the issues of gender and learning styles, teachers can individualize their pedagogies so that students can learn best according to their needs. This is particularly important today as schools should be more accountable to students' academic achievement in collaboration with other stakeholders. Fantini (2001) contended that "the design of programs that are compatible with the style of the learner is increasingly the responsibility of the school in conjunction with the major interested parties closest to the learner, including parents and other advisors" (p. 29). As pointed out by Gess-Newsome and Lederman (1999), a good teacher has to possess pedagogical content knowledge which involves knowing not only subject matter, but also ways in which individuals experience, understand or misunderstand the subject.

This paper also provides insights into the need for catering to learner differences in the context of recent curriculum development. As noted in some curriculum document (Hong Kong Curriculum Development Council, 2003), it seems that little suggestion has been provided by curriculum guidelines as to how to measure and address learner differences. This paper attempts to address this issue by using gender and learning styles as measures of learner differences. The advantage of this approach is that many instruments, which are designed with different principles for use in different settings, are available to measure learning styles. It is hoped that this paper provides practical suggestions to improve student learning through individualization in terms of gender and learning styles and to develop a more learner-focused curriculum.

Conclusion

This paper establishes the importance of gender, learning styles, and programming environment in modeling programming performance by proposing and discussing a gender-focused programming performance model based on the three variables. We believe that our model can make significant contributions to Computer Science education for researchers and practitioners alike. For researchers, it enhances our knowledge of learning and teaching of computer programming, in particular the gender and learning styles issues in the process of learning to program. For practitioners, it helps to improve student learning through individualization of pedagogy and programming environment in terms of gender and learning styles, and ultimately lead to more student-centered teaching as advocated by the education community. For example, would a user interface specifically designed for a gender enhance performance of that gender? Would a pedagogy tailor-made for a gender enhance performance of that gender?

While we acknowledge that this parsimonious model has its own limitations, the implications for researchers and practitioners are significant and could bridge the growing gender digital divide in the context of computing course participation and performance. We encourage further research effort to test our parsimonious model empirically in an authentic learning context. Computer Science education is a relatively new research area. Studies based on different learning theories and research methodologies have been conducted over the past few decades. The model discussed here will undoubtedly add to the knowledge and development of this unique discipline.

References

Ala-Mutka, K. M. (2005). A survey of automated assessment approaches for programming assignments. *Computer Science Education,* 15(2), 83-102.

Ames, P. C. (2003). Gender and learning style interactions in students' computer attitudes. *Journal of Educational Computing Research,* 28(3), 231-244.

Beckwith, L. (2007). *Gender HCI issues in end-user programming.* Unpublished Ph.D. thesis, Oregon State University, USA.

Beckwith, L., & Burnett, M. (2004). *Gender: An important factor in end-user programming environments?* Paper presented at the IEEE Symposium on Visual Languages and Human-Centric Computing Languages and Environments, Rome, Italy.

Birenbaum, M., Breuer, K., Cascallar, E., Dochyd, F., Dori, Y., Ridgway, J., et al. (2006). A learning integrated assessment system. *Educational Research Review,* 1(1), 61-67.

Bishop-Clark, C. (1995). Cognitive style and its effect on the stages of programming. *Journal of Research on Computing in Education,* 27(4), 373-386.

Bishop-Clark, C., & Wheeler, D. D. (1994). The Myers-Briggs personality type and its relationship to computer programming. *Journal of Research on Computing in Education,* 26(3), 358-370.

Carter, J., Ala-Mutka, K., Fuller, U., Dick, M., English, J., Fone, W., & Sheard, J. (2003). How shall we assess this? *ACM SIGCSE Bulletin,* 35(4), 107-123.

Charlton, J. P., & Birkett, P. E. (1999). An integrative model of factors related to computing course performance. *Journal of Educational Computing Research,* 20(3), 237-257.

Chinn, D. (2005). Peer assessment in the algorithms course. *ACM SIGCSE Bulletin,* 37(3), 69-73.

Cuniff, N., Taylor, R. P., & Black, J. B. (1989). Does programming language affect the type of conceptual bugs in beginner's programs? A comparison of FPL and Pascal. In E. Soloway & C. S. James (Eds.), *Studying the Novice Programmers* (pp. 419-430). Hillsdale, NJ: Lawrence Erlbaum Associates.

Daly, C., & Waldron, J. (2004). *Assessing the assessment of programming ability.* Paper presented at the 35th SIGCSE Technical Symposium on Computer Science Education, Norfolk, VA, USA.

Fantini, M. D. (2001). A contemporary approach to individualization. *Theory into Practice,* 19(1), 28-31.

Ford, N. (2001). The increasing relevance of Pask's work to modern information seeking and use. *Kybernetes,* 30(5), 603 - 630.

Gess-Newsome, J., & Lederman, N. G. (1999). *Examining pedagogical content knowledge.* The Netherlands: Kluwer Academic Publishers.

Giddens, A. (1993). *Sociology.* Cambrige, UK: Polity Press.

Gomes, A., & Mendes, A. J. (2007). Learning to program - difficulties and solutions. In *Proceedings of the 10th International Conference on Engineering Education* (pp. 283-287). Coimbra, Portugal: University of Coimbra.

Hong Kong Curriculum Development Council. (2003). *Computer and information technology curriculum and assessment guide (Secondary 4-5).* Hong Kong: HKSAR Government Logistics Department.

Honigsfeld, A., & Dunn, R. (2003). High school male and female learning-style similarities and differences in diverse nations. *The Journal of Educational Research,* 96(4), 195-206.

Houston, D. M. (1993). *An exploration and analysis of the relationship among learning styles, teaching styles, gender and performance in a college computer science course.* Unpublished Ph.D. thesis, Kansas State University, USA.

Jonassen, D. H., & Grabowski, B. L. (1993). *Handbook of individual differences, learning and instruction.* Hillsdale, NJ: Lawrence Erlbaum Associates.

Keri, G. (2002). Male and female college students' learning styles differ: An opportunity for instructional diversification. *College Student Journal,* 36(3), 433-442.

Lister, R., & Leaney, J. (2003). Introductory programming, criterion-referencing, and bloom. *SIGCSE Bulletin,* 35(1), 143 -147.

Ma, L., Ferguson, J., Roper, M., & Wood, M. (2007). Investigating the viability of mental models held by novice programmers. *SIGCSE Bulletin*, 39(1), 499-503.

Mahmoud, Q. H., Dobosiewicz, W., & Swayne, D. A. (2004). Making computer programming fun and accessible. *IEEE Computer,* 37(2), 106-108.

McCracken, M., Almstrum, V., Diaz, D., Guzdial, M., Hagan, D., Kolikant, Y. B.-D., et al. (2001). A multi-national, multi-institutional study of assessment of programming skills of first-year CS students. *SIGCSE Bulletin,* 33(4), 125-180.

McDowell, C., Werner, L., Bullock, H. E., & Fernald, J. (2003). The impact of pair programming on student performance, perception and persistence. In *Proceedings of the 25th International Conference on Software Engineering* (pp. 602-607). Portland, OR: IEEE Computer Society.

Messick, S. (1994). The matter of style: Manifestations of personality in cognition, learning, and teaching. *Educational Psychologist,* 29(3), 121-136.

Miller, J. A. (2004). *Promoting computer literacy through programming Python.*Unpublished Ph.D. thesis, The University of Michigan, USA.

Nuby, J. F., & Oxford, R. L. (1996). *Learning style preferences of Native American and African-American secondary students as measured by the MBTI.* Paper presented at the Annual Meeting of the Mid-South Educational Research Association, Tuscaloosa, AL, USA.

Oliver, R. (1993). Measuring hierarchical levels of programming knowledge. *Journal of Educational Computing Research,* 9(3), 299-312.

Parvez, S. M., & Blank, G. D. (2008). Individualizing tutoring with learning style based feedback. In *Proceedings of the 9th International Conference on Intelligent Tutoring Systems* (pp. 291-301). Berlin: Springer.

Pioro, B. T. (2004). *Performance in an introductory computer programming course as a predictor of future success for engineering and computer science majors.* Paper presented at the International Conference on Engineering Education, Gainesville, FL, USA.

Prasad, C., & Fielden, K. (2002). *Introducing programming: A balanced approach.* Paper presented at the 15th Annual Conference of the National Advisory Committee on Computing Qualifications, Hamilton, New Zealand.

Ramalingam, V., LaBelle, D., & Wiedenbeck, S. (2004). *Self-efficacy and mental models in learning to program.* Paper presented at the 9th Annual Conference on Innovation and Technology in Computer Science Education, Leeds, UK.

Reeves, T. C. (2000). Alternative assessment approaches for online learning environments in higher education. *Journal of Educational Computing Research,* 23(1), 101-111.

Riding, R., & Rayner, S. (1998). *Cognitive styles and learning strategies: Understanding style differences in learning and behaviour.* London: David Fulton Publishers.

Ross, J., & Schulz, R. (1999). Can computer-aided instruction accommodate all learners equally? *British Journal of Educational Technology,* 30(1), 5-24.

Satratzemi, M., Dagdilelis, V., & Evagelidis, G. (2001).A system for program visualization and problem-solving path assessment of novice programmers. In *Proceedings of the 6th Annual Conference on Innovation and Technology in Computer Science Education* (pp. 137-140). New York, NY: ACM Press.

Severiens, S. E., & Ten Dam, G. T. M. (1994). Gender differences in learning styles: A narrative review and quantitative meta-analysis. *Higher Education,* 27(4), 487-501.

Sloan, R. H., & Troy, P. (2008). *CS 0.5: A better approach to introductory computer science for majors.* Paper presented at the the 39th SIGCSE Technical Symposium on Computer Science Education, Portland, OR, USA.

Smith, P., & Webb, G. (2000).The efficacy of a low-level program visualization tool for teaching programming concepts to novice C programmers. *Journal of Educational Computing Research,* 22(2), 187-215.

Thomas, L., Ratcliffe, M., Woodbury, J., & Jarman, E. (2002). Learning styles and performance in the introductory programming sequence. In *Proceedings of the 33rd SIGCSE Technical Symposium on Computer Science Education* (pp. 33-37). New York, NY: ACM Press.

Webber, A. B. (1996).The Pascal Trainer. *SIGCSE Bulletin,* 28(1), 261-265.

Wehrwein, E. A., Lujan, H. L., & DiCarlo, S. E. (2007). Gender differences in learning style preferences among undergraduate physiology students. *Advances in Physiology Education,* 31, 153-157.

WGBH Educational Foundation and the Association for Computing Machinery. (2009). New for computing image: Report on market research [Electronic Version]. Retrieved November 14, 2013 from www.acm.org/membership/NIC.pdf.

Wu, C. C., Dale, N. B., & Bethel, L. J. (1998).Conceptual models and cognitive learning styles in teaching recursion. In *Proceedings of the Twenty-ninth SIGCSE Technical Symposium on Computer Science Education* (pp. 292-296). New York, NY: ACM Press.

In: Horizons in Computer Science Research. Volume 9
Editor: Thomas S. Clary
ISBN: 978-1-63321-522-1

Chapter 7

A METHODOLOGIES AND PROCESSES LANGUAGE FOR THE SOFTWARE INDUSTRY

Sandro J. Bolaños*[1,*]*, Rubén A. González*[2,†]*,
***Carlos A. Arismendi*[1] *and Edwin J. Castañeda*[1]**
[1]Faculty of Engineering,
Distrital Francisco José de Caldas University, Bogotá, Colombia
[2]College of Engineering and Architecture,
Pontificia de Salamanca University, Madrid, Spain

Abstract

This paper presents a Software Methodology-and-Process Modeling Language, also referred to as −SMPML−. A brief description of the vocabulary is provided, followed by a set of perspectives that are applied directly to a case study. Some of the most relevant results, obtained from an actual project, are discussed and analyzed. The modeling language presented in this document is suggested to be used as a wrap for the modeling and computational languages that are utilized within the current software industry.

This language appears as a powerful alternative proposal even for parallel-process modeling such as that involving BPMN (for industrial processes) or SPEM (for software processes).

Keywords: Process language, modeling, vocabulary, viewpoints, software industry

1. Introduction

The use of various computational and modeling languages has allowed software engineers to make the abstractions of ideas that can be expressed using natural language (NL). These ideas are then represented in machine language (ML), and so complex solutions can be proposed implemented over software- based systems. As software engineering

* E-mail address: sbolanos@udistrital.edu.co (Corresponding Author).
† E-mail address: ruben.gonzalez@upsam.es.

evolved, abstraction levels improved by using models of solutions that closely resemble NL evermore. The problem is that there are so many intermediate languages in between NL and ML –UML [1, 2], Archimate [3], programming languages [4], among others –,that each software process ends up requiring specialized personnel that already knows the languages, namely "software architects, process engineers, programming staff etc...". With this wide variety of languages, in time, achieving traceability among different models becomes more complex, making it more difficult for the people involved in a particular process to communicate. In the present study, there is a motivation to solve a particular problem, namely the use of a language together with its proposed viewpoints in order to model a process. A case study is described including a set of results, future work and some conclusions.

2. An Ever-Growing Problem

In software engineering, languages represent a fundamental tool that allows not only transferring ideas but also easy abstraction processes. This permits capturing the most important ideas that ultimately contribute to successful problem-solving. In the path from the problem domain to the solution domain, within a software engineering process, different languages may appear: the first is natural language NL, then, after a first abstraction, architecture languages AL appear (e.g., Archimate), subsequently, design languages DL (such as UML), and finally, programming languages PL, which are used to accurately describe specific tasks that are to be translated into machine language ML, at this point the process is already in its solution-domain stage.

Even though there is an established route between natural language NL and machine language ML, closing the gap between NL and ML is still a challenge due to two fundamental reasons: firstly, the appearance of new languages is being permanently encouraged; secondly, traces between the two (NL and ML) are not always clear. This motivates the so called–Missing Link Paradox–, which can be stated as follows: *"every time a an intermediate language (along the NL-ML path) is proposed, such a language will appear as the link that finally completes the chain; however, the findings reveal that the real achievement is a realization that more languages can be defined motivated by the newly proposed language"*. By following this trend, we are only extending the problem.

3. A Methodology-and-Process-based Solution

Methodologies as well as software processes serve as a wrap for the languages that appear between LN and LM. These processes contribute to the articulation of languages and represent good solutions to the "missing link paradox". An convenient aspect of having methodology-and-processes diversity lies in the consolidation of common vocabulary. By synthesizing such a common vocabulary, the Software Methodology-and-Process Modeling Language SMPML was proposed, and it is precisely through this language that we put forward a categorization of a solution to management, structure and innovation within software processes and methodologies.

In this study, we present the Software Methodology-and- Process Modeling Language –SMPML– by using a set of viewpoints proposed for its own use. Through such viewpoints it is possible to represent any methodology or process in a unified manner. SMPML allows constructing a weave for the languages involved in the path from NL to ML, including important considerations such as responsibilities, products and services, incidents and contributions, improvements, accumulated knowledge and experiences, and even the possibility of producing customized processes according to the project's conditions.

Another widely recognized proposal for modeling software processes is SPEM –Software & Systems Process Engineering Metamodel Specification–, which was developed by OMG in order to define software development processes, systems and their components. This proposal becomes a solution to model, document, manage and improve software processes [5]; however, its deployment has faced strong criticism. Most of such criticism is due to the extremely generalized and ambiguous semantic (meta-model-based) descriptions, which resulted in a language that is difficult to use [6]. Even in its second version, SPEM 2.0, there is a framework that is only applicable to process description. The framework is process-and-activity-flow- centered but neglects other fundamental aspects such as the participants, the products, the generated knowledge, the associated information, and the guidelines of different mechanisms in use, which can be seen as categories and sub-categories for activities themselves. SMPML does address all these aspects [7]. On the other hand, SPEM has observable disadvantages when compared to SMPML, for instance SPEM lacks views, as opposed to the well-defined views offered by SMPML, which are grouped into three characterization categories as follows: management, structure, and innovation. These categories are proposed to go beyond the simple description of the processes and methodologies in use. Moreover, from SMPML, it is possible to model SPEM as a stereotyped sub-set.

Nowadays, software processes are a subject of particular interest. This area of study includes optimization of software processes, analysis of their behavior, improvements to communication between clients, analysts, and developers, and also addresses causes of delay, resource management, and cost reductions [8]. Some trends are identified such as process-centered environments PSEE [9] and software development process automation, resulting in proposals like MDA –Model Driven Architecture– [10, 11], MDD –Model Driven Development–, BDD –Behaviour Driven Development– and TDD –Test Driven Development–, which show the importance of creating a software-process engineering and even a software- process architecture. SMPML is regarded as an option that closely meets the needs that gravitate around the software process and methodology.

The following sections describe the implementation of SMPML when guiding the software process engineering that was applied to creating the information system of a DNA Bank (in Colombia). This software engineering project was managed by the biodiversity and genetical resource group at the genetics institute of Universidad Nacional de Colombia.

4. SMPML

Language SMPML –Software Methodology-and-Process Modeling Language– puts forward a new vide-open level of abstraction that is independent of other languages. The language is intended to strengthen the software engineering discipline by facilitating the expression of ideas that pertain to software methodology-and-process modeling based on the creation of a wrapping environment for the languages that get involved throughout the dialectical path from NL to a particular ML (figure 1).

The main objectives set by SMPML include:

- Modeling software-development methodologies and processes.
- The unification of a common vocabulary for the architects, managers and innovators involved in software processes and methodologies, facilitating communication.
- Integrating programming, design, architecture and other programming languages that take part in a development process.
- Keeping records of the most important phenomena that occur while applying software methodologies and processes; promoting methodology/process control while configuring an improvement-and-maturity base for new applications.
- Structuring software methodologies and processes based on software methodology/process patterns already defined that may be expressed and documented using the SMPML vocabulary.
- Promoting the development of new ways of conducting software methodologies and processes by defining them as the subject of study.

The most remarkable strength of SMPML is its common, simple, and summarized vocabulary, which has been defined with the purpose of facilitating communication [12] (figure 2).

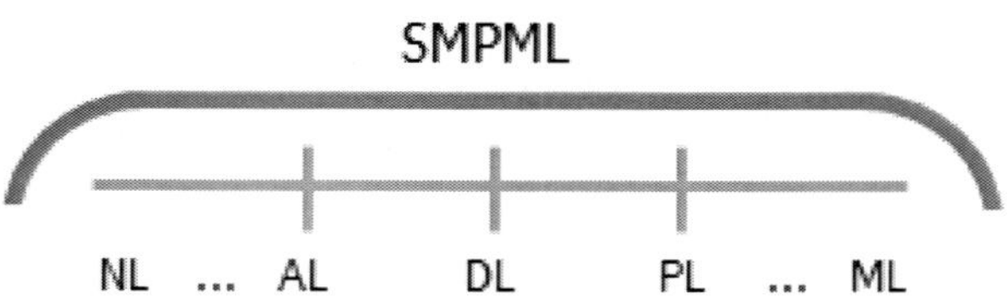

Figure 1. Wrapping Language SMPML.

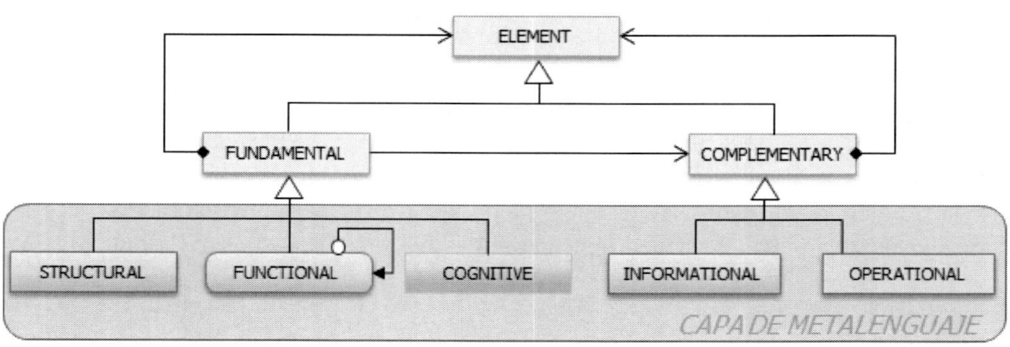

Figure 2. SMPML meta-language.

SMPML consists of two elements, namely a grammar that allows the formal expression of language and a graphical representation of such grammar, which exploits the advantages of graphs.

The graphical representation consists of three fundamental building blocks, namely elements, interactions and viewpoints.

Element: An element represents the base concept in SMPML, which can be either Structural −actor, role, input, result−, Functional −process, methodology, phase, activity, task, instruction, pros, cons−, Cognitive −hard knowledge, soft knowledge−, Informative −document, note, text− , or Operational−transactional, relational−. These concepts constitute the meta-language vocabulary and the object language.

Interaction: Interaction establishes the way language elements are connected. Interaction can be represented by Relations −use, possession, composition, realization, generalization−, or Transactions −flow, generation−.

Viewpoints: Viewpoints configure the well-defined graphs recommended by the language as key angles that must be considered and that constitute a valuable semantic character for processes and methodologies.

5. Case Study

In order to show the operation of SMPML when applied to a case study, we present the results obtained from using SMPML to document the information-system development process for a DNA Bank. This software project was aimed at developing an information system that permits maintaining biological samples well organized and also supports administrative, sample management, and information-access processes.

The team that was put together to conduct the project included the participation of various universities, namely Universidad Distrital (Bogot, Colombia), Universidad Nacional de Colombia y Universidad de Pontificia de Salamanca (Spain). The whole problem was formulated by the Biodiversity and Genetic Resource Group -GBRG- at Universidad Nacional, whereas the participants from Universidad Distrital and Universidad Pontificia de Salamanca made up the supporting engineering team.

Following the framework proposed in SMPML [13, 14, 15], the development of the project was addressed from the management, structuring and innovation perspectives, as illustrated in the following subsections:

5.1. Management

Management focuses on the process participants, identifying participants as the main information source. By identifying the people involved, it is possible to clearly assign responsibilities and distribute the various tasks according to the expected production during the process. This type of information can be seen in the four viewpoints that make up this category, namely strategy, organization, production and documentation.

5.1.1. Strategy

Regarding this viewpoint, the methodology adopted during development is represented by showing the process as a constituent part of the methodology. the main purpose is to bring the process-configuring guidelines to the foreground. This viewpoint reflects the findings from the study about methodologies/candidate processes for the software project [16, 17, 18,19].

The selected methodology to be followed in the project was RAD (Rapid Application Development) [20, 21, 22]. This methodology is agile and prototype-activity-based. RAD contemplates three main phases that are represented as processes (figure 3).

Each of these phases can be matched to certain activities, tasks and instructions depending on the desired detail level (figure 4).

RAD was selected mainly in order to exploit the advantages associated to the use of prototypes during a development process, generating greater interests within the user group while closely satisfying their needs.

5.1.2. Organization

Through the organization viewpoint, the actors that take part in the process are established together with their specific roles [23]. Actors are regarded as the main information source, representing the most important resource within the project. A clear understanding of the organization's dynamics (knowledge) allows proper administration of such a particular resource [24, 25].

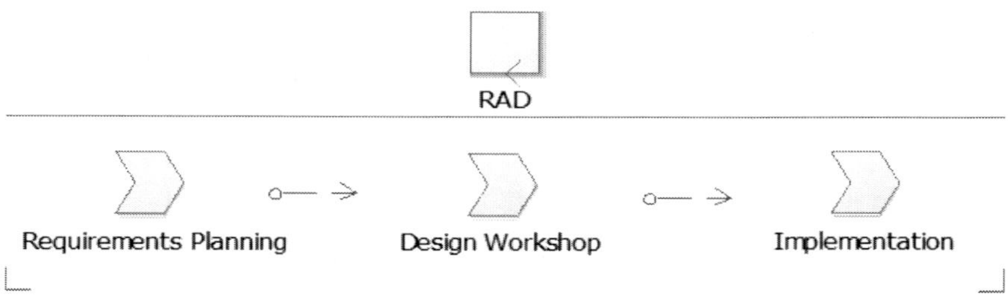

Figure 3. Methodology.

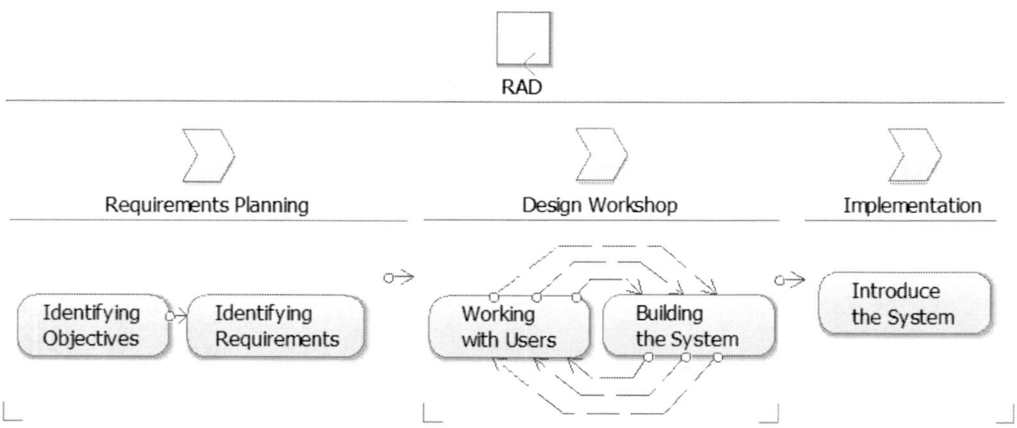

Figure 4. Methodology with Activities.

In order to facilitate the distribution of responsibilities within the project, the actors involved were classified according to two main roles, namely the "Users" role and the "Development team" role (figure 5a).

Role configuration occurs through a hierarchical structure, allowing the prioritization of responsibilities according to the capabilities available [26, 27, 28]. Thus, responsibilities associated to the role "Development team" are distributed among its corresponding sub-roles, namely: Project Director, Analyst, Designer and Developer (figure 5b).

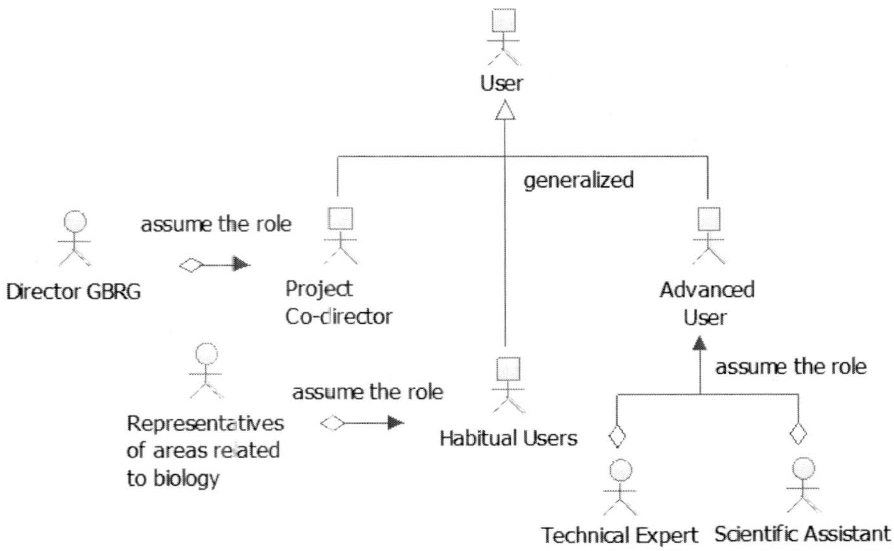

Figure 5a. Users.

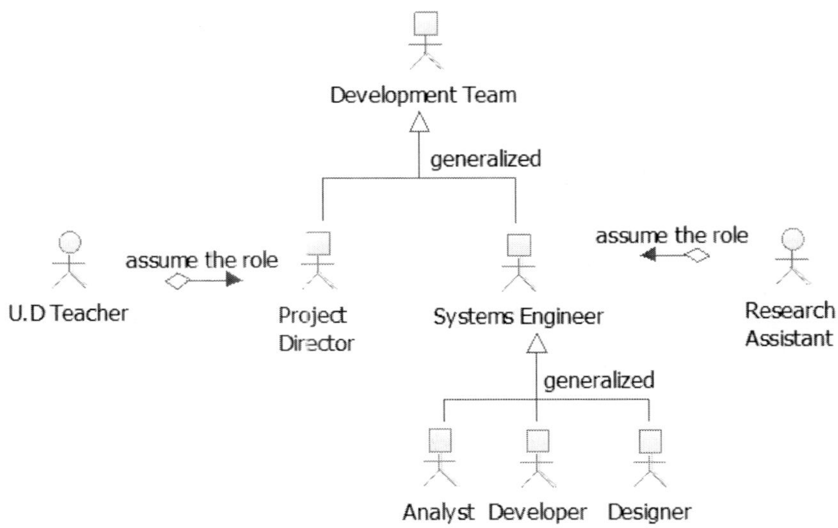

Figure 5b. Development Team.

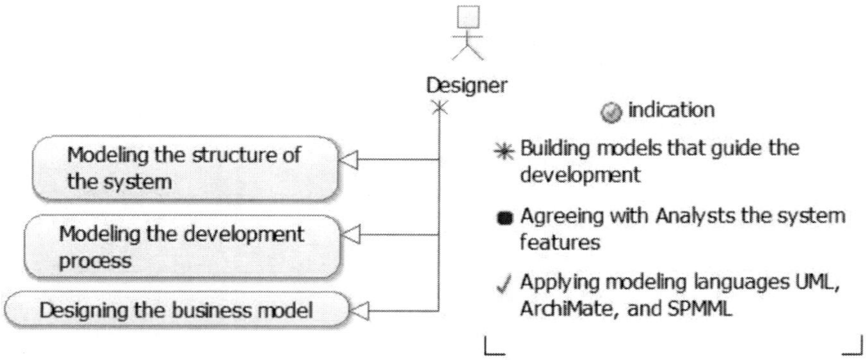

Figure 5c. Designer Characteristics.

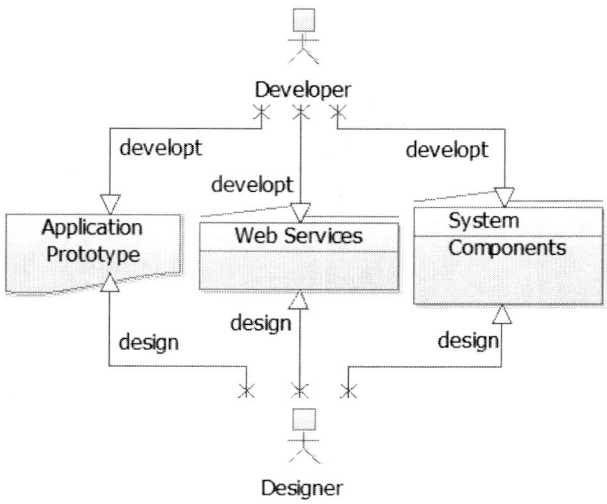

Figure 6a. Products.

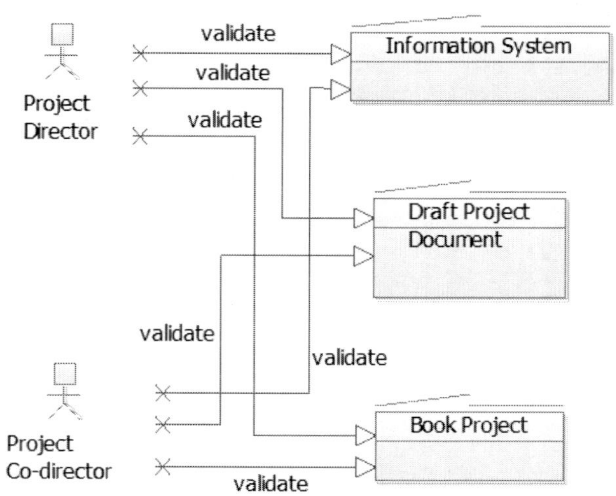

Figure 6b. Product Collaboration.

Over this same viewpoint, activities and tasks are assigned to each of the roles, together with indicators that are represented by functions, objectives and practices. The organization viewpoint provides the necessary information about participants so that the project can be successfully executed (figure 5c).

5.1.3. Production

The production viewpoint permits specifying the products and/or services –artifacts– that are generated by each role while performing his/her functions [29]. In addition to highlighting the value of the actions performed by each role, it is also possible to visualize the necessary collaborative links during the production of artifacts [30], it is even possible to specify the type of contribution made by assigning a particular value to each relationship between a role and an artifact (figure 6a). In this last diagram, it is possible to see the way a greater artifact production is being carried out by the designer and developer roles.

The viewpoint includes the most frequent variations that occur over the "Realize" relationship – specifies, produces, validates, develops, tests, maintains y and designs –, also allowing the addition of a new relationship at any time (figure 6b).

The importance of this point lies in the level of control and understanding it provides. This allows a global overview of the relationships that occur between the process roles and artifacts.

5.1.4. Documentation

Documentation is highlighted through this viewpoint [31, 32]. In this viewpoint, all documents/notes/texts written or consulted by users are defined. In this particular case, documentation is centered on assistant researchers playing their role of Information and Technology engineers, who are the people with the highest workload in terms of document revision and production, which is fundamental in process understanding [33]. (figure 7a)

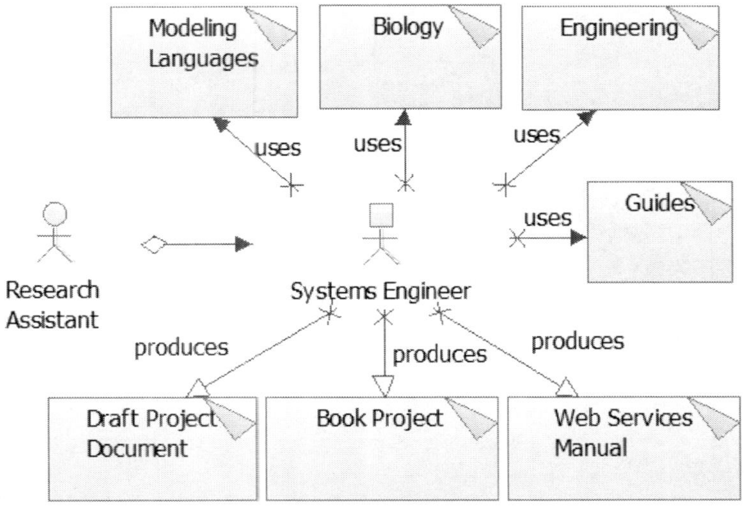

Figure 7a. Documentation.

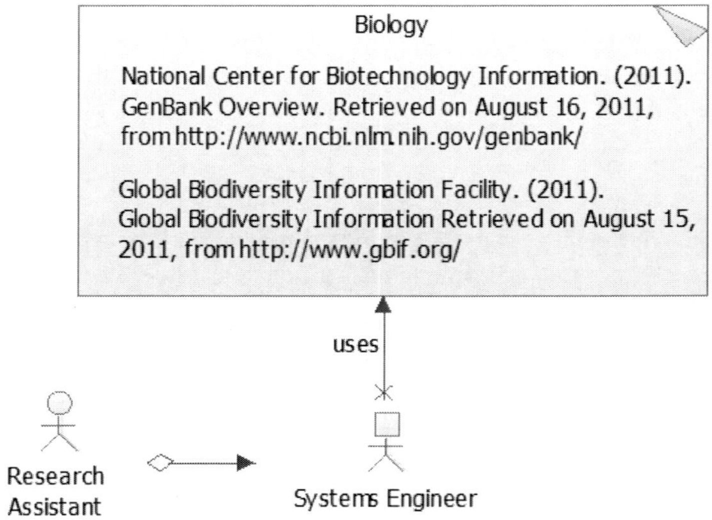

Figure 7b. References.

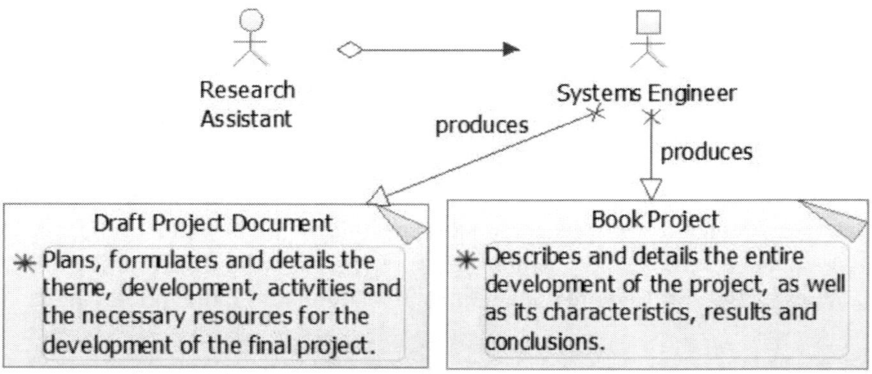

Figure 7c. Indicators.

The language also allows adding value to diagrams by using texts or notes, where additional information can be include (e.g., a list of the most relevant references) (figure 7b).

It is also possible to add indications −functions, objectives and practices− or contradictions −restrictions, limitations and risks−, according to the type of information to be represented (figure 7c).

Complementary to the artifacts being produced, the documents that support the process are recorded, including not only the documents produced but also the existing documents that were consulted [34].

5.2. Structuring

Through process-and-methodology structuring, it is possible to define the building blocks and the way they interact [35, 36, 37, 38]. the viewpoints included in this category focused on defining the architecture, architecture-configuring mechanisms, the proposed contribution for each process, and artifacts interdependence.

5.2.1. Architecture

This viewpoint offers the possibility to customize processes [39, 40], allowing software-process architecture design. besides representing standards or stiff rules, methodologies offer valuable guidelines that can be followed so that it is possible to configure a process. Every single project is different and it has its own particularities and requirements, thus there are a few occasions where a particular methodology can be closely followed in full. Based on this viewpoint, it is possible to construct and detailed the building blocks of the corresponding development process (figure 8a).

Modifications were added to the process aimed at minimizing user participation time during prototype development. More concrete tasks were defined for the Requirement Planning phase centered on the construction of organization and business models (figure 8b).

During the design-workshop phase we propose to focus the work on the system's graphic component. This allows finishing the requirement elicitation stage while users get familiar with the final aspect of the system (figure 8c).

For the closing part of component development, the Programming phase was added. The development of each component stems from this phase (figure 8d).Whereas the integration of components is included in the final implementation phase (figure 8e).

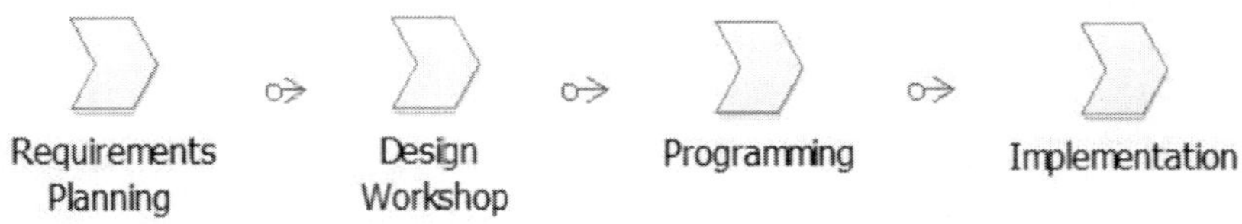

Figure 8a. Architecture.

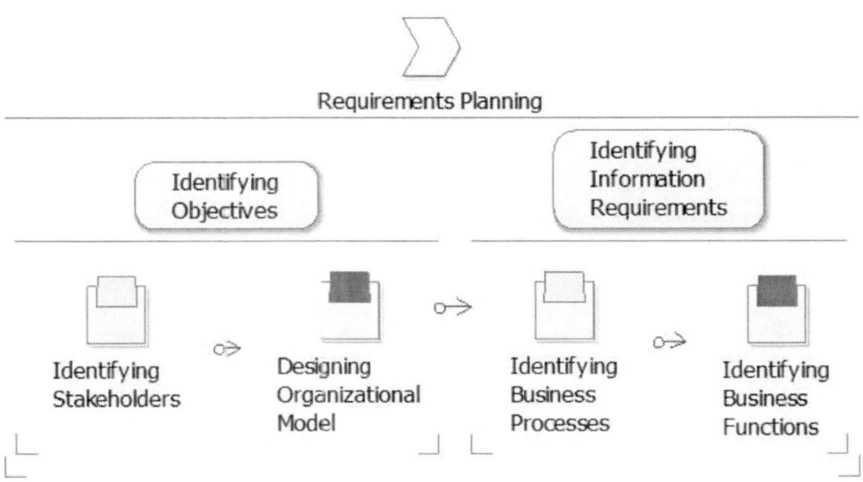

Figure 8b. Planning.

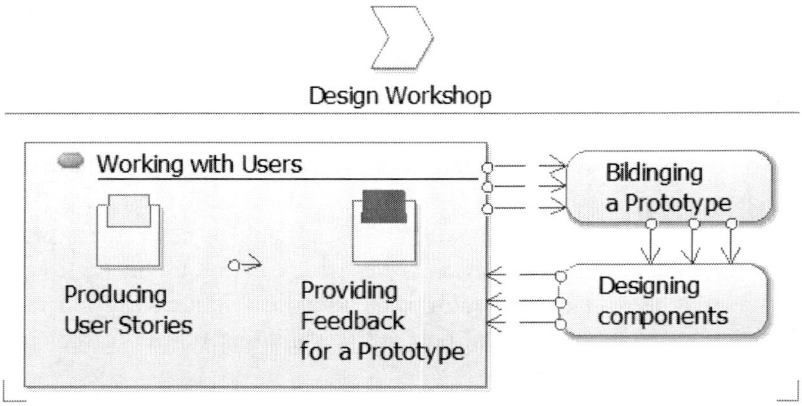

Figure 8c. Graphic Component.

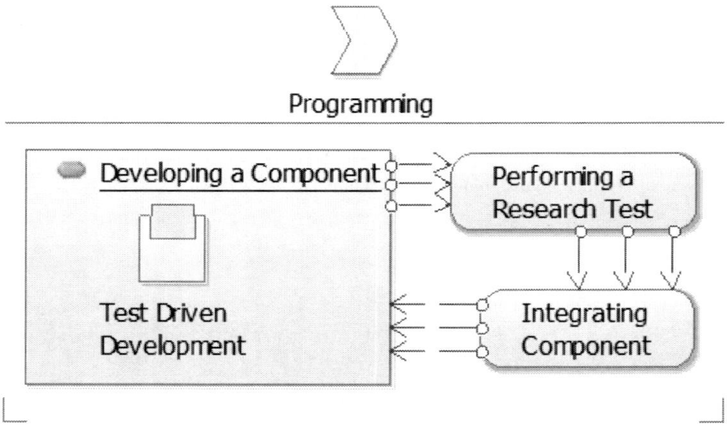

Figure 8d. Programming.

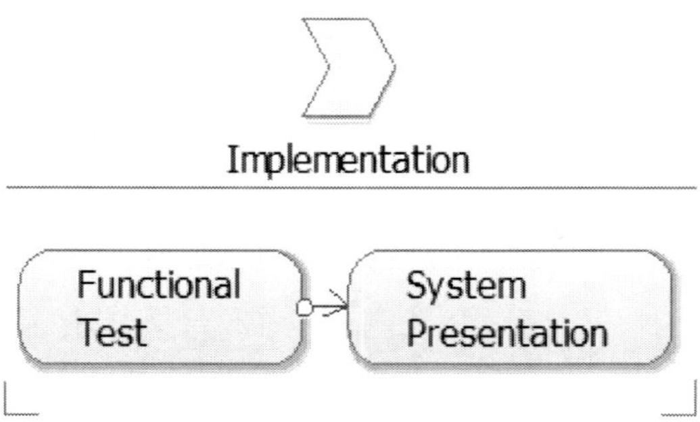

Figure 8e. Implementation.

The overall result is a coherent process that exhibits the characteristics of the project, which represents a practice that promotes changing situations, with processes that disappear and other new processes that appear, involving adaptations and/or improvements.

5.2.2. Guidelines

In the guidelines viewpoint, the pros and cons of methodologies are established. The methodology is not an absolute solution anymore; instead, it becomes part of the problem. The methodology itself becomes a subject of study to be examined, and its strengths and weaknesses are assessed.

This viewpoint permits displaying the strengths associated to the use of RAD in a project sobre. The viewpoint also considers the practices, values and principles that most contributed to the development of the DNA-bank information system (figure 9a).

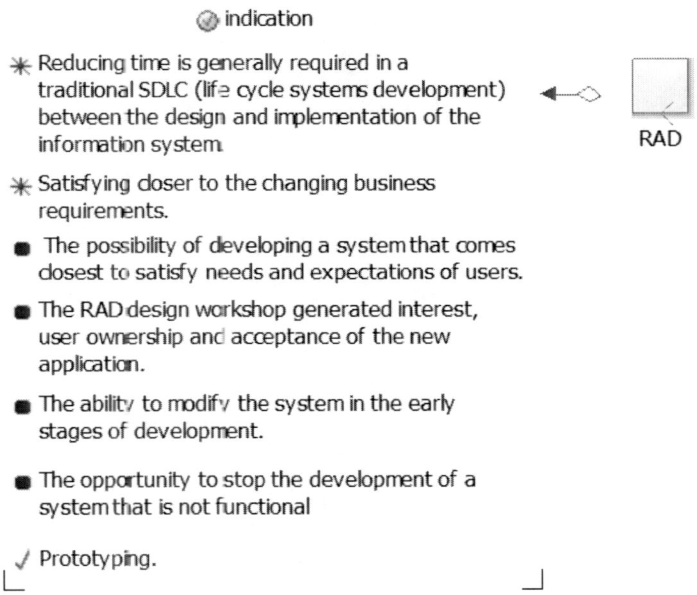

Figure 9a. Pros.

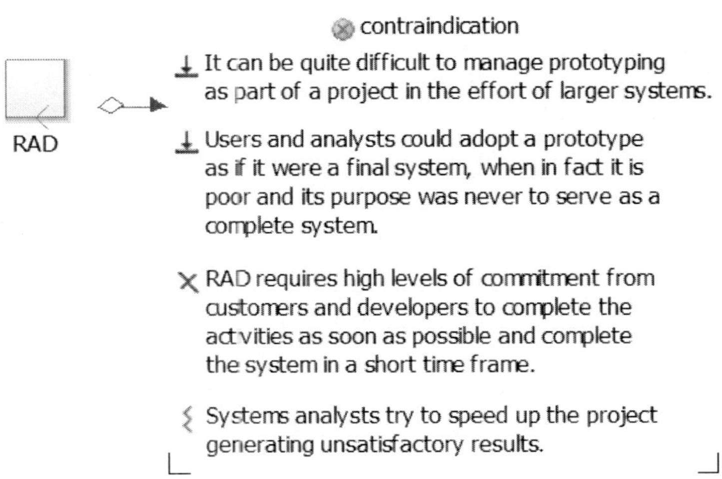

Figure 9b. Cons.

The following are the RAD elements that favored the project the most. These elements are classified into risks, restrictions and limitations.

This viewpoint is oriented towards maintaining permanent assessment of processes and methodologies, providing support for innovation processes (figure 9b).

5.2.3. Artifact Roadmap

In this viewpoint, the most relevant artifacts of the software development process are modeled. The viewpoint focuses on the inputs of the process as well as on the results obtained by adopting an input-output model [41] (figure 10a).

By following the artifact route, it is possible to see what the necessary work is before producing an artifact and the elements that follow after producing such an artifact. This permits monitoring the whole process more easily (figure 10b).

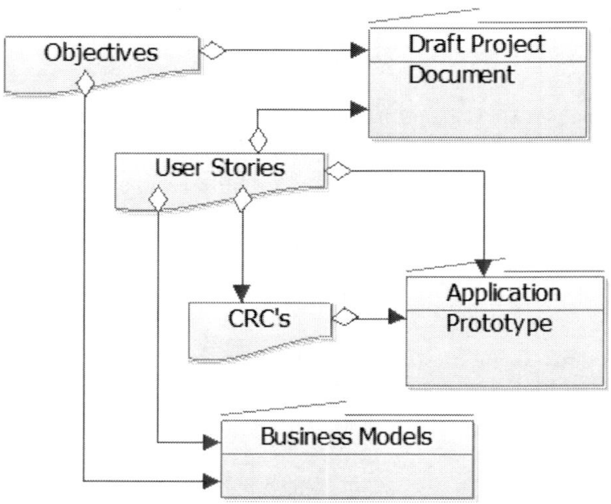

Figure 10a. Inputs.

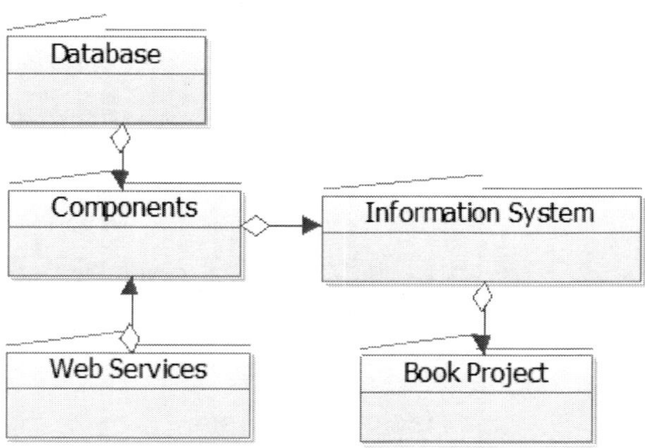

Figure 10b. Results.

In the case of the present project, the first set of artifacts to be developed is easy to identify; namely the objectives and user history records constitute the basis for all artifacts. In order to reach crystallization of the information system; components, web services and a database must be developed, which will be reflected in the final documentation of the project.

5.2.4. Contribution

This viewpoint combines the functional elements of the chosen strategy with the mechanisms, inputs and results obtained from such elements. The overall result is a an input-output model where intermediate results are overlooked in order to emphasize the elements required by the strategy as well as the generated outputs (figure 11).

The initial elements (found at the beginning of the project) can be easily identified: a group of people with certain needs and the intention of working towards meeting those needs; and a group of people capable of providing high quality solutions based on ICTs. The objectives to be attained are also made clear by accurately establishing the intended products.

5.3. Innovation

It is impossible to conceive a software factory with a stiff structure within its production line [42]. Software requirements are ever more complex and demand the use of new processes. Innovation addresses the promotion of software process-and- methodology re-inventions so as to find new alternatives or even new disciplines that allow handling the problems occurring during software development.

Innovation processes focus on the knowledge exchange analysis, namely the recording of problems and the conception of improvement.

5.3.1. Communication

Communication [43, 44, 45] is the basis for knowledge exchange, which is a key aspect in understanding problems and also in designing solutions (figure 12).

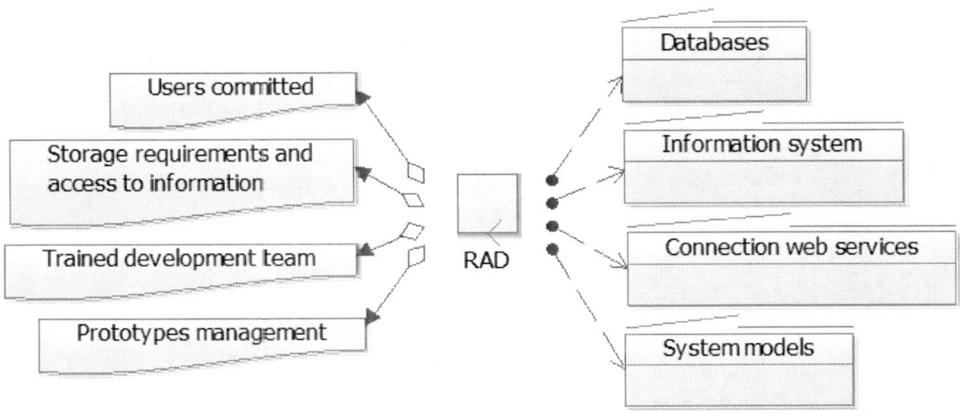

Figure 11. Contribution.

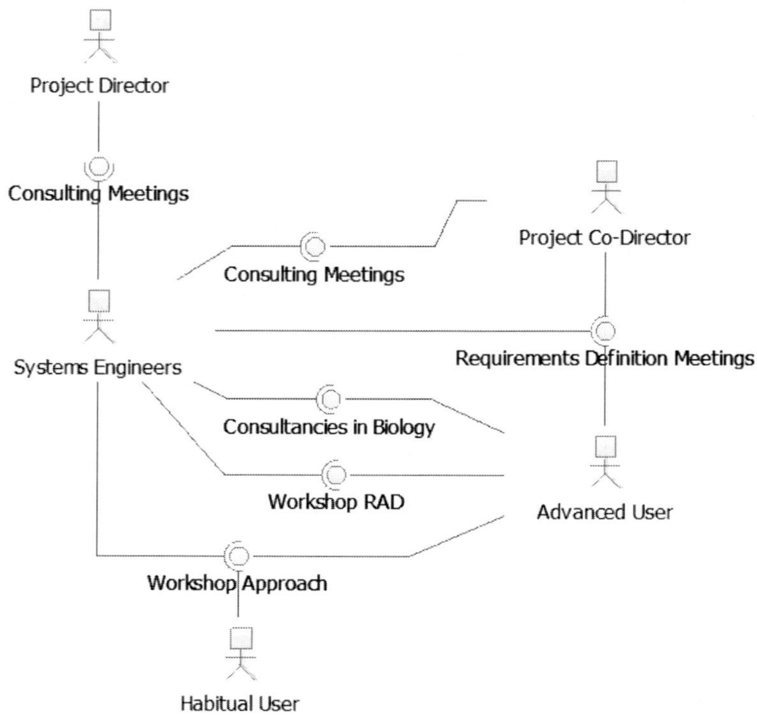

Figure 12. Communication.

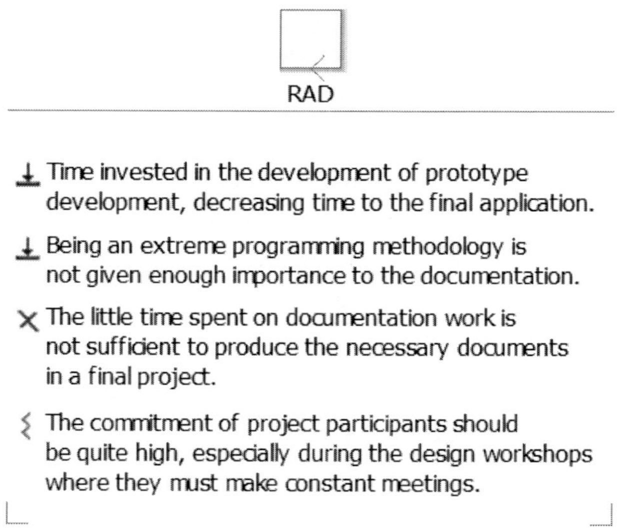

Figure 13. Problems/Solutions.

In this viewpoint, interaction between the project's actors is set up, and represented by an interface. These interfaces serve the purpose of representing a various events ranging from design workshops (where prototype evaluation is conducted) to informal meetings (such as the gatherings where the team was advised on the basic biological terms that allow proper understanding of the whole business).

5.3.2. Problem/Solution Definition

Keeping record of the incidents that arose during the execution of the proposed development process permits establishing the type of deficiencies that should be addressed in future projects, either about the chosen processes or about the applied methodology.

This viewpoint reflects the limitations, restrictions and risks [46] that were faced during the development process of the DNA-bank information system (figure 13).

The main incidents arose when adjusting the working time span intended for document production while the time of users supporting the development was spent. The use of a prototype to accelerate requirement elicitation allowed a quick identification of the system's needs; however, in many occasions the momentum around improving the prototype leads to neglect of documentation tasks.

5.3.3. Improvement

By retrospectively analysing the development process, good practices that facilitated process flow are considered while changes that allow overcoming the recorded problems are proposed. The analysis permits continuous improvement of the development process and even promotes the design of new methodologies.

Figure 14. Improvement.

The improvement viewpoint offers freedom to suggest changes and/or incorporate novelties within the methodologies and development processes. Such new elements are based on the experience gained during the process as well as on the deficiencies spotted in the problem/solution viewpoint (figure 14).

5.3.4. Knowledge

One of the proposals associated to SMPML consists in integrating a knowledge viewpoint where the capabilities of the people participating in the development are highlighted [47]. Knowledge is considered as the main resource for the project, which promotes the design of a strategy that matches the capabilities of participants.

Knowledge is represented in a graphical way and two categories are clearly established, namely soft knowledge and hard knowledge [48, 49]. This includes a clear and concise description of how useful this knowledge really is for the project (figure 15).

The development of the information system for the DNA bank would not have been possible without the knowledge provided by the members of GBRG, who took the role of users and cooperated during the whole process, from the business analysis to the design of various user interfaces.

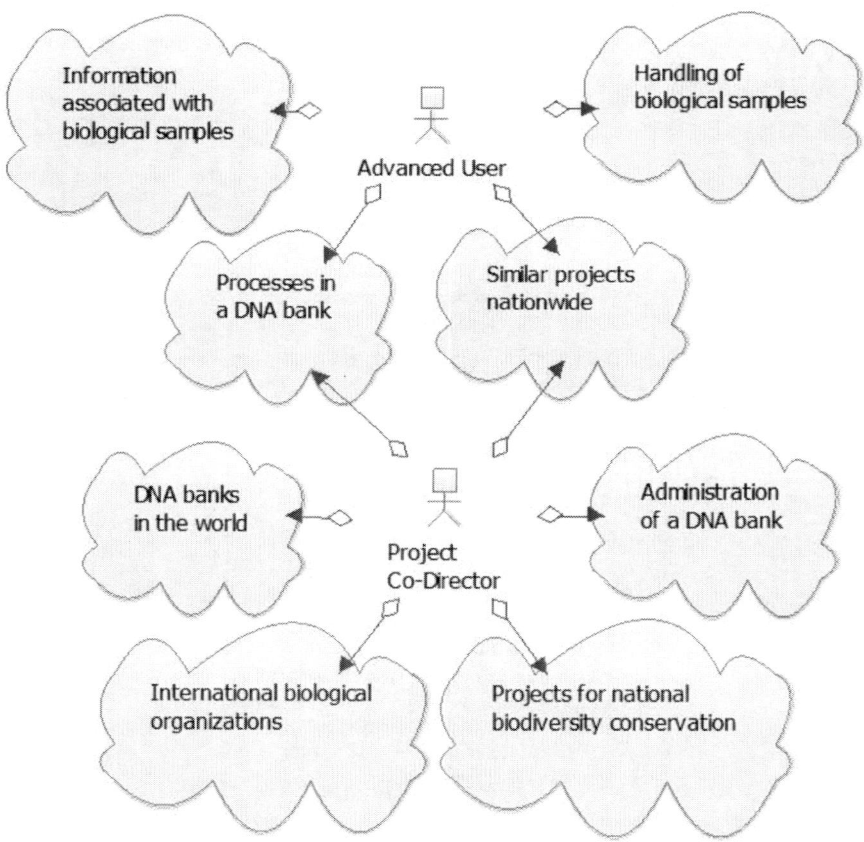

Figure 15. Knowledge.

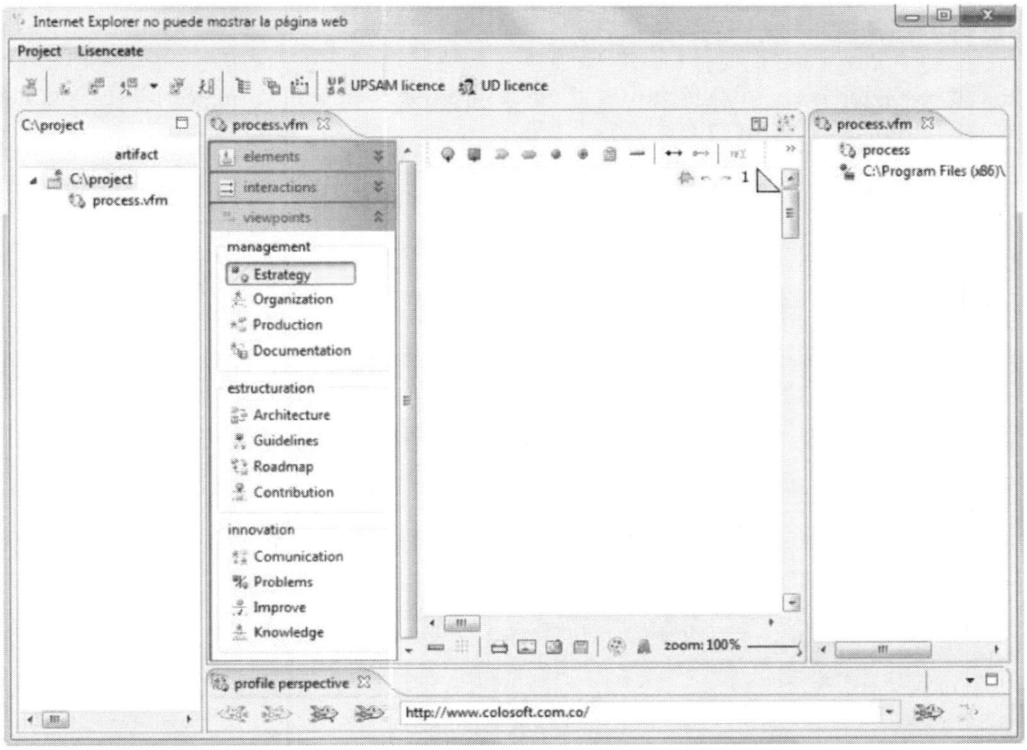

Figure 16. Coloso Platform.

6. A Platform for SMPML

There is a long list of PSEE [50] that emphasize a consistent reflection of software-development-process evolution in the particular model that represents the process. This is achieved by using a PML -Process Modeling Language-, whose purpose is to articulate the activities involved in the process; the proposal associated to SMPML is to offer a wider range of possibilities from a set of perspectives that encourage the use of existing processes or the creation of methodologies/processes that fit into a particular software project. From SMPML it is possible to address new approaches to the understanding of an organization, to product definition that results from knowledge, and also to the search for new solutions to the problem of software creation and evolution. These approaches are modeled in SMPML by using concepts and viewpoints that permit engraving people's intentions on the artifacts that make up the software project. In order to achieve such an integrating concept (as proposed in SMPML) an environment that allows binding Archimate (architecture), UML (design), and Java (programming) views from SMPML has been developed. Such a platform, referred to as Coloso [51] (figure 16), is built under a flexible architecture [52] that permits extending its functionalities and components in a simple way. This platform was used for the development of the project presented herein.

7. Results

The following is a set of the most relevant results observed while using SMPML as guide language throughout a software project.

7.1. Documentation Reduction

The first visible result of applying SMPML to the information-system development process (conducted at the DNA bank) is the integration of the process' most relevant elements with a high-level (yet easy-to-understand) vocabulary.

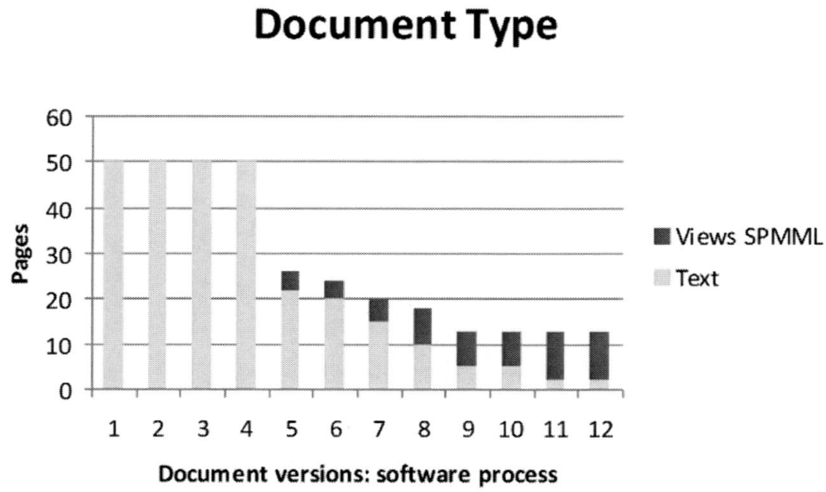

Figure 17a. Inputs.

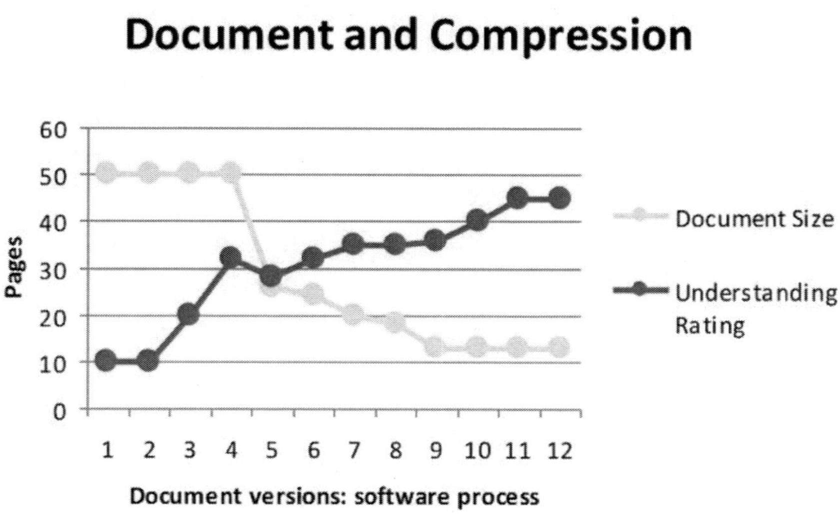

Figure 17b. Document and Compression.

The communication processes between participants involved in a technical way improve when using SMPML, which reduces the amount of documents without affecting the information contained in them. This also favors an easy understanding of the process. It is worth noting that it was possible to reduce a 50- page written document that required four different versions to be written (and contained the written explanation of the objectives, scope and methodology) down to 13 views by using a graphic (clear and expressive) language –SMPML– (figure 17a).

In a technical way within the software process, simple feed- back was agreed with the people involved, using a score that ranged from 0 - 50 and represented an assessment on how understandable the presented documents actually were, the conventions were as follows:

- 0 non-existing
- 10 ambiguous
- 20 vague
- 30 understandable
- 40 clear
- 50 very clear

In order to obtain a Compression Assessment curve (figure 17b), four initial versions were written in a descriptive document (a text) and, from version 5 onwards, the team started to use SMPML models. Although there is a slight decrease in the initial evaluation, once the constituent elements of the language were understood, performance increased rapidly in terms of its indicators. This improvement was also reflected in the perceived motivation of the development team. The Document Size curve shows average results from the assessment with respect to the reduction of the physical size of documents (about the software process). Of course, the reduction in the amount of documentation is considerable after the fourth version, where SMPML was introduced.

7.2. Time Spent in Meetings

The time spent in (working-team) meetings was optimized by using SMPML views for the understanding of the development process, which also empowered decision making with regard to changes and innovation within the process. During the development of the whole project, 12 meetings were held, each lasting 120 minutes, except for the very first meeting, which lasted about 180 minutes. Various topics were discussed during the meetings and the first set of meetings were crucial to define the software process. The amount of time devoted to software- process-related topics decreased from one meeting to the next, not only due to the natural stabilization inherent to project development but also due to the impact of using SMPML as common communication vocabulary (figure 18).

7.3. Integration of Other Languages

One of the most remarkable characteristics of SMPML, is its capabilities to operate as integrator. By modeling software processes, it is possible to encapsulate the different models built throughout the lifecycle as artifacts of the process itself. Within the viewpoints of the project (for the DNA bank), the following models can be found: business model, web-service model, components, databases and prototypes. These models are represented as artifacts of the software process, and are also visible within the viewpoints of Production and Artifact Roadmap (figure 19).

The integration achieved in the SMPML viewpoints permits visualizing the purpose and use of each model, configuring a guide for the execution of processes. The Production viewpoint allows visualizing the people responsible for the construction of these artifacts; whereas the Artifact Roadmap viewpoint permits visualization of the interdependence between artifacts, creating a path between them, which makes the existing traceability between models visible.

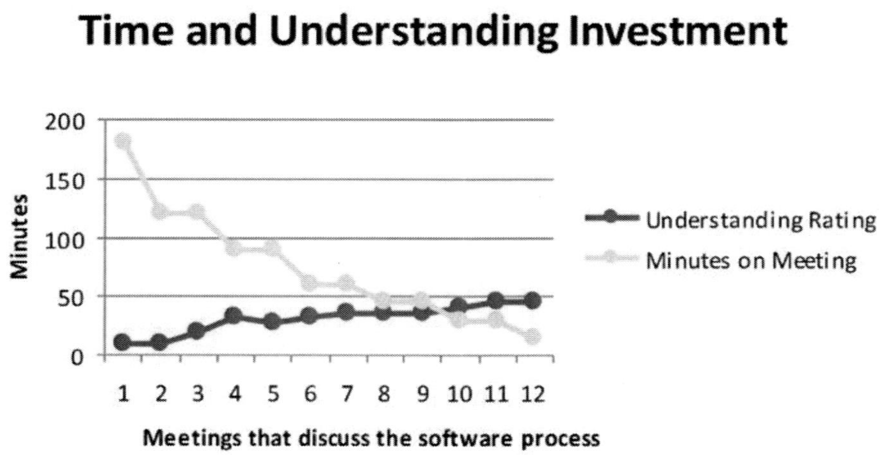

Figure 18. Time and Understanding.

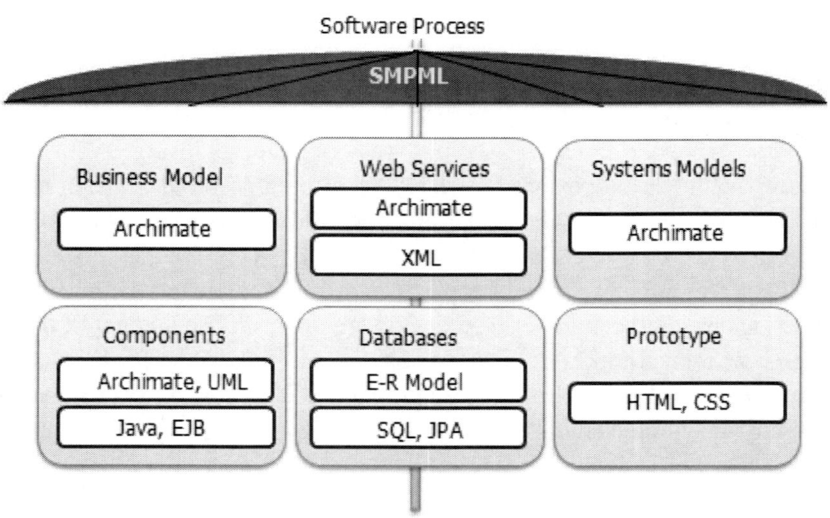

Figure 19. Integration.

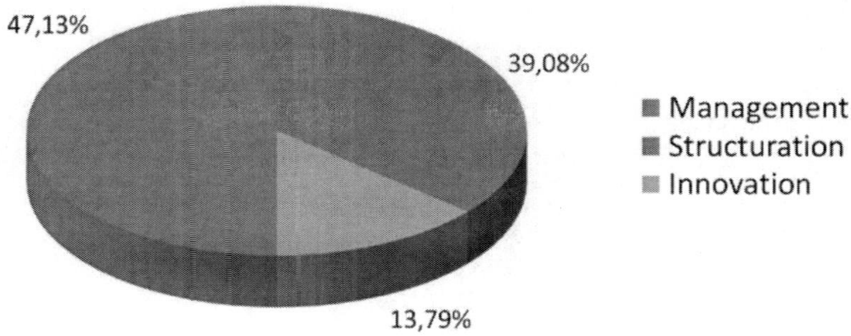

Figure 20. Software Process.

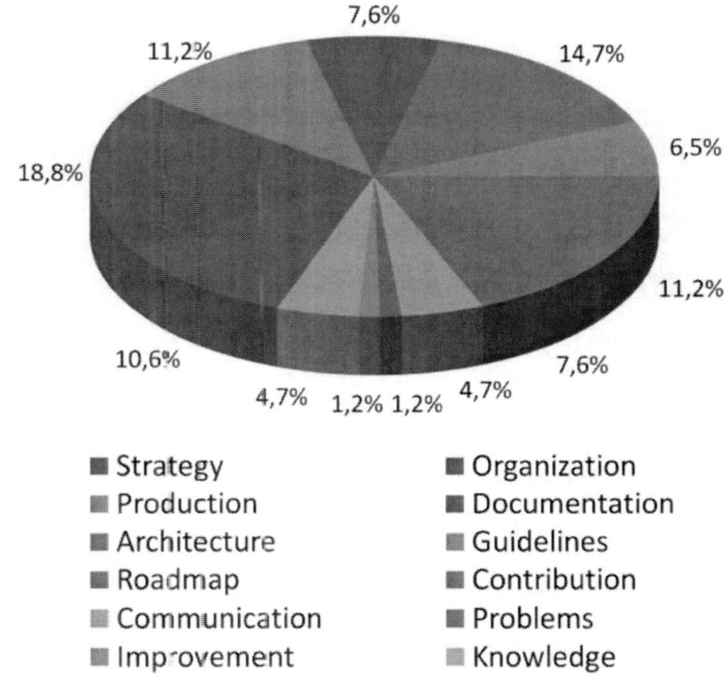

Figure 21. Viewpoints.

7.4. Impact

On the whole, there are 12 viewpoints proposed by SMPML, but not all of them were as relevant during the development of the project. According to the objectives initially set, the use of SMPML during the project focused on the documentation and organization of the development project; hence, the most relevant viewpoints were those associated to the Management and Structuring groups, whereas the Innovation processes were not addressed with enough maturity as these processes were out of the project's scope (figure 20).

The most relevant viewpoints regarding process documentation were those included in the Management category, where the most basic process elements were represented, namely participants, roles, methodology, production throughout the whole process, and the documents supporting the project. These viewpoints gather the most significant and, at the same time, general elements of the process.

In the Structuring category, it was possible to represent the process in more detailed manner, allowing the definition of the most relevant concepts that needed to be considered during development. The Guidelines viewpoint represents the expected benefits when applying the selected methodology and also assesses the deficiencies that pertain to such a decision. The guidelines-viewpoint analysis contributes to defining a better process according to the characteristics of the project, which becomes visible within the Architecture viewpoint. Simultaneously, the Artifact Roadmap and Contribution viewpoints become additional guidance for process flow, defining inputs and outputs at each part of the process and for each artifact.

The viewpoints associated to the Innovation category are oriented towards improving software processes, thus their contribution is envisioned for future executions of the process (figure 21).

The Knowledge and Communication viewpoints highlight new characteristics of the software processes. In this context, knowledge management begins to take special value as one of the most important resources to achieve successful execution of software methodologies and processes.

7.5. Language Expression

As an initial activity when setting up the project, some key terms were identified. These terms gravitate around the conception of the information system for the DNA bank. The purpose was to enquiry about the theoretical implications that lie in these terms as well as creating a term inventory. Subsequently, and as a criterion that indicates the potential scope of SMPML, the team looked for a relationship between the language elements and the key terms already found in such a way that the proposed SMPML elements proved to be enough to span the language that pertained to the problem domain. (figure 22) presents the element proportion (structural, behavioral, cognitive, informational and operational) regarding the SMPML elements employed.

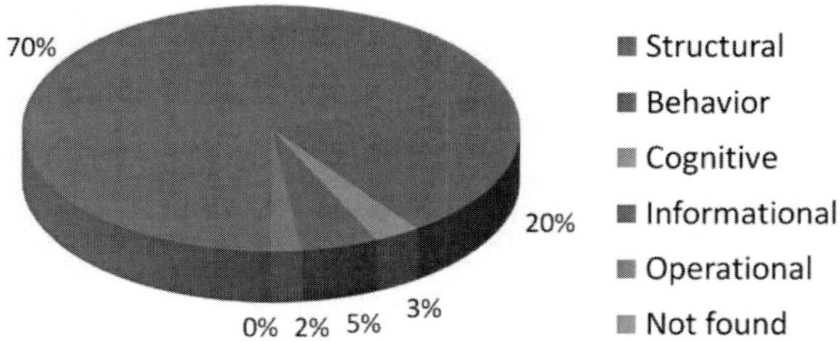

Figure 22. SMPML Elements Employed.

Figure 23. Utilization of SMPML Elements in the Problem.

Figure 22 shows the percentages for specific elements that are used in the solution to the problem, covering the whole range of vocabulary that was found and pertains to the problem domain (figure 23).

8. Future Work

One of the objectives of SMPML is to generalize the whole proposal to industrial processes; hence, short-term work should include the implementation and modeling of a project from an industrial process perspective. This type of work is intended to reduce the gap between the understanding of organizations (from their processes) and the possibilities that arise for the making of their own software systems.

Another project is also suggested to strengthen and open the Coloso platform in order to allow its free use and also to encourage feedback inputs from others. The idea is to achieve a freeware environment together with the possibility of integrating more languages than those proposed so far.

It is important to continue with the growth and maturity of the SMPML proposal, with the help of the academic and industrial communities, as it is utilized in more projects.

Conclusion

SMPML facilitated the modeling and control of the software methodology through which completion of the information system for a DNA bank was achieved. This bank is administered by the biodiversity and genetic resource group at the genetics institute of Universidad Nacional.

Using SMPML to represent the software methodology and process within the project, permitted recording details such as: the methodology's pros-and-cons description, a record of consulted documentation, and even an integration of the other languages (used during the process) as production artifacts.

SMPML permits modeling changes as they occur during the process as well as the implementation of innovations. This makes it easier for engineers to go beyond a simple description; it may even allow engineers to make their own process architecture.

The viewpoints perspective defines a clear framework that favors the analysis and the understanding of methodologies and/or processes.

SMPML facilitated communication among the engineers involved in the software process in such a way that every agreement regarding activities and modifications was made directly over the models smoothly and quickly.

Viewpoints such as Production and Artifact Roadmap offered valuable guidance about the process progress, facilitating control and monitoring tasks, which relates the produced artifacts to the roles in charge (assigned roles), making the interdependence between different artifacts visible.

SMPML is a promising solution to management, structuring and innovation within software methodologies and/or processes; however, the development of a wider range of projects is necessary to receive more feedback about the strengths and weaknesses found on the way.

Acknowledgments

The completion of this research project has been possible thanks to the academic support received from a research group called GICOGE – Grupo Internacional de Investigación en Informática Comunicaciones y Gestióndel Conocimiento. The authors also would like to thank Universidad Distrital de Colombia and Universidad Pontificia de Salamanca de España for their support in terms of research, and also Universidad Nacional de Colombia for their contributions to the project.

References

[1] Booch G., J. Rumbaugh, I. Jacobson, *The Unified Modelling Language Reference*, Addison-Wesley, 2005.

[2] Booch G., J. Rumbaugh, I. Jacobson, *The Unified Modelling Language User Guide*, Addison-Wesley, 2005.

[3] OG, Open group. *Technical standard archimate 2.0 specification*, published by the open group, http://www.archimate.org, accessed 19- february-2012 (2012).

[4] Tucker A., R. Noonan, *Programming Languages Principles and Paradigms*, McGraw Hill, 2002.

[5] OMG, *Software & systems process engineering meta-model specification*, version 2.0, Standard document URL: http://www.omg.org/spec/SPEM/2.0/PDF, oMG Document Number: formal/2008-04-01 (2012).

[6] Benoit X. C., B. C. Alain, Towards a rigorous process modeling with spem, *ICEIS* (2006) 530–533.

[7] Bolaños S., Spml: *Software process modelling language, logic suport register certificate-software*, libro-tomo-partida 13-28-279 (4-marzo-2011).URL http://www.derechodeautor.gov.co/htm/mapa.htm

[8] Prez J. D., Notaciones y lenguajes de procesos. unavisin global, *Tech.rep.,* Research Report submitted to the Department of Computer Languages and Systems of the University of Sevilla (2012).

[9] Derniame J. C., B. A. Kaba, D. Wastell, *Software process: principles, methodology, and technology,* Springer-Verlag Berlin Heidelberg, 1999.

[10] Kleppe A., W. Warmer, J. and Bast, *MDA explained the model driven architecture: practice and promise,* Addison- Wesley, 2003.

[11] Singh Y., M. Sood, Model driven architecture: A perspective, in: Advance Computing Conference, 2009. IACC 2009. *IEEE International*, 2009, pp.1644–1652.

[12] Brooks F., *The Mythical Man-Month*, Addison-Wesley, 1995.

[13] Bolaños S., V. Medina, Software development process based on knowledge management, in: KMO '2010, *Fifth International KMO Conference*, Veszprm Hungary, 2010.

[14] Bolaños S., V. Medina, J. Soto, Metaproceso para el desarrollo de software, in: V Simposio Internacional de Sistemas de Informacion e Ingeniera de Software en la Sociedad del Conocimiento SISOFT, 30 sep, Bogot Colombia, 2010.

[15] Bolaños S., V. Medina, J. Soto, Marco conceptual para el metaproceso de desarrollo de software, in: *the ninth Latin American and Caribbean Conference for Engineering and Technology* LACCEI, 3 Aug, Medell´ın Colombia, 2011.

[16] McChesney I. R., Toward a classification scheme for software process modelling approaches, *Information and Software Technology* 73 (7) (1995) 363–374.

[17] García F., M. Piattini, F. Ruiz, G. Canfora, C. A. Visaggio, Fmesp: Frame- work for the modeling and evaluation of software processes, *Journal of Systems Architecture* 52 (11) (2006) 627–639.

[18] Liu C., D. Umphress, Heavyweight or lightweight: a process selection guide for developing grid software, in: *ACM-SE 46: Proceedings of the 46th Annual Southeast Regional Conference on XX, ACM*, 2008.

[19] Ruparelia N. B., Software development lifecycle models, in: *SIGSOFT Software Engineering Notes*, Vol. 35, ACM, 2010.

[20] Pressman R., *Software Engineering a practitiones's approach*, seventh edition, McGraw Hill, 2009.

[21] Daud N., N. Bakar, H. Rusli, Implementing rapid application development (rad) methodology in developing practical training application system, in*: Information Technology (ITSim), 2010 International Symposium* in, Vol. 3, 2010, pp. 1664–1667.

[22] Thuan N. H., J. Dietz, T. V. Lang, Combining demo models with rad's techniques in the analysis phase of software development process, in: Computing and

Communication Technologies, Research, Innovation, and Vision for the Future (RIVF), *2010 IEEE RIVF International Conference* on, 2010, pp. 1–4.

[23] DeMarco T., T. Lister, Peopleware productive projects and teams, Dorse House Publishing Co, 1999.

[24] Acuña S. T., N. Juristo, Assigning people to roles in software projects, *Software-Practice and Experience* 34 (7) (2004) 675–696.

[25] Zhu H., M. Zhou, P. Seguin, Supporting software development with roles, in: Humans, IEEE Transactions on, *IEEE*, 2006, pp. 1110–1123.

[26] Weinberg G., *The psychology of computer programming*, second edition, Van Nostrand Reinhold Litton Educational Publishing, 1998.

[27] Capretz L. F., F. Ahmed, Making sense of software development and personality types, *IT Professional* 12 (1).

[28] Capretz L. F., F. Ahmed, Why do we need personality diversity in software engineering?, in: SIGSOFT *Software Engineering Notes*, Vol. 35, 2010.

[29] Downey J., N. Power, An artifact-centric framework for software development skills, in: SIGMIS CPR '07: Proceedings of the 2007 ACM SIGMIS CPR conference on Computer personnel research: *The global information technology workforce*, 2007.

[30] Sharp H., H. Robinson, M. Petre, The role of physical artefacts in agile software development: Two complementary perspectives, *Interacting with Computers* 21 (1-2) (2009) 108–116.

[31] vanLoggem B., Placing documentation at the heart of the development cycle, in: *ECCE '11: Proceedings of the 29th Annual European Conference on Cognitive Ergonomics*, ACM, 2011.

[32] Schreck D., V. Dallmeier, T. Zimmermann, How documentation evolves over time, in: IWPSE '07: Ninth international workshop on Principles of software evolution: in conjunction with the 6th ESEC/FSE joint meeting, *ACM*, 2007.

[33] de Boer R. C., H. van Vliet, Writing and reading software documentation: How the development process may affect understanding, in: *CHASE '09: Proceedings of the 2009 ICSE Workshop on Cooperative and Human Aspects on Software Engineering*, 2009.

[34] Parnas D. L., Document driven disciplined development of software, in: Software Engineering Conference, 2005. *Proceedings. 2005 Australian*, 2005, pp. 2–3.

[35] Baldi M., S. Gai, M. L. Jaccheri, P. Lago, Object-oriented software process model design in e3, *Software Process Modelling and Technology*. Research Studies Press, Taunton, England, 1994, pp. 279–290.

[36] Podnar I., B. Mikac, A. Caric, Sdl based approach to software process modeling, in: in R. Conradi, ed., Proceedings of 7th European Work- shop on Software Process Technology (EWSPT 2000), Kaprun, Austria, Springer, 2000, pp. 190–202.

[37] Ribo J. M., X. Franch, Promenade: A pml intended to enhance standarization, expressiveness and modularity in software process modelling, Research report lsi-00-34-r, *Language and systems informatics*, Politechnica of Catalonia (2000).

[38] Choi I., H. Jeong, M. Song, Y. U. Ryu, Ipm-epdl: an xml-based executable process definition language, *Computers in Industry* 56 (1) (2005) 85–10.

[39] Pedreira O., M. Piattini, M. R. Luaces, N. R. Brisaboa, A systematic review of software process tailoring, in: SIGSOFT Software Engineering Notes, Vol. 32, ACM, 2007.

[40] Ferratt T. W., B. Mai, Tailoring software development, in: *SIGMIS-CPR '10:*

Proceedings of the 2010 Special Interest Group on Management Information System's 48th annual conference on Computer personnel research on Computer personnel research, ACM, 2010.

[41] Leontief W., *Input-output economics*, Oxford University Press, 1986.

[42] Clements P., L. *Northrop, Software Product* Lines, Addison-Wesley,2002.

[43] H. H. J., Do you like pina coladas? How improved communication can improve software quality, Software, *IEEE* (2003) 90–92.

[44] Pikkarainen M., J. Haikara, O. Salo, P. Abrahamsson, J. Still, The impact of agile practices on communication in software development, *Empirical Software Engineering* 13 (3) (2008) 303–307.

[45] Abdullah N. N. B., S. Honiden, H. Sharp, B. Nuseibeh, D. Notkin, Communication patterns of agile requirements engineering, in: *Proceedings of the 1st Agile Requirements Engineering Workshop, AREW'11 - In Conjunction with ECOOP'11*, 2011, p. 1.

[46] Agarwal R., J. Prasad, M. Tanniru, J. Lynch, Risks of rapid application development, *Communications of the ACM* 43.

[47] Bolaños S., V. Medina, R. Gonzalez, Emerging concepts between software engineering and knowledge management, *Advances in Intelligent Systems and Computing*, publicado por Springer (2012) 13–21.

[48] Nonaka I., A dynamic theory of organizational knowledge creation, *Organization Science* (1994) 14–37.

[49] Nonaka I., H. Takeuchi, *The Knowledge-Creating Company*, Oxford University Press, 1995.

[50] Zamli K. Z., Process modeling languages: A literature review, *Malaysian Journal of Computer Science* (2001) 26–37.

[51] Bolaños S., R. Crespo, O. Sanjuan Martinez, J. Espada, V. Medina Garcia, Coloso: A development environment centered process and intent, in: Information Systems and Technologies (CISTI), 2012 7th Iberian Conference on, *IEEE Conference Publications*, 2012, pp. 1–6.

[52] Bolaños Castro S., R. Gonzalez Crespo, A software architecture proposal artistic engineering environment -aee-, in: Engineering Applications (WEA), 2012 Workshop on, *IEEE Conference Publications*, 2012, pp. 1–6.

In: Horizons in Computer Science Research. Volume 9
Editor: Thomas S. Clary
ISBN: 978-1-63321-522-1

Chapter 8

DESIGN OF LURIA MEMORY TEST FOR OLDER ADULTS ON MOBILE DEVICES

Amilcar Meneses Viveros[1], Erika Hernández Rubio[2] and J. A. Hijar Miranda[2]
[1]Departamento de Computación, CINVESTAV-IPN., México, D.F.
[2]Instituto Politécnico Nacional, SEPI-ESCOM., México, D.F.

Abstract

Due to increasing life expectancy of the population, it is necessary to have tools that help provide various services to the elderly. Some of these tools are related to health services. In particular, in the area of mental health, specialists use various memory tests, such as Luria, to assess the degree of mental impairment or to prevent it. The use of mobile technology could be of great help to both the specialists and the elderly in the application of Luria tests. However, such solutions involve many details in the implementation for the system to be usable and functional, because older adults may have visual, hearing or motor impairments, among others. Furthermore, the application of some tests requires contextual plasticity, because the memory depends on the user experience, so that the elements of the tests should be tailored to each user use.

1. Introduction

In the last decades of the twentieth century the population of many countries increased their average life expectancy and the birth rate decreased. The aging process is more dynamic in developed countries. This is reflected in the incremental percentage of elderly population [1]. According to United Nations Population Fund (UNFPA), in 2012 the percentage of the world population with more than 60 years old was 11.5 percent, while in the more developed regions reaches 22.6 percent. It is projected that by 2050 the elderly population will be 21.2 percent of the world population [1][2].

In Mexico, for example, adults over 60 years old have with mental problems or mental deterioration are 2.5 percent. Of these, 31% is due to the aging process and 41% per disease [2][3][4][5]. The group of older adults has a higher social risk resulting from the advancement of age the most propensity to present physical or mental limitations. And that is accentuated by the deficiencies that exist in the coverage and quality in social security and health care [3] [4]. Therefore it is important to prevent memory deterioration through treatment by mental health specialists. In addition to developing new technologies that help facilitate treatment and to allow greater coverage of some health services [5].

Currently, doctors and mental health specialists, applied to patients both physically different, listening exercises, and understanding, among others. These exercises can reduce memory loss or determine the level of impairment of cortical functions of individuals [6] [7] [8] [9]. Luria tests are designed for this purpose and are considered neuropsychological research methods for the patient. The Luria memory tests are oriented to the study of motor, visual, auditory features, language and writing, reading, arithmetic and the memory processes and intellectual. The aim of this study of these functions is to find out the fundamental defects caused by local lesions in the brain. This grant allows a diagnosis of the syndrome and that is to determine the deterioration level of psychic functions. The general approach to testing the proposed A. R. Luria in his book Higher cortical functions in man [7]. Luria tests can be applied to older adults to determine the degree of memory deterioration.

The application efficiency of Luria memory tests decreases in older adults owing to biological factors that are pertaining to the human body such as genre, age, and race [5][6]. For example, inability or difficulty moving to the place of performance of testing, or difficulty in solving the test due to visual deterioration or motor skills. Another problem that has been detected is the coverage to meet the demand for health services. Few health centers and specialists are capable of addressing mental deterioration. Each specialist can have a significant number of patients who must apply the tests, which increases the complexity of monitoring patients. In particular, specialists apply the tests and take control and monitoring traditional and face shape (pencil, paper and paper files). One solution is to provide a software tool to assist in this process and have the flexibility to take advantage of mobile technologies.

The use of some mobile devices, especially those with touch screen at least with 7 inches size, such as tablets and some smartphone, can be considered to develop applications for Luria memory test applied to older adults. In [10], an analysis of the Luria memory tests is presented to applications implemented as computer systems and mobile computing. In that work, a feasibility analysis of the Luria memory tests is presented for inclusion in applications that can run on desktops and mobile devices [10]. This analysis reveals that 90% of memory tests may be conducted as applications on mobile devices taking advantage of their different mechanisms and means of interaction (touch screen, use of sensors, microphones and cameras, among others). These solutions enable the specialist to define the sequence of exercises to be performed in the first sessions of patient assessment. And later, the patient can perform exercises from a mobile device, without the presence of specialists. The patient can exercise anytime, anywhere. In addition, if the software sends the results of the assessments to the specialist, then the monitoring of patients can be done remotely. Such solutions help users (patients and specialist) can simplify their time, resulting in better quality of services and better quality of life for older adults.

Such solutions involve applications on mobile devices for applying Luria tests are completely intuitive for users. For this reason, it is necessary that the graphical user interface and means interactions are intended for older adults. In addition, we have two sets of design problems: 1) the adult interaction with system functionality. 2) the plasticity of the system with the user experience. The user interaction with the system functionality refers to its main functions are intuitive (open session, select and load Luria memory tests, to name a few), that the information is appropriate to display any visual limitations that may have the user and the means of interaction can change depending on the capabilities of the elderly.

The plasticity of the system depending on the user experience makes reference to consider the memory of individuals depends on emotional factors or life experiences. For example, it found that for tests where the user must memorize a set of words, individuals have better retention of words related to their experience of life [8]. For this reason the system is responsible for adapting the test to user context.

To create systems that can be used by older adults should be considered latent human factors in the elderly, such as perception, cognition and movement control [11][12]. There are some design guidelines aimed at older adults seeking better usability of devices and applications.

In this work, we discuss the different Luria memory tests and alternatives for application in mobile devices. It begins with a review of the different Luria memory tests and alternatives for application in mobile devices. Subsequently, we present the software design strategy that we use for applications on mobile devices. It starts with developing storyboards for an overview of the system state changes and determine the features and appropriate means of interaction [18][19]. After displays for mayor adults are designed using design patterns and guidelines for applications on mobile devices [11][12][13][14][15][16][17][19]. And also special cases are discussed when the system should automatically adapt their interaction means to user limitations and context of the users [11][12][18].

2. Luria Tests

The Soviet neurologist Alexander Romanovich Luria, trend psychoneurology studied higher cortical functions in man and its relation to the brain mechanisms. He considered the functional systems to be responsible of human behavior such complex systems, plastic, capable of self-regulation resulting from the interaction of a set of areas of the brain. The social environment is a determining factor in these functional systems.

Luria's ideas have achieved wide circulation in our days, mainly by the development of a test, called Luria-Christensen Neuropsychological Test. This test was developed by his disciple, A. Christensen, and widely used in Neurology and Neuropsychology for the diagnosis of various brain functions.

The test is a battery of neuropsychological evaluation that studies, using different exercises five neuropsychological domains or higher-level functions: *Attention, language, movement and action, perception, memory and learning*. The main objective of this test is to analyze and understand the structure of psychic phenomena, to help diagnose abnormalities of the central nervous system as well as the rehabilitation of higher cortical functions. In this paper we will focus on the testing of memory and learning functions.

2.1. Tests for Memory Processes

There are three key parts of research on memory processes: *A study of the direct fixation of footprint, analysis of the processes of fixing repetition and remembrance instrumentalized.* Each of these parts has its own set of tests.

i) Direct-fixation Trace

The purpose of these tests is to establish to what extent the patient is able to maintain direct traces left by the stimuli. Also show whether the patient alterations in the volume and strength of the conservation of the tracks are present, and if symptoms conservation disorders are manifested in a spatial area, such as the visual trace, hearing trace, or tactile trace.

Afterimages. In this test, the patient is shown 3 or 4 bright red geomeric figures on a homogeneous background (gray or white) for 15 or 20 seconds each one; the patient continues to see the imprint of the figure, which appears briefly after removing. Moreover, generally, the print is stained an additional color (cyan in this case). The image displayed in a fixed place in the homogeneous background is called posimagen negative. In this way, it differs from the positive posimagen. Usually, retains a fairly accurate contour that can blur gradually. The image remains some time; then disappears gradually and sometimes recurs once or twice. In healthy people, the visual posimagen remains 15 to 30 seconds and then loses its precision and disappears. The total time of the afterimage and fluctuations depend on individual characteristics of the person, as well as the brilliance of the exciter and the extension of its attachment.

Direct retention of visual trace. In this test, the person presents three or four visual images from 5 to 10 seconds. The figures are simple geometric figures. When the time expires, the figures are removed and the patient should draw the figures even remember.

Direct retention of hearing trace. The user is presented with various rhythmic tones to be played. In order to study the kinesthetic memory, the patient will show several hand positions that should imitate to play.

Direct retention of verbal trace. The study of the stability of retention is performed verbal dictating traces (or showing in writing) a range of 3 to 4 words or numeric digits to be repeated immediately.

This test is presented in three successive stages. In the first stage it is read to the patient, or is presented visually, a series of three, then four and finally five words to listen and repeat immediately. In the second step, a pause of 5 to 10 seconds between reading and the reproduction is made, and the subsequent reproduction of the series to set the degree of stability that traces is retained. In the third stage, the repetition of the series of words separated from his presentation with a break of 10 to 15 seconds, in this pause will be distracting the patient with a conversation. The purpose of this exercise is to determine the ease with which the reproduction of traces can be inhibited with external excitatory. At all stages, the patient has to reproduce the words in the same order that they were submitted.

To determine the ease with which the patient can go from playing a series of words to the reproduction of another, the following is done: After performing the first experiment, the patient is asked to repeat the same set of words but presented in a different order. For example, after the series: "home-forest-cat-table", the patient is presented with the series "table-forest-cat-house". The phenomena of pathological inertia may preclude the patient to move to the new series and instead, continue repeating the previous series, in the same order in which it was shown on that occasion.

Reproduction of the contents of stories. In this test, the patient will read any simple story, and asked him to narrate. Then the same is done with a second story (which includes elements of the first story). The experimenter sets the completeness of the patient conveys the content of each of the stories, and see if the patient does not intertwined with them additional partnerships, i.e., if no mixing elements of the first and second, or contamination of both appears stories. After the patient has narrated the contents of the second story, the patient is asked to remember the first again. Failure to do so indicates a high feedback inhibition.

ii) Retention Process Testing

Retention processes and their alteration in cases of pathological conditions of the brain also constitute one of the best studied sections of modern general psychology.

Words learning. In this test, the patient is shown several words or numerical figures, unrelated, and the number of items exceeds the number that you can remember. Usually the series consists of 10 to 12 words, or 8 to 10 numeric digits. The patient is asked to remember and repeat the series in any order. After recording the number of retained items, the patient is presented with a series of new and re-recorded the results. This process is repeated 8 to 10 times and the data obtained are shown in the form of "memory curve".

iii) Tests for logical or mediated memorization

Study of memory and intellectual processes. Its purpose is to characterize the active auxiliary means, which serve to memorize of material comprised for logical activity.

Mediate memory. The patient is asked to remember a series of 12 to 15 words, using appropriate plates, which serve as a means of support to memorize. The plates used, must not directly represent the contents of the word. The plates are selected so that the patient is forced to establish some relationship between the word sense and the plate. A typical example of this process can be memorizing the word "rain" in the plate "umbrella" or the word "thief" in the plate "bolt".

The mediate memory test can be carried out in two variants. In the first variant, the patient is shown a series of words, each of which corresponds to a sheet which should serve to remind. In the second, standing 15 to 20 sheets against the person, and must choose the one that best serves to remember the word given. Once the patient has chosen to associate a picture to a word, you should ask the reason why he chose that image, this relationship should be considered and the partnership must be remembered by the patient.

Pictogram. It is a variant of the mediate recall test. The patient is proposed remember several words or expressions, then the patient is asked to draw each time a sign or figure that can be used to remember the word. Must use words or expressions that cannot be represented directly, for example "a deaf old woman" or "a hungry child". After the series finished words are presented to the patient drawings made by him, and should reproduce the necessary words.

3. Older Adults Centered Design

The design of user interfaces is an essential part of software development, which involves concepts such as usability, different forms of interaction, the context of use, and flexibility, among other. On the one hand, the design process must involve the requirements of the final product that seeks to develop. In another hand, the design should consider the characteristics of the end users who will use the product. For this reason, we consider the use of processes to help better designs, for example the design focused on the user. The user-centered design is to use methods that focus on creating designs from the perspective of end users, involving them in the design stages. Universal design is a variant of UCD. The main goal is that universal design products are designed to be flexible enough to be usable for people with or without limitations. A good universal design benefits to anyone and should benefit even more people with disabilities. This idea can be applied when designing products for seniors.

Older adults have different physical impairments. These impairments include reduction of different capacities such as visual, hearing, motor and cognitive. In the literature, it has been found that there is research centered design seniors and have been given a set of design recommendations. These recommendations are grouped for each of the problems identified: Visual, hearing, haptic and cognitive.

Design Recommendations for Visual Problems

Older adults have a gradual impairment of vision, because parts of the eye suffer deformities like lens or cornea. This affects mainly in the use of mobile devices because screens, although no high-resolution, its size is between 5 and 9 inches mainly. Therefore, for text presentation the following recommendations are made:

- *Font size:* recommended 12 points and x-height.
- *Font style*: It is recommended to use Sans Serif fonts like Arial or Times New Roman.
- *Use of capital letters:* Text in uppercase attract much attention and is recommended for major labels.
- *Contrast:* Texts with a heterogeneous color with respect to the background color where present. For example white text on a black background or vice versa.
- Reduce scrolling, because it is more difficult to process information.

Older adults vary greatly in their perceptual abilities, so it is advisable to use multimodal interfaces to seek information. This combined with voice haptics or some other form of interaction.

Design Recommendations for Hearing

The ear suffers gradual deterioration. The user loses ability to hear certain frequencies voice. Recommendations for incorporating auditory interfaces are:

- *Volume Control*: It is important to provide the user with directions on how to adjust the volume levels.
- Frequencies of 4000 Hz or higher.
- *Provide redundant information*: For example, in the case of using caution signs (warnings), use another sensory channel, as the vibration of a device or a light. Also consider at this point, the auditory and visual presentation of a message.
- Minimize background noise or reverberation: The objective is to increase the degree of attention. This can be achieved, staying in rooms with sound-absorbing materials, and maximizing the use of headphones.

For interfaces with reporting by voice, the recommendations are

- *Pauses appropriate grammatical elements*: As after phrases or end of a sentence.
- *Adapting the voices according to the situation*: Using only natural voice timbre. Use male voices to announce information. And using female voices, a little below average in decibels, to attract attention. Avoid synthetic voice messages.

Design Recommendations for Haptic Problems

Haptic interfaces refer to any interface other than visual or hearing. This includes the set of gestures on mobile devices. However, older adults may have diseases like arthritis that prevent gestures occur properly. For this type of interfaces, the main recommendation is:

- Allow sufficient time for entries.

Design Recommendation for Cognitive Problems

Cognitive problems are caused by injury or gradual deterioration in short-term memory and working memory mainly. This affects attention span, spatial cognition is reflected in the navigation application. The design recommendations for these problems are:

- Only provide relevant information.
- Provide a clear indication of where the user is in an information space, as the structure of a menu.
- Do not saturate the capabilities of user attention. Avoid paying too much information in different ways at the same time.
- Use interface techniques that reduce the use of working memory.
- Designing the interface using common metaphors such as tabs or folders.
- Provide multiple ways to access information.
- Use words to indicate some action is better than using icons.

4. Design of Luria Memory Test

Luria tests are sets of exercises that are associated with one of the three major categories: A study of the direct fixation of trace, analysis of the processes of fixing repetition and remembrance instrumentalized. In this section we have included a test of each category. For direct fixation traces was selected direct retention of visual trace test. For retention process was selected learning word test. And, finally, for mediated memorization was selected de pictogram test.

For the design of interfaces memory tests we have relied on the use of the storyboard. This allows us some independence on the specific design patterns to each platform. The Storyboard's main characteristics present the design of the user interface and context [21]. This lets us know the type of information is presented as the user interacts with the application.

4.1. Direct Retention of Visual Trace

For testing visual traces, it is possible to present 3 or 4 random geometric figures (square, circle, pentagon, etc) bright red on the mobile device display, indicating that remain for 15 to 20 seconds and must be indicated in the instructions that the patient should remain viewing this pictures during this time. The application solicits to the patient to draw the figures that was showed before. As mediate memory test, in this test its needed a haptic interface that can be implemented with the touchscreen technology. The draws made by the patient must be saved in a lightweight format such as JPEG and send to the database.

Figure 1 shows the storyboard of this test. It starts with a screen where information is given to the user to perform the test and a button to start. You may notice that the button to start the test is labeled with uppercase text. The second screen shows a sample of how the image sequences will be. The third screen shows the capture screen where the user draw the figures even remember. The last screen allows the user to indicate that the test is over.

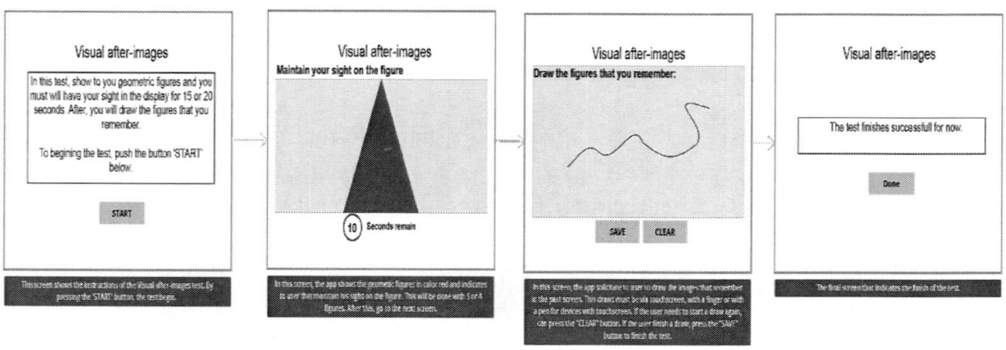

Figure 1. Storyboard of direct retention of visual footprint test.

4.2. Words Learning

Are presented to the person many words or numbers, not linked to each and whose number exceeds the amount that can remember. Usually the series consist of 10 to 12 words of 8 to 10 numbers. The patient is asked to recall and repeat the series in any order. After recording the number of items retained, presents to the patient again the series and re-records the results. This process is repeated 8 to 10 times. After complete all repetitions and spent 50 to 60 minutes, the specialist must ask to the patient the series of words without mentioning it to the patient again. Then the test has two phases: in the first series of words or numbers are presented and the patient should repeat. In second phase, going 50 or 60 minutes, the patient to indicate the words or numbers to remember is requested.

The application must download the series of words in a database containing common series for this test. Must have a variety of these series, so that no repetition between tests. Figure 2 shows the storyboard of the first phase of the test. Four types of test interfaces with the user are presented in storyboard. These four types of interfaces are given by the combinations of the two types of presentation of test information (written or audio) and the two ways in which the user provides the interaction with the test (written or spoken). The test shows that words can be read to the patient or in the form of text. In this analysis we consider two cases:

1. For the case in which the words are presented in the form of text, must take the general considerations of a text in this analysis. The words are displayed on screen with an appearance time for the user to have a chance to read the word and hold it. In this analysis it is proposed that the time of occurrence for word is 5 to 10 seconds.
2. For the case in which the words are presented in the form of audio, playback of sound files is required in the mobile devices. This represents a higher data download and use more features. This form is recommended for this test, because it's similar to testing experience between the patient and the specialist.

Figure 3 shows the storyboard of the second phase of the test. At this stage there is no reporting only the user is asked to indicate the elements of the list even remember. The input of the application can be via voice or keyboard.

These combinations of interaction allow the test to be adaptable to the conditions of the elderly. For example, if the elderly have eyestrain, then you can choose to submit the list through audio. If the user has mobility problems such as arthritis, and can not write, then you can repeat the list via voice.

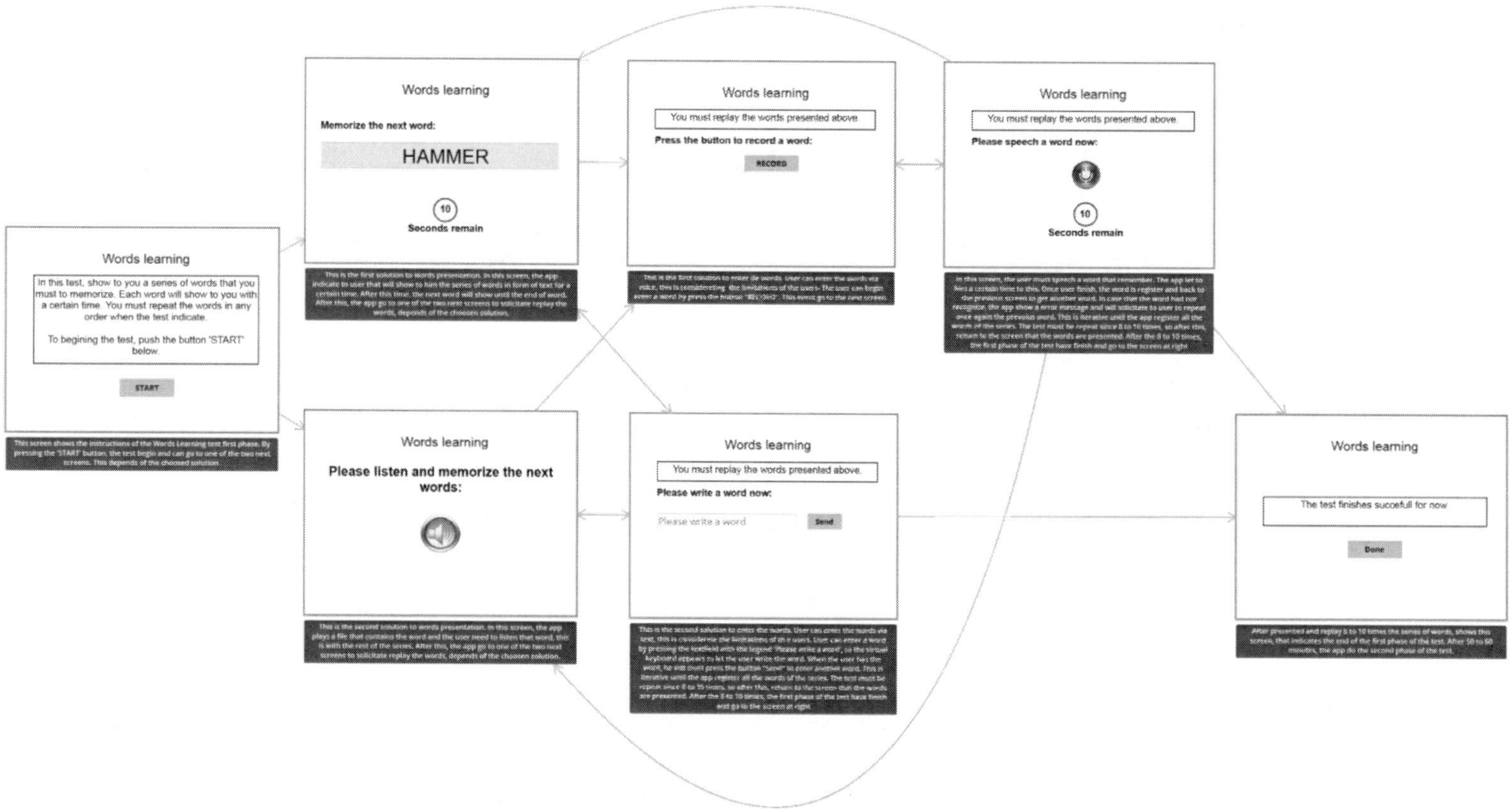

Figure 2. Storyboard of phase one of word learning test.

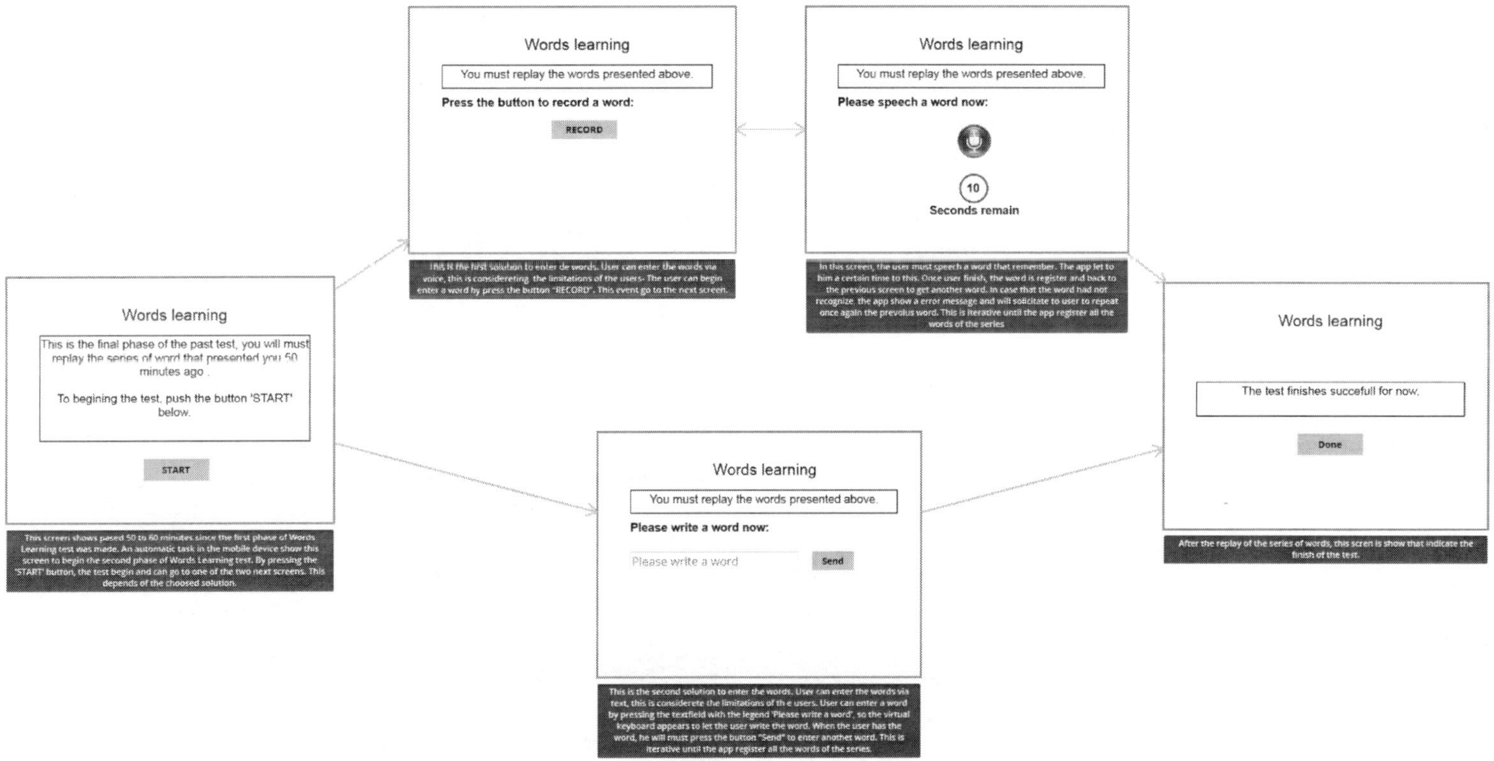

Figure 3. Storyboard of phase two of word learning test.

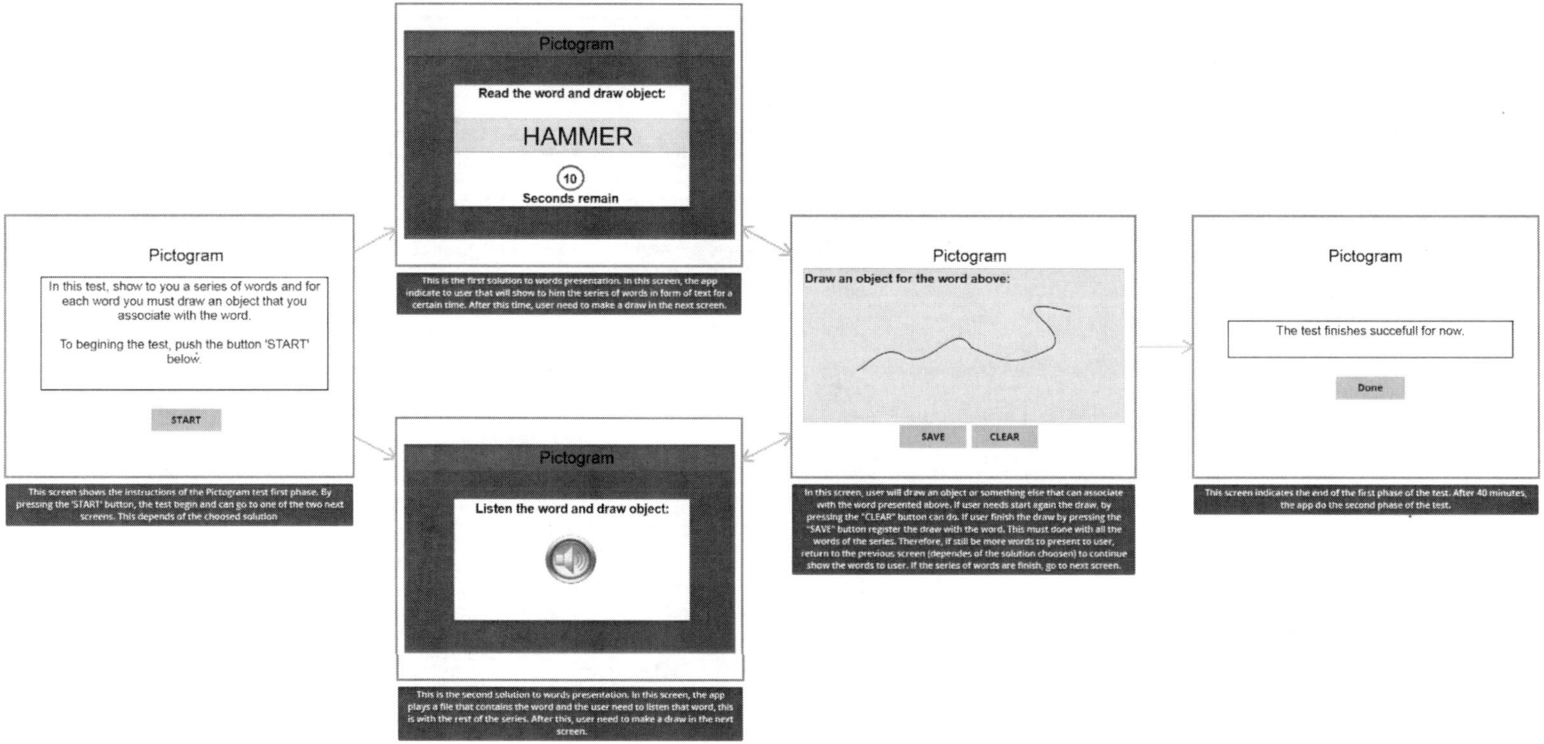

Figure 4. Storyboard of phase one of pictogram test.

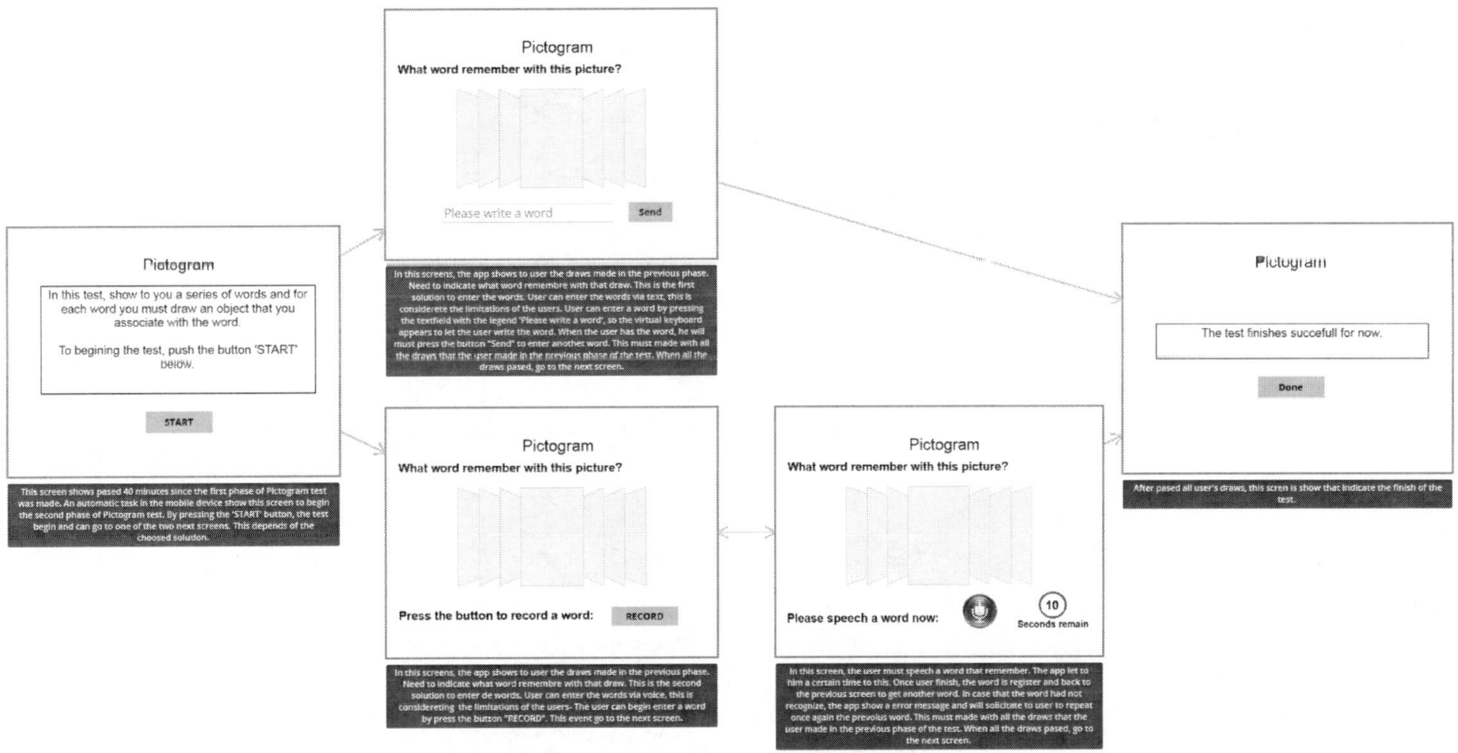

Figure 5. Storyboard of phase two of pictogram test.

4.3. Pictogram

This test is a variant of the mediate memory test. The test consists of presenting to the patient a series of 12 to 15 words. For each word the patient should draw any sign or figure that can be used to remember the word.

To present the words in this test, we can use the analysis in the words learning test. For each word, the application requests the patient draw a figure that associates with the current word. For this a haptic interface is needed. The touch- screen technology allows the user to do actions with the fingers. In this case the action is draw. The draws made by the patient must be saved in a lightweight format such as JPEG. These images will be shown to the patient after 40 minutes just like the words reproduction in the mediate memory test. This test also consists of two phases: the words the user must draw after seeing or hearing the word was presented in the first phase. In the second phase, the user is presented with the figure drew, and then the user must indicate the word associated with the picture.

5. Conclusion

Designs for mobile devices Luria three tests are taken. Each test is representative of the testing for memory cortical functions. The use of storyboards is presented as a suitable tool for such systems because no pattern design avoids any specific mobile platform such as Android or iOS. Storyboards can also follow the rules of the designs focused on seniors and verify the context of use as they interact with the system.

Tests must adapt their mechanisms of interaction with the physical limitations of older adults. Fortunately, for some memory tests no differences in Luria introduce the user to remember the elements of written or spoken form. But for other tests this is not necessarily true. A solution that could help manage the interaction problems of older adults with mobile applications, would have equivalences between different mechanisms of interaction. For example, changing a haptic interface by an hearing interface. Or search equivalent gestures that are viable for different users.

The system must be able to adapt to user capabilities. So the system must be able to meet these constraints through an information system or some inference can be made about a patient's knowledge base. Another feature that the system must know is the patient's life experience to associate sets of words or images on tests. These specifications can be the specialist in the first interview. Therefore, it becomes necessary to have a data model for the different tests of Luria layers and is information related to patients and specialist.

References

[1] Organización de las Naciones Unidas (ONU). (2013). *Perspectivas Mundiales Demográficas: Revisión 2012*. Departamento de Asuntos Económicos y Sociales, División de Población.

[2] ConsejoNacional de Población. (2013). *Proyecciones de la Población en México 2010-2050.* México, CONAPO.

[3] Instituto Nacional de Estadística y Geografía (INEGI). (Octubre 2013). *Estadísticas a propósito del día internacional de las personsas de edad,* Datos Nacionales. México, INEGI.

[4] Instituto Nacional de Estadística y Geografía (INEGI). (2011). Censo de *Población y Vivienda* 2010. Cuestionario ampliado. Base de datos. México, INEGI.

[5] Mario Ulises Pérez Zepeda. (2010). *Deterioro Congnoscitivo*; Instituto de Geriatría. México D.F.

[6] Papalia, D., Wendkos, S. &Feldman, R. D. (2003). *Human Development*; McGraw Hill 9. Ed. New York.

[7] Alexandr R. Luria (1995). *Higher cortical functions in man*; Springer, U.S.A.

[8] Esperanza Bausela Herreras. (2010). *Curva de aprendizaje de Luria en personas con daño cerebral*; *Enseñanaza e Investigación en Psicología*, vol 15, num 1, enero0abril, 147-158, Consejo para la Enseñanaza e Investigación en Psicología, México

[9] Feggy Ostrosky-Solís, Alfredo Ardila & Mónica Rosselli. (1999).*NEUROPSI: A brief neuropsychological test battery in Spanish with norms by age and educational level*; *Journal of the International Neuropsychological Society*, vol. 5, 413433, Cambridge University USA.

[10] Hijar Miranda, J. A., Erika Hernández Rubio & Amilcar Meneses Viveros. (2014). *Analysis of Luria memory test for development on mobile applications*, to be published in proceedings of HCI International, (LNCS proceedings) Springer.

[11] Richard Pak & Anne McLaughlin. (2011). *Designing Displays for Older Adults*; CRC Press, United States.

[12] Arthur D. Fisk, Wendy A. Rogers, Neil Charness, Sara J. Czaja & Joseph Sharit. (2009). Designing for older adults, CRC Press, United States.

[13] Steve Love. (2005). *Understanding Mobile Human-Computer Interaction*; Elsevier.

[14] Theresa Neil. (2012). *Mobile Design Pattern Gallery*, O'Reilly.

[15] Julie A. Jacko. (2012). *Human-Computer Interaction Handbook: Fundamentals, Evolving Technologies, and Emerging Applications*, Third Edition (Human Factors and Ergonomics), CRC Press, Taylor & Francis Group.

[16] Valentino Lee, Heather Schneider& Robbie Schell. (2004). *Mobile Applications: Architecture, Design, and Development*. Prentice Hall PTR, Upper Saddle River, NJ, USA.

[17] Rogers, Y., Sharp, H. & Preece, J. (2011). *Interaction Design: Beyond Human-Computer Interaction*; John Wiley & Son Ltd.

[18] Dimitrios Tzovaras, editor. (2008). *Multimodal User Interfaces: From Signals to Interaction*. Springer, Berlin.

[19] Stefano Carrino, Maurizio Caon, Omar Abou Khaled, Rolf Ingold & Elena Mugellini. (2013). *Functional Gestures for Human-Environment Interaction*, Human-Computer Interaction. Interaction Modalities and Techniques. *Lecture Notes in Computer Science*, Volume 8007, 167-176.

[20] Maia, L. A. C. R., Silva, C. F. D., Correia, C. R. & Perea-Bartolomé, M. V. (2006). El modelo de Alexander Romanovich Luria (revisitado) y suaplicación a la evaluación neuropsicológica. *Revista Galego-Portuguesa de Psicoloxía e educación*, No 11-12 (Vol. 13), ISSN: 1138-1663, Universidade da Coruña, 2006.

[21] Truong, K.N., Hayes, G.R. & Abowd, D.G. (2006). Storyboarding: an empirical determination of best practices and effective guidelines. In *Proceedings of the 6th conference on Designing Interactive systems. ACM*, 12-21.

In: Horizons in Computer Science Research. Volume 9
Editor: Thomas S. Clary
ISBN: 978-1-63321-522-1

Chapter 9

SYNCHRONIZING NODS OF A COMPUTER-GENERATED CHARACTER AND A SPEAKER USING THERMAL IMAGE PROCESSING

***Yasunari Yoshitomi*[1,*]*, Ryota Kato*[1]*, Taro Asada*[1]* and Masayoshi Tabuse*[1]**

[1]Division of Environmental Sciences, Graduate School of Life and Environmental Sciences, Kyoto Prefectural University, Shimogamo, Sakyo-ku, Kyoto, Japan

Abstract

We introduce our system for communication between a speaker and a computer-generated (CG) character for making the speaker feel more comfortable. Nonverbal communication, such as a facial expression, a nod, and a hand gesture is very important for reciprocal communication between humans. We used an image registered by infrared rays, which displays the thermal distribution of the face and neck, for communication between a speaker and a CG character.

In our system, the CG character can synchronize its nodding with the speaker's nodding by predicting the speaker's nod angle. The CG character starts predicting the angle just after the human begins to speak and nod, and the CG character stops nodding while maintaining a front-view face when the human maintains a front-view face and is silent. The CG character starts predicting the angle again when the human begins to speak again.

The measured feature parameter is the input to a fuzzy algorithm system to obtain the nod angle of the speaker in front of an infrared ray camera, and then a moving-average model is used to predict the nod angle of the speaker. The average error of the nod angle obtained by our system was estimated as approximately 5 degrees. In addition, the CG character nods its head, not only when a human nods his or her head, but also when a human shakes his or her head left or right.

[*] E-mail address: yoshitomi@kpu.ac.jp.

1. Introduction

Nonverbal communication, such as a facial expression, a nod, or a hand gesture, is very important for reciprocal communication between humans. The realization of suitable communication between a human and a computer will help the development of computers, networking, robots, and, in particular, computer systems that interact with people living alone.

In an aging society, for example, in Japan, something to talk to would help a person advanced in years to live alone peacefully. Embodied communication technologies have been developed using the relationship between a human utterance and a nod [1]–[4]. In addition, several studies have investigated head gesture recognition [5]–[9]. However, in our daily lives, it is more difficult to take visual information from a person's head movements to synchronize the nod of a computer generated (CG) character in comparison with using audio information for the same purpose.

The primary reason for this difficulty is that the nuances of shade, reflection, and local darkness due to the inevitable changes in gray levels strongly influence the accuracy of head gesture recognition.

In this chapter, we introduce our system [10], [11] for synchronizing the nods of a CG character and a speaker. We use an image registered by infrared rays (IR), which display the thermal pattern of the face and neck, to develop a system of communication between a speaker and a CG character.

2. Image Acquisition

The principle of thermal image generation comes from the well-known law by Stefan and Boltzmann, which is expressed by $W = \varepsilon\sigma T^4$, where W is radiant emittance (W/cm^2), ε is emissivity, σ is the Stefan-Boltzmann constant (=5.6705×10^{-12}W/cm^{2}K^4), and T is temperature (K).

For human skin, ε is estimated at 0.98 to 0.99 [12],[13]. In our study, the approximate value of 1 was used as ε for human skin. Therefore, the values of ε for almost all substances are lower than that for human skin [12]. Accordingly, the human face and neck can be easily extracted in a scene when the skin temperatures selected for producing the thermal image have the value of 1 for ε [14]–[16]. Figure 1 shows examples of male face and neck images captured by visible ray (VR) and IR. We can obtain a thermal face and neck image without lighting even at night. In principle, the temperature measurement by IR does not depend on skin color [13], darkness, or lighting condition, resulting in easy extraction of the characteristics of the face and neck from the surrounding area on the thermal image.

3. Synchronizing Nods of a CG character and a Human

In this section, we introduce our system [10] for synchronizing the nods of a CG character and a human by thermal image processing.

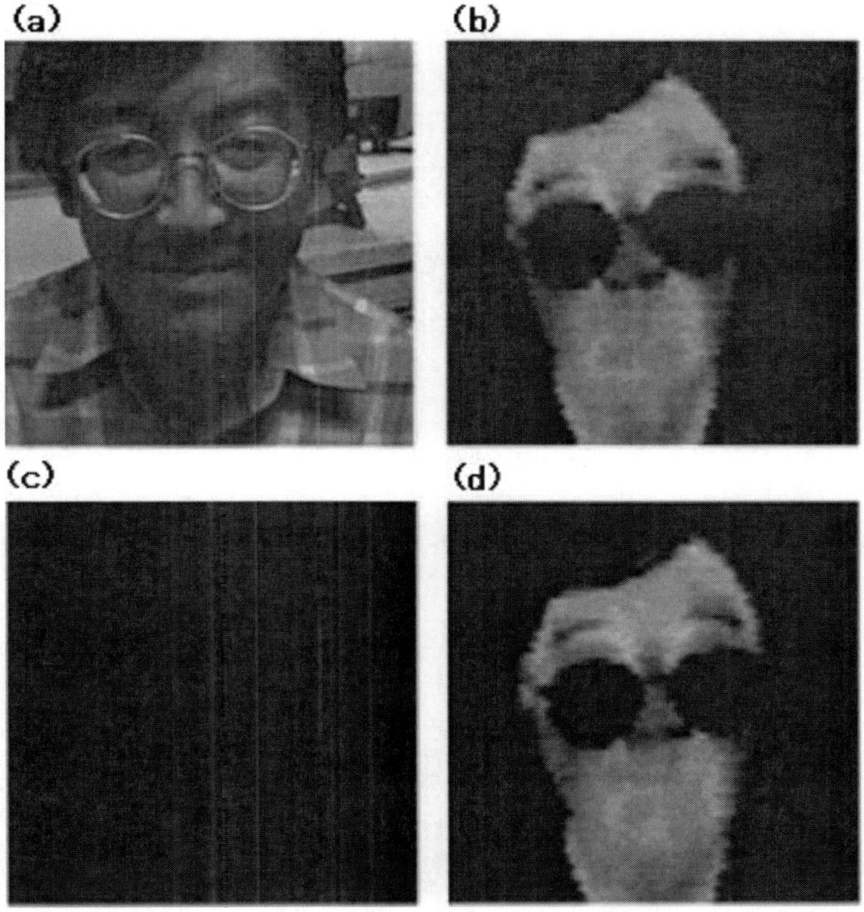

Figure 1. Examples of a face image at night: (a) VR with lighting, (b) IR with lighting, (c) VR without lighting, (d) IR without lighting [16].

3.1. Basic Processing Flow

Figure 2 shows the flow chart of our method. Before the basic processing, we make the fuzzy rules between the ratio (here in after referred as the *nod*) of the horizontal length to the vertical length of the face region on the thermal image and the face direction vector (hereinafter referred as $\boldsymbol{n}$), which has a norm of 1. For making the rules, we prepare a thermal image for measuring the *nod*, while we use a motion capture system for measuring $\boldsymbol{n}$. Using the fuzzy algorithm and the input of the *nod*, the resulting nod of the CG character is expressed by $\boldsymbol{n}$, which is the output of three estimated values of the elements of the vector. We explain the fuzzy algorithm and the process for measuring $\boldsymbol{n}$ in Section 3.2.

First, we obtain a pair of thermal images for the frontal and downward face directions for a subject to normalize the value of the *nod* as 1 in the case of frontal direction, and to transform the value of the *nod* of the subject to that of a typical subject. We explain the normalization and the transformation for the value of the *nod* in Sections 3.2.2 and 3.5.5, respectively.

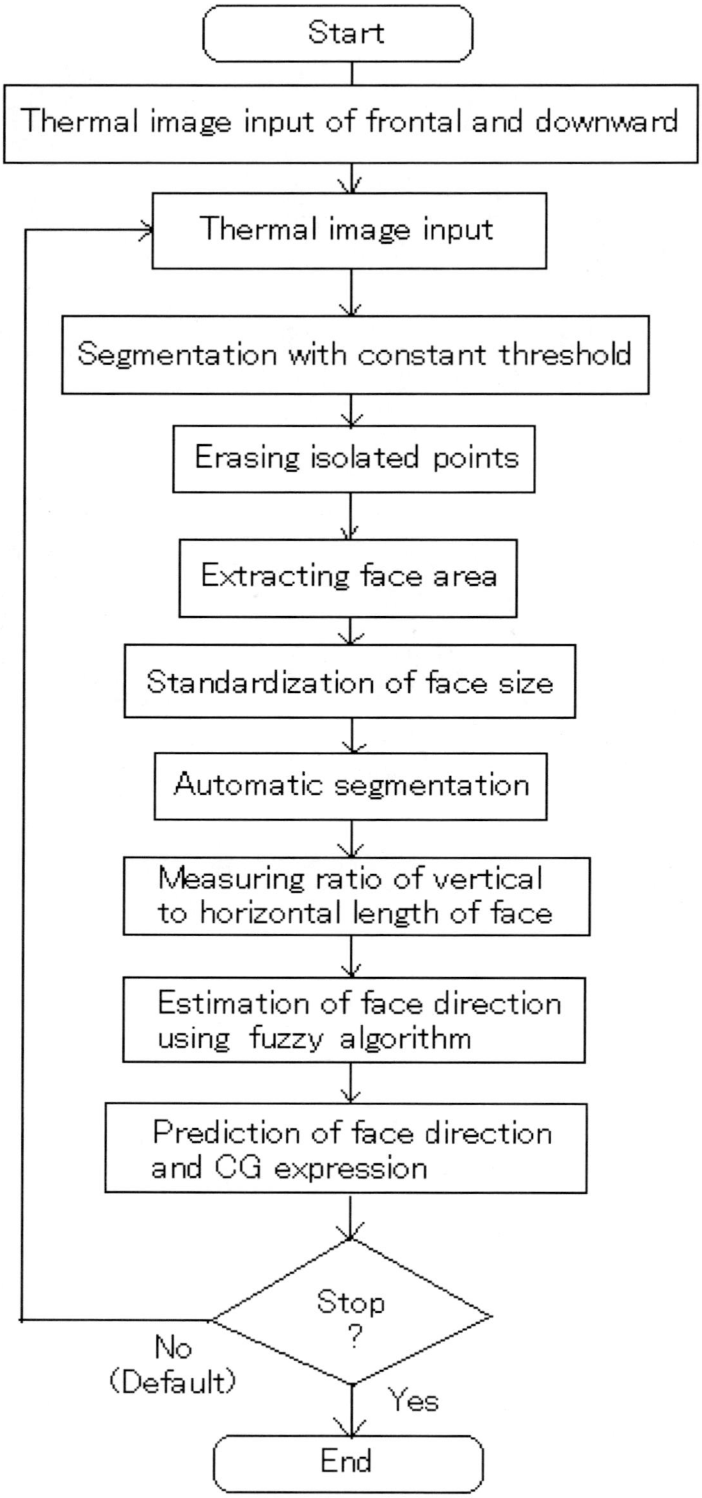

Figure 2. Flow chart of our method for synchronizing nods of a CG character and a human [10].

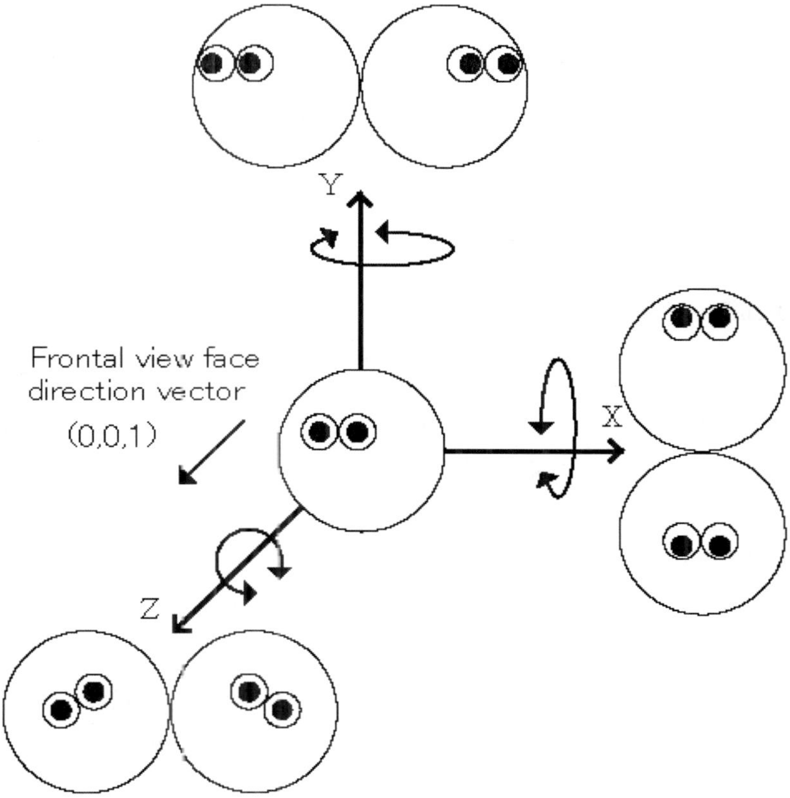

Figure 3. Three-dimensional coordinate system [18].

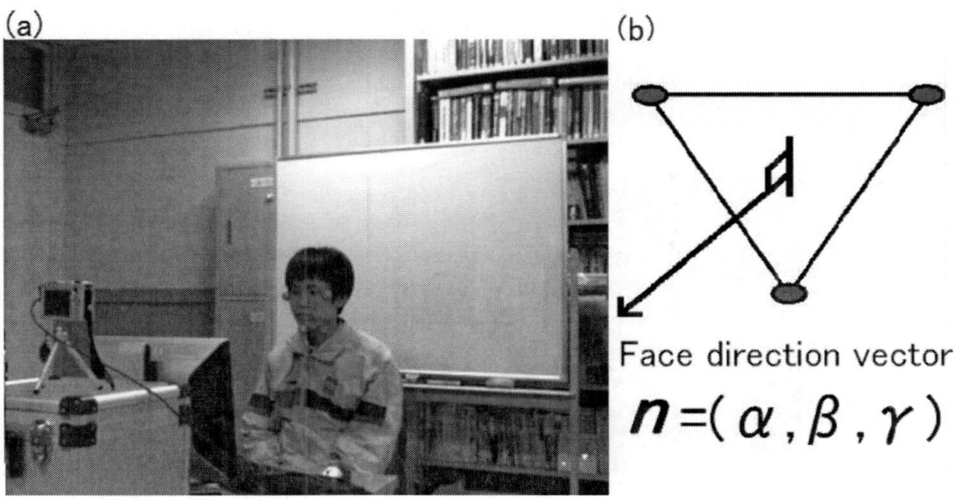

Figure 4. Face direction vector $\boldsymbol{n}$:(a) face image with three markers, whose coordinates are measured, (b) technique for making the face direction vector $\boldsymbol{n}$ [10].

As preprocessing for measuring the *nod*, segmentation with a constant threshold, erasing of isolated points, extracting the face area, standardizing of the size of the face, and automatic segmentation [17] are performed for the thermal image. Then, the *nod* is measured. For predicting the nod of a human, we use the moving average (MA) model. We explain the process for the prediction of the nod of the human in Section 3.3.

3.2. Fuzzy Algorithm for Face Direction Estimation

3.2.1. Parameter Used for Fuzzy Rules

Figure 3 shows the three-dimensional coordinate system used in our method. When the face is frontal, $\boldsymbol{n} = (0,0,1)$ corresponds to the face direction.

Figure 4 demonstrates how to measure $\boldsymbol{n}$ by using the motion capture system. For making the fuzzy rules and evaluating the accuracy of the nod angle obtained by our method, three markers are attached on a subject's jaw and both temples. Figure 4 (a) demonstrates an experimental scene where we place an IR camera and a computer monitor in front of the subject. We also place separately two cameras, which are not seen in Figure 4 (a), of the motion capture system in two diagonal positions from the frontal direction of the subject. By using the coordinates of the three markers, $\boldsymbol{n} = (\alpha, \beta, \gamma)$ is determined by geometric calculation. The three elements of $\boldsymbol{n}$ are used as parameters of the consequent in the fuzzy rules.

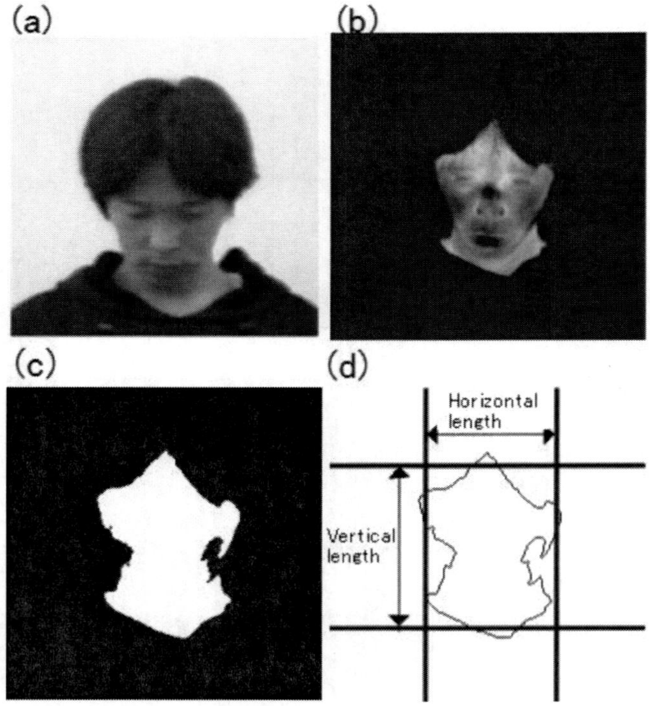

Figure 5. Downward rotation: (a) visible ray image, (b) thermal image, (c) binary image, (d) schematic diagram for explaining parameter *nod*[19].

Figure 5 demonstrates the downward rotation of the face. The *nod* used as a parameter of the antecedent in the fuzzy rules is measured as the ratio of the vertical length to the horizontal length of the face.

For eliminating the influence of the hairstyle and the throat region on the binary image as much as possible, the area having horizontal pixels less than an experimentally decided threshold is ignored in measuring the vertical length of the face, and the area having vertical pixels less than another experimentally decided threshold is also ignored in measuring the horizontal length of the face.

3.2.2. Fuzzy Rules and Algorithm

The fuzzy rules are described in Eq. (1). The fuzzy algorithm is described in Eqs. (2)– (5)[10].

$$\text{If } X = A_i \text{ then } Y_1 = B_{i1}, Y_2 = B_{i2}, Y_3 = B_{i3}, \quad (i = 1, 2, 3) \tag{1}$$

$$\mu^*_{B_{ij}}(Y_j) = W_i \mu_{B_{ij}}(Y_j), (i = 1, 2, 3, \; j = 1, 2, 3) \tag{2}$$

$$W_i = \mu_{A_i}(X^*), \; (i = 1, 2, 3) \tag{3}$$

$$B^0_j = \bigcup_{i=1}^{3} B^*_{ij}, \; (j = 1, 2, 3) \tag{4}$$

$$Y^*_j = \frac{\int \mu_{B^0_j}(Y_j) Y_j dY_j}{\int \mu_{B^0_j}(Y_j) dY_j}, (j = 1, 2, 3), \tag{5}$$

where X denotes a parameter of the antecedent; Y_1, Y_2, Y_3 denote parameters of the consequent; A_i, B_{i1}, B_{i2}, B_{i3} denote the corresponding fuzzy labels for X, Y_1, Y_2, Y_3, respectively; W_i denotes a fitness value of the ith rule to the input of X^*; Y^*_j denotes an output for Y_j. The integral in Eq. (5) is performed in the whole range of Y_j. In our method, $X=nod$, $Y_1=\alpha$, $Y_2=\beta$, $Y_3=\gamma$. We use three fuzzy rules described as "frontal," "rather downward," and "downward."

Figure 6 shows a schematic diagram of the membership functions used for both the antecedent and the consequent. C_i denotes a fuzzy label of the antecedent or the consequent, for example, A_3. Z corresponds to a variable of the antecedent or the consequent, for example, X.

For determining each actual shape of the membership function, we use the measured values for the corresponding parameter. In the case of C_2, the corresponding measured value is neither a maximum nor a minimum value among the three measured values. In the case of C_1 and C_3, the corresponding measured values are the minimum and the maximum, respectively, among the three measured values.

In the case of C_2, whose membership function is a triangle shape, its membership function has a maximum value of 1 at the corresponding measured value and a minimum value of 0 at the corresponding measured value for C_1 and C_3, respectively.

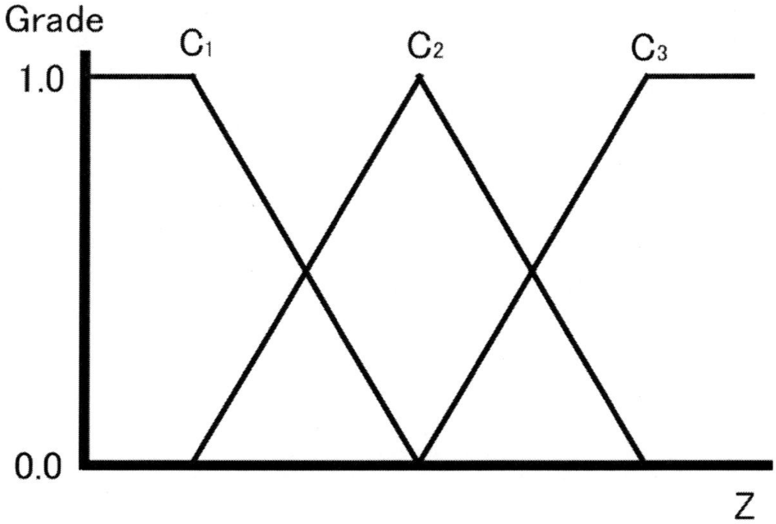

Figure 6. Membership functions [10].

In the case of C_1, its membership function has a maximum value of 1 at its corresponding measured value or less and decreases linearly to a minimum value of 0 at the measured value for C_2.

In the case of C_3, its membership function has a maximum value of 1at the corresponding measured value or more, and decreases linearly to a minimum value of 0 at the measured value for C_2.

In addition, the value of the *nod* is normalized by dividing by the value in the case of "frontal." We use a fuzzy algorithm for outputting ***n*** with three fuzzy rules and the value of the *nod* as an input. For integrating outputs from all rules, we use Eqs.(4) and (5).

3.2.3. Nod Angle Calculation

Eq. (6) defines a nod angle θ (°) that is calculated with γ.

$$\theta = 57.3\cos^{-1}\gamma \tag{6}$$

In the present study, θ is positive in the case of downward rotation.

3.3. Prediction of Nod Angle

For predicting the nod angle of a subject, we use the MA model expressed by Eq. (7).

$$\hat{\theta}(i) = \sum_{j=1}^{J} a(j)\theta(i-j), \tag{7}$$

where $\hat{\theta}(i)$ is a predicted value for $\theta(i)$, $a(j)$ is a coefficient for prediction, and J is a dimension for prediction. J is decided with Akaike's Information Criterion (AIC) expressed by Eq. (8).

$$AIC = n \ln S + 2p, \tag{8}$$

where n is the number of data, S is the summation of the squared error, and p is the number of parameters. J is decided as p, which gives the minimum value of AIC.

3.4. Face Direction Expression Using CG

We use Virtual Reality Modeling Language (VRML) and Java for expressing a CG character. Figure 7 shows examples of the CG expression of a nod.

3.5. Experiment

3.5.1. Experimental Environment

The thermal image produced by a thermal video system (Thermo Shot F30, NEC Avio Infrared Technologies Co., Ltd.) was transformed into a digital signal by an A/D converter (ADVC-300, Thomson Canopus) and then input into a computer with an IEEE1394 interface board (I・O Data Device: 1394-PCI3/DV6).

We used a computer (DELL Optiplex 745, CPU: Intel Core 2 Duo 6600 2.4 GHz, main memory: 2 GB, and OS: Windows XP (Microsoft)). We used Visual C++ 6.0 (Microsoft), Java 2 SDK Standard Edition 1.3, and VRML 2.0 for programming.

The thermal image to be processed in the computer had a spatial resolution of 240×160 pixels and 8 bit gray levels at each pixel. We used the motion capture system (Radish, LibraryCo., Ltd.) for measuring the position of markers attached on the subject' face.

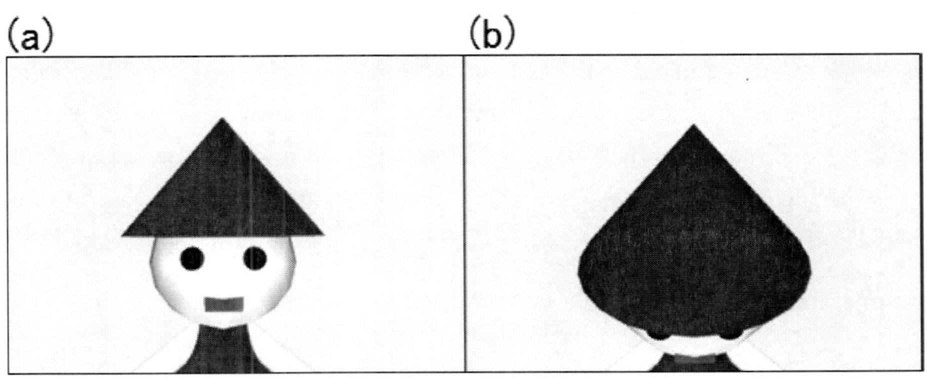

Figure 7. CG expression of nod:(a) frontal view, (b) nod of 30 degree angle [18].

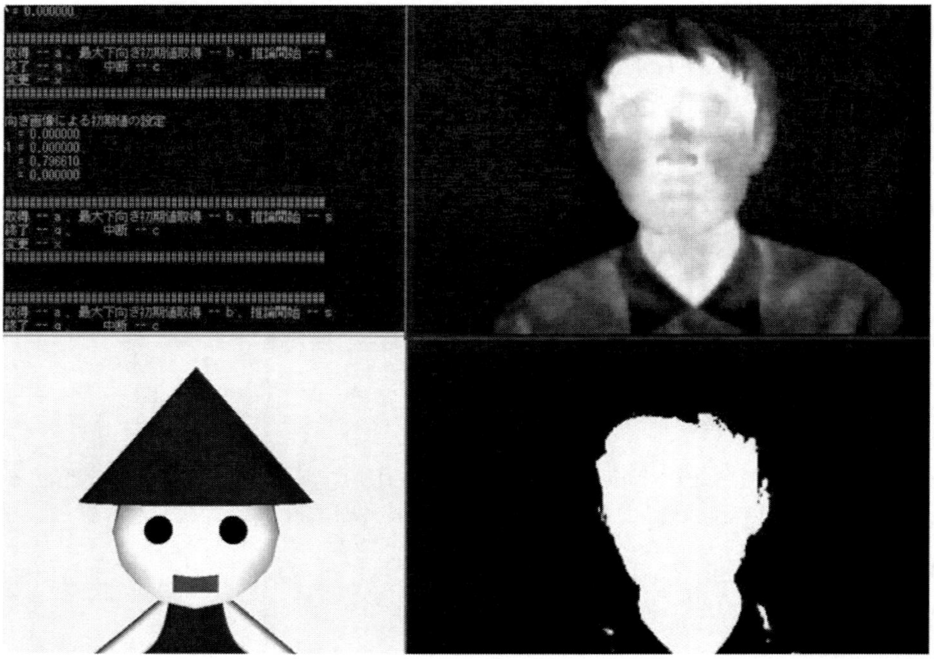

Figure 8. Monitor screen of computer in the experiment. Upper left: expression on command prompt, Upper right: thermal image, Lower left: CG, Lower right: binary image [10].

We also used another computer (Dell Dimension 8300, CPU: Pentium IV 3.2 GHz, main memory: 2.0 GB, OS: Windows XP) for performing the motion capture by Radish. Figure 8 shows a monitor screen of the computer in the experiment.

3.5.2. Measurement of Parameters Used for Fuzzy Labels and Treatment for Input out of Range Decided by Fuzzy Labels

We obtained each fuzzy label as an average value of six subjects: four males (A, B, C, D) and two females (E, F). Table 1 shows the fuzzy labels for each rule [10], [18].

We obtained the nod angle θ by using the output of γ of the fuzzy algorithm, and Eq. (6). Because we use membership functions whose shapes are described in Figure 6, the output of γ is within the range of the maximum and the minimum obtained from the three rules. For a *nod* of 1.000 or above, the output by the fuzzy algorithm was $\gamma = 1.000$. For a *nod* of 0.750 or under, the output by the fuzzy algorithm was $\gamma = 0.925$. To overcome the above problem, when the input of a *nod* was under 0.750, we used a linear equation decided experimentally for getting the nod angle θ from the *nod* having a value of 0.750 or under.

3.5.3. Approximation to Nod Angle θ Obtained by Motion Capture System

Since we used the fuzzy labels shown in Table 1, the nod angle θ inevitably had errors for each individual subject. For predicting the nod angle of a subject as precisely as possible, we used a linear graph approximation method to approximate the nod angle θ to be that obtained by the motion capture system.

For one male subject (G), we calculated the linear graph described in Figure 9 and used the relation for predicting his nod angle.

3.5.4. Prediction of Nod Angle θ of Subject Using the MA Model

According to Eqs.(7) and (8), for subject G, the value of 23 as J gave the minimum value of AIC when J was used for p, as shown in Figure 10. Then, we denoted Eq. (9) for predicting the nod of subject G [10].

$$\begin{aligned}\hat{\theta}(i) = {} & 1.39\hat{\theta}(i-1) - 0.19\theta(i-2) - 0.24\theta(i-3) - 0.11\theta(i-4) + 0.053\theta(i-5) \\ & + 0.032\theta(i-6) - 0.043\theta(i-7) - 0.028\theta(i-8) + 0.024\theta(i-9) + 0.03\theta(i-10) \\ & + 0.12\theta(i-11) - 0.15\theta(i-12) - 0.005\theta(i-13) + 0.0073\theta(i-14) + 0.11\theta(i-15) \\ & + 0.031\theta(i-16) - 0.14\theta(i-17) - 0.041\theta(i-18) + 0.18\theta(i-19) - 0.056\theta(i-20) \\ & + 0.052\theta(i-21) - 0.18\theta(i-22) - 0.14\theta(i-23)\end{aligned} \tag{9}$$

We did not have the value of $\theta(i-1)$ at the timing position of $i-1$ because it took approximately 0.13 s to get $\theta(i-1)$. Accordingly, we used $\hat{\theta}(i-1)$ instead of $\theta(i-1)$, as described in Eq. (9).

Table 1. Fuzzy labels for each rule [10], [18]

Rule \ Variable	***nod***	α	β	γ
1 (frontal)	1.000	0.000	0.000	1.000
2 (rather downward)	0.908	0.027	0.147	0.989
3 (downward)	0.750	0.042	0.379	0.925

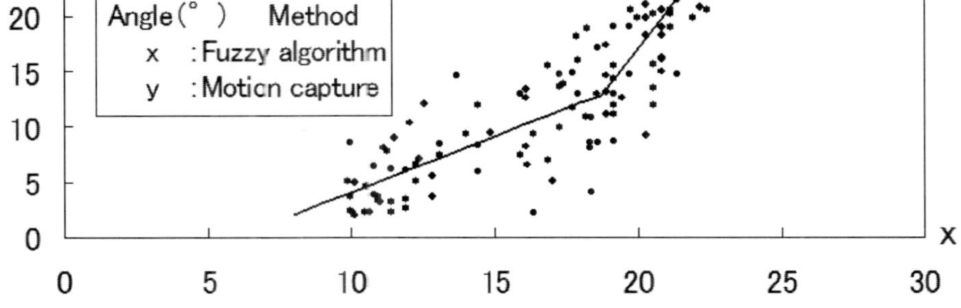

Figure 9. Line graph approximation of nod angle from output using the fuzzy algorithm [10].

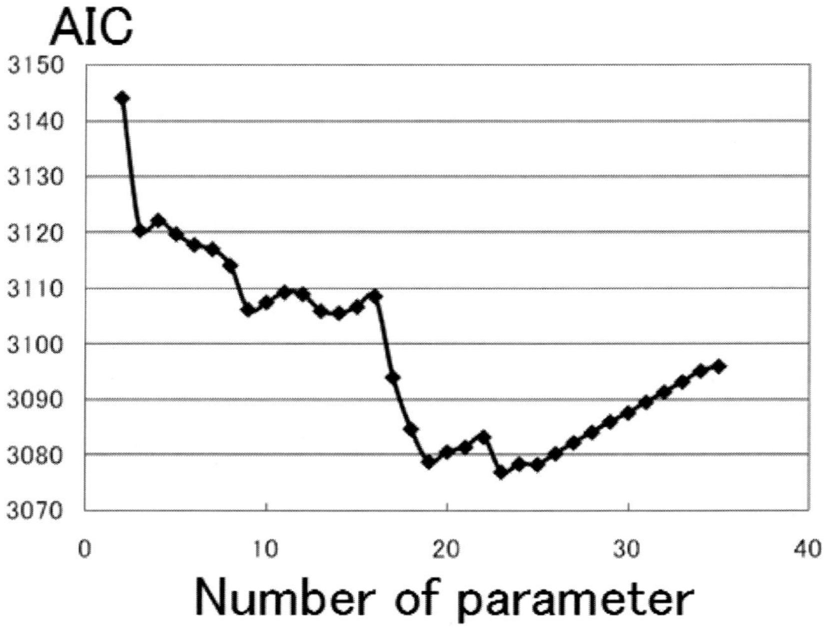

Figure 10. AIC [10].

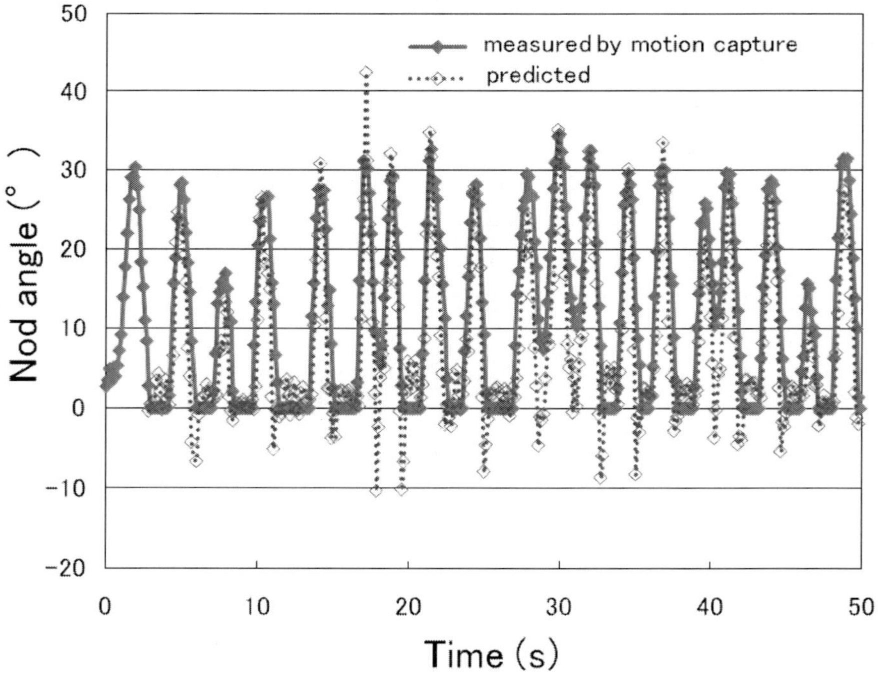

Figure 11. Accuracy of predicted nod angle for subject G [10].

Figure 11 shows the accuracy of the predicted nod angle for subject G using Eq. (9), as determined beforehand with the data for subject G in the previous experiment. The average error for the predicted nod angle was 5.1°. For the CG expression, the nod angle is transformed to 0 when $\hat{\theta}(i)$ is negative.

3.5.5. Application to Other Subjects

We used the line graph approximation, shown in Figure 9, for getting the nod angle from the output of the fuzzy algorithm. The line graph obtained for subject G may not be appropriate for other subjects. However, it is time consuming to get the line graph for each subject using the motion capture system. To overcome this problem, when we used our system for another subject, we approximately transformed the value of the nod for another subject to that for subject G by using a linear equation decided experimentally with two pairs of nod values of subject G and another subject in the frontal and downward cases and following the same procedure as that for subject G for getting the predicted nod angle.

For two male subjects (H and I), we used the above method for getting the predicted nod angle. Figures 12and 13 show the accuracy of the predicted nod angle for subjects H and I, respectively. The average errors of subjects H and I for the predicted nod angle were 4.4° and 5.5°, respectively. The difference between the errors for subject G and for subjects H and I was within 1.0°. This result shows that the method using the line graph approximation of the nod angle made for a typical subject (G) and the transformation of the nod value from another subject to the typical subject is useful.

3.6. Summary

We introduced our system for communication between a human and a CG character.

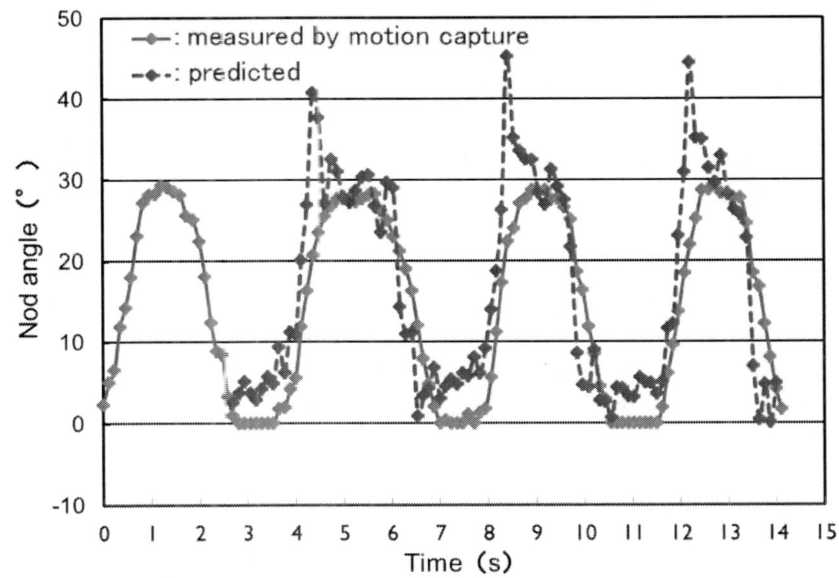

Figure 12. Accuracy of predicted nod angle for subject H.

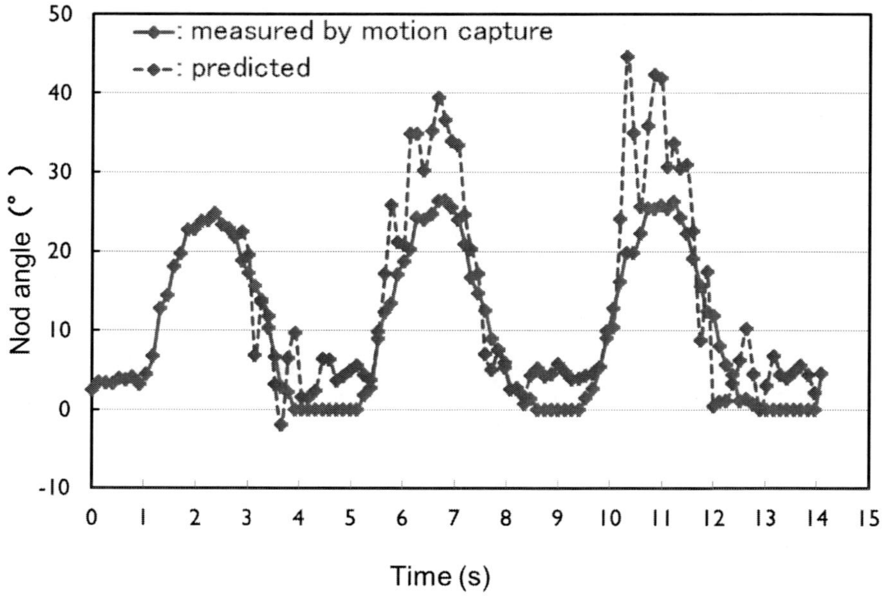

Figure 13. Accuracy of predicted nod angle for subject I.

In our system, the CG character can synchronize its nod with a human's nod by predicting his or her nod angle. The measured feature parameter is inputted to the fuzzy algorithm system to estimate the nod angle of the person in front of the IR camera, then we use the MA model for predicting the nod of the person. The average error of the nod angle obtained by the present system was estimated as approximately $5°$.

The appearance of the CG character had a great influence on the impression of the subject. It is necessary to improve the appearance of the CG character so that it makes a good impression to the user. In addition, the target of not only appearance but also movement of the CG character depends on the intended usage of the system.

In future systems, we assume usage of the CG character (agent) as a phone answering service using a computer and as a virtual friend for a person living alone. In our system, the movement of the CG character is just a nod. We will add other movements besides nodding according to the usage.

We adopt the fuzzy algorithm for estimating ***n*** from the *nod* because it is easy to improve its accuracy by adjusting the rules, the membership functions, and the procedure for integrating the outputs from the rules for the input. In Section 3, we introduce a system for synthesizing the nods of a CG character and a human. Then, we investigate the suitable embodied communication between a human and a CG character.

4. Synchronizing Nods of a CG Character and a Speaker

In this section, we introduce our system [11] for synchronizing the nods of a CG character and a speaker using thermal image processing. To make the communication between the speaker and the CG character more natural, we added some modules to detect the utterance of a human to our system described in Section 3.

4.1.Basic Processing Flow

Figure14 shows the flow chart of our method. We use the fuzzy rules of the ratio of the horizontal length to the vertical length of the face region on the thermal image and the face direction vector, which has a norm of 1. By the fuzzy algorithm and the input of the *nod*, which are described in Section 3.2, $\boldsymbol{n}$ is output as three estimated values of the elements of the vector and is used for expressing the nodding of the CG character.

First, as described in Section 3.5.5, we obtain a pair of thermal images of the frontal and downward face directions of a subject to normalize the value of the *nod* as 1 in the case of the frontal direction, and to transform the value of the *nod* of the subject to that of a typical subject.

Then, after capturing sound data to obtain constant thresholds, the sound data are judged by the thresholds to determine whether the subject has spoken an utterance.

The preprocessing operation for measuring the *nod* includes segmentation with another constant threshold, erasing the isolated points, extracting the face area, standardizing the size of the face, and automatic segmentation [17], all of which are performed on the thermal image. Then, the *nod* is measured.

To predict the *nod* of a human, we use the MA model described in Section 3.5.4. Then, if the subject maintains a frontal face for longer than approximately 0.7 second, the CG character maintains a frontal face until the sound is judged to indicate an utterance. When the sound is judged as an utterance, the processing is restarted from the thermal image input. Otherwise, the processing is set back to the sound input and judgment of the utterance. The processing of utterance-driven nodding of the CG character is explained in detail in Section 4.2.

4.2. Utterance-Driven Nodding of the CG Character

The thresholds for the sound data values are set as $\bar{x}_s - 5\sigma_s$ and $\bar{x}_s + 5\sigma_s$, where $\bar{x}_s$ and σ_s express the average and the standard deviation, respectively, of the sound data value for one second under the condition of no utterance. The sound data for 0.5 second with an interval of approximately 0.2 second are performed to erase noises, and then two series of samplings with an interval of 0.084 second are performed by using the method reported in [20]–[22].

Then, it is determined whether every sampled data falls within $[\bar{x}_s - 5\sigma_s, \bar{x}_s + 5\sigma_s]$, which is considered to be the range of no utterance. When at least one sampled datum has a value outside $[\bar{x}_s - 5\sigma_s, \bar{x}_s + 5\sigma_s]$, our system judges that the sound data contain an utterance. Once the sound data are judged as containing an utterance, the preprocessing operation for measuring the *nod* is started.

When the subject maintains a frontal face for longer than approximately 0.7 second, the CG character maintains a frontal face until the sound is judged as an utterance. When the sound is judged as an utterance, the processing is restarted from the thermal image input. Otherwise, the processing is set back to the step of the sound input and the judgment of the utterance.

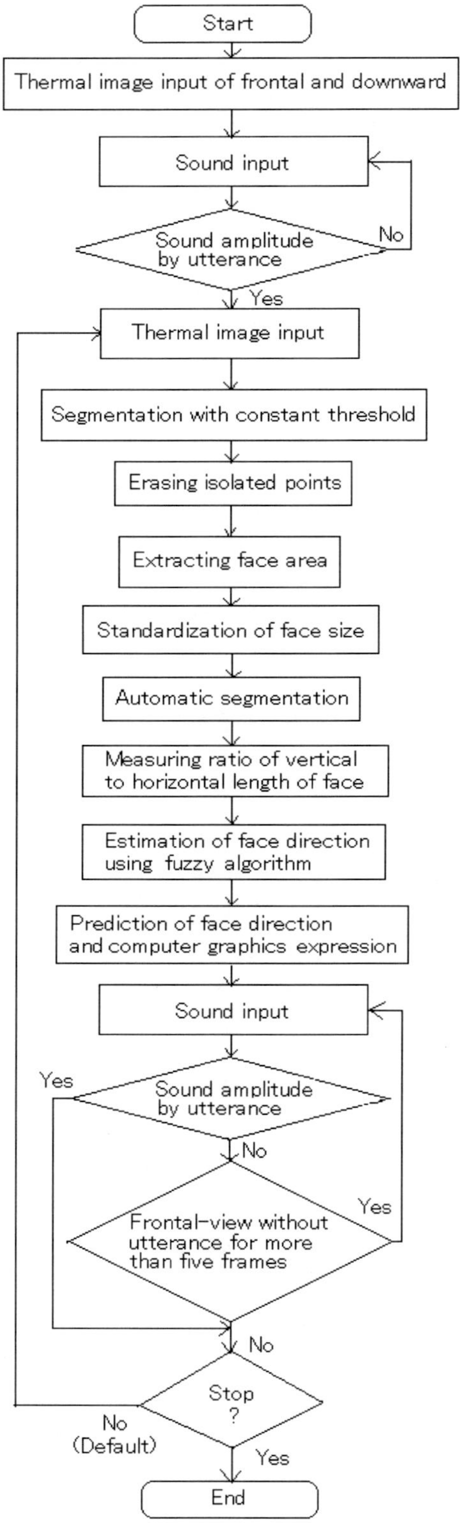

Figure 14. Flow chart of our method for synchronizing nods of a CG character and a speaker [11].

4.3. Prediction of Nod Angle

We use fuzzy rules and the algorithm described in Section 3.2 and the MA model described in Section 3.3 for predicting the nod angle of subject G. In addition, we use the method described in Section 3.5.5 for getting the predicted nod angle for another subject.

4.4. Face Direction Expression Using Computer Graphics

We use the virtual reality modeling language (VRML) and Java for expressing the CG character. Figure 7 shows examples of the CG character expressions of nodding. When $\hat{\theta}(i) < 5°$ in Eq. (9), $\hat{\theta}(i)$ is converted to 0° because the CG character having $\hat{\theta}(i) < 0°$ throws its head back and the character having the small value of $\hat{\theta}(i)$ fluctuating near 0° displays an unnaturally shaking attitude. Therefore, in this study, all nodding values of the CG character are restricted to be above 5°.

4.5. Experiment

4.5.1. Experimental Environment

The thermal image produced by a thermal video system (Thermo Shot F30, NEC Avio Infrared Technologies Co.) was transformed into a digital signal by an A/D converter (ADVC-300, Thomson Canopus) and the signal was input into a computer with an IEEE 1394 interface board (I • O Data Device: 1394-PCI3/DV6). We used a computer (Dell Optiplex 745, CPU: Intel Core 2 Duo 6600 2.4 GHz, main memory: 2 GB, and OS: Windows XP, Microsoft). Hereinafter this is referred to as PC1. For programming, we used Visual C++ 6.0 (Microsoft), Java 2 SDK standard edition version 1.3, and VRML 2.0. The thermal image to be processed in the computer had a spatial resolution of 240 × 160 pixels and an 8-bit gray level at each pixel. The sound data captured by a wireless microphone (WM-1320, TOA Corporation) and a wireless tuner (WT-750B, TOA Corporation), were amplified by a blender (AT-PMX5P, Audio-technica) and transformed into a digital signal by the A/D converter, and the signal was input into a computer with the IEEE 1394 interface board (I • O Data Device: 1394-PCI3/DV6). We used a second computer (Dell OptiplexGX620, CPU: IntelPremium 43.4 GHz, main memory: 1.99 GB, and OS: Windows XP, Microsoft). Hereinafter, this is referred to as PC2. The CG character was expressed on PC2, which used Microsoft Internet Explorer 7.0 and Parallel Graphics Cortona VRML Client 3.1.

PC1 was connected to PC2 by a cable to form a local area network. The thresholds for sound amplitude were decided in PC2. When the sound data were judged to be above the threshold and therefore coming from an utterance, PC1 started a series of processing for measuring the *nod* just after receiving the signal from PC2 through the cable. Moreover, when the signal indicated that the subject was judged to have maintained a frontal face for longer than approximately 0.7 second, the signal was sent from PC1 to PC2 through the cable. Then, the CG character on PC2 maintained a frontal face until the sound was judged in PC2 as an utterance. When the sound was judged as an utterance in PC2, PC1 restarted the series of processing for measuring the *nod* from the thermal image input, just after receiving the signal from PC2 through the cable.

4.5.2. Conditions

The 11 subjects participating in the experiments consisted of the following: 2 males in their 20s, subjects J and K; 3 females in their 20s, subjects L, M, and N; 1 male in his 30s, subject O; 1 female in her 30s, subject P; 1 male in his 40s, subject Q; 1 female in her 50s, subject R; 1 male in his 60s, subject S; and 1 female in her 60s, subject T. When the CG character synchronized its nodding to that of the subject during speaking, the subject's impression of the CG character's reaction was investigated with two kinds of experiments. The first experiment (hereinafter referred to as Experiment No. 1) was as follows. After watching a video digesting the soccer finals of the 2011 FIFA Women's World Cup for approximately five minutes, each subject verbally gave a summary and an impression of the video while in front of the computer monitor on which the CG character of our system was shown. The CG character synchronized its nodding to that of the subject.

The second experiment (hereinafter referred to as Experiment No. 2) was as follows. Each subject watched a video for approximately two minutes. The video was a comic skit by the Sandwich Man, a Japanese comedy duo. The subject sat in front of the computer monitor, on which the CG character of our system was shown. The CG character synchronized its nodding to that of the subject. Figure 15 shows a scene of Experiments No. 1 and No. 2. These two experiments were performed to investigate the effect and the challenges of our system. After the two experiments, all subjects answered a questionnaire.

4.5.3. Results and Discussion

Figures 16–18 show the results of the questionnaire for Experiment No. 1. In the questionnaire, 27.3% of the subjects were encouraged or very encouraged to say something to our system, whereas an equal number (27.3%) were discouraged from saying anything to our system (Figure 16). The movement speeds of the CG character were considered to be slightly low by approximately one-third of the subjects, as shown in Figure 17. One of the reasons why the reaction of the CG character was considered to be unnatural or slightly unnatural by 54.5% of subjects, as shown in Figure 18, was that the CG character only nodded and did not change its facial expression.

Furthermore, when the hand of a subject appeared in the thermal image, the CG character nodded. This reaction could give the subject an unnatural impression of the CG character. At the initial stages of Experiments No. 1 and No. 2, the thermal images of the frontal and downward faces of each subject were captured for calculating the feature parameter *nod* of the subject. In our system, the degree of nodding of the CG character was obtained with the thermal images and the technique for converting the feature parameter *nod* of the subject to that of subject G. Therefore, when the degree of nodding of the CG character was overly large for the initial downward face of the subject, the nodding of the downward face in the experiments became greater than that of the nodding of the subject. This situation happened with Subject R, and it resulted in the highest nod angle (157.2°) of the CG character in Experiment No. 1. In contrast, the nod angle of the CG character in Experiment No. 1 was within 60° for the other subjects. A ratio of a nod angle more than 5° was assumed to express a degree of communication between a subject and the CG character. The ratio seemed to depend on the subject. As shown in Table 2 [11], the ratio was in the range of 0% to 53.4%. Subjects J, K, M, and Q, who had relatively small ratios of a nod angle more than 5°, had the impression that the CG character moved slowly, and subjects J, K, and M had the impression that the total expression of the CG character was neutral. These impressions might be caused by the fact that the CG character could nod only when the subject nodded. However, subjects L, N, R, and S, who had relatively large ratios of a nod angle more than 5°, had the impression that the CG character moved well, and subjects L, N, and Rhad the impression that the reaction of the CG character was unnatural or slightly unnatural. According to the comments of some subjects, the appearance and the static facial expression of the CG character did not give a natural impression.

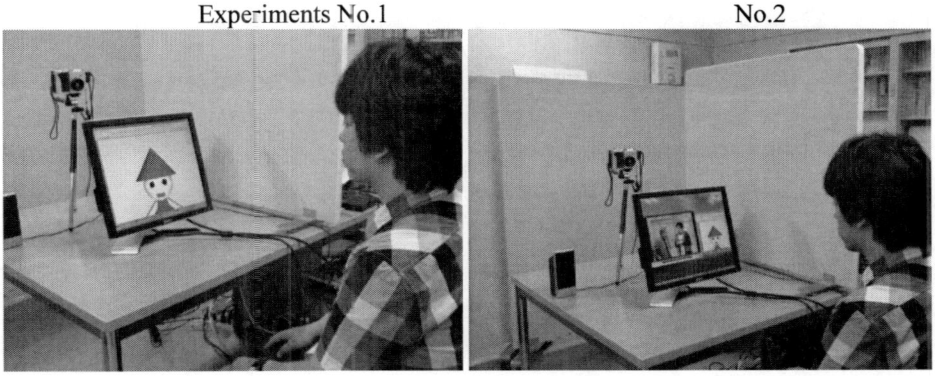

Figure 15. Scenes of Experiments No. 1 and No. 2 [11].

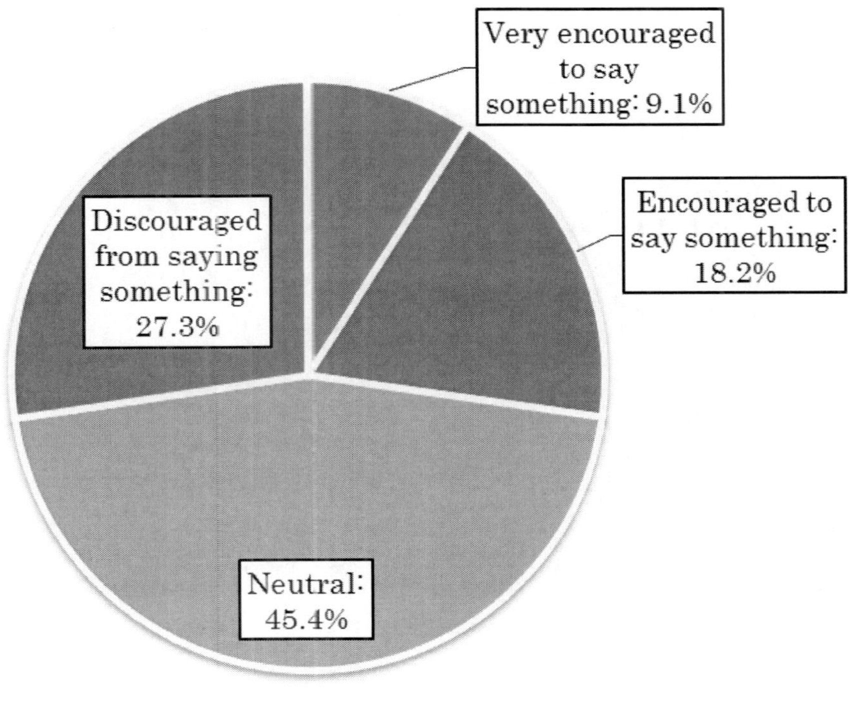

Figure 16. Total impression of the CG character [11].

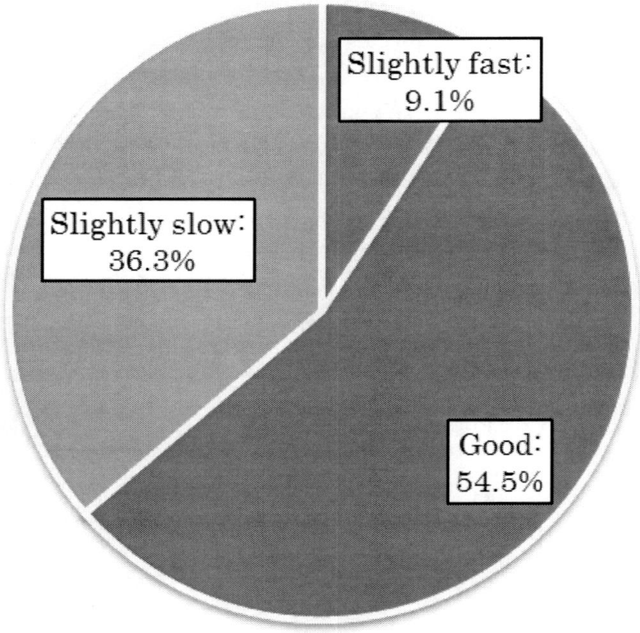

Figure 17. Impression of speed of the CG character [11].

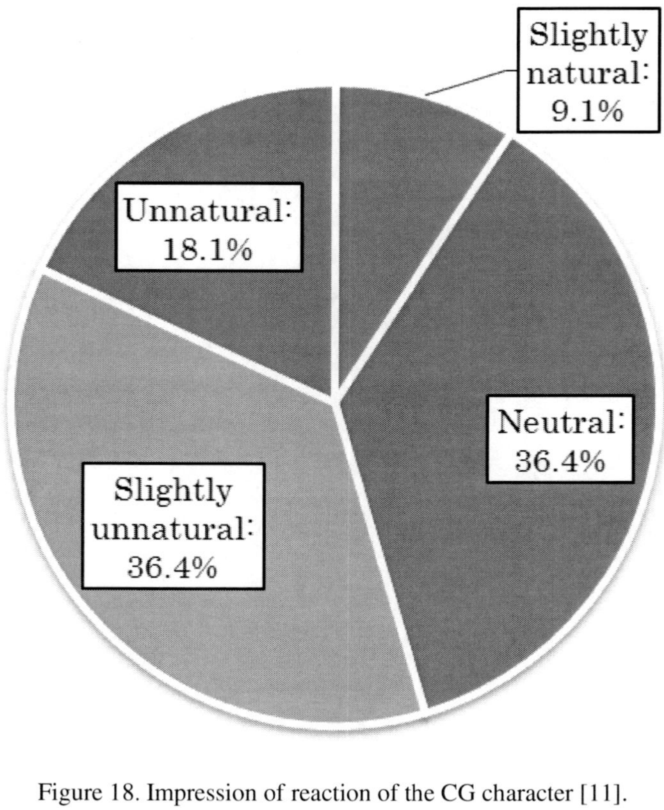

Figure 18. Impression of reaction of the CG character [11].

Table 2. Ratio r of nod angles above 5° in Experiment No. 1

Subject	**J**	**K**	**L**	**M**	**N**	
r (%)	0.0	1.7	53.4	9.3	42.9	
Subject	**O**	**P**	**Q**	**R**	**S**	**T**
r (%)	20.4	16.5	2.9	45.8	38.4	10.6

Table 3. The ratio r of nod angle above 5°in Experiment No. 2

Subject	**J**	**K**	**L**	**M**	**N**	
r (%)	9.8	78.7	51.0	35.1	41.0	
Subject	**O**	**P**	**Q**	**R**	**S**	**T**
r (%)	18.1	29.2	0.9	46.2	19.6	16.8

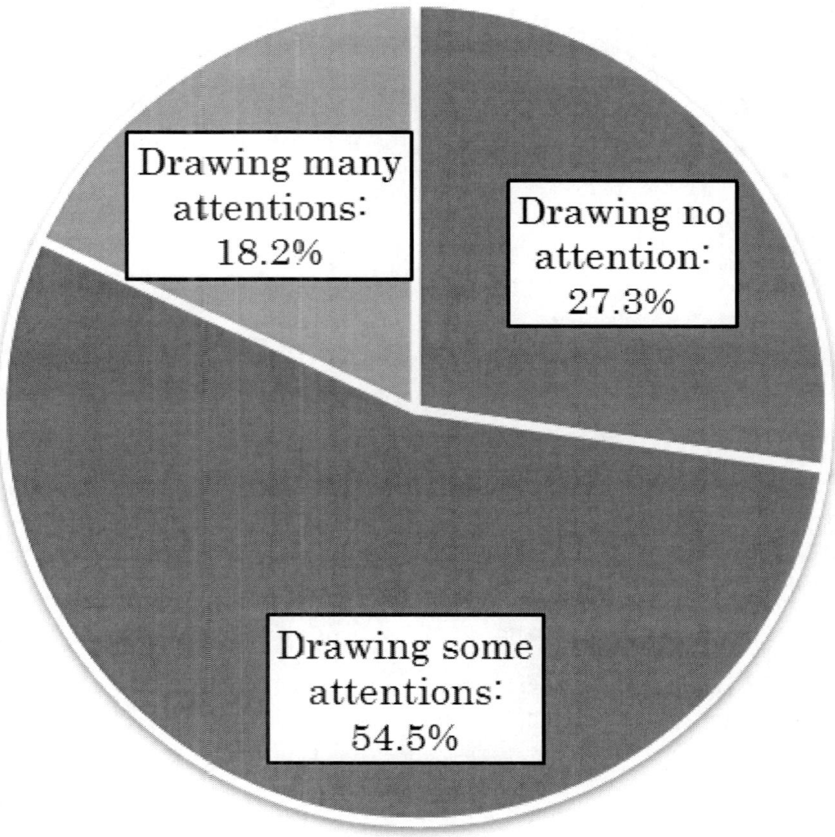

Figure 19. Attention level to the CG Character [11].

Figures 19–21 show the results of the questionnaire for Experiment No. 2. Because the sound from the loudspeakers of PC2 could influence the judgment of the utterance of a subject, the volume of the loudspeakers was kept at a low level. Therefore, some subjects commented that the voice of the video was not easy to hear.

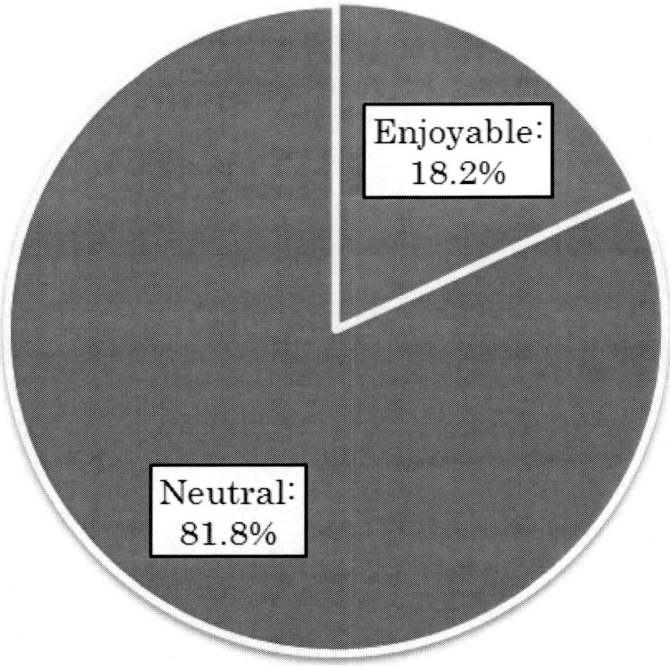

Figure 20. Mental influence by the CG character [11].

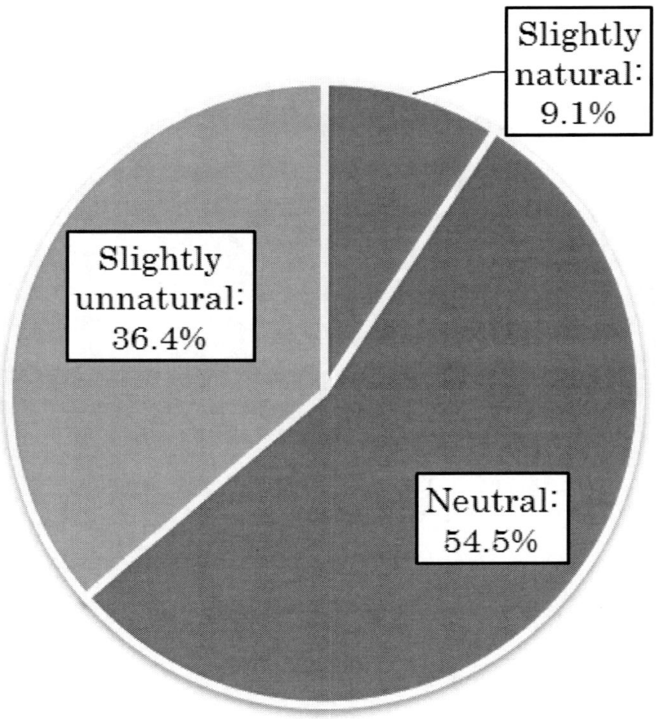

Figure 21. Impression on movement of the CG character [11].

Most subjects concentrated their attention on the video of the comic skit while sitting still, so that the CG character maintained a frontal face. The ratio of a nod angle more than 5° seemed to depend on the subject's personality and fell in the range of 0.9% to 78.7%, as shown in Table 3 [11]. Subjects K, L, N, and R, who had a relatively large value of the ratio of the nod angle more than 5°, had the impression that their attention was drawn to the CG character.

According to the comments by some subjects, the CG character needed more kinds of appearances, reactions, facial expressions, and voices, so that their attention might be more drawn to the CG character and thus result in less attention to the video.

Figure 22 [11] shows the subject's personality expressed by the nodding of the CG character. Subject K concentrated her attention on the video and sat almost still through Experiment No. 1, while she sat nodding to some extent in Experiment No. 2. For the other subjects, we found that the easiness of the interaction between the subject and the CG character depended on the subject's personality.

4.6. Summary

We used an image registered by IR, which displays the thermal pattern of the face and neck, to develop a system of communication between the speaker and the CG character. To make the communication between the speaker and the CG character more natural, we added some modules to detect the utterance of a human to the system described in Section 3.

In the future, we will compare the present method with embodied communication technologies using the relationship between a human utterance and a nod [1]–[4].

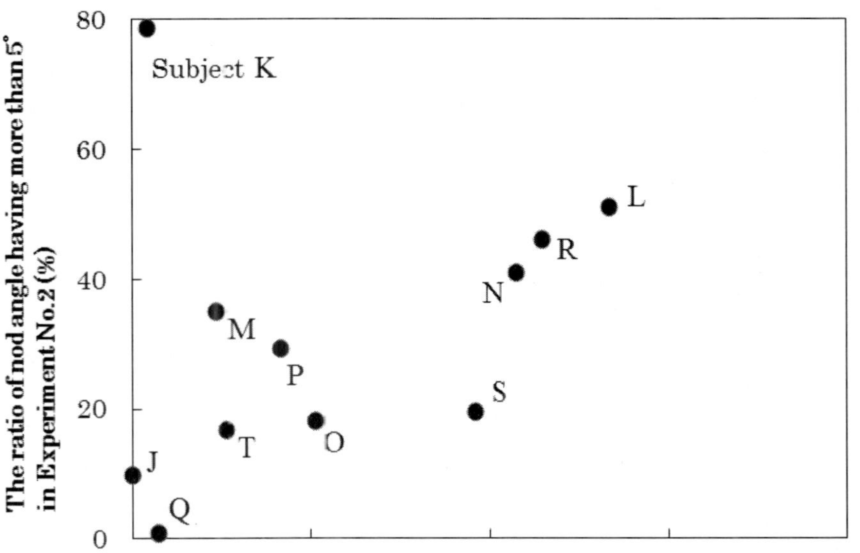

Figure 22. Subject's personality expressed by the nodding of the CG character.

5. Conclusion

We introduced our system for communication between a speaker and a CG character by exploiting thermal image processing. The CG character can synchronize its nodding with a speaker's nodding by predicting the speaker's nod angle. The measured feature parameter is inputted to a fuzzy algorithm system to estimate the nod angle of the speaker in front of the IR camera, then we use the MA model for predicting the nod of the speaker. The CG character itself had a great influence on the users' impressions. In future work, we need to improve the CG character by considering the use of the system and the individual user's preferences.

Acknowledgment

We would like to thank the people who gave their cooperation as subjects in our experiments.

References

[1] Watanabe T, and Yuuki N, A voice reaction system with a visualized response equivalent nodding. *Advances in Human Factors/Ergonomics*, 12A:396-403, (1989).

[2] Watanabe T, Okubo M, and Ogawa H, An embodied interaction robots system based on speech. *J. Robotics and Mechatronics*, 12(2):126-134, (2000).

[3] Watanabe T, Danbara R, and Okubo M, InterActor: speech-driven embodied interactive actor. *Proceedings of 11th IEEE Int.* Workshop on Robot and Human Interactive Communication, Berlin, Germany, Sep. 25-27, 2002, pp430-435, (2002).

[4] Watanabe T, Okubo M, Nakashige M, and Danbara R, InterActor: speech driven embodied interactive actor. *Int. J. Human-Computer Interaction*, 17(1):43-58, (2004).

[5] Zelinsky A, and Heinzmann J, A novel visual interface for human-robot communication. *Advanced Robotics*, 11(8):827-852, (1998).

[6] Choi HI, and Rhee PK, Head gesture recognition using HMMs. *Expert Systems with Applications*, 17(3):213-221, (1999).

[7] Nonaka H, Communication interface with eye-gaze and head gesture using successive DP matching and fuzzy inference. *J. Intelligent Information Systems*, 21(2):105-112,(2003).

[8] Lin CS, Ho CW, Chang KC, Hung SS, Shei HJ, and Yehd MS, A novel device for head gesture measurement system in combination with eye-controlled human-machine interface. *Optics and Lasers in Engineering*, 44(6):597-614, (2006).

[9] Jia P, Hu HH, Lu T, and Yuan K, Head gesture recognition for hands-free control of an intelligent wheelchair. *Industrial Robot Int. J.*, 34(1):60-68, (2007).

[10] Kato R, Yoshitomi Y, Asada T, and Tabuse M, A system for synchronizing the nods of a CG character and a human using thermal image processing and a moving-average model. *J. of Artificial Life and Robotics*, 15(1):10-16, (2010).

[11] Yoshitomi Y, Kato R, Asada T, and Tabuse M, A system for synchronizing nods of a computer-generated character and a speaker using thermal image processing.

Proceedings of 17th Int. Symposium on Artificial Life and Robotics, Beppu, Oita, Japan, Jan 19-21, 2012, pp 216-221, (2012).

[12] Kuno H (1994) Infrared rays engineering (in Japanese). Tokyo, IEICE, pp 22.

[13] Kuno H (1994) Infrared rays engineering (in Japanese). Tokyo, IEICE, pp 45.

[14] Yoshitomi Y, Kimura S, Hira E, and TomitaS, Facial expression recognition using infrared rays image processing. *Proceedings of the Annual Convention IPS Japan*, Osaka, Japan, Sep 4-6, 1996, 2:339-340, (1996).

[15] Yoshitomi Y, Kimura S, Hira E, and Tomita S, Facial expression recognition using thermal image processing. *IPSJ SIG Notes*, CVIM103-3, Kyoto, Japan, Jan 23-24, 1997, pp 17-24, (1997).

[16] Yoshitomi Y, Miyawaki N, Tomita S, and Kimura S, Facial expression recognition using thermal image processing and neural network. *Proceedings of 6th IEEE Int. Workshop on Robot and Human Communication*, Sendai, Japan, Sep 29-Oct 1, 1997, pp 380-385, (1997).

[17] Yoshitomi Y, Tanijiri T, A machine for automatic segmentation of image and its method (in Japanese). Japan patent application 2002-344185, 2002.

[18] Kato R, Yoshitomi Y, Asada T, Fujita Y, and Tabuse M, A method for synchronizing nods of a CG character and a human using thermal image processing", P*roceedings of 18th IEEE Int. Symposium on Robot and Human Interactive Communication*, Toyama, Japan, Sep. 27-Oct. 2, 2009, pp 848-853, (2009).

[19] Yoshitomi Y, Tsuchiya A, Tomita S, Face recognition using dynamic thermal image processing. *Proceedings of 7th IEEE Int. Workshop on Robot and Human Communication*, Takamatsu, Kagawa, Japan, Sep.30-Oct.2, 1998, pp 443-448, (1998).

[20] Ikezoe F, Nakano M, Yoshitomi Y, and Tabuse M, Facial expression recognition using thermal face image automatically acquired in speaking (in Japanese). *Proceedings of Human Interface Symposium 2005*, Fujisawa, Kanagawa, Japan, Sep.15-17, 2005, pp 7-12, (2005).

[21] Nakano M, Yoshitomi Y, and Tabuse M, Efficient facial expression recognition using thermal face image in speaking and its application to analysis of individual variations (in Japanese). *Proceedings of Human Interface Symposium 2006*, Kurashiki, Okayama, Japan, Sep.25-28, 2006, pp1151-1156, (2006).

[22] Nakano M, Robust facial expression recognition for various speakers (in Japanese). Master's thesis, Dept. of Environmental Information Graduate School of Human Environmental Sciences Kyoto Prefectural University, pp1-70, (2008).

In: Horizons in Computer Science Research. Volume 9 ISBN: 978-1-63321-522-1
Editor: Thomas S. Clary

Chapter 10

EVALUATION OF EFFECTIVE PARAMETERS OF ENERGY CONSUMPTION IN WIRELESS SENSOR NETWORKS

***Ali Norouzi*[1,*], *Ahmet Sertbas*[1,†] *and A. Halim Zaim*[2,‡]**
[1]Computer Engineering Department, Istanbul University, Istanbul, Turkey
[2]Computer Engineering Department, Istanbul Commerce University, Istanbul, Turkey

Abstract

The development of wireless sensor networks (WSNs) has never been free of challenges and many researchers have been interested in overcoming these challenges. The energy consumption, longevity, and performance of the networks are among the main challenges and have drawn a great deal of attention from researchers. Delving deeper into the issues we encounter more detailed parameters that are the cause of these challenges. To put it another way, there are trivial but at the same time effective parameters whose improvement can enhance the network and overcome the challenges. This chapter tries to introduce and survey all the parameters from a technical viewpoint and presents a general report on the previous works. In addition, advantages and weaknesses of the factors and approaches to improving WSNs are discussed. The study proposes a classification of the parameters and processes that affect different layers of the networks. Furthermore, a comparison of the common methods and further recommendations are represented. Each comparison is concluded by a proposal of the best method to deal with the challenges and improve the networks.

1. Introduction

A collection of nodes arranged into a cooperative network constitutes a wireless sensor network (WSN) [1, 2]. Every node is capable of carrying out processing and may possess

* E-mail address: norouzi@ieee.org.
† E-mail address: asertbas@istanbul.edu.tr.
‡ E-mail address: azaim@iticu.edu.tr.

different types of memories, an radio frequency (RF) transceiver, a power source, and variety of sensors and actuators. The nodes are capable of wireless communication and are usually arranged automatically following deployment in an ad hoc fashion. It is notable, however, that the network has to deal with serious limitations of energy, memory size, and bandwidth. These limitations challenge the networks with regard to collecting and processing the data. The networks are used in a variety of fields such as the military, medicine, environment, and household monitoring. The common aspects of the networks in these different fields are the determining roles of energy, data loss, and delay. In many cases, it is not possible to determine an optimized network, and consequently several protocols have been proposed to achieve better optimized networks.

An objective of wireless networks is detecting and reporting events, which is done by all the nodes in the network. A considerable challenge is routing, which aims to map a suitable route between the source and destination. This goal is usually achieved by using several algorithms and protocols. A direct and effective routing affects other factors such as longevity and consumption of energy. Dealing with this challenge means considerable changes in the network performance. The fact that studying transmission, selection of neighbouring nodes, and proper node selection may help find a better solution for routing, which in turn affects energy consumption, longevity, traffic, time, and so on, explains the need for present study [3, 4].

Regardless of the application, routing protocols of WSNs need to maximize longevity and minimize overall energy consumption. Many key issues must be taken into account in the design of WSNs. In many applications it is not possible to replace or recharge the sensors. In view of this, several articles have been published regarding the improvement of energy consumption and longevity [5].

Based on an examination of the challenges of longevity and energy consumption, in the rest of the chapter, recommendations and solutions are proposed (setting the selection parameters) for setting the routing.

The rest of the paper is organized as follows. The effective parameters in energy consumption are discussed in Section 2, while Section 3 discusses the determination and estimation of distance. Section 4 proposes a solution and discusses it in detail regarding energy in WSNs. The influence of a number of sources is examined in Section 5, and Section 6 presents the issue of the number of hops and its effect on the performance of the network. Fianlly, Section 7 presents a summary of the methods introduced in this chapter.

2. Effective Parameters in Energy Consumption

Route discovery is one of the main functions in WSN routing in which the proper hop is selected by sending and receiving path request packages to the neighbouring nodes. A notable point to take into account in routing by sending a package is that depending on the route, it induces different levels of effects. In general, sending a routing package is feasible in two directions in WSNs: first, sending from the source to the sink node, and second, sending from the sink to the neighbouring nodes. The former mode happens when the routing node sends a routing package to the sink; in the latter mode, a response for routing is sent from the sink to the neighbouring node and then it returns to the source. These two routing modes have different effects on the network [5–7].

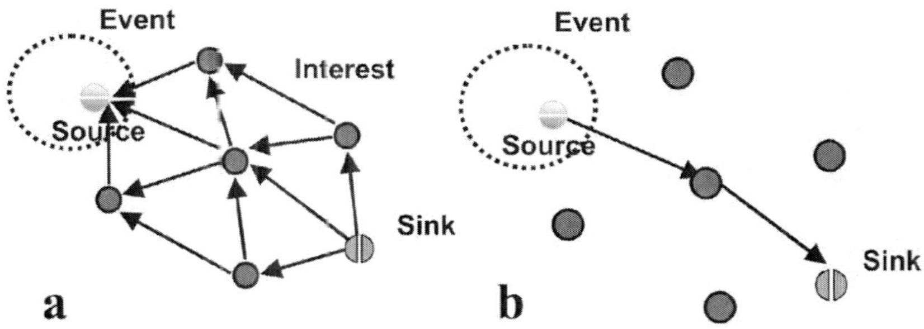

Figure 1. (a) transmission of interest data to discover the source; (b) transmission of discovery data from source to sink.

The sink node in Figure 1a acts as a transmitter and propagates an interest message to the neighbouring nodes, and in Figure 1b the source node acts as a transmitter. Therefore, adoption of the proper neighbouring node can be approached from two different viewpoints.

As pictured in Figure 1, to find the sources, the nodes send out a set of interest packages toward their neighbours and, upon finding the source node, send the discovery data to the sink node.

We assume that the concept of an optimum step implies that the node selected for surveying at the moment of transmission must be the best possible choice. Therefore it is necessary to take into account a set of factors and parameters, some of which are introduced below.

The present chapter is an attempt to survey the parameters and the factors that play notable roles in routing and mapping. Technical assessment of the parameters reveals some of the challenges ahead of WSNs and improving these factors results in better routing. A list of the influential and influenced factors along with a brief introduction on the function of the parameters and common methods is presented in what follows

2.1. Distance between Neighbouring Node and Sink Node

A neighbouring node in a WSN is a node at the frequency range of the transmitter node, as well as part of the geographical position of the transmitter. In this network, the transmitting node needs to know the position of the neighbouring node for routing. Whether or not the neighbouring node is on the route of the sink has a great effect on navigation of the package and establishment of the routing map. For instance, average energy consumption and delay in establishment of a routing map are much higher for sink nodes which are farther away.

2.2. Distance between Each Node and the Transmitter Node

For shorter distances between the neighbouring nodes – closer nodes – the transmitter needs less energy. This means that this parameter leads to better selection.

2.3. Energy of Neighbouring Node

Taking into account the physical limitations of sensors (battery capacities), energy plays a key role in wireless networks. Thus, the Low Energy Adaptive Clustering Hierarchy (LEACH) model was adopted to evaluate the received energy [1, 10]. So, when the distance between transmitter and receiver (d) is longer than d_0 (reference distance), the multi-path model (α as waste of energy coefficient of the path) is adopted; otherwise an open environment model (waste of energy coefficient of the path = 2) is adopted:

$$E_{Tx}(l,d) = E_{Tx-elec}(l) + E_{Tx-amp}(l,d) = \begin{cases} lE_{elec} + l\varepsilon_{fs}d^2 & d < d_0 \\ lE_{elec} + l\varepsilon_{mp}d^4 & d \geq d_0 \end{cases} \tag{1}$$

where E_{elect} is the energy required to activate electronic circuits, and ε_{fs} and ε_{mp} are the activating energy of the power amplifier for multiple-path and open space modes, respectively. The more general form of (2) and (3) with "p" and "q" as fixed coefficients is:

$$E_{Tx}(l,d) = p + qd^{\alpha} \tag{2}$$

On the receiver side, the energy consumed in receiving "l" bit of data is:

$$E_{Rx}(l) = E_{Rx-elec}(l) = lE_{elec} = p \tag{3}$$

2.4. Capacity of Buffer of the Neighbouring Node

The parameters regarding economic energy consumption are among the critical elements in the network structure. The parameters principally deal with the traffic load at each node and are obtained based on the occupied space of the buffer.

As the traffic load increases, the number of inputs in the line that the processor is able to process increases.Because the memory is an expensive element in the sensors, the available memory in each sensor is limited. Therefore, a proper algorithm must be used to manage this type of buffer.

A buffer is a temporary memory and is commonly found in any device that performs processing. The buffer maintains a balanced and equal processing pace for different processors. A notable matter before sending data to the buffer is to determine the status of the buffer (full or empty). When the buffer is full, the packages sent to the buffer are dropped and lost, and consequently result in a heavier traffic load that causes a negative effect on the longevity of the network. At any rate, the high price of buffers increases the costs of the device. Moreover, where several nodes are deployed in the network, it is not feasible to increase the size of the buffer, while a larger buffer space means a reduction in package loss.

Among the proposed solutions for managing buffers of sensors are queuing theory, genetic algorithms, and reducing the headers of transmitted and received packages.

2.5. Delivery Time

The time taken to deliver a package is called the delivery time; the shorter the delivery time, the better the selection rate.

The time needed for a package to travel between the sources and reach the destination node is the delivery time. In other words, the time required to travel through the network and reach the destination intact is the delivery time. The importance of the parameter lies in the fact that the longer the delay time, the higher the traffic load of the network, which influences the longevity of the network. In addition, this parameter helps to find proper neighbouring nodes. Delivery time, moreover, is influenced by other parameters such as noise in the environment, signal power, bandwidth, volume of the transmitted package, collisions, and distance between the nodes. There are a variety of ways to decrease the delivery time including reducing noise of the path or using amplifiers. The path between the nodes also affects the delivery time so that the delivery time between closer nodes is shorter and that between nodes which are further apart is longer.

Delivery time= time of propagation – time of complete reception

Still, it is notable that delivery time directly affects the quality of service and better delivery time means higher performance and less traffic load.

2.6. Success or Failure in Path Election

By modifying a variable in the header of the package, the number of successes and failures can be recorded and reported. Therefore, a record of every node can be checked (success/failure rate) before transmission. In this way, the nodes with a high failure rate have less chance of being elected. This is another effective parameter in the election function.

The ratio of success to failure is a practical parameter that logs and reports the number of successful deliveries compared with the number of failed deliveries. The parameter is recorded in the header. Before transmitting a package, the log of each node is checked and nodes with a higher rate of failure have a smaller chance of being selected. That is, the parameter is effective in the route selection function. This parameter, however, is not free of drawbacks as it increases the volume, traffic, and processing load. In addition, the parameter helps find the best route. For instance, take a node located on a riverbank that appears to be an optimum choice regarding the required energy and other factors; however, the node is still not accessible and the packages sent to the node are dropped. This means that the loss rate of the node increases and it is less likely that the node will be selected in future.

Finally, the parameter can be used in a more applied way and this is necessary where there are no considerable geographical and environmental changes. On the other hand, the parameter is very helpful where the environment is volatile whether naturally or unnaturally.

2.7. Number of Passed Hops

The sink node can use the variable to estimate the number of passed hops and length of the path that the package has passed to reach the sink. Based on the policies and purposes of running the network, this parameter may be considered positive or negative. For instance, more hopping might be preferred to balance the energy (the purpose); in other words, more hopping is preferred for specific applications while some applications such as emergencies and medical applications prefer less hopping.

2.8. Delay in Transmission

This parameter refers to end-to-end delay – the time between complete transmission and complete delivery of packages. Factors such as environmental noise and traffic load affect this parameter.

The parameters (e.g., distance between gap and source, energy level, buffer volume, time to deliver, success and failure rate) as discussed above are all effective in this type of transmission, although the main point is that some of the effective parameters exert different influences. There are also additional parameters that exert greater influences, such as the probability of risk and number of references.

2.9. Risk and Probability of Transmission-Reliability

This parameter is applicable where the sink nodes send queries about an event based on the main stream of data and tries to send them through more reliable positions with less risk. For instance, to check on an outbreak of fire in a ship, question/answer messages are mainly sent to the engine room. That is, routing is initiated from the point where the probability of an event is highest.

2.10. Number of Sources

The parameter is set depending on the sink node; the sink node tries to give priority to the node that covers more sources within its range. This prevents the energy of the irrelevant nodes from being wasted.

3. Determining and Estimating Distance between Two Nodes

A list of the parameters which are effective in the performance of WSNs has been introduced. The parameters are determined depending on the application. To put it another way, these parameters show different features and have different effects depending on the application.

The following sections present an in-depth and more accurate survey of the parameters to gain a revealing insight into their role in the WSNs under study.

3.1. Signal Power

Upon receiving a propagated packet, the node first checks the signal power and estimates the distance using the power obtained by [4, 6]. Naturally, the signal power received by a receiver from the farther nodes is less than that of the nearer nodes. Actually, there is direct relation between the signal power and the distance, as shown in [8, 17].

(4)

where P_t and P_r are the power of transmitted and received signals respectively, G_r and G_t are the signal gain of the receiver and transmitter respectively, λ is the wavelength, and L is the network wastage rate. The larger P_r is, the closer the transmitter.

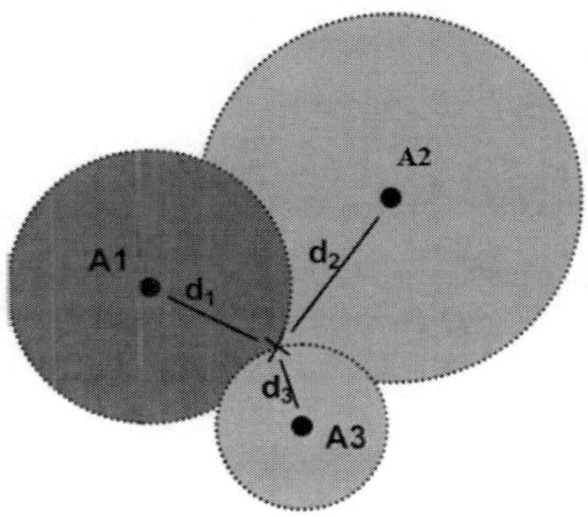

Figure 2. Schematic view of propagations with different signal power.

As pictured in Figure 2, node *A2* with a weaker signal is farther away than the two other adjacent nodes and the neighbour of node *x*.

3.2. Average Delay between Two Nodes

The term "delay" refers to end-to-end delay (complete transmission to complete reception of the package). Different factors such as noise in the environment and traffic load may influence the length of delay.

In other words, end-to-end delay commences from the moment the package leaves the source and ends the moment the package reaches the receiver node. The delay is obtained as follows:

$$
\begin{gathered}
AVG\_D_{end\text{-}end} = [\, d_{trans} + d_{prop} + d_{proc}] \\
AVG\_D_{end\text{-}end} = \textit{end-to-end delay} \\
AVG\_D_{trans} = \textit{transmission delay} \\
AVG\_D_{prop} = \textit{propagation delay} \\
AVG\_D_{proc} = \textit{processing delay}
\end{gathered} \tag{5}
$$

3.3. GPS

By equipping each sensor with a GPS, the sensor can estimate the distance of every node. GPS technology uses satellites to compare transmission and reception times and the difference between the two shows the position of the GPS receiver relative to the satellite. Therefore, by measuring distance using several satellites, the system can locate the sensor and display the result on an electronic map. GPS satellites orbit the earth twice every 24 hours and send the information signal to Earth.

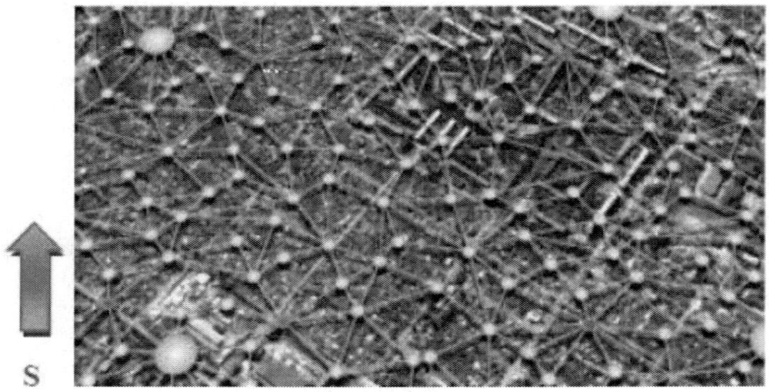

Figure 3. Distribution of sensors at urban areas.

Signals from at least four satellites are required to obtain the latitude, altitude, and longitude. The figure above, for instance, shows the distribution of sensors in an urban area. Figure 3 portrays how GPS can be used to obtain longitudes and latitudes of sensors in a city using a positioning map.

3.4. Layout and Distribution

In general, WSNs can have different distributions including uniform, random, and grid distributions. In the case of grid distribution, the distance between every pair of nodes can be estimated and the position of each node is determined stepwise based on the header information. Figure 4 displays a layout where the distances between the nodes are fixed.

Usually, the layout is determined based on the application for which the network is designed. For example, in military applications, airplanes carry sensor nodes randomly over the region, while in other cases (e.g., underwater sensor networks), a uniform layout is the best choice, and for urban networks a grid (Figure 4) is the choice.

Random distribution is another type of distribution in WSNs. Many random events may use a Poisson distribution; This type of distribution also may generate an estimate of binominal probabilities. In addition to being an estimator of distribution, the Poisson distribution is a reliable probability model for the accidents that happen randomly in time and place. It is commonly used to gain a deeper insight into WSN behaviours or simulation of such behaviours.

The Poisson distribution is defined as: $P(X = x) = e^{-mmx}/x$ and $x = 0, 1,\ldots, n$, where "e" is an exponential number (2.71828).

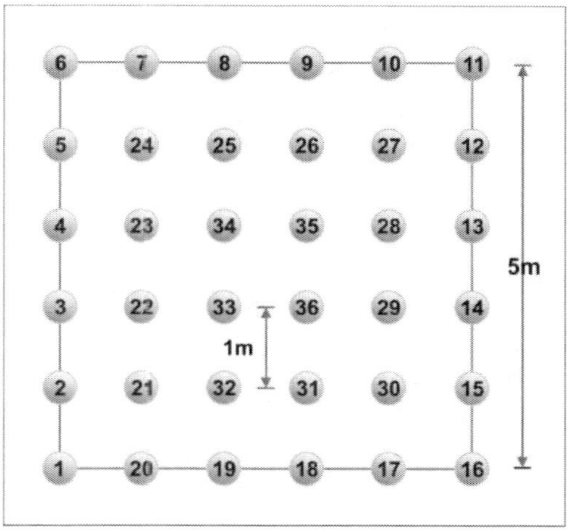

Figure 4. Grid layout in a wireless sensor network.

3.5. Probability

In some cases, distance can be estimated based on probability of occurrence. In case of a fire outbreak, for instance, the probability of finding the fire in engine room is high enough that makes it possible to estimate the distance to the place of event based on the probability. In general, due to high risk, probability estimate is made along with other estimates.

3.6.Number of Cluster Heads

The clusters of passed head is logged in the header of each package in the cluster networks. So the distance may be obtained based on the density of the network and using related, adjacent, and non-adjacent clusters.

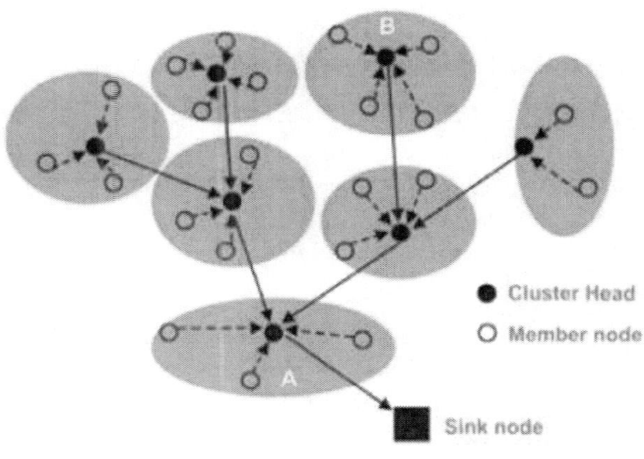

Figure 5. Number of passed steps by the head-cluster nodes.

Once a package is received from a node, the information of the cluster head in each package's header records the number of passed cluster heads. In addition, the boundaries of each cluster are given by the definite borders of the network. Therefore, the distance of each cluster head can be estimated [13,20].

For example, node A (Figure 5) receives a package from head cluster 2, and the approximate distance of each cluster is about 10 m; therefore, the distance between node B and node A is about 20 m.

3.7. Comparison of Results

Many different types of distance estimation methods (Table 1) were studied in the previous sections. The methods are suitable for specific applications; however none of them are perfect. For instance, the GPS method is not recommended for the implementation of distance estimation as it is too costly (equipping each sensor with GPS is too costly with a large number of sensors). However, for important and critical purposes such as water exploration on Mars, such costs are negligible, and when the purpose of the network is to monitor or find wildlife, the costs may be considered enormous.

Table 1. Distance Estimation methods

	Limitation	**Application**	**Processing volume**	**Accuracy**
GPS	Cost	Positioning	Low	High
Signal power	Processing	Determining distance	Moderate	Good
Distribution layout	Implementation	Distribution of sensors in urban area, battle fields, under water	Depending on the layout, so low for grid	Good just for girds
Probability	Reliability	Estimating distance of event	High	Low
Head-cluster step	Processing and transmission	Estimating passed steps	Moderate	Moderate
End-to-end delay	Processing	Delay estimate	Moderate	Good

On the other hand, determining distance based on layout and distribution suits a grid network; however, in many applications, the implementation of grid networks is not feasible (e.g., distribution of sensors in remote areas to discover an event). Consequently, such estimates are not feasible for random layouts such as urban utilization, gardens, parks (natural/non-natural), sport fields, and farms.

The probability estimate method suits specific applications. Because of the risk of inaccurate results, the method may be misleading; therefore, it is not recommended for many applications. However, for estimating distance using the steps passed by the package, the method is helpful where there is clustering. As mentioned earlier, the signal power method is suggested for estimating distances. In spite of requiring more complicated computations, the results obtained are more logical and accurate compared with the results of other methods.

4. Energy and Sensor Networks

Due to its direct and considerable effects on longevity, reliability, and adoption of the optimum route, energy is a great challenge for WSNs. Therefore, energy management in WSNs has drawn considerable attention.

For wireless networks, the parameter of energy can be approached differently, such as by estimating energy to elaborate on competition between nodes in adopting cluster heads and adopting the proper neighbours for routing. However, the issue of energy is not limited to a single node as it deals with estimation of the average energy consumption (energy consumption of all nodes) of the network. In other words, energy can be considered in two different ways: first, as the energy of a single node, and second, as the total energy of the network.

It is noticeable that there is a direct relation between network longevity and the remaining energy of the network. However, one way to calculate longevity is to consider a node dead when less than 10% of the energy remains. Therefore, this parameter and the way in which it is obtained are crucial [15, 18].

4.1. Calculation of Energy of Node

Recent developments in wireless communication technology have made it possible to build networks with small sensors. The networks can be used in different fields such as military, health, industrial, and weather monitoring, tracking of items such as commodities, and home security [6, 8]. Although this technology promises great opportunities, there are still several challenges to deal with before making a WSN applicable.

One key limitation of sensor networks is their dependency on batteries. Another that can be named is that sensors may be positioned in inaccessible places and there may be many of them, which means that maintaining the sensors will be too difficult if not impossible. Therefore, minimizing energy consumption is one of the top priorities in designing the systems. Heinzelman et al. brought in one of the most well known energy consumption models, which has received great attention as a basis for designing communication protocols with low power consumption [4, 11]. Section 2.2 deals with some other models, although there is a paucity of studies on measuring energy consumption by the sensors. Anastasi et al. used average current consumption measured with a voltmeter to measure the energy consumed by a sensor node [14]. In another work, power consumption by the sensors in different states was measured with the use of an oscilloscope. Unfortunately, these tests were carried out on a short-term basis and no statistical proof is available [12].

4.2. Types of Energy Consumption

The energy consumed can be measured on different bases, such as watts, joules, and voltage. By introducing different measures of energy consumption, the calculation of energy in its different forms is discussed here. Moreover, a comparison between the efficiency of the performance of the models is made in a table.

Table 2. Radio Characteristics, Classical model

Radio mode	Energy Consumption
Transmit Electronics ($E_{Tx\text{-}elec}$) Receiver Electronics ($E_{Rx\text{-}elec}$) $E_{Tx\text{-}elec} = E_{Rx\text{-}elec} = E_{elec}$	50 nJ/bit
Transmit Amplifier (ε_{amp})	100 pJ/bit/m^2
Idle (ε_{amp})	40 nJ/bit
Sleep	0

Table 3. Sensor states for μAMPS model

State	SA-1110	Sensor, A/D	Radio	Pk (mW)
Active	Active	sense	tx/rx	1040
Ready	Idle	sense	Rx	400
Monitor	Sleep	sense	Rx	270
Observe	Sleep	sense	Off	200
Deep Sleep	sleep	Off	Off	10

4.2.1. The Classical Energy Consumption Model

An energy consumption model was introduced by Heinzeman et al. based on the results of an observation that showed data communication subsystems can have a determinant role in energy consumption [4, 11]. The model is represented in Table 2..

The model adopts a radio with lower power consumption, which allows it to slightly outperform some standard definitions (e.g., Bluetooth) [8, 17]. A usual starting point is adopted by the model, although it is still to be confirmed regarding the behaviour of a physical radio in a WSN. Based on the application, the CPU and the sensor are either neglected or used to obtain the consumption of energy by a node. Therefore, some figures on consumption of energy by those elements must be employed jointly with the radio model. The reason is that the whole system, rather than the radio, must be powered by the power supply.

4.2.2. μAMPS Specific Model

A model designed for a specific platform (the μAMPS Wireless Sensor Node) was proposed by Shih et al. The platform is equipped with a powerful microprocessor (ARM SA 1110, clock speed 59–206 MHz) [9]. The energy consumption of the microcontroller, radio, and energy lost by leakage are taken into account by the model (Table 3).

The energy consumption for transmission/reception of one bit is not obtained by the model. At any rate, a transmission rate of 1 Mbps is used by the platform by definition; this means that by using the method the energy required for one bit is obtainable. Having obtained the power value, the energy consumption for transmission/reception of one bit can be calculated [11, 19]:

Time taken to send or receive one bit = 1/1 Mbps = 1 μsec

$$Energy = Power \times Time \tag{6}$$

where power is in watts and time is in seconds

$$Energy_{Txonebit} = 1040 \times 1 \times 10\text{-}3\ W \times 1 \times 10\text{-}6\ sec$$
$$Energy_{Txonebit} = 1.04\ \mu J/bit$$
$$Energy_{RxonebitReadystate} = 0.4\ \mu J/bit$$
$$Energy_{RxonebitMonitorstate} = 0.27\ \mu J/bit$$

4.2.3. Mica2 Specific Model

The model introduced by Polastreet al. gives the total energy consumed for Mica2 by adding the energy of transmission, reception, listening, data sampling, and sleeping [8,16]. The values are obtained using the expected energy consumption by the CPU and the radio. A summary of current consumption is listed below (Table 4).As the authors present current consumption and time, and assuming that Mica2 is powered by a 3 V source [16], the energy of transmitting and receiving one bit is calculated as (Relation 7):

$$Energy = Current \times Voltage \times Time \qquad (7)$$

where the current is in amperes, the voltage is in volts, and time is in seconds

$$Energy_{Tx} = 20 * 10^{-3}\ A * 3\ Volts * 416 * 10^{-6}\ sec / 8\ bits = 3.12\ \mu J/bit$$
$$Energy_{Rx} = 15 * 10^{-3}\ A * 3\ Volts * 416 * 10^{-6}\ sec / 8\ bits = 2.34\ \mu J/bit$$

The difference from the Heinzelman model is two orders of magnitude [11]. With the µAMPS model, energy for transmission is comparable, while energy for reception is one order of magnitude bigger in the Mica2 case.

Table 4. Current consumption for Mica2 model

Operation	Time (s)		I (mA)	
Initialize radio (b)	350 E-6	t_{rinit}	6	c_{rinit}
Turn on radio (c)	1.5E-3	t_{ron}	1	c_{ron}
Switch to RX/TX (d)	250E-6	$t_{rx/tx}$	15	$c_{rx/tx}$
Time to sample radio (e)	350E-6	t_{sr}	15	c_{sr}
Evaluate radio sample (f)	100E-6	t_{ev}	6	c_{ev}
Receive 1 byte	416E-6	t_{rxb}	15	c_{rxb}
Transmit 1 byte	416E-6	t_{txb}	20	c_{txb}
Sample sensors	1.1	t_{data}	20	c_{data}

4.2.4. Mica2 Specific Model with Actual Measurements

Shnayder et al. presented a current consumption model based on measurements on the Mica2 platform [12]. A summary of the model is shown in Table 5.

The figures listed in the table above have been calculated separately. Summing energy consumption by each active component gives the total current. For example, only the CPU is in active mode and seven radios transmitting at +10 dBm (worst case) is sufficient to obtain the energy required to transmit and receive one bit. The bit rate is not determined, so the same time as that used in the previous model is employed. The energy cost based on each bit transmitted using Relation (8) is:

$$\text{Energy}_{Tx}=(8+21.5) * 10^{-3}\ \text{A} * 3\ \text{Volts} * 416 * 10^{-6}\ \text{sec} / 8\ \text{bits} = 4.602\ \mu\text{J/bit}$$
$$\text{Energy}_{Rx}=(8+7) * 10^{-3}\ \text{A} * 3\ \text{Volts} * 416 * 10^{-6}\ \text{sec} / 8\ \text{bits} = 2.34\ \mu\text{J/bit} \quad (8)$$

Table 5. Current consumption with actual measurements

Mode	Current	Mode	Current
CPU		Radio	
Active	8.0 mA	Rx	7.0 mA
Idle	3.2 mA	Tx (-20 dBm)	3.7 mA
ADC Noise Reduce	1.0 mA	Tx (-19 dBm)	5.2 mA
Power-down	103 μA	Tx (-15 dBm)	5.4 mA
Power-save	110 μA	Tx (-dBm)	6.5 mA
Standby	216 μA	Tx (-dBm)	7.1 mA
Extended Standby	223 μA	Tx (dBm)	8.5 mA
Internal Oscillator	0.93 mA	Tx (+dBm)	11.6 mA
LEDs	2.2 mA	Tx (+dBm)	13.8 mA
Sensor board	0.7 mA	Tx (+dBm)	17.4 mA
EEPROM access			
Read	6.2 mA		
Read Time	565 μs	Tx (+10 dBm)	21.5 mA
Write	18.4 mA		
Write Time	12.9 ms		

Table 6. Energy consumption models

Models	**Energy model**	**Cost of transmitting**	**Cost of receiving**	**Energy consumption at standby mode**	**Option and operation**
Classical	joule	50 nJ/bit	50 nJ/bit	0	Low
μAMPS	Watt	1.04 μJ/bit	0.4 μJ/bit	10 mW	Moderate
Mica2	Volt	μJ/bit3.12	μJ/bit 2.34	0	High
Mica2 with actual measurements	Volt	μJ/bit4.602	μJ/bit 2.34	216 μA	Very high

The obtained figures for the model are like those gained for the model proposed in [17]. The different results for the energy taken to transmit one bit are probably because Polastreet al. did not determine how much power is used for transmission, which is probably different from what is used in [8,12].

4.2.5. Comparison of Results

What makes the above models worthy of attention is their different forms of energy consumption; even the sensors' estimate of energy consumption is based on a variety of models. However, recent technological and electronic advances have simplified the estimation of energy consumption so that every sensor may report its percentage residual energy and, using software, longevity. As listed in Table 6, the classic energy model has low operational power and uses lower energy for transmitting and receiving data. Still, it is noticeable that the classic energy model does not consume energy in standby mode, which is not the case in other models. On the other hand, what distinguishes the classical energy model is that it measures energy in joules, while μAMPS and Mica2 use voltage and watts respectively. Again, the table above represents energy cost increases with increases in operational power, and clearly more processing requires more energy. For instance, a noise-checking operation consumes less energy as it conducts little processing.

4.3. Network Energy Consumption

One of the important criteria of a network (assessed based on the diagram) is the energy consumption of the network. Energy consumption in a network is the total energy consumption divided by the number of nodes in the network (Relation 9).

$$E_T = \frac{\sum_{i=0}^{n} Ei}{N} \tag{9}$$

E_T= Total Average Energy Consumption of Network

In fact, all nodes start off with equal energy – all nodes use similar batteries or other sources of energy. Therefore, when the network commences its function, the starting energy of each node is equal to the maximum level of energy.

4.4. Network Longevity

The short life of the sensor network is one of disadvantages of these networks, and is mainly due to limited power sources. In addition, the specific position of a node may be a great threat to the longevity of the network. For instance, a node located close to the sink dies much sooner than the other nodes, as it consumes its energy faster due to the heavier processing load. In addition, failure of such nodes results in cutting the sink's line of communication with the whole network and consequent failure of the network. Some of the energy management solutions are structure dependent. For the case mentioned here, an automatic structure is effective; the majority of the decision making is conducted locally, which relieves the traffic load on the critical node and consequently increases the longevity of the node and the network. Early running-out of energy is also common for the nodes in areas with lower traffic load and where nodes are scattered. In such cases, a power management resident in each node and use of energy-aware solutions to ensure that critical nodes carry out fewer operations may help [10, 15].

The longevity of the network can be assessed from different viewpoints; that is, there are different ways of calculating it.

1. First sensor death: the time at which the first death among the sensors occurs, so that the network is dead when the first sensor is dead.
2. When the remainder of the sensor nodes have less than 10% of full energy. This method is more applicable as the method holds, the sensor keeps 10% of its energy for emergency situations, which means that the residual energy is only used for reporting events at critical moments.
3. The network dies when the last sensor dies. This method does not sound logical and is barely used.
4. When the network fails to function, which means when a node close to the sink dies and the sink losses connection with the whole network, the whole network fails to carry out the designated function.

One of the most common ways to improve the longevity of the network is to balance energy consumption among the nodes in a network. Fair energy consumption, discussed in previous works, is implemented through optimization algorithms such as genetic algorithms, fuzzy algorithms, and neural networks.

5. Number of Sources

One of the parameters that affect node election is the number of sources. This refers to the number of sources or number of events that happen simultaneously in the network. For example, a military field is invaded by the enemy several times (simultaneous event) and the nodes that report the event are connected to each other. In other cases, a node may monitor several events and report them all to the sink. This feature has both advantages and weaknesses. For one thing, the fact that one node can observe several events simultaneously gives other nodes the chance to remain on standby and save more energy. Also, when undertaking the whole load of reporting, the node loses its energy faster and this results in the death of key nodes in the network. There are several mechanisms and management tools that can be used to achieve a balance between the two extremes.

5.1. The Mechanisms

The two-phase pull protocol (Figure 6) establishes a route or routes between the sources and sink using interest and gradient packages, and a high quality route is adopted using the amplification mechanism. In the first phase, the transmitter/destination node propagates an interest message in the network and when a node finds a match between its data collected by its sensor and the interest message, a discovery data message is sent toward the source. Among the formed gradients, the source/sink node try to find a gradient with the shortest delivery time and highest channel quality. Upon reaching the source, the source node sends the collected data to the source.

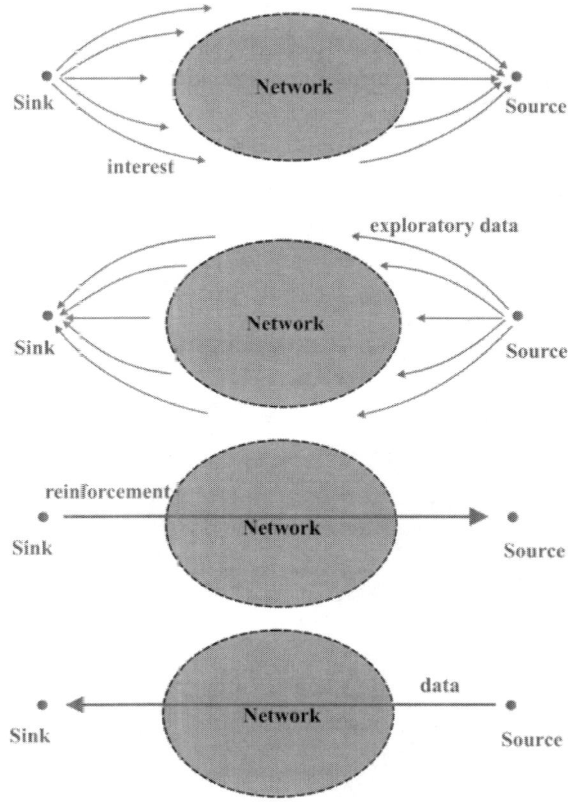

Figure 6. Function of one phase pull propagation method.

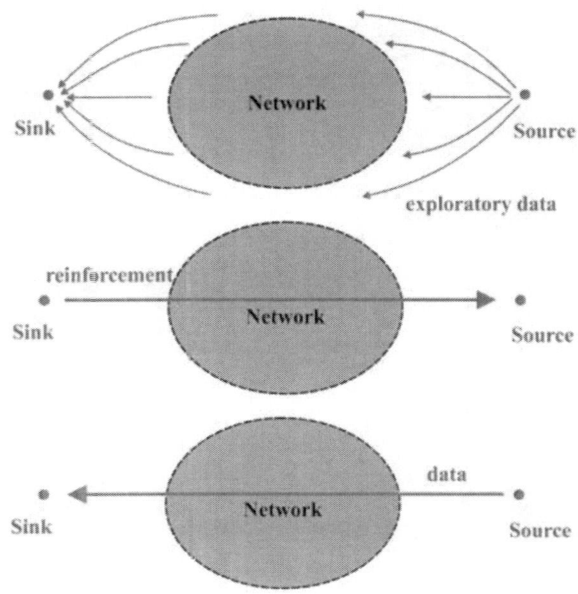

Figure 7. Output propagation method.

The two-phase pull method is the best choice for many, while it gives a poor performance for some other usages; in particular, usages that feature many sources, receivers, and receivers' specific connections increase the volume of data traffic to a great extent. To deal with the problem, push diffusion was introduced, where the roles of information propagator and users are replaced. This makes the data sources actively search for users.

An advantage of push diffusion is the propagation of control packages to find the receivers (Figure 7). In fact, the method sends packages throughout the network in single mode (discovery data), while in the two-stage pull method, packages are sent in two modes. The push diffusion method suits a small number of sources and several receivers (sinks). Another development in the two-phase pull method was the introduction of one-phase pull.

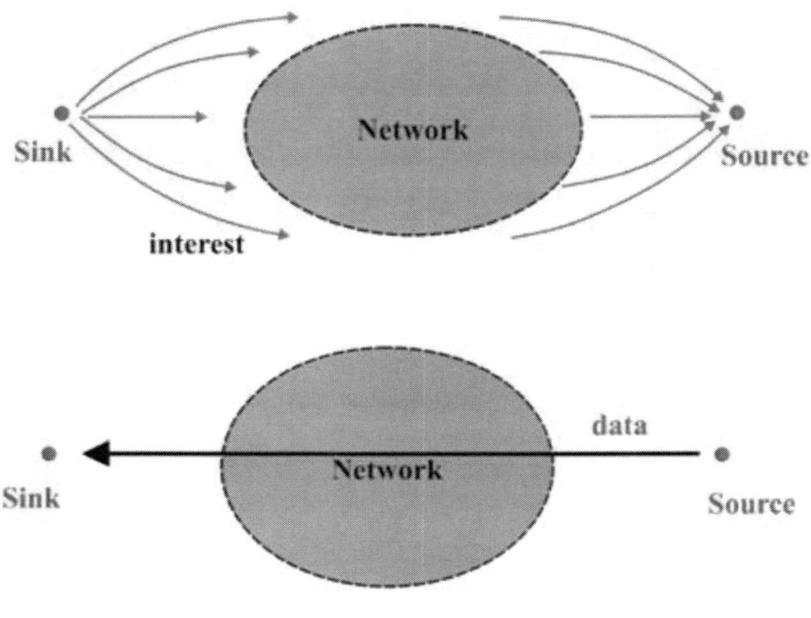

Figure 8. Function of one phase pull method.

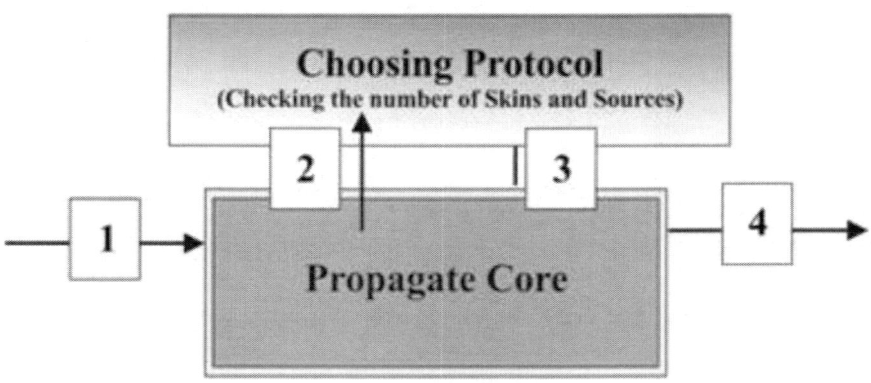

Figure 9. Choosing the proper propagation method based on the number of sinks and sources.

As pictured in Figure 8, one of the phases of the two-phase pull method is omitted depending on the request. Like the two-phase pull method, the requesters send the interest messages throughout the network and form the gradient; however, in spite of the two-phase pull method, once an interest reaches the source, it does not take the source of the first package of data as the discovery data. Instead, it sends the package as the main data to the destination through the gradients that have been formed earlier. Using this procedure, the method does not need to amplify messages. The method is suitable for a large number of sources and few receivers.

5.2. Choosing a Filter Based on the Source and Sink

Depending on the number of sources, sensor networks use proper filters for data propagation along with a set of mechanisms and management methods. In fact, the network adopts the proper propagation filter depending on the operation.

As illustrated in Figure 9, upon the occurrence of an event in the network, the propagation core starts checking the number of sources and sinks in the network to find the best possible filter, infuses it into the propagate core, and finally propagates the interest package in the network.

5.3. Compression of Results

As listed in Table 7, when the number of sources is high, the one-phase pull method outperforms the two-phase pull. In addition, the push diffusion method is not as good as other methods in reporting events; however, it is the best choice when the number of the sinks is too high. Moreover, the one-phase pull method cannot report events properly to the base station.

As shown in Figures 10a and 10b, compared with the push diffusion method, the one-phase pull method does not have good performance with a large number of sinks, nor is it good at reporting events. Figure 11b reveals that with an increase in the number of sources, the performance of the push out diffusion method is almost linear and has poor performance compared with the one-phase pull method. In fact, the reported performance of the former is improved with an increase in the number of sources compared with the latter. However, as pictured in Figure 11, with an increase in the number of sources, the one-phase pull method fails to report events properly when the number of the event grows.

Table 7. Propagation methods based on number of sources and sinks

	Number of source	Number of receivers (sinks)
One phase pull	High	Low
Two phase pull	1	1
Push diffusion	Low	High

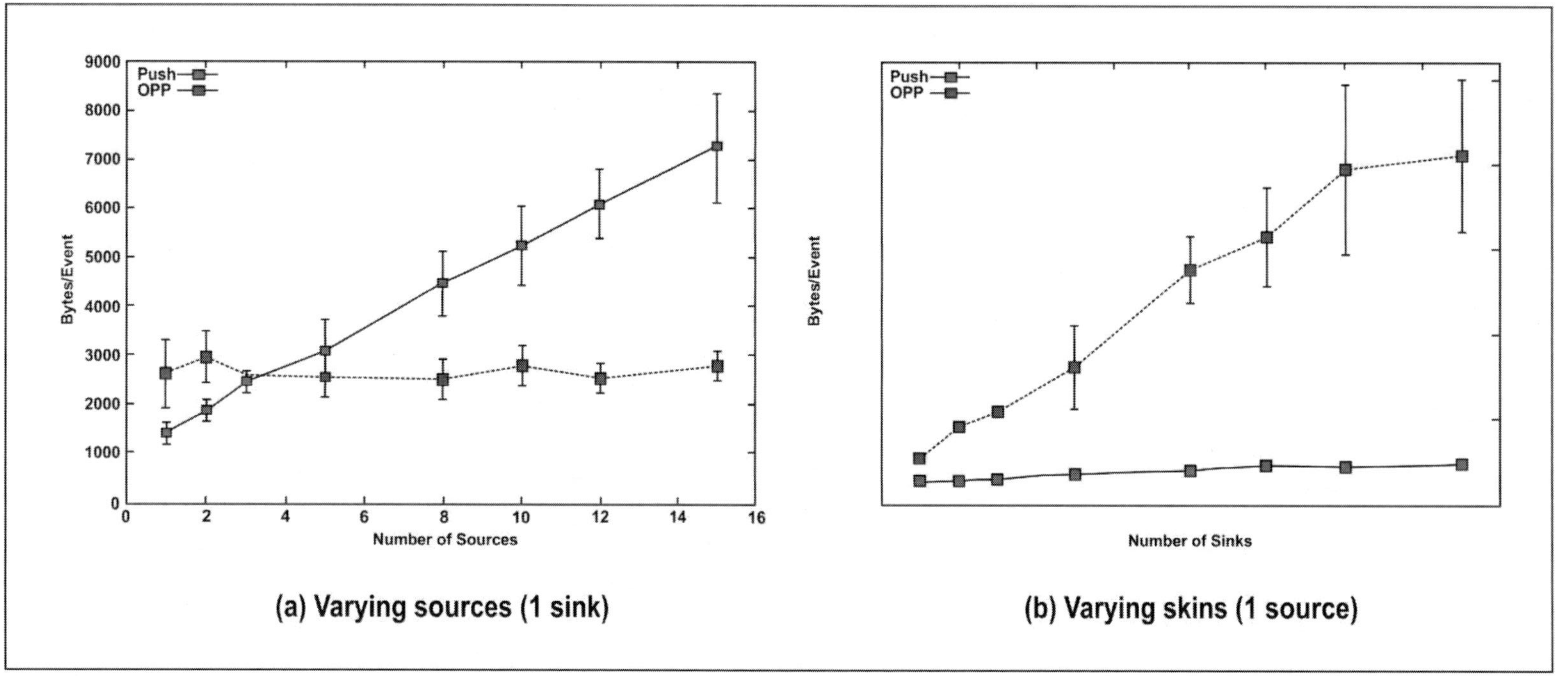

Figure 10. Diagrams of push out diffusion and one phase pull methods.

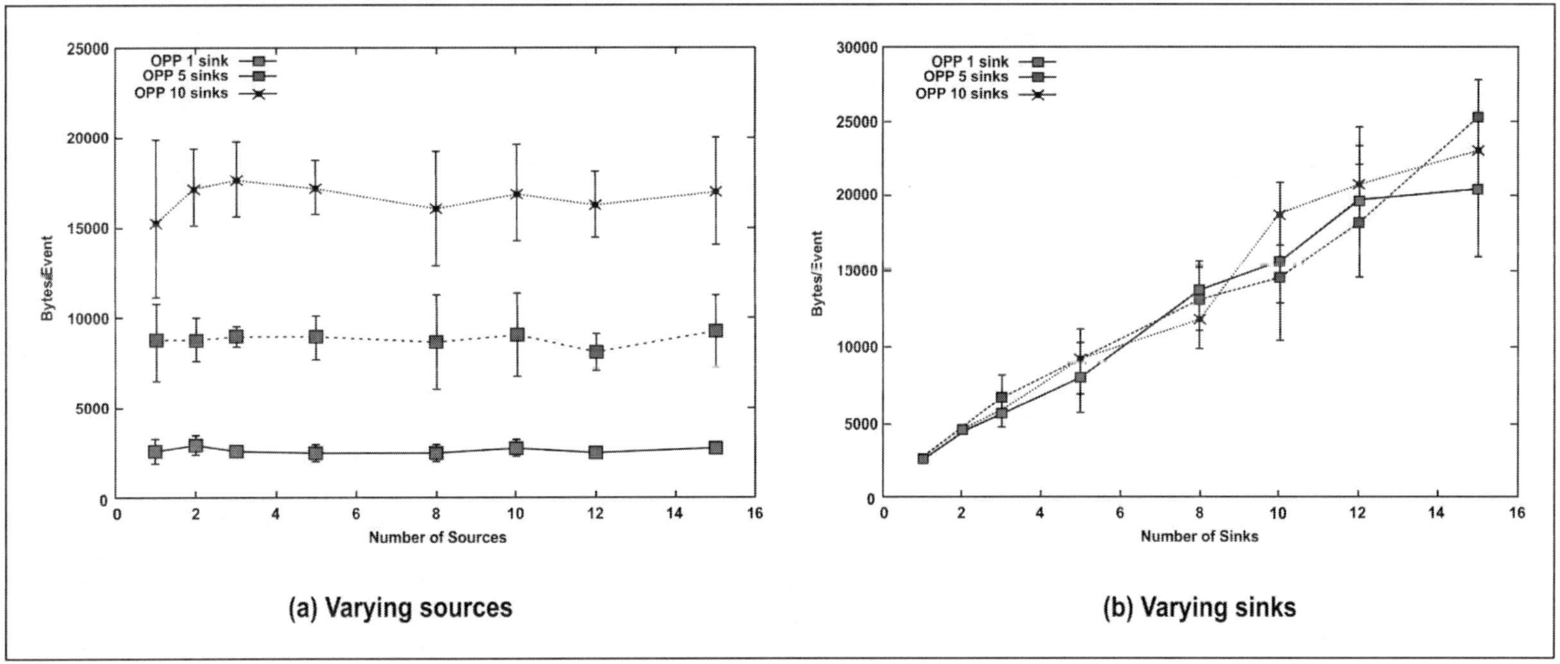

Figure 11. One phase pull method with varying number of sources and sinks.

6. Number of Hops

One of the main points regarding the number of hops is that it is used for determining the passed hops. So each node updates the specification of the package by changing the variables in the header and reports to its neighbours the number of the passed hops from the sink or source node. In the case of uniform layout, the parameter is used to measure the distance. One of the main applications of this parameter is in choosing the route between the sources and sink nodes.

6.1. The Mechanisms

In general, the source node chooses the path that needs less step energy. The noticeable point is that adopting a route with few hops has both advantages and weaknesses. One advantage of a shorter route is that the package reaches the destination faster. This means there is less end-to-end delay, which is of great importance for applications that put more emphasis on the delay.

Another advantage of this parameter that can be mentioned is that the fewer hops there are in the route, the fewer nodes participate in the transmission – more nodes remain in standby state and more energy is saved. Regarding the weaknesses, we may mention that by taking routes with more nodes, nodes may live longer as there is a better energy balance in the network. Therefore, instead of over-loading a node, more nodes participate in the operation. On the other hand, adopting a route with more nodes causes problems such as a heavier traffic load and longer delay. This seriously decreases the quality of the service, although there are advantages such as a better delivery rate and energy balance and decrease in packet loss. Finally, all the advantages and weaknesses mentioned here may be evaluated depending on the application and type of network management.

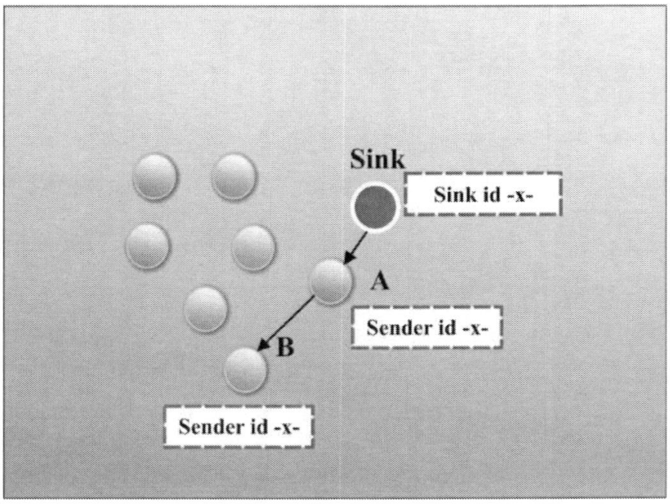

Figure 12. Propagation of interest package and updating of the number of hops.

As Figure 12 shows, the number of hops is recorded in the package's header and updated by every node located on the route until it reaches the sink so that the sink can determine the number of hops.

6.2. Comparision of Results

A source node chooses its route based on the parameters and comparisons listed in Table 8 and the policies of the network. As an example, the source node usually tries to choose a route with the minimum energy requirement; however, it needs to take into account both advantages and weaknesses. A shorter route has the advantage of using a path with fewer hops, which results in faster delivery of the message. The faster delivery means shorter end-to-end delay, which is vital for applications that emphasize delay. Another advantage of choosing a shorter path is that fewer nodes are engaged in the transmission and more nodes remain on standby.

Table 8. Parameters of quality of service based on the number of hops

	Energy	Delay	Delivery	Traffic	Longevity
Increase of number of hops	Energy is balanced	Increase due to high number of propagation	Increase due to better access to node and decrease of packet loss	Increase in traffic due to more transmission	Better longevity due to prevention of over-use of one node
Decrease in number of hops	Over-use of a node	Decrease in delay due to fewer transmission	Dependency of long-range transmission, increase/decrease of packet loss	Prevention of increase in traffic load	Decrease of longevity due to early discharge of batteries

Conclusion

An outstanding opportunity to collect an enormous volume of data from the world around is promised by WSNs. The specially designed sensors can be easily deployed in the network. However, WSNs are not free of drawbacks as they are tightly limited by resource constraints regarding power, memory, and bandwidth. Such disadvantages make collecting and processing the data a serious challenge. WSNs are everywhere nowadays especially when it comes to ubiquitous and pervasive applications. They are used in different fields such as the military, medicine, environment, and households. However, all these applications have energy, data loss, and delay as the determinant factors in their performance. WSNs are application-specific, which means the design varies depending on the application. These networks mainly have to deal with scalability, latency, throughput, resource awareness, data aggregation, optimal routing, overhead, and other related metrics as the main challenges. The necessity of these metrics varies depending on the application. Many applications feature the impossibility of replacing or recharging the sensors. In addition, the role of several factors (e.g., network architecture and protocols, data collection initiation, definition of longevity, channel characteristics, and the energy consumption model) in longevity makes it impossible to estimate the longevity of the network.

The parameters that may affect network performance were discussed. Ten key parameters including the distance between the neighbouring node and the sink node, the distance between each node and the transmitter node, the energy of the neighbouring node, the capacity of buffer of the neighbouring node, delivery time, number of sources, delay in transmission, number of passed hops, success or failure in path election, risk, and probability of transmission-reliability were examined and optimized.

Several distance-estimation methods were reviewed, each of which was better for specific applications, although none of them were the perfect option. At any rate, for critical applications such as water exploration on Mars, these costs are trivial, but where the objective of the network is, for instance, to search for and find wildlife, the costs are notable.

After discussing different measures of energy consumption, the methods of calculating energy in its different forms were introduced. In addition, the performance and efficiency of the models were also compared.

The performance of the one-phase pull method with many sinks is not comparable with that of the push diffusion method; it is also not good at reporting events. The results showed that an increase in the number of sources had no effect on the performance of the push out diffusion method, so the performance is not comparable with the one-phase pull method. Still, there is an increase in the number of sources, which causes failure to report events properly after the number of events increases.

An advantage of the path with fewer hops is a shorter route, which leads to faster delivery of the message. Faster delivery results in shorter end-to-end delay; this feature is critical for applications that emphasize delay. Another notable advantage of adopting a shorter path is the need for fewer nodes to participate in the transmission and consequently more nodes remain on standby.

Taking into account the high cost of buffers, adding more buffer capacity means the network is more expensive. Furthermore, when there are many nodes in the network it is not possible to increase the size of the buffer. However, a larger buffer size prevents loss of packages and also improves balanced energy consumption.

There are other factors in delivery time including environmental noise, signal power, bandwidth, volume of the transmitted package, collisions, and distance between nodes. Improving delivery time is feasible through different methods including reducing noise on the path or adding amplifiers. Still, it is noticeable that there is a direct relationship between delivery time and quality of service, so improving this parameter leads to improved delivery time, higher performance, and lower traffic load.

The success to failure ratio parameter is a practical parameter that mirrors the rate of achievement to refraction by modifying a variable in the header. Before transmission, the record of each node is checked to obtain the success/failure rate. Thus, the nodes with a higher rate of failure are less likely to be selected, which means that this parameter plays an effective role in the route selection function.

The risk and probability of successful transmission, which is known as reliability, is of concern when the queries about an event are sent by the sink nodes based on the main stream of data; in this scenario, the sink nodes try to send the enquiries via more reliable positions with lower risk. The parameters of delay (e.g., distance between gap and source, energy level, buffer volume, time to deliver, success and failure rates), as mentioned earlier, are effective in this type of transmission. However, the main point is that different effective parameters induce different effects.

References

[1] Akyildiz, I. F. and Vuran, M. C. (2010) Front Matter, in *Wireless Sensor Networks*, John Wiley & Sons, Ltd, Chichester, UK. doi: 10.1002/ 9780470515181.

[2] C. Zhi-yan, J. Zhen-zhou, H. Ming-zeng "An energy-aware broadcast scheme for directed diffusion in wireless sensor network", *Journal of Communication and Computer*, ISSN1548-7709, USA 2007.

[3] K. Akkaya and M. Younis, "A Survey of Routing Protocols in Wireless Sensor Networks, " in the Elsevier *Ad Hoc Network Journal*, Vol. 3/3, pp. 325349, 2005.

[4] W. B. Heinzelman, A. P. Chandrakasan, and H. Balakrishnan. An Application-Specific Protocol Architecture for Wireless Microsensor Networks. *IEEE Transactions on Wireless Networking*, 1(4): 660–670, 2002.

[5] A. Norouzi, A. H. Zaim, A. Sertbas, "A comparative study based on power usage performance for routing protocols in wireless sensor network," in *Proceedings of the International Conference on Technological Advances in Electrical, Electronics and Computer Engineering (TAEECE 2013)*, May 2013.DOI: 10.1109/ TAEECE.2013.6557137.

[6] I. F. Akyildiz, W. Su, Y. Sankarasubramaniam and E. Cayirci. "A Survey on Sensor Networks", *IEEE Communications Magazine*, August 2002.

[7] Ali Norouzi, Faezeh Sadat Babamir, A Halim Zaim, An Interactive Genetic Algorithm for Mobile Sensor Networks, *Studies in Informatics and Control*, ISSN 1220-1766, vol. 22 (2), pp. 213-218, 2013.

[8] J. Polastre, "*Sensor Network Media Access Design*", Computer Science Division. EECS Department, University of California, Berkeley2003.

[9] E. Shih, S. Cho, N. Ickes, R. Min, A. Sinha, A. Wang, A. Chandrakasan, *Physical Layer Driven Protocol and Algorithm Design*.

[10] Ali Norouzi, Faezeh Sadat Babamir, A Halim Zaim, An Interactive Genetic Algorithm for Mobile Sensor Networks, *Studies in Informatics and Control*, ISSN 1220-1766, vol. 22 (2), pp. 213-218, 2013.

[11] W. R. Heinzelman, A. Chandrakasan, and H. Balakrishnan, "Energy-efficient communication protocol for wireless microsensor networks" in *IEEE Hawaii International Conference on Systems Sciences*, 2000.

[12] V. Shnayder, M. Hempstead, B. Chen, G. Werner Allen, and M. Welsh, "Simulating the Power Consumption of Large Scale Sensor Network Applications", *SenSys'04*, Baltimore, Maryland, USA, November 3–5, 2004.

[13] Z.Orman, A.Norouzi, F. S. Babamir,Intelligent Node Placement using GA (INPGA) Protocol in Wireless Sensor Networks, in *Proceedings of the International Conference on Wireless Networks* (ICWN'11) ISBN #: 1-60132-187-2 .

[14] G. Anastasi, M. Conti, A. Falchi, E. Gregori, A. Passarella., "Performance Measurements of Mote Sensor Networks" *MSWiM'2004,* October 4-6, 2004, Venezia, Italy.

[15] A. Norouzi, F. S.Babamir, A. H.Zaim, A Novel Energy Efficient Routing Protocol in Wireless Sensor Networks, *journal of Wireless Sensor Network*, Vol 3 No 10 ,PP 1-10 , 2011 .

[16] *XBOW Smart Dust Product Information Guide*, MOOG CROSSBOW Company, available in http://www.xbow.com/Support/Support_pdf_files/XBOW_Smart_Dust_ProductInfoGuide.pdf.

[17] J. Polastre, J. Hill, D. Culler, "Versatile Low Power Media Access for Wireless Sensor Networks", *SenSys'04*, Baltimore, Maryland, USA, November 3–5, 2004.

[18] A. Norouzi, F. Babamir and Z. Orman, "A Tree Based Data Aggregation Scheme for Wireless Sensor Networks Using GA," *Wireless Sensor Network*, Vol. 4 No. 8, 2012, pp. 191-196. doi: 10.4236/wsn.2012.48028.

[19] U. Rawat, M. Sharma ,Directed Diffusion: Features, Current Developments, Issues and Analysis, *International Journal of Computer Applications* (0975 – 8887) Volume 49 – No.12, 2012.

[20] A. Norouzi, F. Babamir and A. Zaim, "A New Clustering Protocol for Wireless Sensor Networks Using Genetic Algorithm Approach," *Wireless Sensor Network*, Vol. 3 No. 11, 2011, pp. 362-370. doi: 10.4236/wsn.2011.311042.

In: Horizons in Computer Science Research. Volume 9
Editor: Thomas S. Clary ISBN: 978-1-63321-522-1

Chapter 11

COMPUTER AIDED-THERMAL MODULE DESIGN

Jung-Chang Wang
Department of Marine Engineering, National Taiwan Ocean University,
Keelung, Taiwan

1. Introduction

The aims of this chapter is to depict how a thermal module comprised with high heat transfer efficiency device design effectively to reduce the temperature of Personal Computer (PC), Note Book (NB), and Server including central processing unit (CPU) and graphic processing unit (GPU), and LED lighting lamp of smaller area and higher heat flux utilizing related computer-aided design tools. The research approach focuses on various thermal modules. For traditional cooling techniques, the extended surface, such as fin is usually added to increase the rate of heat removal. Significant advances in the design theory of heat sinks have been made over the past some decades. The heat capacity from heat source conducted and transferred through heat sink to the surroundings by convection. Thus, the point of adding fin is to help dissipate heat flow from heat source. The extended heat transfer fins are made from several materials including metals, plastics or special substance. The proper CAD/CAE tools employed in thermal modules are important. The computer-aided thermal design of heat sink with high heat transfer device such heat pipe and vapor chamber developed a composite approach ensuring the thermal conditions to provide a high-quality development. There are several theoretical models of thermal modules developed to predict their thermal performance respectively with Software and algorithms in the computer-aided design system. The programs and methods for computer-aided thermal module design are being introduced in the chapter. The developed complex provides for high quality and short time of development owing to the lesser number of iterations of the design procedures. Based on the theoretical models with empirical formula, the author had developed a computer program coded by Virtual Basic version 6.0 to develop window programs and convenience for industrials.

An analytical all-in-one asymptotic model to predict the hydraulic and thermal performance of a practical traditional heat sink including a rectangular base plate and parallel fins with a non-uniform heat source has been developed, which proposed for a wide range of Reynolds and Nusselt numbers, including laminar, transition, and turbulent flows [1, 2].

However, increasing the surface area results in an increase in cost and boosting the fan speed results in noise, vibration and more power consumption, which increases the probability of failure. Its total thermal resistance is usually over 0.3 °C/W not adjust high heat capacity; A two-phase flow heat transfer module with high heat transfer efficiency, to effectively reduce the temperature of heat sources of smaller area and higher power. In recent years, technical development related with the application of two-phase flow heat transfer assembly to thermal modules has become mature and heat pipe-based two-phase flow heat transfer module is one of the best choices [3-7]. A heat sink with embedded heat pipes transfers the total heat capacity from the heat source to the base plate with embedded heat pipes and fins sequentially, and then dissipates the heat flow into the surrounding air. Wang et al. [8-10] have experimentally investigated the thermal resistance of a aluminium heat sink with horizontal embedded two and four U-shape heat pipes of 6 mm diameter; they showed that two heat pipes embedded in the base plate carry 36 percent of the total dissipated heat capacity from Central Process Unit (CPU), while 64% of heat was delivered from the base plate to the fins. Furthermore, when the CPU power was 140 W, the total thermal resistance was at its minimum of 0.27 °C/W. And using four embedded heat pipes carry 48 percent of the total dissipated heat capacity from CPU; the total thermal resistance is under 0.24 °C/W. The total thermal resistance of the heat sink with embedded heat pipes is only affected by changes in the base to heat pipes thermal resistance and heat pipes thermal resistance over the heat flow path; that is, the total thermal resistance varies according to the functionality of the heat pipes. If the temperature of the heat source is not allowed to exceed 70 °C, the total heating powers of heat sink with two and four embedded heat pipes will not exceed 131 Wand 164 W respectively. And the thermal performance of a heat sink with embedded heat pipes has been developed a Windows program for rapidly calculating through Visual Basic commercial software. The superposition principal analytical method for the thermal performance of the heat sink with embedded heat pipes is completely established [11].

Moreover, one set of risers of the L-shape heat pipes were functioning as the evaporating section while the other set acted as condensing section. Wang [12, 13] arranged vertically the six L-type heat pipes in such a way that the bottom acts as the evaporating section and the risers act as the condensing section. It describes the design, modeling, and test of a heat sink with embedded L-shaped heat pipes and plate fins. This type of heat sink is particularly well suited for cooling electronic components such as microprocessors using forced convection. The mathematical model includes all major components from the thermal interface through the heat pipes and fins. It is augmented with measured values for the heat pipe thermal resistance. A Windows-based computer program also uses an iterative superposition method to predict the thermal performance. The sum of the bypass heating power ratios is 14.4% for Q1 and Q2, 20.8% for Q3 and Q4, and 52% for Q5 and Q6, obtained using both the experimental results and the software program based on VB6.0. Thermal performance testing shows that a representative heat sink with six heat pipes will carry 160W and has reached a minimum thermal resistance of 0.22 °C/W. The computer software predicted a thermal resistance of 0.21 °C/W, which was within 5% of the measured value. Moreover, the total thermal resistance of the heat sink with six embedded L-type heat pipes is only affected by changes in the base to heat pipes thermal resistance and heat pipes thermal resistance over the heat flow path. That is, the total thermal resistance varies according to the functionality of the L-type heat pipes. Wang [14] defined the index of the thermal performance of a heat pipe for a thermal module manufacturer, which is the temperature difference between the evaporation and condensation sections of a single heat pipe and maximum heat capacity. The maximum heat capacity reaches the highest point, as the amount of the non-condensation gas of a heat pipe is the lowest value and the temperature difference between evaporation and condensation sections is the smallest one. The temperature difference is under 1°C while the percentage of the non-condensation gas is less than 8×10^{-5}%, and the single heat pipe has the maximum heat capacity.

Another two-phase heat transfer device is the Vapour Chamber (V.C.) inside vapour-liquid working, which has better thermal performance than metallic material in a large footprint heat sink. The overall operating principle of V.C. is defined as follows: at the very beginning, the interior of the vapor chamber is in the vacuum, after the wall face of the cavity absorbing the heat from its source, the working fluid in the interior will be rapidly transformed into vapour under the evaporating or boiling mechanism and fill up the whole interior of the cavity, and the resultant vapor will be condensed into liquid by the cooling action resulted from the convection between the fins and fan on the outer wall of the cavity, and reflow to the place of the heat source along the capillary structure. The effectiveness and better thermal performance of vapour chamber has been already confirmed according up-to-date researches and mass production application in server system and VGA thermal module [16-18]. Wang and Wang [19] derived a novel formula for effective thermal conductivity of vapor chamber by use of dimensional analysis in combination with thermal-performance experimental method. It respectively discussed these values of one, two and three-dimensional effective thermal conductivity and compared them with that of metallic heat spreader. For metallic materials as the heat spreaders, their thermal conductivities have constant values when the operating temperature varies not large. The thermal conductivities of pure cooper and aluminum as heat spreaders are 401 W/m°C and 237 W/m°C at operating temperature of 27 °C, respectively. When the operating temperature is 127 °C, they are 393 W/m°C and 240 W/m°C, respectively. Results show that the two and three-dimensional effective thermal conductivities of vapor chamber are above two times higher than that of the copper and aluminum heat spreaders, proving that it can effectively reduce the temperature of heat sources. The maximum heat flux of the vapor chamber is over 800,000 W/m^2, and its effective thermal conductivity will increase with input power increasing. Thermal performance of V.C. is closely relate to its dimensions and heat-source flux, in the case of small area vapour chamber and small heat-source flux, the thermal performance will be less than that of pure copper material. It is deduced from the novel formula that the maximum effective thermal conductivity is above 800 W/m°C, and comparing it with the experimental value, the calculating error is no more than ±5%.

A vapour chamber is a two-phase heat transfer components with a function of spreading and transferring uniformly heat capacity so that it is ideal for use in non-uniform heating conditions especially in LEDs [20]. The solid-state light emitting diode (SSLED) has attracted attention on outdoor and indoor lighting lamp in recent years. LEDs will be a great benefit to the saving-energy and environmental protection in the lighting lamps region. A few years ago, the marketing packaged products of single die conducts light efficiency of 80 Lm/W and reduces the light cost from 5 NTD/Lm to 0.5 NTD/Lm resulting in the good market competitiveness. These types of LED lamps require combining optical, electronic and mechanical technologies. Wang et al. [21-23] introduce a thermal-performance experiment with the illumination-analysis method to discuss the green illumination techniques requesting on LEDs as solid-state luminescence source application in relative light lamps. The temperatures of LED dies are lower the lifetime of lighting lamps to be longer until many decades. The thermal performance of the LED vapour chamber-based plate is many times than that of LED copper- and aluminum- based plate. The results are shown that the experimental thermal resistance values of LED copper- and vapour chamber-based plate respectively are 0.41 °C/W and 0.38 °C/W at 6 Watt. And the illumination of 6 Watt LED vapour chamber-based plate is larger 5 % than the 6 Watt. Thus, the LED vapour chamber-based plate has the best thermal performance above 5 Watt. The thermal performance of the LED vapor chamber-based plate is worse than that of the LED copper-based plate of less than 4 Watts. In additional to having the best thermal performance above 5 Watts, the luminance of the LED vapor chamber-based plate is the highest. The temperature of the LED rises about 12 °C per Watt. Wang et al. [24] utilizes experimental analysis with window program VCTM V1.0 to investigate the thermal performance of the vapor chamber and apply to 30 Watt high-power LEDs. Results show that the maximum effective thermal conductivity is 870 W/m°C, and comparing it with the experimental value, the calculating error is no more than ±5%. And the LED vapor chamber-based plate works out hot-spot problem of 30 Watt high-power LEDs, successfully. Thermal performance of the thermal module with the vapour chamber can be determined within several seconds by using the window program VCTM V1.0, exactly. The theoretical models with empirical formula for computer-aided thermal module have coded by Virtual Basic version 6.0 to develop window programs HSHPTM V1.0 and VCTM V1.0 and convenience for industrials in this chapter.

2. Heat Pipe

There are three sections, evaporation section, adiabatic section, and condensation section, in a heat pipe as shown in Figure 1. Heat pipe absorbs large amounts of latent heat through the phase change of working fluid and transfers rapidly heat flow to the other side by vapor form without any fluid machinery. Thus, the heat pipe may be regarded as the passive component of a self-sufficient vacuum closed system, which includes the wick structure and working fluid wet the entire capillary structure. The working fluid is pure water with low oxygen content. At the beginning, the heat pipe is in a vacuum. After the wall surface of evaporation section absorbs the heat from heat source, the working fluid in the interior will be rapidly transformed into a high pressure vapor which fills the entire interior of a heat pipe and flow through adiabatic section to condensation section.

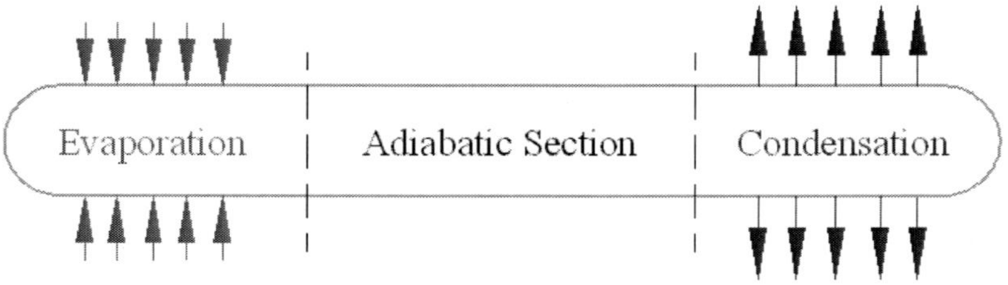

Figure 1. Three sections of a heat pipe.

The high temperature and pressure vapor is produced at the condensation section after the adiabatic section. During the cooling phase, vapor releases latent heat; condense into liquid by the cooling action, and flows back to the location of the heat source of evaporation section because of the capillary force along the capillary structure. The capillary force depends on the capillary structure, the viscosity, the surface tension, and the wetting ability of working fluid. Therefore, the capillary force and the high vapor pressure are the main driving force to make the circulation in a heat pipe. There are two-phase model of the vapor and liquid occurred in a heat pipe. They are regarded as the saturated state. It is usually assumed that the temperatures of the vapor and liquid are equal in their interface.

2.1. Characteristics and Limits

The heat pipe consists of a vacuum-tight container lined with a wick structure on the inner surface and filled with a working fluid, which exists in both liquid and vapor states within the container. The working fluid absorbs heat capacity and evaporates from heat source and condenses into a liquid through condensation section to complete a thermodynamic cycle under slight temperature difference. There are various benefits for a heat pipe. Heat pipe is a uniform temperature device due to the latent heat. Its thermal response time is faster than the solid materials. And it is quiet, reliable and long-time operating device. Finally, heat pipe is smaller volume, lighter weight, and higher usability. Although the heat pipe has good thermal performance for lowering the temperature of the heat source, its operating limitation is the key thermal design issue called the critical heat flux or the greatest heat capacity quantity. This is because temperature drop depends on the pressure drop that the vapor experiences as it flows through the vapor core. A heat pipe may bump into four kinds of heat transport limits, sonic limit, entrainment limit, capillary and boiling limit.

The speed of the vapor flow increases as larger the heat capacity of the heat source. At the same time, the vapor speed and pressure achieves maximum at the interface between vapor and liquid. When the pressure inside is high, the high pressure at the interface blocks the liquid to reflow to the evaporation section. The vapor temperature inside the evaporation section will increase while the liquid is trapped in the condensation section. But when the driving forces, gravity and capillary, of the liquid are large enough to overcome the shear stress in the interface, the liquid would be able to reflow to the evaporation section. Thus, the entrainment limit is that when the heat capacity is increased and the flow speed of vapor is higher than the gateway value, forcing it to bear the shear stress in the liquid; driving force of vapor being larger than the surface tension of the liquid in the wick structure and interface. This phenomenon will lead to the entrainment of the liquid, affecting the flow back to the evaporation section. This is also called flooding phenomenon. When flooding happens, the vapor temperature and pressure oscillate with time. The occurrence of flooding phenomenon limits the performance of a heat pipe. As soon as the reflowing of liquid recovers, the vapor temperature drops. This phenomenon is similar to the flux of the constant mass flow rate at conditions of shrinking and expanding in the nozzle neck. Therefore, the speed of flow in this area is unable to arrive above the speed of sound. This is called sonic limit. When the sonic phenomenon happens, flow choking phenomena maybe to occur and cause the remarkable axial temperature to drop, decrease the thermal performance of the heat pipe.

The boiling limit often takes place for the traditional metal, wick structured heat pipe, which means the initiation of bubble generation inside the wick structure, and it may result in a locally burned out if the bubbles are trapped inside the wick. If the vapor flow rate increases in the evaporation section, the working fluid between the wick and the contact surface of wall will achieve the saturated temperature of vapor in order to produce boiling bubbles. This kind of wick structure will impede the vapor bubbles to leave and have the vapor layer of the film encapsulated. The boiling limit phenomenon causes large thermal resistance resulting in the high temperatures of the heat pipe. The capillary limit is also called the water power limit, which is used in the heat pipe of the low temperature operation. Specific wick structure provides for working fluid in circulation limiting that proposes a pressure balance amongst the wick and vapor core within the heat pipe including the maximum capillary pumping pressure $\Delta P_{cap,\max}$ (Pa), the vapor pressure drop along the heat pipe ΔP_{vl} (Pa), the pressure drop due to the evaporation and condensation sections at the liquid-vapor interface ΔP_{ll} (Pa), the pressure drop of the liquid flow in a wick structure due to the frictional drag ΔP_{wick} (Pa), and the pressure drop in the liquid die to the effect of the gravitational force in the direction of the heat pipe axis ΔP_{g} (Pa) defined as equation (1).

$$\Delta P_{cap,\max} = \frac{2\sigma}{r_c} \geqslant \Delta P_{vl} + \Delta P_{ll} + \Delta P_{wick} + \Delta P_{g} \qquad (1)$$

where σ is the surface tension of working fluid (N/m) and r_c is effective capillary radius (m).

The capillary limit means that loading heat capacity is larger than the capability of capillary pressure rise to drive back the working fluid from the condensation section to evaporation section. The maximum heat transfer attainable in a heat pipe is achieved under conditions such that the capillary pressure head is greater than or equal to the sum of pressure losses along the vapor-liquid path as shown in the Eq. (1). Once the heat loads over the capability of capillary pressure rise, the supply of working fluid will be not enough, and evaporation section will be dried out. The failure normally happens at the far end of the evaporation section first, drying out the wick from the evaporation section towards the condensation section. The index is dry-out point for failure causing a reduction in the heat transfer in the evaporation section in order to stop functioning. A failure mechanism in which the capillary pressure is no longer sufficient to feed the evaporation section, or in other words, the mass flow rate of vapor leaving the evaporation section exceeds the mass flow rate of liquid feeding the evaporation section from condensation section, causing the evaporation section to dry out. The dry out point leads to a large and rapid reduction in the ability to transfer heat capacity into the evaporation section. The high thermal resistance for lower heat loads results from the lower merit number of water at temperatures lower than its boiling point whereas the high thermal resistance at higher powers results from compromising the capillary limit.

The selection of a heat pipe has also some important considerations besides the above four operating limits. Tables 1 to 4 present the major choice points of a heat pipe for the best working substance selection. Firstly, the working environment can usually have high temperature or low temperature conditions accordingly affecting to require a high temperature operating heat pipe or a low temperature operating heat pipe. After confirming the operating environment, the material, internal sintered body, and the type of working fluid for a heat pipe are determined. Therefore, in order to prevent the heat pipe's expiration, the consideration of the selection of a heat pipe is very important. Table 1 reveals the operating temperature of working fluid for compatible materials. Table 2 shows the operating pressure drop of working fluid in a heat pipe. Table 3 exhibits the merit number of the working fluid. Table 4 demonstrates the capillary parameter of the working fluid.

Table 1. Operating temperature of working fluid

Types	Melting Point(°C;1atm)	Boling Point(°C;1atm)	Range(°C)	Compatible Materials
Water	0	100	30~200	Cu, SUS, Ni Si
NH_3	-77.6	-33.2	-60~100	Al, SUS, Ni,Ti
Methanol	-98	64.7	10~130	Cu, SUS, Ni, Fe, Si
Ethanol	-114.4	78.5	0~130	— —
Acetone	-93.1	56.3	0~120	Al, SUS, Cu, Si

Table 2. Operating pressure of working fluid

Operating temperature	0°C	100°C	Types
dP/dT	0	2.5	Water
	18	180	NH_3
	0	10	Methanol
	0	5	Ethanol
	1	16	Acetone

Table 3. Merit number of working fluid

Operating temperature	0°C	100°C	Types
$Mx10^3$	0	5.2	Water
	0.8	0.2	NH_3
$M = \frac{\rho_l \sigma_l h_{fg}}{\mu_l}\left(\frac{KW}{m^2}\right)$	0.4	0.6	Methanol
	0.2	0.5	Ethanol
	0.3	0.4	Acetone

Table 4. Capillary parameter of working fluid

Operating temperature	0°C	100°C	Types
$C_H x10^{-5}$ $C_H=\sigma/\rho$ (m^3/sec^2)	7.6	5.8	Water
	4.0	1.0	NH_3
	3.0	2.5	Methanol
	3.0	2.5	Ethanol
	3.5	2.5	Acetone

2.2. Heat Sink-Heat Pipe Thermal Module

A heat sink-heat pipe thermal module can transfer the total heat capacity from the heat source to the base plate with embedded heat pipes and fins sequentially, and then dissipates heat flow into the surrounding air. Nowadays, it had been applied in PC, Server, CPU, GPU and specific consumer-electronic products successfully. For a traditional air cooling thermal module consisted with simple aluminum heat sink and fan, is to solve the problem of heat load from heat source, adding the fan speed to quickly take away more heat capacity from heat source in order to increase the thermal efficiency of thermal module. However, a noise problem will occur and the performance is unfavorable. The difference between heat sink-heat pipe and traditional heat sink thermal modules is that the most amount heat capacity of the heat source firstly transfers to the evaporation section of heat pipe, so that the liquid of working fluid within evaporation of the heat pipe produces steam. Steam releases heat in the condensation and re-condenses into liquid backing to the evaporator driving by the capillary force of capillary structure to complete this thermal cycle; and the rest of the heat capacity take away from heat sink through forced convection of fan. Therefore, the heat-sink heat pipe thermal module has better thermal performance at the same rotational speed of fan and lower noise. This chapter utilizes Visual Basic commercial software with theoretical thermal resistances and iterant method to develop a window program named HSHPTM version 1.0 for rapidly calculating accurate the thermal performance of heat sink-heat pipe thermal module through input simple parameters.

The longitudinally-finned heat sink-heat pipe thermal modules studied in this article are shown in Figure 2. One end of the heat pipes are inserted into the base plate as the evaporation section and the other end protrude through the upper portion of the fins as the condensation section.

Figure 2. Various heat sink-heat pipe thermal modules.

The proportion of the total heat capacity carried away via the embedded heat pipes has first to determine by iteration and theoretical thermal resistances. These input parameters have dimensions of heat sink, heat pipes, heat source and fan. The computing core of this window program employs the theoretical thermal resistance analytical approach with iterative convergence stated in this article to obtain numerical solution.

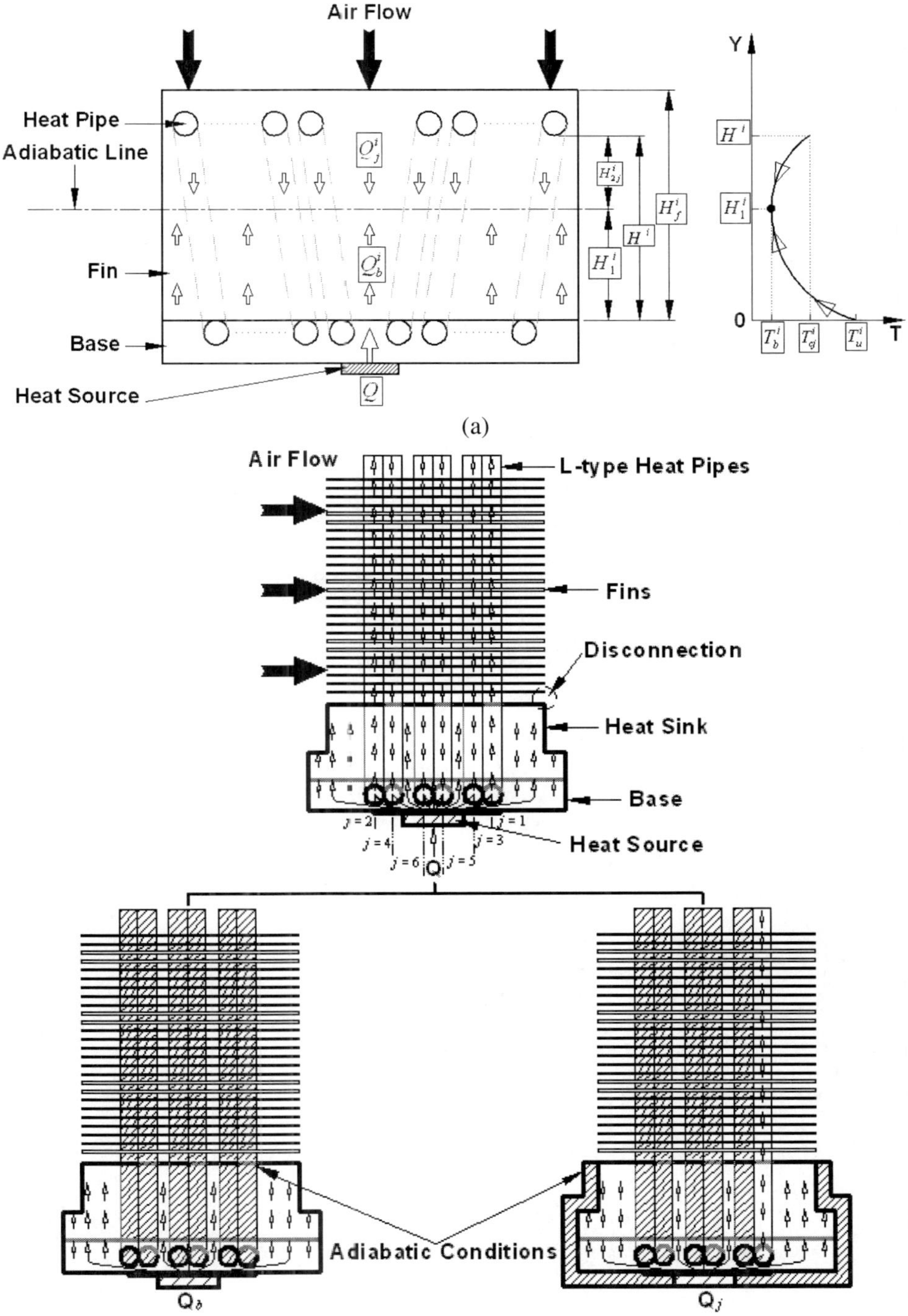

Figure 3. Continued on next page.

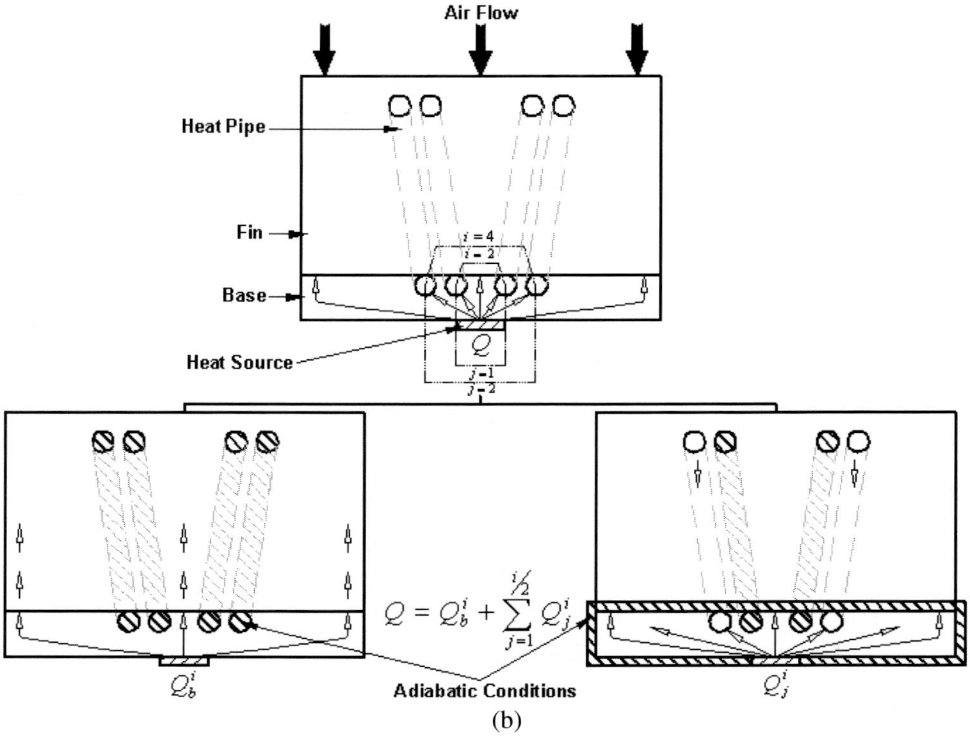

Figure 3. Heat sink-heat pipes thermal module heat flow and superposition method.

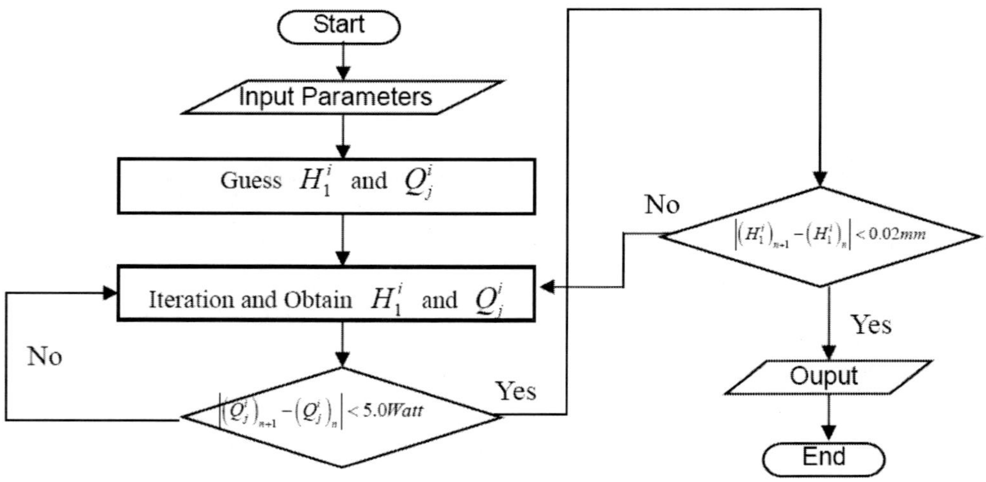

Figure 4. Iterative flowchart of program.

And these individual thermal resistances of contact, base plate, and base to heat pipes, heat pipes, fins and the total thermal resistance can be obtained through this window program HSHPTM V1.0 in this chapter. This window program was coded with Microsoft® Visual Basic™ 6.0 and calculated the thermal performance of a heat sink-heat pipe thermal module in this chapter.

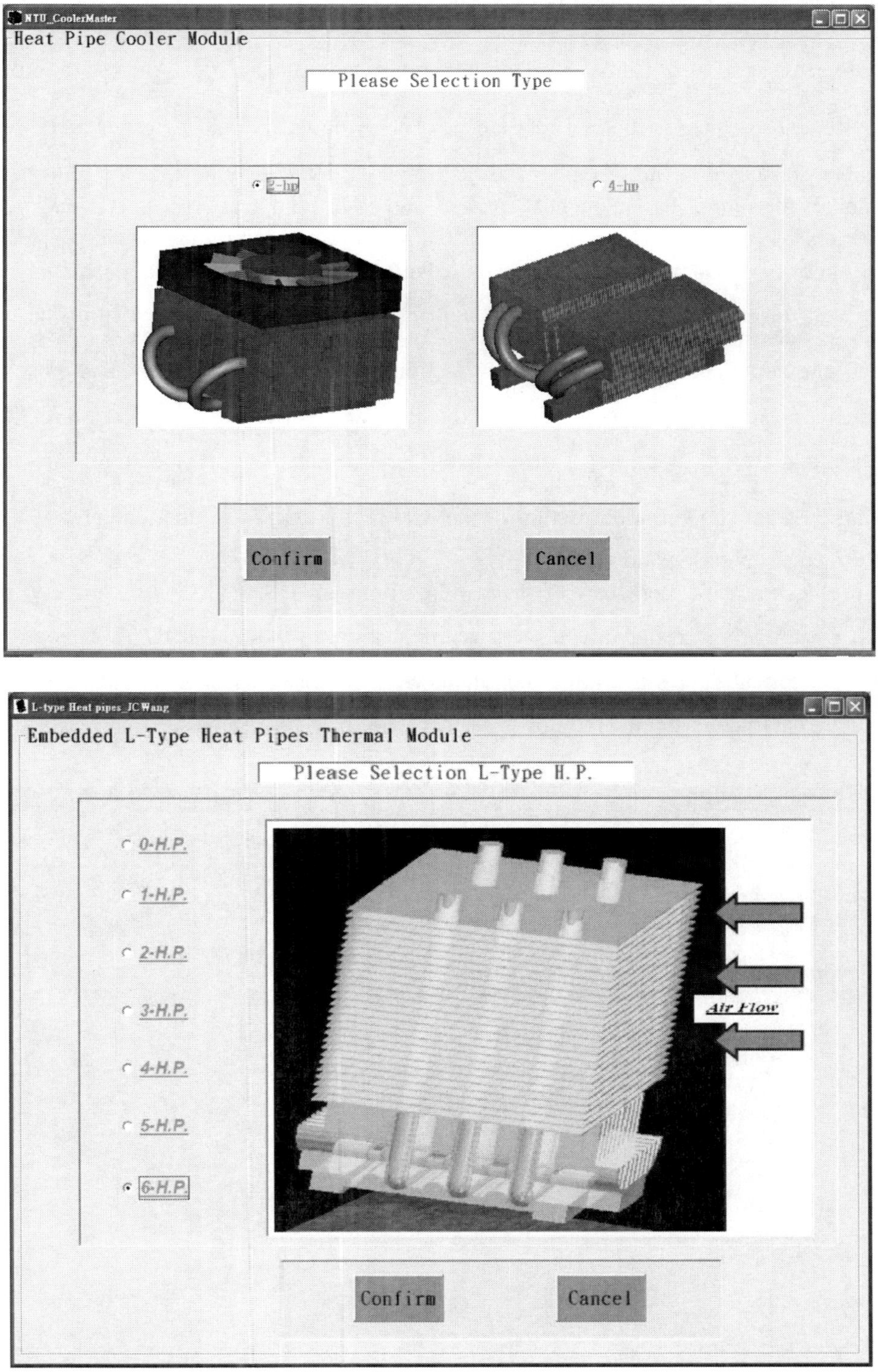

Figure 5. Selection heat sink type window.

From the energy conservation theorem, the total heating power Q equals the sum of base plate heat capacity Q_b^i and embedded heat pipes heat capacity Q_j^i. And the ratio of Q_b^i and Q_j^i depends on theses thermal resistances. The symbols i and j respectively denote the number and position of the embedded heat pipes. Figure 3 shows that the total heating power equals the sum of base plate heat capacity and embedded heat pipes heat capacity from the superposition method. The region where temperature gradient equals to zero appearing between these two heat transfer pathways is called adiabatic line. The fins in this adiabatic position will not have heat transfer. The height of fin is H_f^i.The distance from the upper surface of the base plate to the condensation section of the heat pipes is H^i, and those from the adiabatic position to the upper surface of the base plate and to the condensation section of the heat pipes are H_1^i and H_{2j}^i respectively. T_b^i is adiabatic temperature, T_{cj}^i is the temperature of the condensation section of the heat pipes, and T_u^i is the temperature of the upper surface of the base plate.

Figure 4 shows the flowchart of the window program HSHPTM V1.0. Initially, these H_1^i and Q_j^i are the guessing values and give one percent of the H_f^i and Q. This program estimates numerical values including individual thermal resistances via the guessing values, input simple parameters and the ratio of Q_b^i and Q_j^i.

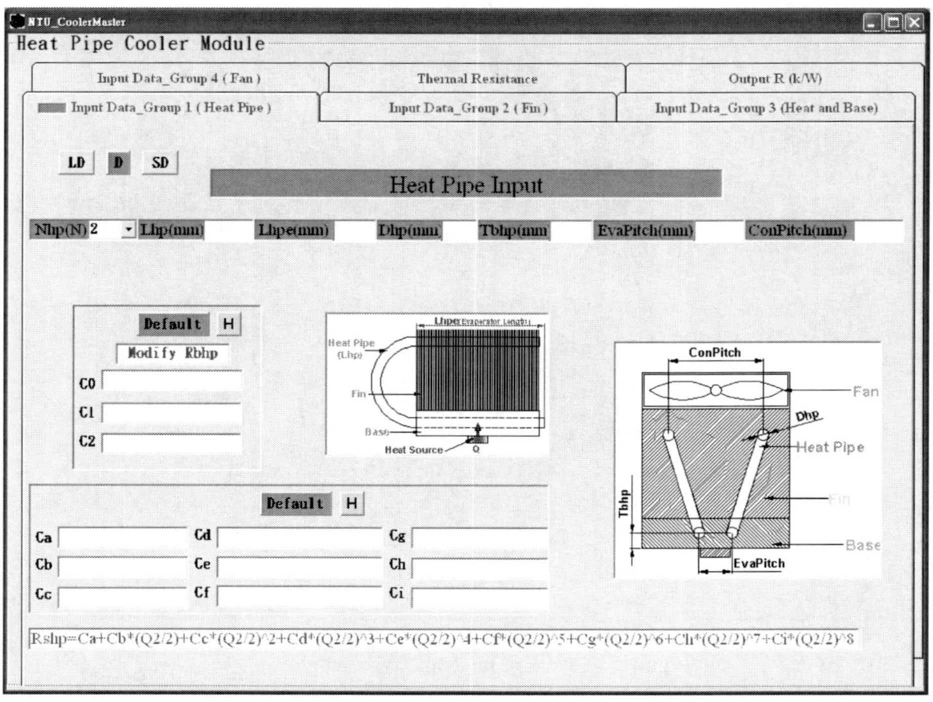

Figure 6. Continued on next page.

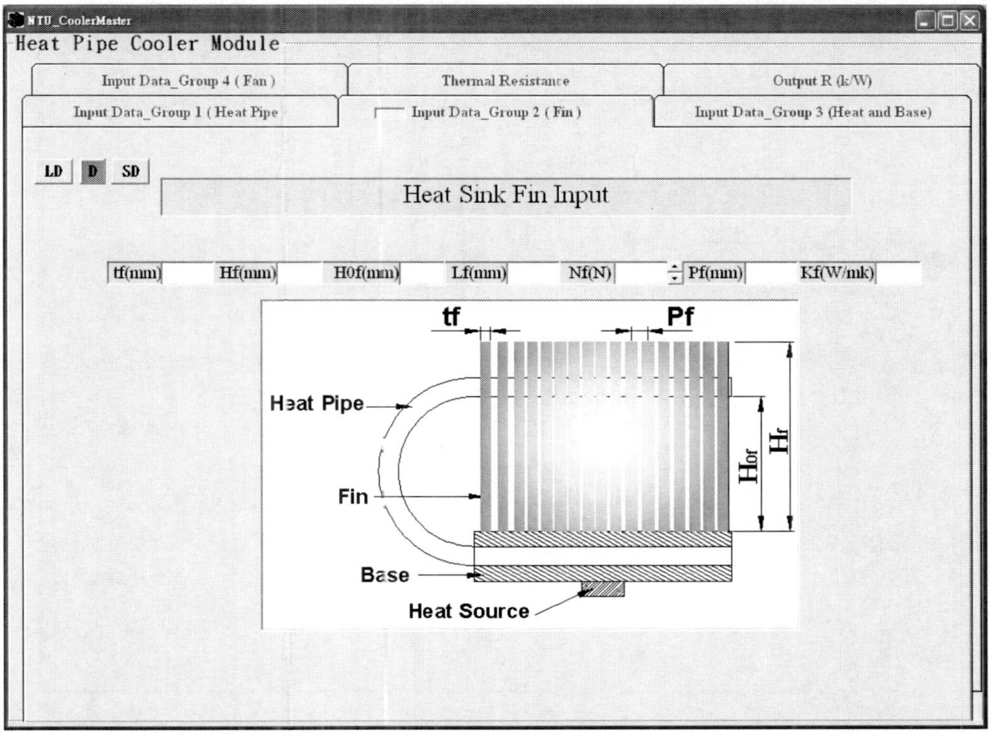

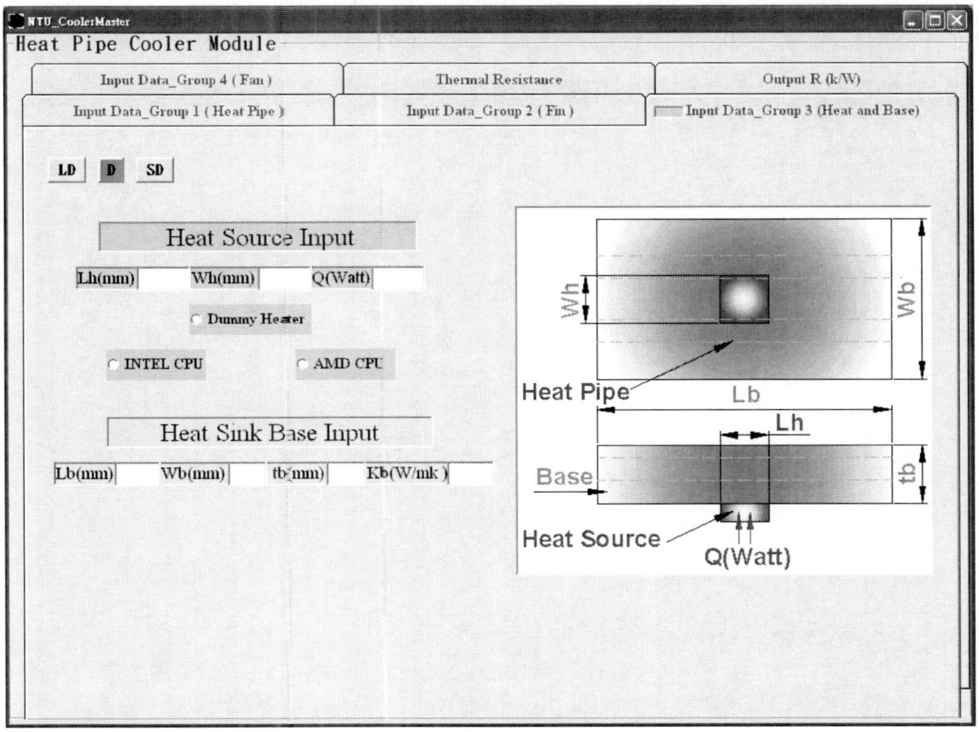

Figure 6. Continued on next page.

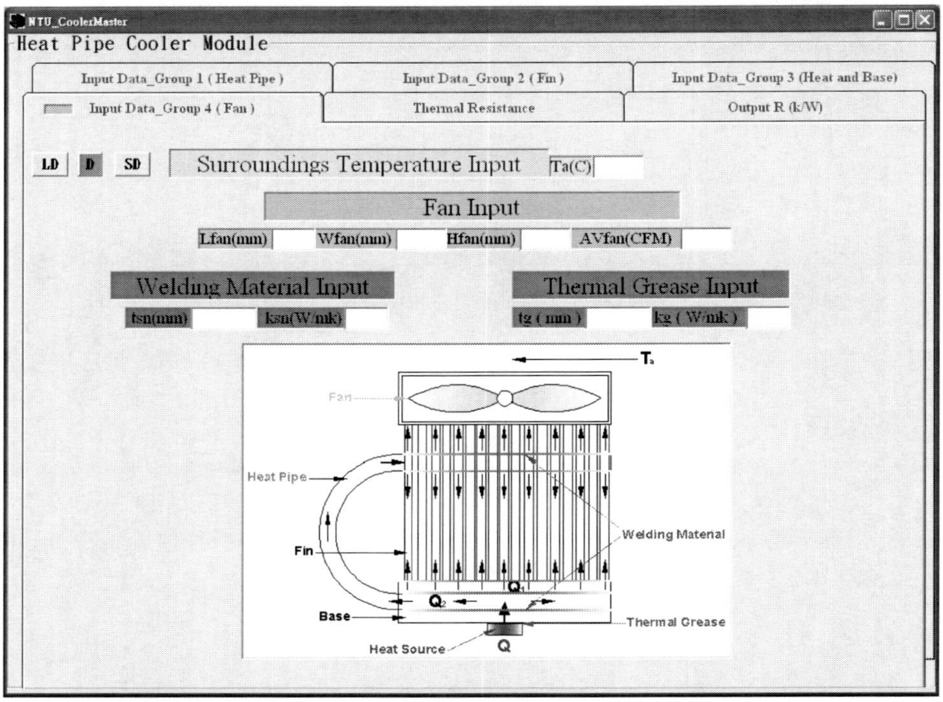

Figure 6. Input parameters before operation (a) Dimensions, position and thermal performance of embedded heat pipes (b)Dimensions and materials of heat sink (c)Dimensions, input power and materials of heat source and base plate (d)Performance and materials of fan and welding grease.

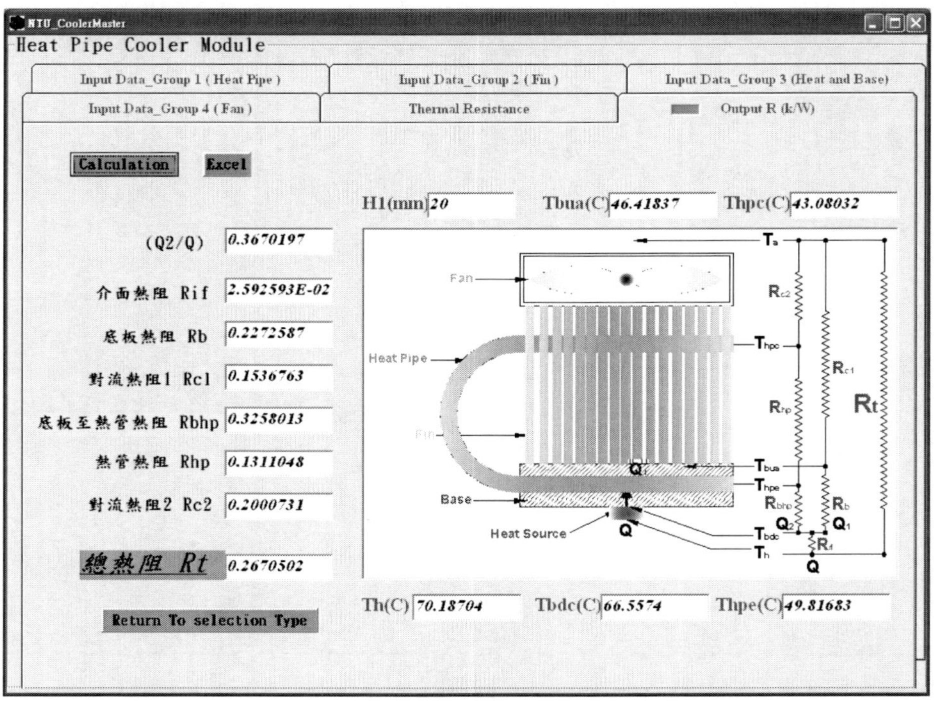

Figure 7. Main menu of program after operation.

Secondary, according to these data, inversely calculating next step values of the H_1^i and Q_j^i. Repeating these steps until satisfying conditions that the absolutions of the $\left[(Q_j^i)_{n+1}-(Q_j^i)_n\right]$ and $\left[(H_1^i)_{n+}-(H_1^i)_n\right]$ are smaller than 5.0Watt and 0.02mm respectively. Finally, these numerical values including the individual thermal resistances and temperatures of the heat sink-heat pipe thermal module and heat capacity of base plate and embedded heat pipes are obtained through this window program.

These parameters affect its thermal performance including the dimensions, thermal performance and position of embedded heat pipes. Thus it is very important for the optimum parameters to be selected to receive the best thermal performance of the heat sink-heat pipe thermal module. The program contains two main windows. The first is the selection window adjusted in the program as the main menu as shown in Figure 5.

In this window, the type of the heat sink-heat pipe thermal module can be chosen separately. The second window has five main sub-windows. There are four sub-windows of the input parameters for thermal module as shown in Figure 6. The first sub-window is the simple parameters of heat pipes including dimensions and thermal performance as shown in Figure 6(a). Figure 6(b) shows the second sub-window involving detail dimensions of a heat sink. The third and fourth sub-windows are the simple parameters containing input power of heat source, materials of thermal grease and solder and performance curve of fan as shown in Figs. 6(c) and 6(d). All the input parameters required for this study of the window program were given and the window program starts. Later, the program examines the situation by pressing calculated icon. The fifth sub-window is the window showing the simulation results. In this sub-window, when it is pressed at calculate icon for making analysis of the thermal performance of a heat sink with embedded heat pipes, we can see a figure as it is shown in Figure 7. According to the necessary iterative calculation and analog method, the heat capacity Q_j^i transferred by embedded heat pipes is found. According to these calculations of the heat sink-heat pipe thermal module, the simulation operation can be done through the HSHPTM V1.0.

3. Vapor Camber

Vapor chamber has uniquely high thermal performance and an isothermal feature; it has been developed and fabricated with low-cost due to a mature manufacturing process for several years. The vapor chamber is essentially a flat-plate type heat pipe made of copper as shown in Figure 8. Water is enclosed as the working fluid and filled up in the interior of vapor chamber. Its advantages are embodied in its thermal-physics properties such as extremely high latent heat and thermal conductivity and low viscosity, as well as its non-toxicity and incombustibility. The overall operating principle is that the interior of the vapor chamber is in the vacuum at the very beginning and after the wall face of the cavity absorbing the heat from heater, the working fluid in the interior will be rapidly transformed into vapor under the evaporating or boiling mechanism and fill up the whole interior of the cavity, and the resultant vapor will be condensed into liquid by the cooling action resulted from the convection between the fins and fan on the outer wall of the cavity, and reflow to the place of the heat source along the capillary structure.

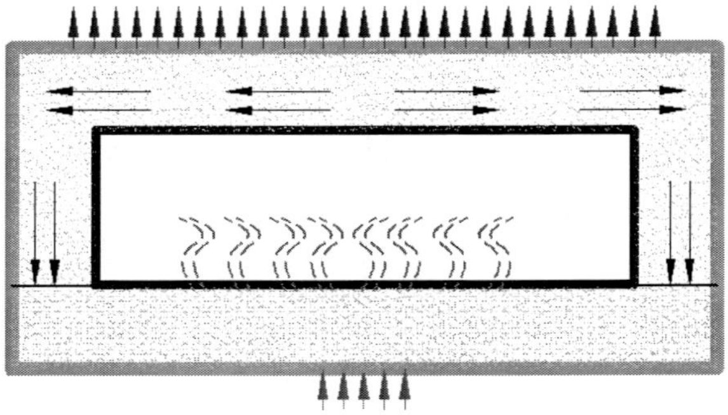

Figure 8. Vapor Chamber.

3.1. Vapor Chamber Thermal Module

This paragraph describes how to evaluate the thermal performance of a vapor chamber-based thermal module, which has existed in the thermal-module industry for several years. Thermal performance of the thermal module with the vapor chamber can be determined within several seconds by using the final formula associated with thermal-performance experimental method deduced in this chapter. Estimating effective thermal conductivity of vapor chamber is very important for getting the thermal performance of vapor chamber-based thermal module. The objective of this chapter is to derive a novel formula for the effective thermal conductivity of vapor chamber and rapid computing its value application in simulating the vapor chamber-based thermal module. This formula is dependent on the characteristics of vapor chamber and input power and dimensions of heat source. A zip-fin aluminum heat sink is soldered upon the heat spreader as thermal module for the heat dissipation, and tested in a wind tunnel to examine its thermal performance. According to the formula to obtain effective thermal conductivity of vapor chamber as heat spreader, there is a numerical value of thermal performance of the thermal module. The comparison with numerical values to experimental data will help us to understand the effectiveness and thermal performance of a vapor chamber and this novel formula is excellent agreement with experimental results in this study.

This chapter utilizes the [F.L.T.θ.] in Buckingham Π Theorem to deduce the thermal performance empirical formula of the vapor chamber. The repeating variables method is the most common method for the dimensional analysis, its related procedures are as follows: firstly, determine there are m variables related functions in certain physical phenomenon or equation, and r basic functions of related variables, and select the so-called repeating variables from all related variables; secondly, multiply the remaining of i related variables by different-power of repeating variables one by one to produce i parameters of Pi; finally, determine the powers of related variables to enable all Pi items to become the non-dimensional parameter groups. The point to choose repeating variables is giving priority to relatively common variables, for which the reason is that they will repeatedly occur in Pi variables. If certain related variable is correlated to other ones, we had better not to choose such related variable as the repeated variable. If we can deduce the proper non-dimensional parameter group by use of the dimensional analysis, the relational expression of the whole functional equation can be effectively deduced by the database of related data inferred from the above-mentioned experimental parameters.

The related variables of the vapor chamber to be confirmed are shown as equation (2) in this article. The symbol k_{eff} in the equation is the value of effective thermal conductivity of the vapor chamber, the k_b is the thermal conductivity of the material made of the vapor chamber, the symbol k_w is the value of effective thermal conductivity of the wick structure of the vapor chamber, the unit of these thermal conductivities are W/mk. The symbol q_{in} is the heat flux of dummy heater and its unit is W/m^2. The symbol h_{fg} is latent heat of working fluid which has unit of J/k. The P_{sat} is saturated vapor pressure of working fluid with unit of N/m^2. The t is the thickness of vapor chamber and the symbol h is the height of working fluid inside vapor chamber. Their unit is m. The symbol A is the area of vapor chamber and its unit is m^2.

$$K_{eff} = Function\{k_b, k_w, q_{in}, h_{fg}, P_{sat}, t, A, \phi h\} \tag{2}$$

$$\left(\frac{k_{eff}}{k_b}\right) = \alpha \cdot \left(\frac{k_w}{k_b}\right)^{\beta} \cdot \left(\frac{q_{in}}{P_s \cdot h_{fg}{}^{0.5}}\right)^{\gamma} \cdot \left(\frac{A}{t^2}\right)^{\lambda} \cdot \left(\frac{\phi h}{t}\right)^{\tau} \tag{3}$$

It can be inferred from equation (2) that there are nine related variables, and the following equation (3) can be inferred by making use of [F.L.T.θ.] system to do a dimensional analysis of various parameters in the above-mentioned equation and combining the analysis result with the equation (2). The $\alpha, \beta, \gamma, \lambda, \tau$ in the equation (3) indicate the constants determined based on the experimental parameters. This study is designed to firstly use thermal-performance experiment to determine the thermal performance and related experimental controlling parameters of the vapor chamber-based thermal, and sort them into the database of these experimental data, then combine with equation (3) to obtain the constants of the symbols. The constants $\alpha, \beta, \gamma, \lambda, \tau$ in equation (3) can be deduced by using the dimensional analysis with thermal-resistance performance experiment, and the formula of effective thermal conductivity coefficients of the vapor chamber can be inferred by combining such constants with known experimental data, as shown in the following formula (4).

The $\alpha, \beta, \gamma, \lambda, \tau$ in the equation (3) indicate the constants determined based on the experimental parameters. We can know from the equation (3) that effective thermal conductivity of the vapor chamber is related to controlling parameters of the experiment, fill-up number of the working fluid influencing symbol ϕh, volume of the cavity influencing symbol t, input power and area of the heat source influencing q_{in}, area of the vapor chamber influencing symbol A. Thus, this study is designed to firstly use thermal-performance experiment to determine the thermal performance and related experimental controlling parameters of the vapor chamber-based thermal, and sort them into the database of these experimental data, then combine with equation (3) to obtain the constants of the symbols

$\alpha, \beta, \gamma, \lambda, \tau$. Let the constant α be 1. And these constants $\beta, \gamma, \lambda, \tau$ are equivalent to 0.13, 0.28, 0.15, and -0.54 based on some specified conditions in this article, respectively.

$$k_{eff} = 46.1 \cdot \left(L_{vc} \cdot W_{vc}\right)^{0.15} \cdot \left(t_{vc}\right)^{0.24} \cdot \left(q_{in}\right)^{0.28} \tag{4}$$

This window program VCTM version 1.0 was coded with Microsoft® Visual Basic™ 6.0 according to the empirical formula (4) and calculated the thermal performance of a vapor chamber-based thermal module in this chapter. These parameters affect its thermal performance including the dimensions, thermal performance and position of the vapor chamber.

Thus it is very important for the optimum parameters to be selected to receive the best thermal performance of the vapor chamber-based thermal module. The program contains two main windows. The first is the selection window adjusted in the program as the main menu as shown in Figure 9. In this window, the type of the air direction can be chosen separately. The second window has five main sub-windows. There are four sub-windows of the input parameters for the thermal module as shown in Figure 10. The first sub-window is the simple parameters of the vapor chamber including dimensions and thermal performance as shown in Figure 10(a). Figure 10(b) shows the second sub-window involving detail dimensions of a heat sink. The third and fourth sub-windows are the simple parameters containing input power of heat source, soldering material, and materials of thermal grease and performance curve of fan as shown in Figures 10(c) and 10(d).

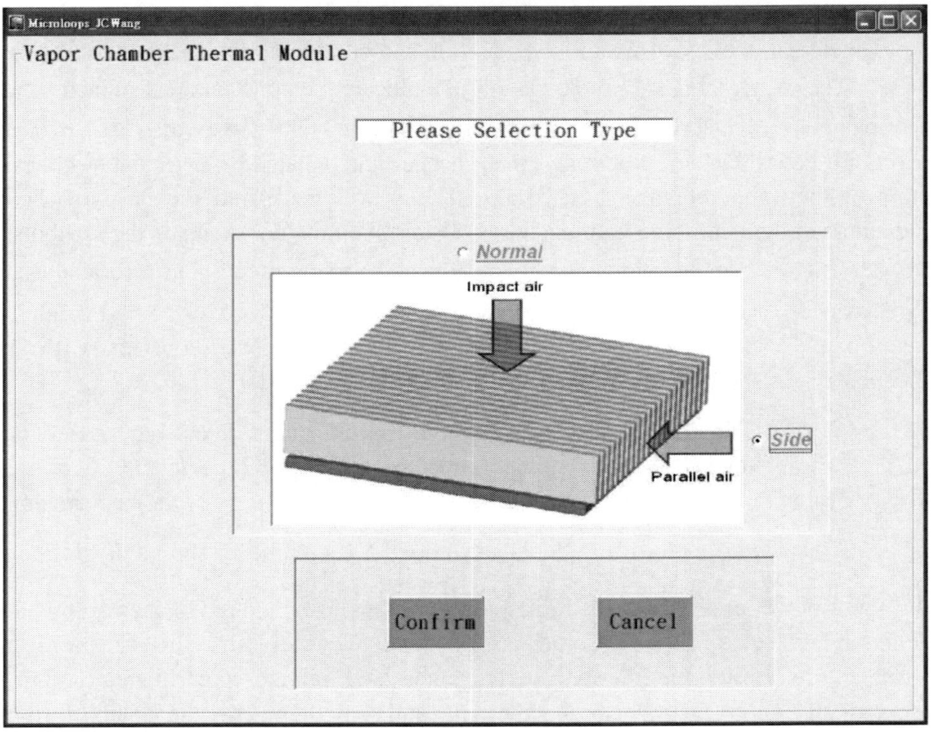

Figure 9. Selection air direction window.

All the input parameters required for this study of the window program were given and the window program starts. Later, the program examines the situation by pressing calculated icon. The fifth sub-window is the window showing the simulation results. In this sub-window, when it is pressed at calculate icon for making analysis of the thermal performance of a vapor chamber-based thermal module, we can see a figure as it is shown in Figure 11.

The heat flux and temperature differences influence its calculation accuracy based on the thermal resistance equation. And certain error necessarily exist between the data measured during experiment, value deriving from experimental data and actual values due to artificial operation and limitation of accuracy of experimental apparatus. In other words, the measurement accuracy of the heat flux and temperature is the key point. For these reasons, it is necessary take account of experimental error to create confidence of experiments before analyzing experimental results. The concept of propagation of error is introduced to calculate experimental error and fundamental functional relations for propagation of error. According to the good thermal insulation, the heat flux measurement has very high accuracy. Therefore, the measurement error of the heat flux nearly can be ignored for making conclusions in this paper. During the experiment, various items of thermal resistances are utilized to analyze the heat transfer characteristics of various pars of thermal modules. In respect to the measurement accuracy of temperature, the errors mainly lay in the measurement error of the thermocouples and the reading error of the digital data acquisition system. A thermal resistance belongs to derived variable and includes temperature and heating power, which are measured with experimental instruments.

The error of experimental instruments is propagated to the result value during deduction and thus become the error of thermal resistance value. Therefore, an error is represented with a relative error and the maximum relative error of thermal resistance defined is within 5 %.

This VCTM V1.0 would also like to design the optimum vapor chamber-based thermal module applying in high-end VGA card through 3-D numerical methods. Nowadays, traditional thermal modules of VGA card are designed and modified according to the experience of engineers in the VGA card industry. However, improvements of thermal performance need further manufacturing more experimental testing activities. For rapid development-period market of VGA card industry, costs of repeated samples and time taken for waiting for samples preparation do not assent to the cost-efficiency. In view of this point, numerical analysis is a subject belonging to computational fluid dynamics (CFD), in which fluid mechanics, discrete mathematics, numerical method and computer technology are integrated by applying computer aided design (CAD) and analytical software tools (Icepak), it is possible to reduce much cost of manufacture and rapid design VGA thermal modules or improve the thermal performance of existing modules within a short period.

CI) card. Thus, a dual-slot side-cooling thermal module for VGA card is chosen to achieve a better thermal performance. The three dimensions of heat sink thermal module are 118 x 83 x 32 mm^3. The thermal design parameters are bare-die GPU type of 18 x 16 mm^2, thermal input power of 165 Watt and under total thermal resistance of 0.273 °C/W. Ambient inlet temperature Ta to fan assumes 45°C, and the performance curve of blower are maximum air volume flow of 30 CFM and static pressure of 360 Pa. The size of the centrifugal fan is 90 x 25 mm^3; rotational speed is 3000 RPM. Reference flow rate will be 15 CFM to consist the optimum fin efficiency. The mean air velocity $\overline{V}_a$ is about 3.5 m/s. The Reynolds number is about 104.

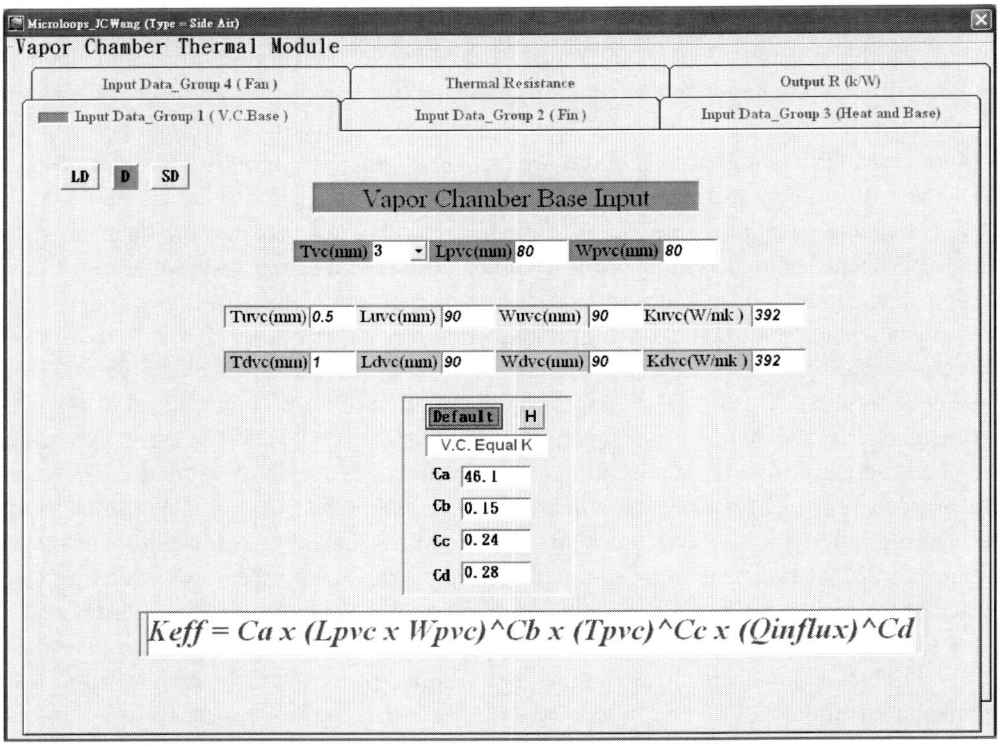

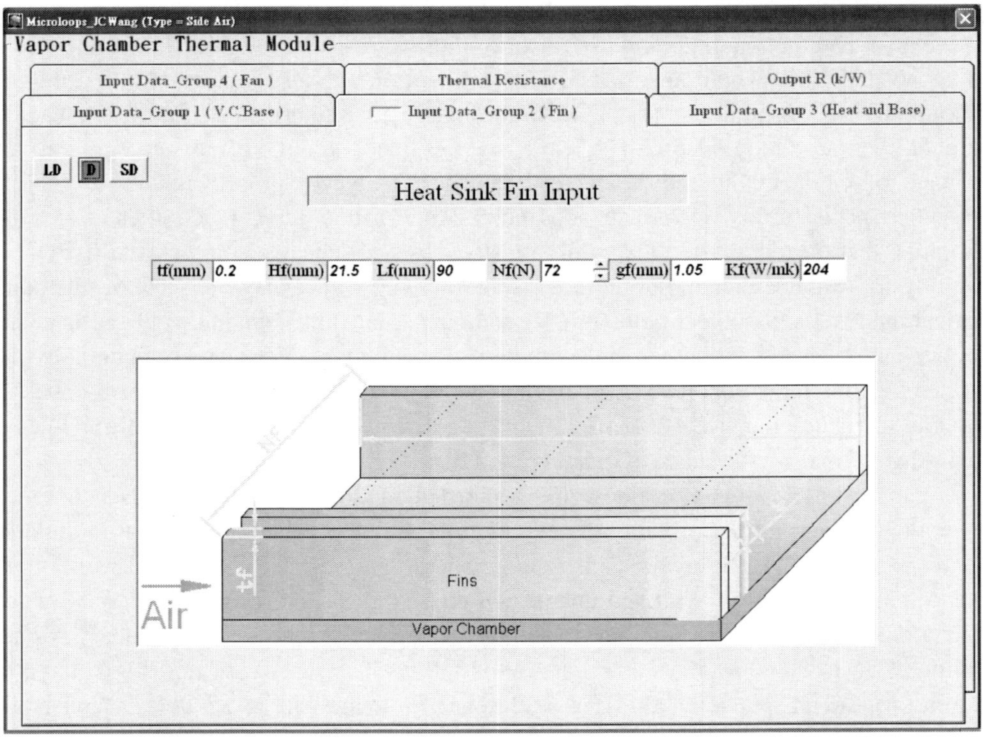

Figure 10. Continued on next page.

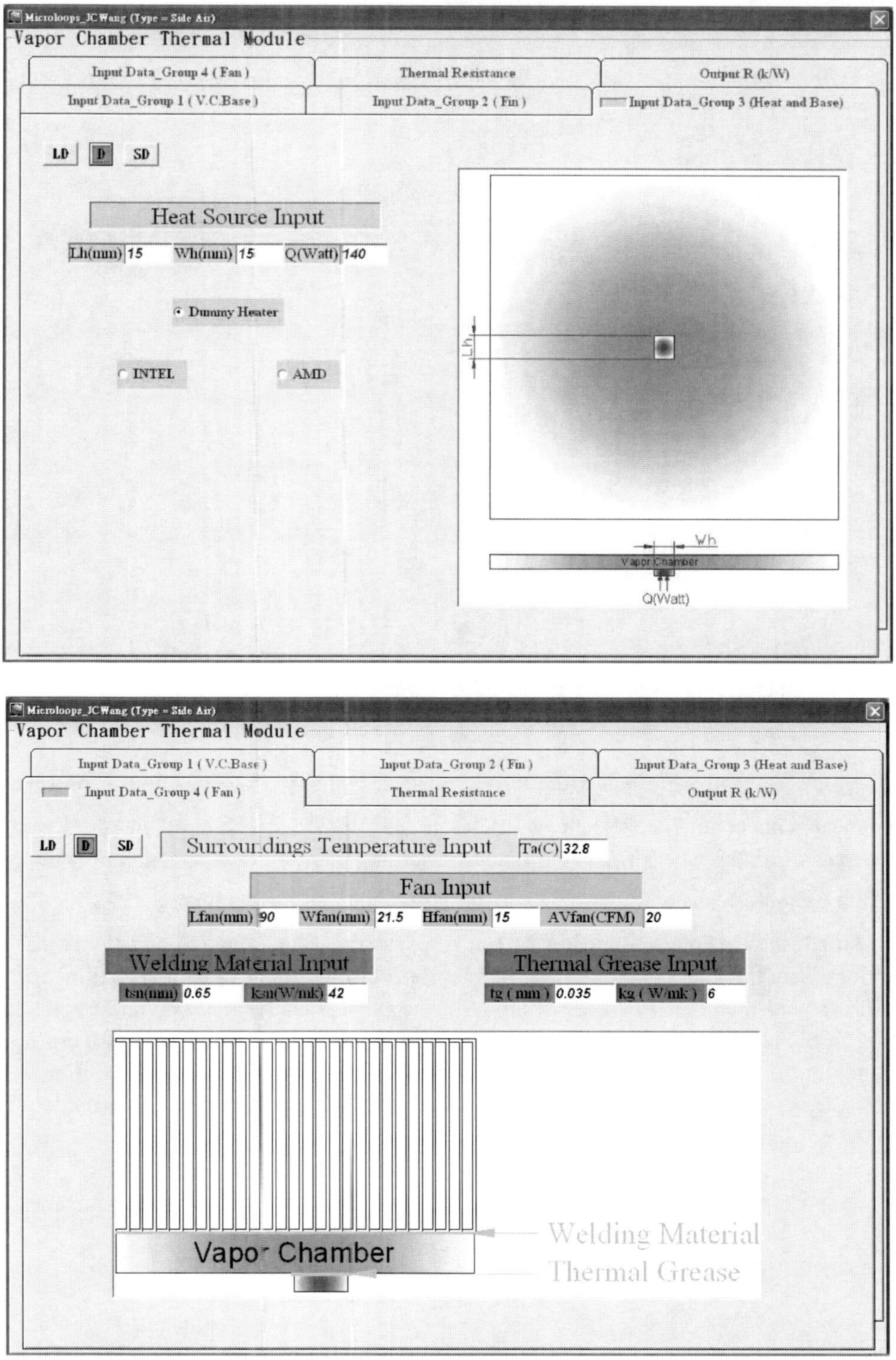

Figure 10. Input parameters before operation (a)Dimensions and thermal performance of the vapor chamber (b)Dimensions and materials of the fins (c)Dimensions, input power and materials of the heat source (d)Performance and materials of the fan and welding grease.

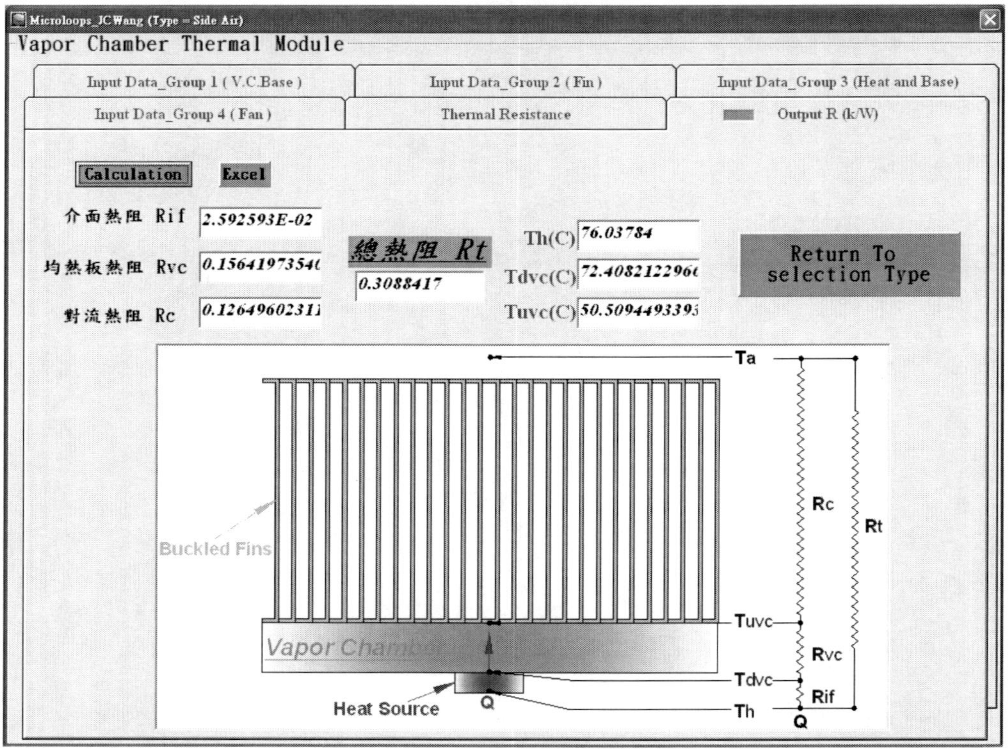

Figure 11. Main menu of program after operation.

Hi-end VGA card coordinates the dimensions of dual-slot protocol control information (PThe mean convection coefficient $\overline{h}$ is about 35 W/m^2°C. The pressure drop can be considered as Eq. (5), where f_{app} is the fanning-friction factor, K_c and K_e are contraction and expansion pressure loss coefficients, $\overline{V}_a$ is the air velocity in the channel, and L_f and D_h are the fin length and hydraulic diameter of fin, respectively. Equations (6) and (7) reveal the estimation of fin thickness and optimum fin gap for rectangle fin at force convection. Studies have shown that the error involved in one-dimensional fin analysis is negligible (less than about 1 %). For optimum fin efficiency, C_s obtains 0.01. Thus, the material of fins is aluminum and fin thickness has to employ under 0.295 mm. This study selects 0.3 mm as fin thickness. C_o is 0.03 and the optimum fin gap is about 1.63 mm. Therefore, the range of fin gap may be 1.3 to 2.1 mm step of 0.2 mm.

$$\Delta P = \left[\left(4 f_{app} \cdot \frac{L_f}{D_h} \right) + K_c + K_e \right] \cdot \left(\frac{1}{2} \cdot \rho_a \cdot \overline{V}_a^2 \right) \tag{5}$$

$$t_f \le C_s \cdot \left(\overline{h} \big/ 5 \cdot K_f \right) \tag{6}$$

$$S_o \cong C_o \cdot \left(t_f \cdot H_f\right)^{0.25} \tag{7}$$

Icepak commercial electronic heat transfer analysis software developed by American Fluent Inc. is adopted in this study. The entire analytical model is established by utilizing file conversion skill between CAD/CFD. There are two types of thermal modules. The overall size of vapor chamber is 70 x 70 x 3 mm^3 and its thermo physical property can be entered from Eq. (4). A comparison with vapor chamber-based thermal module is the embedded heat pipes thermal module as shown in Figure 12.

The 3-D embedded heat pipes thermal module is composed copper plate of 50 x 50 x 3 mm^3 with embedded a U-type heat pipe of 6 mm diameter and two bending heat pipes of 6 mm diameter cross-connecting to fins. The interior of plastics housing for these thermal modules has a structure with a throat. A throat functions as forcing air to flow toward another side at pressurized condition. All conditions of CFD models containing fins, heat sink, cover and blower are the same except based plate.

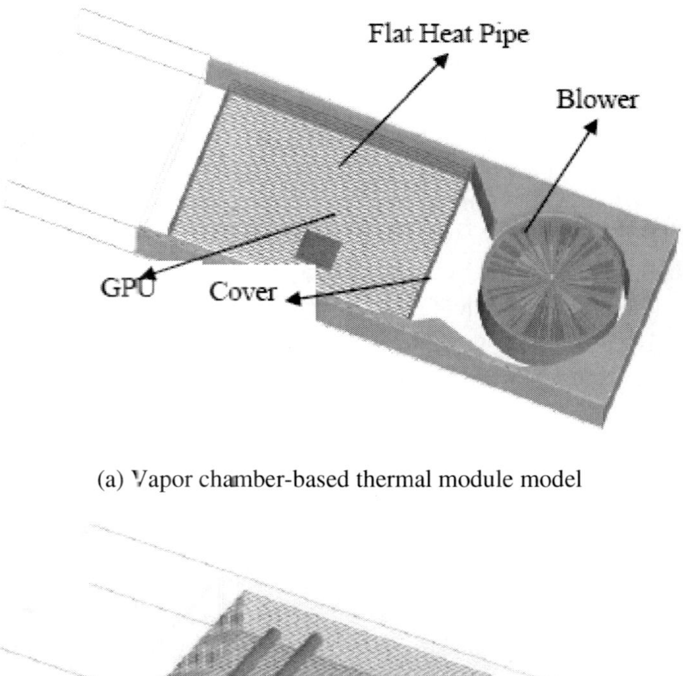

(a) Vapor chamber-based thermal module model

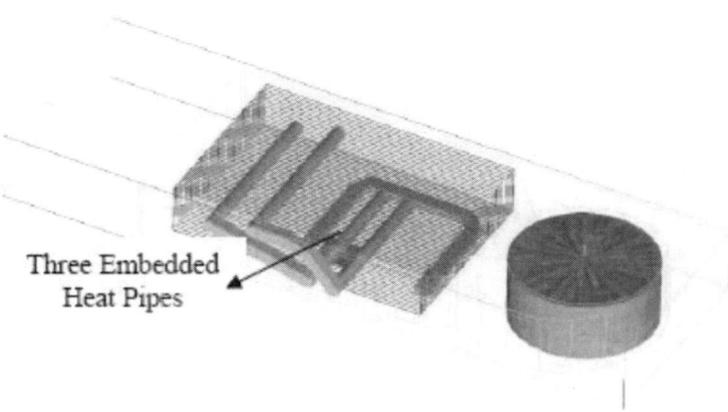

(b) Three embedded heat pipes thermal module model

Figure 12. CFD models.

The numerical simulation analysis can be divided into pre-processing, numerical solving and post-processing. With regard to pre-processing, first of all, a geometrical model is established for 3D VGA card thermal module. Generally, in order to reduce computation grid elements and time taken for simulation and solving, some minor characteristics without influence or with a little influence will be ignored when establishing 3-D geometrical model. And input the boundary conditions and thermo-physical properties, which the ambient temperature is set to 45°C, turbulent model is the k-ε two-equations, the grid pattern is non-structural one and the entire simulation analysis type is steady state. For the entire module, about 2,200 thousands grid elements are used, iterations is about 1000 and it will take about 36 hours to simulate every scenario. Thermal resistance is commonly used to evaluate thermal performance of thermal modules and also an important parameter in thermal module design. The larger the total thermal resistance is, poorer the thermal performance of thermal modules is, and higher the temperature of heat source is. Thermal resistance is defined as follows in Eq. (8).

$$Q = \frac{\Delta T}{R} \tag{8}$$

which R is the thermal resistance (°C/W), ΔT is temperature difference (°C), and Q is the input power (Watt).

Figure 13 is the apparatus of thermal performance experiment in this study. The experimental values are obtained from the AMCA wind tunnel testing system of actual mass-production goods of the flat heat pipe or embedded three heat pipes thermal modules, which applied to high-end VGA card as shown in Fig 13(a). The AMCA wind tunnel system follows AMCA 210 standard manufactured by Taiwan LonGwin Corp., which its overall dimensions are 850 × 3600 × 1800 mm^3. The maximum operating flow rate and static pressure are 250 CFM and 200 mm-H_2O, respectively. The accuracy is within ±2 % and repeatability error is ±1 %. There are three types inclined angles of 0° (Horizontality), 90° (Verticality) and 180° (Anti-gravity) as shown in Figs. 13(b) to 13(d). The thermal design parameters are bare-die GPU type of 18 × 16 mm^2. Thus, the dummy heat source for simulation GPU is a heated copper block 36.5mm × 25.5mm × 11mm and the area of heat source is 18mm × 16mm. Two electrical heating tube are provided copper block and a T-type thermocouple is embedded to measure the temperature of dummy heater (T_h). Another thermocouple measures the ambient temperature (T_a). When the temperature was in the range from -30 to 180 °C, the measurement error of T-type thermocouple was about ±0.2 °C. A pressure of about 9 to 11 Kg/cm^2 is applied upon the fixture fixing thermal module with simulated heat source during experiment to control and maintain thermal contact resistance of the system. Three kinds input power are 150, 165 and 180 Watts in this experiment.

The thermal performance experiments are conducted upon the results obtained from vapor chamber-based thermal module to demonstrate the difference between thermal performance of that and the one of embedded three heat pipes thermal module. The procedures of the experiment introduced in the study are as follows. Step1. Set up and calibrate the equipments of AMCA wind tunnel testing system. Step2. Apply thermal grease on the surface of dummy heater uniformly. Step3. Fix the thermal module on the fixtures. Step4. Turn on the wind tunnel system. Step5. Adjust the pressure applied upon the fixture to stabilize thermal contact resistance. The thermal contact resistance can be minimized by applying thermal greases such as silicon oil, soft metallic foil such as tin, silver, copper, nickel, or aluminum. Step6. Adjust the voltage and current of the power supply unit till the heating power of the simulated heat source is 150W. Step7. Record the steady-state temperature value through wind tunnel system. Step8. Change the inclination angles to 90° and 180° in order. Step9. Repeat Step6 to adjust the heating power to 165W and 180W in order.

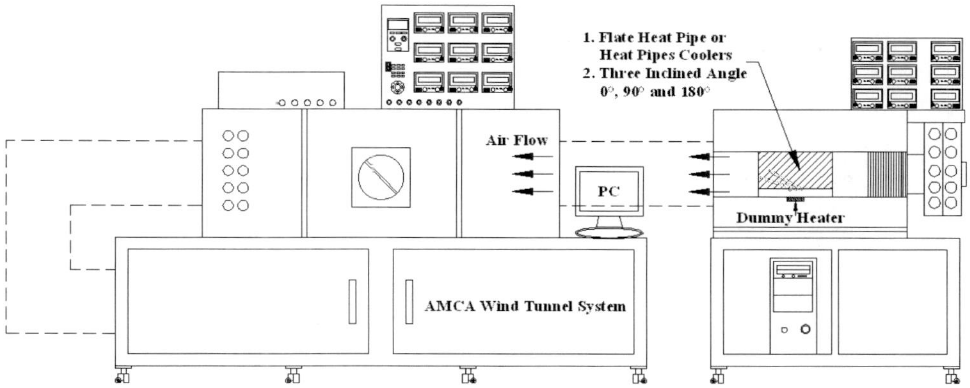

(a) Wind tunnel system

(b) 0°

(c) 90°

(d) 180°

Figure 13. Experimental equipment and testing angles.

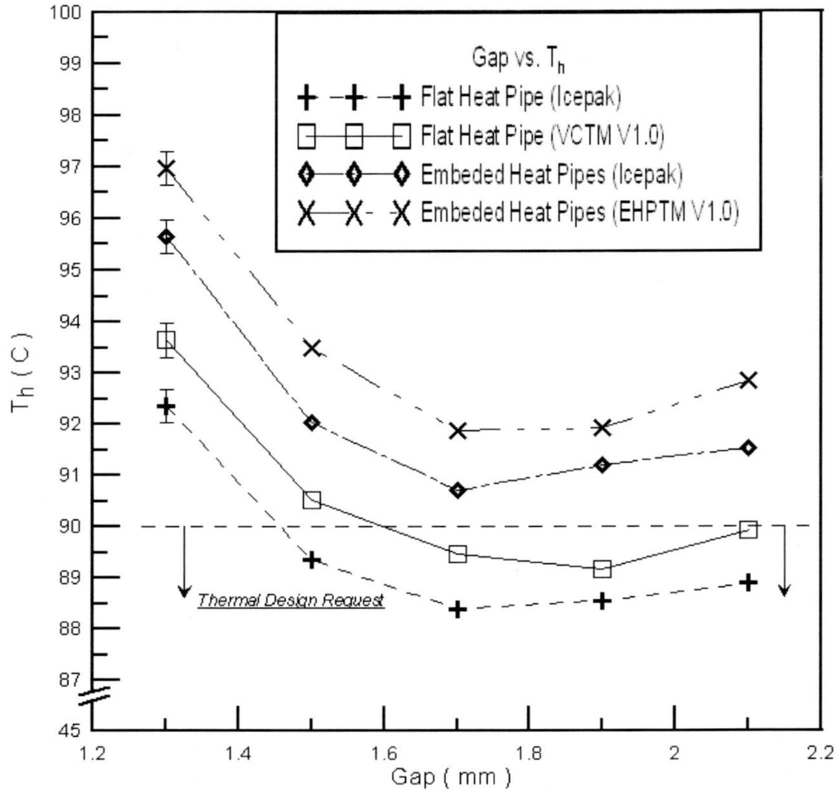

Figure 14. Relationships of T_h and space for vapor chamber-based and embedded heat pipes thermal modules.

Figure 14 shows the simulated results of curve fitting and the fitting equation is shown as Eq. (9). The symbol S means space. The error has about 2 % between the numerical data of VCTM V1.0 and simulated data of Icepak. And there has better thermal performance of 1.9 mm fin gap than 1.7 mm fin gap based on the numerical data from VCTM V1.0.

Therefore, for a vapor chamber-based thermal module solution, considering cost and performance, 0.3 mm Al fin and 1.9 mm fin gap is recommended. In this condition, there are 37 pcs fin counts, and it saves around 12 % fin cost. Therefore, the experiment chooses the optimum fin design of 1.9 mm gap and 37 counts to manufacture the prototype of vapor chamber-based thermal module. The vapor chamber-based and embedded three heat pipes thermal modules are analyzed and designed to optimization in high-end VGA card cooling system at without changing fan performance through CFD simulation with thermal resistance analysis and experiment in this study. And the vapor chamber-based thermal module can achieve the optimum heat dissipation and the maximum heat flux may exceed 60 Watt/cm^2.

From the experimental results, when Al fins are 29 mm in height, 0.3mm in thickness, 37 in number and spaced out 1.9 mm apart, the optimum total thermal resistance of a vapor chamber-based thermal module is 0.232°C/W in this study.

Through numerical and experimental results, the thermal performance of a vapor chamber-based thermal module has above 8 % improvement comparing to that of an embedded three heat pipes thermal module. The optimization process is done and checked by

VCTM V1.0 and EHPTM V1.0 window software in the chapter. Finally, the simulation analytical results and experimental data show that the error of the total thermal resistance value is within 5 %.

$$T_h = 227.345 - 219.175 \times S + 114.317 \times S^2 - 19.688 \times S^3 \quad (9)$$

3.2. LED Application

Vapor chamber (VC) has been proven the excellent heat spreading performance utilized in PC, NB, and Server, particularly in high-power light-emitting diode (LED). As high-power LEDs array are utilized for more general lighting systems, more significant amount of heat flux being generated while it is operating. The main challenge is that the lifetime of high-brightness LEDs is easily shortened by thermal problem generated at the device junction and ambient temperature. As shown in Figure 15, host of the vapor chamber may compose of the aluminum, copper or stainless steel, and the LED has the junction of electric circuits under the surface of vapor chamber with high thermally conductive and insulated grease between them; This high thermally conductive and insulated grease may construct from the aluminum nitride, the boron nitride with the agglutination material.

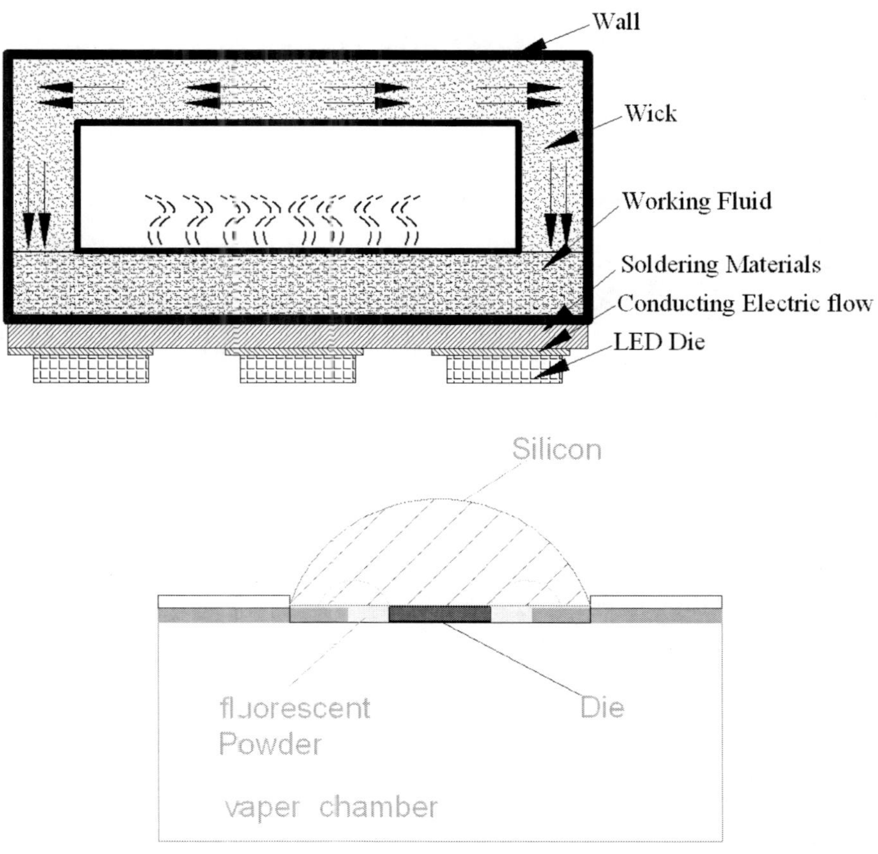

Figure 15. LED vapor chamber-based plate.

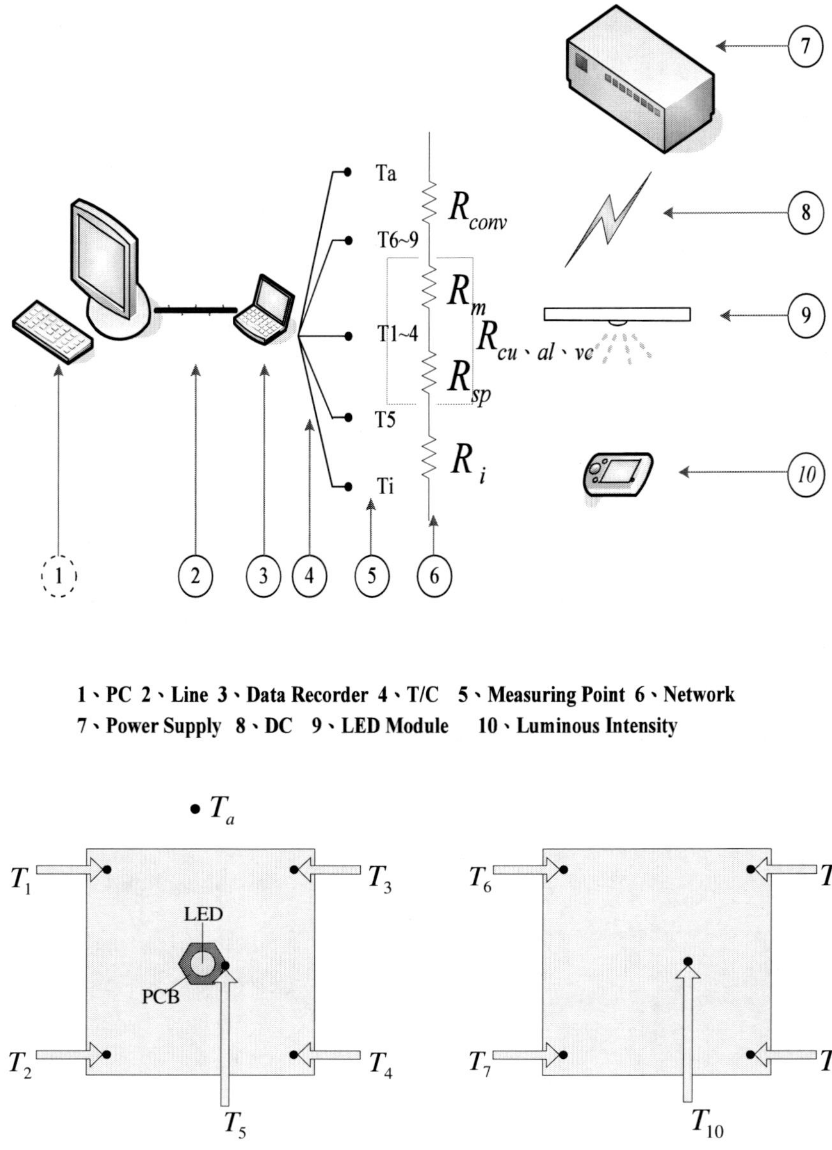

Figure 16. Experimental apparatus for LED based plate.

This electric circuit meets the point-system to be possible LED constitutes the electrical connection using the silver rubber or eutectic method. Figure 16 shows the experimental apparatus and thermal resistance network of LED based plate. Utilizing these materials of copper, aluminum and vapor chamber as LED based plate respectively and LEDs are four white dies operating voltage is 5.4 which the area of each die is 1 x 1 mm^2, having 4 dies, placing center symmetry with pitch 2 mm. The heating power from LEDs is 1 Watt with step gap 1 Watt up to 6 Watt. The TES1330A test luminous intensity for LED laying 10 cm from LED based plate. There are 11 measuring temperatures including surroundings Ta, based plate T1, T2, T3, T4, T6, T7, T8, T9, T5, T10, as shown in Figure 16.

This research also analyzes these thermal performances of three kinds of based plate by the commercial software Flotherm Version 8.1, respectively. The boundary conditions, properties of material and input parameters all tally with these experimental conditions. Obtaining the velocity distribution and temperature from the simulation results calculates the simulation thermal resistances of based plate. By the above results of experiment, theory and simulation may know this error range in order to judge this applies of this LED vapor chamber-based plate feasibility in the thermal module. The Vapor chamber has uniquely high performance and an isothermal feature; it has been developed and fabricated with low-cost due to a mature manufacturing process for several years. The window program VCTM V1.0 is to calculate the thermal performance of a vapor chamber-based thermal module. These LEDs are direct bounded with vapor chamber as shown in Figure 17. The LED vapor chamber-based plate has 7 x 7 LEDs and the dimension of each LED chip is 1 x $1mm^2$. The operating current and voltage are 0.96 A and 51 V. Another LED cooper based-plate will compare the thermal performance with LED vapor chamber-based plate through experimental method of a heating power 50 W.

(a)

(b)

Figure 17. 50 Watt high-power LEDs vapor chamber-based plate thermal module.

These LEDs have high heat flux above 300 W/cm^2. Results show that the effective thermal conductivity of the VCPCB is many times higher than that of the AlN, copper and aluminum PCB, proving that it can effectively reduce the temperature of the LEDs and obtain more uniform illuminance. And the thermal performance of the LEDs VCPCB is better than that of the LEDs Copper PCB and has the highest effective thermal conductivity of 965 W/m°C at 187.5 W/cm^2 from VCTM V1.0. The LEDs VCPCB works out hot-spot problem of 100 Watt high-power LEDs, successfully.

The printed circuit board (PCB) composite made up variables of dielectric, copper and solder layer thicknesses affected the thermal performance of high-power LEDs lighting system. Therefore, combination VC and PCB (VCPCB) can perfectly serve the high-power LEDs package system. One of these next-generation PCBs is the VCPCB application in high-power LEDs. This study reports the manufacturing characteristics and utilizes experimental analysis with window program VCTM V1.0 to investigate the thermal performance of VCPCB applying in a high-brightness LED array package module.

This study utilizes a thermal-performance experiment with the illumination-analysis method to discuss the thermal performance of VCPCB. The VCPCB is composed variables of against-welding layer, copper wire, solder layer, dielectric layer and vapor chamber as shown in figure 18. There have heat treatment of annealing and tempering for 45 μm-Copper 170 °C, 21 μm-dielectric layer 150 °C, and 35 μm-solder mask 130 °C taking 30 minutes and 1000 hours for 1000 cycles between -20 °C and +100 °C. The Cu wire can be printed on the vapor chamber. And the dielectric layer has a breakdown of the ability of anti 4 KV.

LEDs can be soldered on the VCPCB using low temperature solder paste resulting from heat treatment of 180 °C for vapor chamber. In last, the VCPCB can be employed the Surface Mount Technology (SMT) operation for the automatic manufacture. Soldering VCPCB on the AL die-casting heat sink with asymmetry radial fins is to compose LEDs bulb lamp as shown in figure 19, which has 4 pieces of LED up to 12 Watt. The size of VCPCB is a diameter of 9 cm and a thickness of 3 mm with thermal conductivity above 700 W/m°C according to the window program VCTM V1.0.

Figure 18. Photos of VCPCB.

Figure 19. LED bulb lamp with VCPCB.

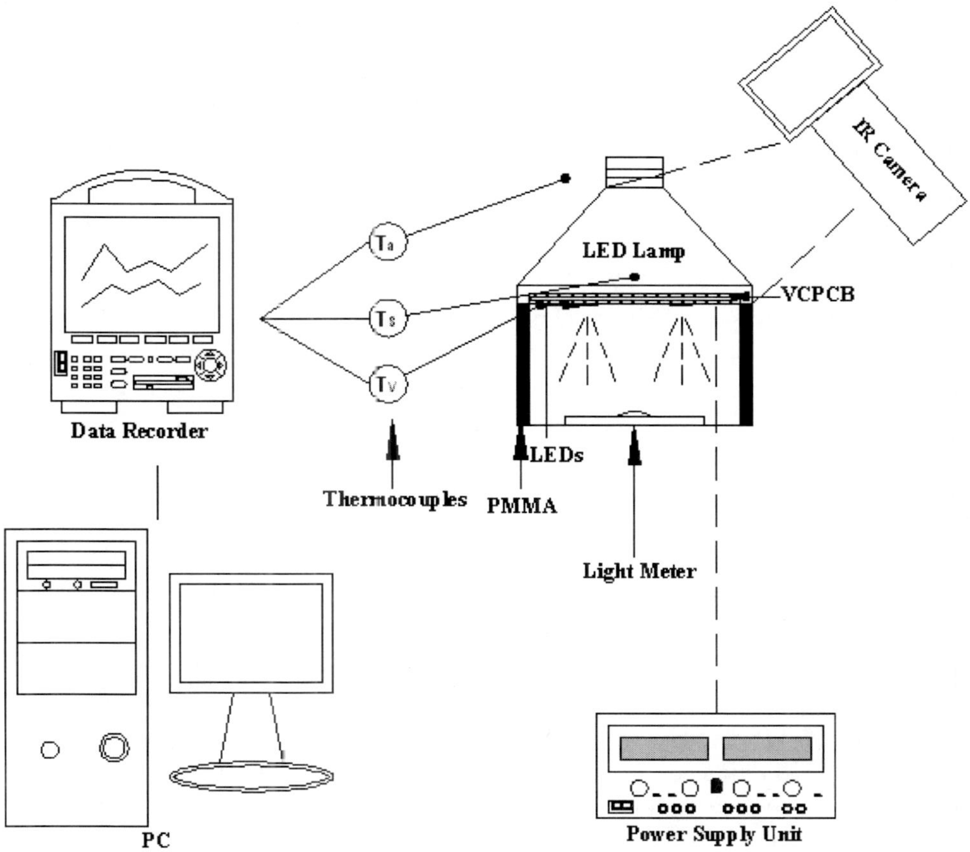

Figure 20. VCPCB experimental apparatus.

Figure 20 shows the LEDs bulb lamp experimental apparatus. There are four dies of white LEDs color used in VCPCB. The operating voltage is about 6 and the area of each die is about 2.5 x 2.5 mm^2, placing center symmetry with pitch of 12 mm. The power supply of

ADC50-10 has a maximum voltage and ample of 50 and 10 respectively to employ these four dies as the heat source in this experiment, with error within 0.5 % + 3 mV. The heating power from the LEDs is 2 Watt with a step gap of 2 Watt up to 10 Watt. Experimental temperatures are measured by T-type thermocouples composed of the materials of copper and nickel. The T-type thermocouple has a maximum measuring range from -200 °C to +350 °C and an error range of 0.5 °C.

These measuring temperatures are recorded through the GL-800 recorder, which has 40 measuring channels and the recording time is 0.1 ms. The thermography is employed to record all experimental process, which has a 150 x 150 Pixel IR camera and a maximum measuring range from -10 °C to +300 °C with an error range of 3 °C. The TES1330A test luminous intensity for LED laying 10 cm from the LEDs VCPCB and the luminous range is 0.01 to 20000 Lux with error within 1 %.

Firstly, place the LED bulb lamp in the experimental system and turn on the power supply to offer LEDs input power. Then, start to measure these temperatures with the recorder. There are 3 measuring temperatures including the surroundings of T_a, VCPCB of T_v, and heat sink of T_s as shown in Figure 20. When the temperatures and illumination of LED are in a steady state and their recording curves appears as a horizontal line, one experimental team stops. Every team spends about one hour. The maximum temperature of T_{max} is recorded by thermography as the LEDs temperature. And the luminous intensity of this LED lamp is also recorded by TES1330A.

Conclusion

This chapter investigates thermal-module methodologies of Personal Computer (PC), Note Book (NB), Server including central processing unit (CPU) and graphic processing unit (GPU), and LED lighting lamp of smaller area and higher power in the electronics industry. This approach presented a method of dealing with the tremendous amount of number crunching requirement posed by the thermal design of thermal modules. HSHPTM V1.0 and VCTM V1.0 are also expected to help them make decisions related to the lifetime and reliability of them in a right, reasonable and systematic way.

The preliminary results presented here are very encouraging. Among the many thermal analysis and simulation approach techniques, HSHPTM V1.0 and VCTM V1.0 seem to be the only one which will make the real-time thermal design of electronics industry possible. The author is looking for contributing to the LED industry, government and academia for the green energy-saving lamps through vapor chamber-based thermal module design. The author's future efforts could be dedicated to developing a LED green energy-saving lamps system.

A detail consideration of designing procedure development features and thermal designing operations let us develop the computer-aided thermal designing structure, to choose necessary methods, to develop appropriate models and methods of thermal conditions analysis of technical objects, furthermore decision acceptance with the aim of providing their thermal-physic characteristics. Finally, the author would like to mention a few points as the contribution of this study. This can serve as a reference for future researchers.

Acknowledgments

This chapter originally appeared in these References and is a major revised version. Some of the materials presented in this chapter were first published in these References. The authors gratefully acknowledge Prof. J.-C. Wang and his Thermo-Illuminanace Lab for guidance their writings to publish and permission to reprint the materials here. The work and finance were supported by National Science Council (NSC) and National Taiwan Ocean University (NTOU). Finally, the author would like to thank all colleagues and students who contributed to this study in the Chapter.

References

[1] V. Lin and S.-L. Chen. 2003, Performance analysis, optimum and verification for parallel plate heat sink associated with single non-uniform heat source, *ASME 2003 International Electronic Packaging Technical Conference and Exhibition, InterPACK2003,* Vol. 2, pp.229-236.

[2] H.-H. Wu, Y.-Y. Hsiao, H.-S. Huang, P.-H. Tang and S.-L. Chen, 2011, A practical plate-fin heat sink model. *Applied Thermal Engineering,* Vol.31, Issue 5, pp.984-992.

[3] J.-C. Wang, 2008, Novel Thermal Resistance Network Analysis of Heat Sink with Embedded Heat Pipes, *Jordan Journal of Mechanical and Industrial Engineering,* Vol. 2, No. 1, Mar., pp. 23-30.

[4] J.-C. Wang, H.-S. Huang and S.-L. Chen, 2007, Experimental Investigations of Thermal Resistance of a Heat Sink with Horizontal Embedded Heat Pipes, *International Communications in Heat and Mass Transfer,* Vol.34, Issue 8, October, pp. 958-970.

[5] J.-C. Wang and S.-L. Chen. 2007, Thermal Performance of Two-Phase Closed Thermosyphon Cooling System, *Proceedings of the Third International Conference on Thermal Engineering: Theory and Applications,* May 21-23, Amman, Jordan.

[6] R.-T. Wang and J.-C. Wang, 2012, Analyzing the Pressure-Difference Phenomenon between the Condensing and Boiling Sections in a Heat Pipe Cooling System, *International Communications in Heat and Mass Transfer,* Vol. 39, Issue 3, March, pp.390-398.

[7] H.-S. Huang, J.-C. Wang and S.-L. Chen, 2007, Experimental Investigation on Thermal Performance of Heat Sink with Two Pairs of Embedded Heat Pipes, *Proceedings of IPACK2007,* ASME InterPACK`07.

[8] J.-C. Wang, 2009, Developing Window Program of Heat Sink with Embedded Heat Pipes, *Proceedings of the Fourth International Conference on Thermal Engineering: Theory and Applications,* January 12-14, 2009, Abu Dhabi, UAE, P.1-P.7.

[9] J.-C. Wang, R.-T. Wang, C.-C. Chang and C.-L. Huang, 2010, Program for Rapid Computation of the Thermal Performance of a Heat Sink with Embedded Heat Pipes, *Journal of the Chinese Society of Mechanical Engineers,* Vol. 31, Issue 1, February, pp.21-28.

[10] J.-C. Wang, T.-L. Chang and Y.-K. Chang, 2010, Window Program of Heat Sink Heat Pipes Thermal Module, *7th International Conference on Heat Transfer, Fluid Mechanics and Thermodynamics, HEFAT2010,* 19-21 July 2010, Antalya, Turkey.

[11] J.-C. Wang, 2009, Superposition Method to Investigate the Thermal Performance of Heat Sink with Embedded Heat Pipes, *International Communications in Heat and Mass Transfer,* Vol.36, Issue 7, August, pp. 686-692.

[12] J.-C. Wang, 2011, L-type Heat Pipes Application in Electronic Cooling System, *International Journal of Thermal Sciences,* Vol.50 , Issue 1, January, pp.97-105.

[13] J.-C. Wang and W.-J. Chen, 2011, Thermal Analysis for L-type Heat Pipes Heat Sink with Dual Fans, *11th International Conference on Fluid Control, Measurements, and Visualization (FLUCOME 2011),* December 5th to 9th, 2011, in Keelung, Taiwan.

[14] J.-C. Wang, 2011, Investigations on Non-Condensation Gas of a Heat Pipe, *Engineering,* Vol. 3, pp.376-383.

[15] R.-T. Wang, J.-C. Wang and T.-L. Chang, 2011, Experimental Analysis for Thermal Performance of a Vapor Chamber Applied to High-Performance Servers, *Journal of Marine Science and Technology-Taiwan,* Vol. 19, No. 4, July/August, pp.353-360.

[16] J.-C. Wang, 2010, Development of Vapour Chamber-based VGA Thermal Module, *International Journal of Numerical Methods for Heat and Fluid Flow,* Vol.20, Issue 4, May, pp.416-428.

[17] J.-C. Wang and W.-J. Chen, 2011, Vapor Chamber in High-end VGA Card, *Microsystems, Packaging, Assembly and Circuits Technology Conference,* 2011. *IMPACT 2011. 6th International,* pp.393-396.

[18] J.-C. Wang and T.-C. Chen, 2009, Vapor Chamber in High Performance Server, *Microsystems, Packaging, Assembly and Circuits Technology Conference,* 2009. *IMPACT 2009. 4th International,* pp.364-367.

[19] J.-C. Wang and R.-T. Wang, 2011, A Novel Formula for Effective Thermal Conductivity of Vapor Chamber, *EXPERIMENTAL TECHNIQUES,* Vol. 35, Issue 5, September/October, pp.35-40.

[20] J.-C. Wang, 2011, Applied Vapor Chambers on Non-uniform Thermo Physical Conditions, *Applied Physics,* Vol. 1, pp.20-26.

[21] J.-C. Wang and C.-L. Huang, 2010, VAPOR CHAMBER IN HIGH POWER LEDS, *Microsystems, Packaging, Assembly and Circuits Technology Conference,* 2010. *IMPACT 2010. 5th International,* pp.1-4.

[22] J.-C. Wang, 2011, Thermal Investigations on LEDs Vapor Chamber-Based Plates, *International Communications in Heat and Mass Transfer,* Vol.38, Issue 9, November, pp. 1206-1212.

[23] J.-C. Wang, T.-S. Sung and W.-P. Chen, 2011, Hyper-Generation LEDs VCPCB, *Microsystems, Packaging, Assembly and Circuits Technology Conference,* 2011. *IMPACT 2011. 6th International,* pp.332-335.

[24] J.-C. Wang, R.-T. Wang, T.-L. Chang, D.-S. Hwang, 2010, Development of 30 Watt High-Power LEDs Vapor Chamber-Based Plate, *International Journal of Heat and Mass Transfer,* Vol. 53 , Issue 19/20, September, pp.3900-4001.

In: Horizons in Computer Science Research. Volume 9 ISBN: 978-1-63321-522-1
Editor: Thomas S. Clary

Chapter 12

HFAT: A HIGH PERFORMANCE HYBRID FAT32 FILE SYSTEM

Wasim Ahmad Bhat* **and S. M. K. Quadri**†*
Department of Computer Sciences, University of Kashmir, India

Abstract

Magnetic disk drives are mechanical at heart and hence have performance limitations. However, a hybrid storage system that combines the advantages of the inexpensive random seek of solid state storage device with the inexpensive sequential access of the magnetic disk drive, can significantly improve the performance of a file system in a variety of situations. In this paper, based on this idea, we propose *a high-performance hybrid FAT file system*, namely hFAT, which stores the most frequently accessed metadata of files in a FAT file system on a flash drive while as actual contents on the magnetic drive in order to eliminate the head positioning latency incurred by file system operations in FAT file systems. The empirical evaluation of hFAT using Sprite LFS small-file benchmark indicates that hFAT file system can reduce the latency incurred by FAT32 file system operations by a minimum of 25 %, 10 % and 90 % during writing, reading and deleting a large number of small files respectively, if a solid state storage device having latency lesser or equal to 10 % of that of magnetic disk is used in addition.

PACS: 05.45-a, 52.35.Mw, 96.50.Fm

Keywords: FAT File System, Hybrid Storage, File System Performance, Disk File Systems

AMS Subject Classification: 53D, 37C, 65P

1. Introduction

FAT file system is the primary file system for various operating systems including DR-DOS, FreeDOS, MS-DOS, OS/2 (v1.1) and Microsoft Windows (upto Windows Me). FAT file system being simple in design, chronologically old and primarily supported by

*E-mail address: wab.cs@uok.edu.in
†E-mail address: quadrismk@kashmiruniversity.ac.in

Microsoft OSes has made it most compatible and widely used file system. Almost all operating systems support FAT file systems. Furthermore, digital devices like mp3 players, digital cameras and so on, all need to store and process persistent data. These devices exchange this data frequently with desktop computers. This is only possible if the file system used in the device is supported by the PC's operating system, and no file system full-fills this requirement as FAT file systems do. Similarly, among solid state storage devices such as pen drives and removable magnetic disk drives which communicate with PCs via USB interface, FAT file systems are common for compatibility reasons. However, because of the same simple and chronologically old design FAT file systems face performance challenges. As compared to other file systems, the performance of FAT is poor in situations where large number of small files are being processed. Furthermore, for large file sizes it also does not perform so well. Logically, the design of FAT file system is similar to that of Old Unix file system (UFS). In FAT file systems, the metadata necessary to locate the contents of every file and directory are placed at the beginning of the volume. As a consequence, the seek distance between this metadata and actual contents of files and directories is large. Moreover, no effort is made to place the contents of a file or directory at rotationally optimal positions. Furthermore, the directory entries are arranged as an unordered linear list. Therefore, finding a particular file within a directory requires a linear search with an algorithm complexity of `O(n)`. Worst, the metadata necessary to locate all the clusters belonging to a file (or directory) is scattered in a long FAT Table. As a consequence, this table needs to traversed from the head to the tail until sufficient entries are read to locate the contents of that file (or directory). Though being *Update-in-place* file system, FAT file system does not achieve *logical locality*. However, depending upon the state of the file system, *temporal locality* may be possible for userdata but can't be exploited for performance.

Since, the inception of FAT file system in 1981, this performance problem has been there in its design. Although, UFS received many performance patches to address such problems, however no such effort was made for FAT file system. The concepts of FFS and other related proven techniques which enhanced the performance of UFS can be applied to FAT file systems, however this will create a high performance but incompatible version of FAT file system which is not desirable after achieving the spot of highly compatible file system. Nevertheless, other techniques which do not demand modification of file system design or need little affordable source modification are feasible. This paper describes the design, simulation and evaluation of a new FAT file system, namely hFAT, which stores the most frequently accessed metadata of files in a FAT file system on a flash drive while as actual contents on the magnetic drive. Specifically, the idea is to store the contents of directories and small amount of most frequently accessed FAT Table of FAT file systems on the solid state drive to eliminate the head positioning latency incurred by file system operations in FAT file systems.

The rest of this paper is organised as follows. Section 2 discusses the background of FAT file systems followed by various proposals to exploit the advantages of hybrid storage system. Section 3 highlights various performance problems in FAT32 file system. Section 4 discusses the design of *a high performance hybrid FAT32* file system called hFAT file system. Section 6 presents the simulation of hFAT file system for performance evaluation while section 7 discusses the experiment. Finally, section 8 discusses the results, section 9 presents the conclusion and section 10 highlights the limitation and future scope of the work.

2. Background & Related Work

FAT is a proprietary computer file system originally developed by BILL GATES and MARC McDONALD in 1976/1977 for managing disks in Microsoft's BASIC program. In 1980, IBM approached BILL GATES to discuss the state of home computers and what Microsoft products could do for IBM. Since Microsoft had never written an operating system before, GATES suggested that IBM investigate an OS called CP/M (Control Program for Microcomputers), written by GARY KILDALL of Digital Research. Kildall had his Ph.D. in computers and had written the most successful operating system of the time, selling over 600,000 copies of CP/M. IBM contacted GARY KILDALL but he refused. IBM soon returned to BILL GATES and gave Microsoft the contract to write a new operating system, one that eventually wiped GARY KILDALL'S CP/M out of common use [Hamm and Greene 2004].

In 1981, Microsoft bought QDOS from TIM PATTERSON of Seattle Computer Products to develop MS-DOS 1.0 for IBM and IBM compatible PCs. QDOS was a `16-bit` *Quick and Dirty* clone of Gary Kidall's `8-bit` CP/M. TIM PATTERSON had bought a CP/M manual and used it as the basis to write his operating system in six weeks. QDOS was different enough from CP/M to be considered legally a different product. In addition to other parts, QDOS had a slightly different file system than CP/M which was based on the file system of Microsoft Disk BASIC program that used an organisation method called FAT (File Allocation Table) to write its files to floppy disks. In fact, FAT was the main difference between CP/M and MS-DOS when it was released, and it was definitely the key to success of the new OS [Bellis].

The first FAT version called FAT12 file system was released with MS-DOS 1.0 in 1981. As primarily designed for floppy disk, it had limited features. Hierarchical file structure (directories and sub-directories) was added to FAT12 with the introduction of MS-DOS 2.0 in 1983 when IBM released the PC-XT with a built-in hard disk. In 1984, MS-DOS 3.0 was released along with IBMs new PC-AT with an updated FAT16 file system which allowed much larger file sizes and supported 1.2 MB 5.25" floppy disks. In January 1986, MS-DOS 3.2 introduced extended partition. In 1987 and 1988, FAT16 file system received more enhancement patches and was finally released with MS-DOS 4.0 and OS/2 1.1 [Kirps 2008].

One of the major drawbacks of the FAT file system was its 8 character filename limit (plus a 3 character extension). 255 character long filenames were made possible using VFAT (or "Virtual FAT") which stored the long filenames as meta information visible to the user while the OSes actually operated with 8 character filenames. VFAT was introduced with the more user friendly Windows 95 in 1995. Although, Microsoft had also designed a very efficient file system named NTFS v 1.0 in 1993, but it was only released with NT line of OSes and was released with Windows 3.1 NT.

In order to overcome the volume size limitation of FAT16 file system, Microsoft decided to implement a newer generation of FAT, known as FAT32, with cluster counts held in a `32 bit` field, of which `28 bits` are currently used. In theory, FAT32 file system supports a total of approximately `268,435,456 clusters`, allowing for drive sizes in the range of 8 TBs with 32 KB clusters (2^{28}). However, the boot sector uses a 32 bit field to limit volume size to 2^{32} sectors (2 TB on a hard disk with 512 byte sectors). The maximum possible size for a file on a FAT32 volume is 4 GB minus 1 byte. FAT32 was introduced with Windows 95 OSR2 [Tomov].

Microsoft has continued its support to FAT file systems even though they have developed other high performance file systems. They also designed a specialised FAT file system, namely FATX, for XBOX in 2002. Recently, the FAT32 file system was reworked to support large volume sizes, large file sizes and file system reliability. This FAT file system, namely exFAT, was released in 2006 with Windows Vista. In addition, KFAT [Kwon et al.2005], TFAT [Microsoft b] and FATTY [Alei et al. 2007], all are reliability enhancements to the actual FAT file system design by the Microsoft and other individual researchers. Also, standards such as ECMA-107 and ISO/IEC 9293 for FAT12 and FAT16 without long filename support have been drafted.

Based on the idea of hybrid storage system many proposals have been made. [Baker et al.1992] proposed using a small amount of battery-backed RAM to act as a small write buffer to reduce disk accesses. The motive was to prevent losing recent updates to file caches without having to continuously write data back to the disks as soon as updates occur. Similarly, [Miller et al.2001] designed a system called HeRMES which uses a form of non volatile RAM called Magnetic RAM (MRAM) to act as a persistent cache for a magnetic disk drive. They used MRAM to cache the file system metadata and also buffer writes to the magnetic disk drive. Furthermore, [Wang et al. 2006] proposed Conquest which uses a simple partitioning approach in which they place all small files and metadata (e.g. directories and file attributes) in NVRAM (Non-Volatile Random Access Memory) while the remaining large files and their associated metadata are assigned to the magnetic disk drive. Though these approaches significantly improve the performance of a file system, however these demand some file system source modification in addition to physical overhaul of the machine to support new pieces of hardware.

Moreover, Microsoft Windows 7 utilises hybrid drives with an option known as ready boost [Matthews et al. 2008]. The idea is to use flash memory as a persistent buffer or cache to absorb all read and write requests. This was primarily developed to improve the power usage of laptop systems by allowing the magnetic disk drive to spin down during low workload times. Similarly, [Soundararajan et al. 2010] proposed a hybrid solid state device and magnetic disk drive system that accumulates a log of changes on the magnetic disk drive before writing them in bulk onto the solid state device at a later time. Finally, [Fisher et al. 2012] proposed to optimise the I/O performance of a system by using a large magnetic disk drive and limited size solid state drive in tandem to store data. They proposed a drive assignment algorithm which determines which device to place data on in order to take advantage of their desirable characteristics while trying to overcome some of their undesirable characteristics. Though these proposals can be added to any file system on the fly without any hardware overhaul, however they only use the other device as an auxiliary log until the updates are committed to the actual device. Hence, this procedure demands house-keeping work to be done at sometime later.

3. Performance Problems in FAT32 File System

The FAT file system design is very simple. Although, there are many flavours of FAT file systems, but all of these share same logical design. This subsection and following subsections refer to the most compatible and widely used FAT file system, namely FAT32 file system, for reference [Microsofta].

The performance of FAT32 file system as compared to other file systems is very poor. Specifically, FAT32 file systems can't handle a workload which comprises accesses to large number of small files. Some of the main and significant reasons for this are as follows:

1. The complete metadata and userdata of a file (or directory), even in best case, is scattered at three different places, i.e. directory entry, FAT Table and userdata clusters. This allows head positioning latencies to creep in at various junctures of a file system operation.

2. There is a large seek distance between the frequently accessed metadata store, i.e. FAT Table, which is required to locate clusters associated with every file and directory, and the contents of those files and directories. Furthermore, this distance is covered twice as FAT Table is located at one extreme end of the volume as shown in Figure 1.

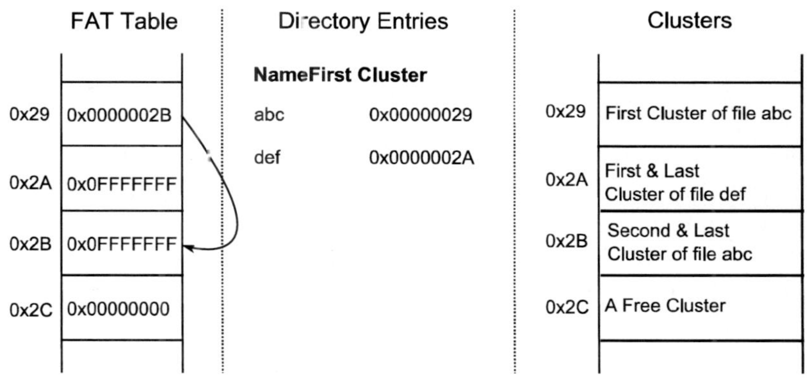

Figure 1. Relationship between various on-disk structures of FAT32 file system.

3. FAT32 file system design makes no effort to place all clusters belonging to any file or directory contiguously to avoid intra-file seeks. Moreover, this creates a probability that to locate the chain-of-clusters associated with the file or directory in the FAT Table may incur head positioning latencies as the entries may span over multiple sectors.

4. Similarly, no design effort exists to place the clusters belonging to all files and directories residing in the same directory contiguously. This leads to inter-file latency while accessing the contents of these directories and files. Furthermore, this also creates a probability that the information necessary to locate chain-of-clusters associated to each such directory and file in the FAT Table may incur head positioning latencies.

5. In a workload where files are created and deleted frequently or their lengths often changed, the volume becomes increasingly fragmented over time. This exaggerates the presence of head positioning latencies between directory entry and FAT Table, between various entries of FAT Table and between data clusters allocated to the file or directory.

6. Moreover, FAT32 file system design neither achieves *logical locality* nor *temporal locality*, gives no regard to rotational latency, uses simple data structures and so on.

4. Design of hFAT File System

The design of FAT32 file system is logically similar to that of Old Unix file system (UFS). As an analogy, FAT32 keeps FAT Table at the beginning of the volume like UFS keeps the inode store. Moreover, in both file systems directory entries hold filenames. However, inodes only maintain information regarding a particular file or directory while as the allocation/deallocation list is maintained individually by UFS within *Superblock*. In contrast, the FAT Table records both free and allocated clusters within the volume along with the chain-of-clusters associated with a particular file or directory, while as directory entries in addition to filename contains other information such as attributes, size, first cluster in chain and so on [Heybruck]. So logically, the design of FAT32 file system is bit better than UFS. In-spite of this, FAT32 file system suffers from performance problem mainly because of the large seek distance between FAT Table and clusters. Furthermore, the percentage of storage space occupied by FAT Table is very small as compared to clusters (`32 bits/cluster`). As such, as the size of volume increases, the maximum seek distance increases significantly. Furthermore, this seek distance is covered twice as FAT Table is located at the beginning of the volume. The figure 2 shows the impact of large volume size on maximum seek distance between FAT Table and clusters. Also, because directory

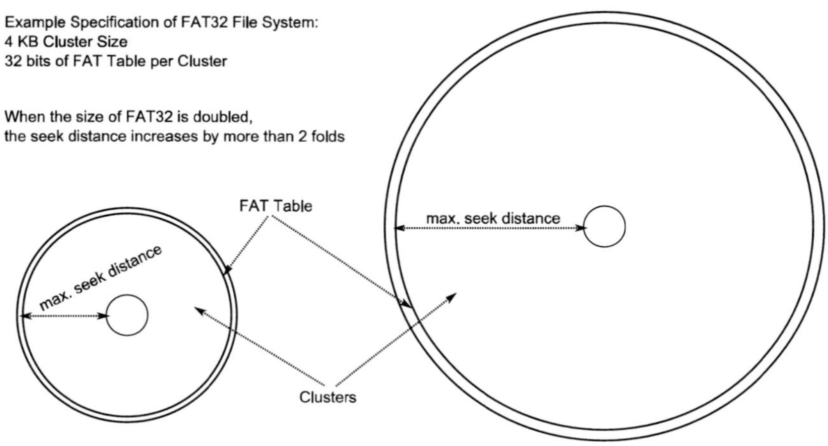

Figure 2. Effect of large volume size on seek distance between FAT Table & Clusters.

entries hold actual key to locating the clusters allocated to a file (or directory), by naming them and locating the first cluster in the chain, access to this metadata is mandatory. As clusters allocated to a directory can also be scattered, latency is inevitable. Furthermore, in a workload wherein large number of small files, whose size is less than cluster size of FAT32 volume, are accessed, there are more frequent accesses to directory entries than FAT Table. In fact, all the requests can be satisfied from directory entries. However, deletion operations require access to FAT Table. In contrast, a workload wherein large files (atleast 2-3 clusters long) are accessed, there are more frequent requests to FAT Table than directory entries. Nevertheless, in both cases, the latencies incurred during access to FAT Table and directory entries deteriorate the performance of FAT32 file system.

One possible solution to this would be to modify the FAT32 file system same way as UFS was modified. In other words, re-engineering FAT32 file system using the concepts of FFS and CFFS can yield significant performance gains. However, this is much complex as FAT Table can't be put near every file and directory. Furthermore, this will rigorously modify the FAT32 file system design and FAT file system so modified, will lose its identity. Moreover, as mentioned earlier FFS overcomes latency problems by making certain assumptions about magnetic disks which no more hold true.

Another possible solution to reduce these latencies would be to pre-cache and delay-write the whole FAT Table. This is beneficial because this FAT Table is a central metadata store that is needed by every individual file and directory residing on the volume. However, the size of FAT Table can impose serious limitations. As an example, for a `2 TB` FAT32 volume having `8 KB` cluster size, cache memory required for FAT Table is `1 GB`. Furthermore, FAT32 is not reliable and thus, any unanticipated crash can result in data loss and possible file system corruption.

In contrast, directory clusters can be placed near the contents of files and directories them name by modifying the source of FAT32 file system. However, the algorithmic complexity involved and assumptions to be made make it less appealing.

hFAT is a *high performance hybrid FAT32 file system design* that overcomes the performance problems faced by plain vanilla FAT32 file systems. The hFAT file system intends to exploit the advantages of the solid state device's small and flat random access time with the large sequential access speed and storage capacity of the magnetic disk drive to improve the performance of FAT32 file system. In other words, hFAT intends to distribute the workload of FAT32 file system between solid state and magnetic storage devices by placing the small *hot zone* of the file system i.e. FAT Table and directory entries, on the solid state storage device while the large *cold zone* on the magnetic disk drive. Although there exist proposals to use hybrid storage for performance gains, but all of these proposals either propose using solid state storage device as a cache or an auxiliary log until the changes are committed to actual storage. Furthermore, they demand design and/or source modification. However, hFAT proposes using solid state storage device as a persistent store for the most frequently used FAT Table and directory entries of a FAT32 file system. The motive of this design is to satisfy all the accesses to FAT Table and directory entries from a small and low latency solid state storage device without modifying the design or source. As such, it totally eliminates the head positioning latencies incurred during access to FAT Table and directory entries. The Figure 3 shows the logical layout of hFAT file system. In order to accomplish this, hFAT has two choices; 1) modify the source of FAT32 file system, or 2) modify the block device driver. As a matter of fact, modifying the source of either FAT32 file system or block device driver has several problems and thus is not feasible. However,

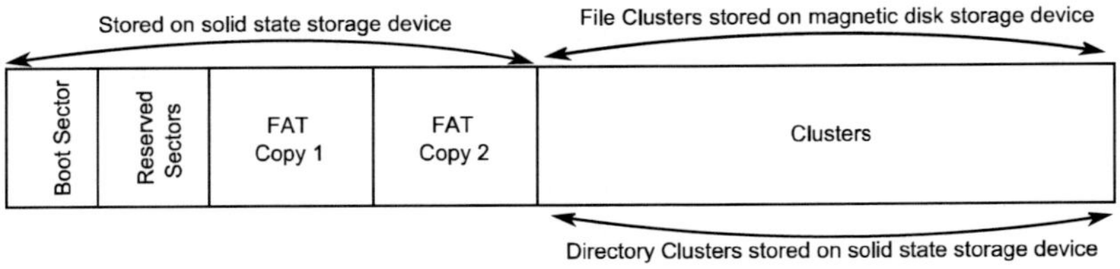

Figure 3. Logical on-disk layout of hFAT file system.

adding a layer of abstraction just below the FAT32 file system and above the block device driver can do the job. The technique called *driver stacking* enables one driver to be stacked on top of another driver just like file system stacking, in which one file system module can be stacked on top of another file system module. File system stacking is not feasible here as the requests made by FAT32 file system should be pre-processed rather than pre-processing the requests made to FAT32 file system. The stacked block device driver acts like fan-out file system by overlaying over two block device drivers; one responsible for doing I/O with solid state storage drive and another responsible for doing I/O with magnetic disk drive. The driver so stacked can forward the request to appropriate block device driver depending upon the request made by FAT32 file system and return the results to upper layers.

5. Working of hFAT Stackable Device Driver

When a volume is formatted with FAT32 file system with hFAT slipped in, all the read requests are satisfied from magnetic disk. This is done so to allow FAT32 file system code set appropriate values for the size of FAT Table, cluster size and so on. However, all the write requests are for metadata and hence hFAT redirects them to solid state storage device to zero-fill FAT Table, initialise BPB and root directory, and so on. With its completion, hFAT reserves some space on solid state storage device to act as a log that maintains the list of clusters allocated to directories and there corresponding mapping into solid state storage device. This mapping serves two functions; 1) It allows hFAT to utilise the space on solid storage device effectively, and 2) it addresses the question how the stackable device driver will identify whether the request is for data clusters or metadata clusters? In case of FAT Table it is quite simple as there is a clear boundary between FAT Table and rest of the FAT32 volume. However, identifying requests for clusters containing directory entries is difficult as directory clusters may be scattered around with data clusters of files. To overcome this, hFAT uses this `log`. The `log` is populated by hFAT in following situations; 1) When a newly created FAT32 volume is mounted for the first time along hFAT, the first request made to hFAT that crosses the FAT Table boundary pertains to root directory. Thus, hFAT gets the first cluster number of the root directory and can locate rest of clusters from FAT Table. As further requests arrive for any cluster of root directory, hFAT can analyse the contents to identify the allocation/deallocation of any new subdirectory. In case, hFAT finds one, it records its cluster number(s) in the `log` along with mapping in solid state storage device. 2) To further validate that a cluster is a directory cluster, hFAT can analyse the contents of that cluster for directory entry signatures. This procedure applies not only to root directory but for all those clusters who have an entry in `log`. The figure 4 shows the logical design of hFAT file system with a driver stacked on top of two block device drivers. One may argue that this may add performance overhead to the working of FAT32

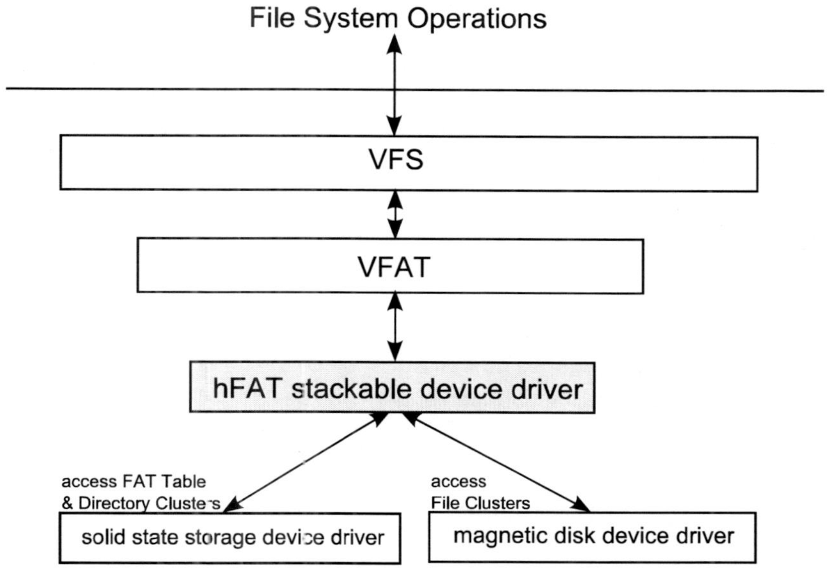

Figure 4. Design of hFAT file system using driver stacking.

file system. However, because most of the processing is simple and doesn't require any I/O to magnetic disk, the performance overhead is expected to be low and will be amortised by faster hardware. Furthermore, it is clear that the space actually meant for FAT Table and directory clusters on magnetic disk is lost. However, in general scenario, the space lost is less than 1% of total space of magnetic disk and thus, is affordable. Moreover, it is mandatory for hFAT that the FAT32 file system be created newly.

6. Simulation of hFAT Stackable Device Driver

Device driver stacking is possible in Linux but unfortunately there is no well defined interface to perform it. This can lead to many performance and technical problems during the operation of stacked driver. In contrast, *Windows Driver Model* introduced in Windows 98 and 2000 and *File System Filter Manager* introduced in Windows XP Service Pack 2 provide a clean, flexible and efficient driver stacking support. However, Windows OSes have there own limitations. Nevertheless, the behaviour of hFAT stackable device driver can be simulated because of the minimal functionality embedded in it. hFAT stackable device driver has to perform only one task; forward the request of upper layer (i.e. FAT32 file system) to one of the two below existing device drivers depending upon the type of request. This behaviour can be simulated if FAT32 file system block trace of some workload or benchmark is fed to the simulator along with the information necessary to qualify the request as metadata or userdata.

As the motive of this simulation is to identify the number of requests satisfied from solid state storage device and magnetic disk drive, we provide both block trace and the necessary information. Also, as hFAT makes no changes to FAT32 file system design and works below a level at which FAT32 file system operates, the efficiency will be achieved if hFAT sends more requests to solid state storage device than magnetic disk drive. Indeed, this information is reported by our simulator. However, we need to further evaluate the efficiency of hFAT by assigning each block access to solid state device and magnetic disk drive some latency values to identify the reduction in latency of operations.

Algorithm 1 shows the simplicity if algorithm used during the simulation of hFAT stackable device driver.

Algorithm 1 Algorithm used during simulation of hFAT stackable device driver

Input: *blockTrace*, *Information*

Output: *ssdBlockRead*, *ssdBlockWrite*, *hddBlockRead*, *hddBlockWrite*

```
while blockTrace contains more blocks do
    if blockTrace.blkNum is metadata then
        if blockTrace.blkNum is read then
            ssdBlockRead ← ssdBlockRead + 1
        else
            ssdBlockWrite ← ssdBlockWrite + 1
        end if
    else
        if blockTrace.blkNum is read then
            hddBlockRead ← hddBlockRead + 1
        else
            hddBlockWrite ← hddBlockWrite + 1
        end if
    end if
end while
```

7. Experiment

In order to illuminate specific operations which improved by hFAT, the FAT32 file system was exercised using Sprite LFS small-file microbenchmark to get block trace. However, instead of writing, reading and deleting `1 KB` files, the benchmark wrote, read and deleted `4 KB` files. This is in accordance to repeatedly reported observation that file system workloads are dominated by accesses to small files, typically `4 KB` or less in size [Agrawal et al. 2007]. Furthermore, Sprite LFS small-file microbenchmark was implemented as a simple shell script using `bash-version 4.1.7(1)`. Moreover, the caches were flushed after every phase of Sprite LFS small-file benchmark. The block trace was captured via `/proc/sys/vm/block_dump` interface of Linux kernel to log only those blocks whose request was not satisfied by the buffer cache. However, the size of ring buffer of Linux was changed from default `4096 bytes` to `8192 bytes` to avoid loss of any block trace due to overflow. Furthermore, because of the simplicity of the simulation, the simulator was implemented in-house as a shell script using `bash-version 4.1.7(1)`.

The experiment was conducted on an Intel based PC with Intel Core i3 CPU 550 @ 3.20 GHz processor with total 4 MB cache and 2 GB DDR3 1333 MHz SDRAM. The hard drive used is a 320 GB SATA drive with on board cache of 8 MB and 15.3 ms of reported average access time. The drive is partitioned into 20 GB primary partition to hose the Fedora Core 14 operating system kernel version 2.6.35.14-95.fc.14.i686 and another 5 GB partition to mount FAT32 file system. The partition is large enough to hold all the files and small enough to fit in one zone of the disk. Moreover, the experiment was run on a newly created file system. Furthermore, during the execution of Sprite LFS small-file microbenchmark, the Linux was set to run at run-level 1 to reduce the random effect of other applications and demons. Also, the experiment was repeated atleast 5 times and all the results were averaged; the standard deviation was less than 3 % of the average in all cases.

8. Results & Discussion

The result of the simulation is shown in Table 1 and 2. Table 1 shows the number of block reads satisfied by non-HDD device and by HDD device against each operation of the Sprite LFS small-file microbenchmark. Similarly, Table 2 reports the same statistics but for blocks written. Moreover, in each category, the percentage of block accesses absorbed by non-HDD device is calculated. There are many things worth noticing here. First, in

Table 1. hFAT simulation report showing distribution of read blocks

Operation	Blocks Read (non-HDD)	Blocks Read (HDD)	Access %age of non-HDD
Create 10,000 4 KB Files	1380	0	100 %
Read 10,000 4 KB Files	643	10,000	6.04 %
Delete 10,000 4 KB Files	721	0	100 %

Table 2. hFAT simulation report showing distribution of written blocks

Operation	Blocks Written (non-HDD)	Blocks Written (HDD)	Access %age of non-HDD
Create 10,000 4 KB Files	2063	10,000	17.10 %
Read 10,000 4 KB Files	626	0	100 %
Delete 10,000 4 KB Files	785	0	100 %

case of blocks being read, in two phases 100 % of block reads are satisfied from non-HDD device while in one phase the percentage is as low as 6.04 %. This means that 66 % of the operations of this workload can effectively exploit the `100 %` benefits of low and flat latency of non-HDD device for reading.

Second, in case of blocks being written, in two phases `100 %` of blocks writes are satisfied from non-HDD device while in one phase the percentage is as low as `17.10 %`. This means that `66 %` of the operations of this workload can effectively exploit the `100 %` benefits of low and flat latency of non-HDD device for writing.

Third, the phases in which block reads or writes are not `100 %` satisfied from non-HDD device correspond to reading and writing `10,000 4 KB files`. This is expected as in these two phases the ratio of metadata to userdata is very low. However, these phases are mutually exclusive and such an operation within each phase is benefited from other operation of the phase that exploits `100 %` benefits of non-HDD device. As an example, the first phase wherein `10,000 4 KB` files are created, the percentage of blocks read from non-HDD device is `100 %` while as the percentage of blocks written to non-HDD device is `17.10 %` (expected as ratio of metadata to userdata to be written is low). However, the `100 %` block reads from non-HDD device augments the `17.10 %` blocks writes in two ways; 1) the reads in operations experience low and flat latency of non-HDD device, and 2) the repositioning of R/W head of HDD device during such reads is eliminated which otherwise would have created latency for blocks to be written. Similar benefits are exploited in second phase.

Finally, in third phase `100 %` block reads and writes are satisfied from non-HDD device. This is expected as this phase only deals with metadata.

Furthermore, we evaluated the performance of hFAT by assigning various access latencies to non-HDD device. To evaluate over a range of access latencies, we assigned weights in terms of percentage of access latency of HDD device with granularity of `1 %`. In other words, we assigned `100` possible latency values to non-HDD device where each value corresponds to some percent of latency of HDD. As an example, if HDD device has access latency of `200 ms`, then we assigned latencies to non-HDD device ranging from `2 to 200 ms` with the step size of `2`.

Moreover, the read/write latency is not symmetric in either solid state storage device or magnetic disk drive. Although, less expensive solid state storage devices typically have write speeds significantly lower than their read speeds, but higher performing ones have similar read and write speeds. Furthermore, HDDs generally have slightly lower write speeds than their read speeds. Nevertheless, we assigned same latency values to both types of operations in each type of device. Furthermore, we assigned average access latency of HDD to each accessed block of HDD. Unfortunately, this way the benefits gained by removing the repositioning of the head which reduces the inter-userdata block latency can't be calculated. This means that the evaluation will yield the upper bound on the latency incurred by operations and can be expected to go down. Figure 5 shows the graph plotted for three phases of the benchmark against the range of access latencies across x-axis and the latency incurred by operations in terms of percentage of actual latency when only HDD is used. This graph indicates that those phases which have steep slope are highly affected by the latency of HDD device while as others are less affected. In the figure, the phase corresponding to deletion of files is highly affected by the latency of HDD device. Next comes the phase that creates the files followed by the phase that reads these files. This graph also shows that using hFAT with a non-HDD device having latency `10 %` of that of

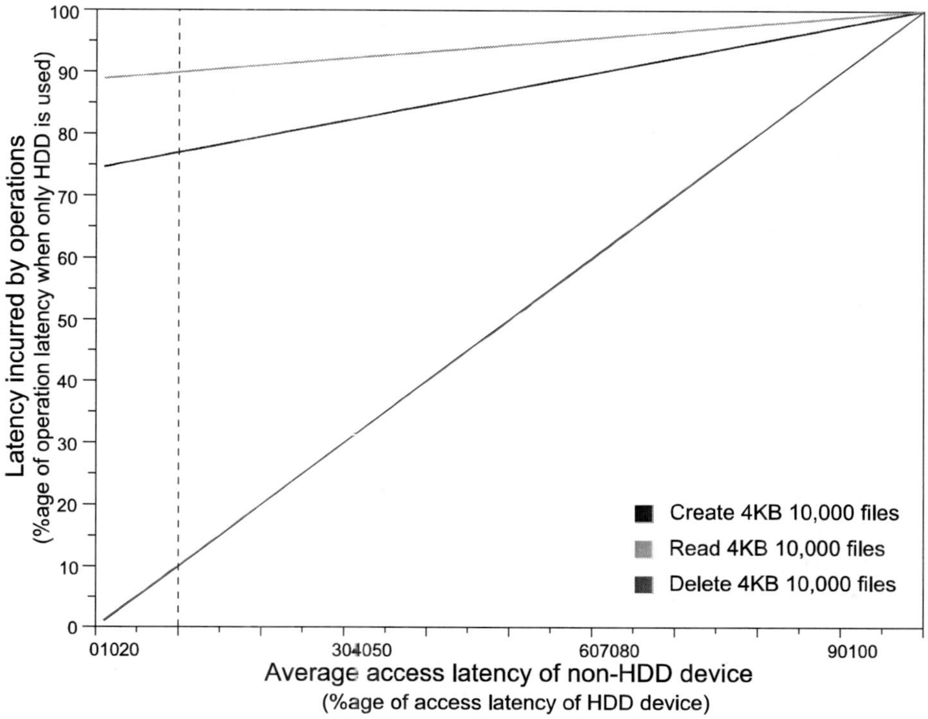

Figure 5. Affect of various latencies on total latency of operations of hFAT.

HDD can reduce the latency of write operations by as minimum as 10 %, read operations by as minimum as 25 % and of delete operations by 90 %. It is to be noted that this reduction is the lower bound as the average access time of HDD is taken into consideration.

Furthermore, the typical access latency of non-HDD is about 0.1 ms while as for HDDs the average access time ranges between 5 to 10 ms. The ratio of 0.1 ms to 5 ms corresponds to 2 % while as the ratio of 0.1 ms to 10 ms corresponds to 2 %, both being lesser than 10 %. This is even lesser than what is required as per our observation.

9. Conclusion

We can conclude that using hybrid storage system for enhancing the performance of disk file systems is valuable. The fact is that the accesses to most frequently used structures of a file system includes a small amount of file system wide metadata. This metadata if stored on solid state storage device can not only eliminate the seeks and rotational delays incurred during its access but will significantly reduce the the total latency incurred by operations.

Based on this idea, we designed and simulated the behaviour of a *high performance hybrid FAT32 file system* called hFAT. hFAT uses a solid state storage device to hold the most frequently used metadata of FAT file systems, namely FAT Table and directory clusters. FAT Table accounts to small amount of the file system space but is used by every operation that reads, writes or deletes files. However, being located at the beginning of volume it creates the performance bottle neck in overall file system. Furthermore, directory clusters need necessarily to be accessed during file system operations and are scattered around the volume of the disk. hFAT places these structures on a solid state storage device in order to eliminate the seeks and rotational delays incurred by operations during their access. However, in order to keep the design of FAT32 file system intact, we propose hFAT to be slipped in as a stackable device driver. Furthermore, we simulated the behaviour of hFAT as stackable device driver and evaluated the performance gains by running the block trace collected by exercising a FAT32 file system using Sprite LFS small-file benchmark. The results indicate that hFAT file system can reduce the latency incurred by FAT32 file system operations by a minimum of 25 %, 10 % and 90 % during writing, reading and deleting large number of small files respectively, if a solid state storage device having latency lesser or equal to 10 % of that of magnetic disk is used as an addition.

10. Limitations & Future Scope

hFAT has been currently simulated and evaluated using Sprite LFS small-file benchmark, however it needs to be evaluated for other microbenchmarks and macrobenchmarks. Also, hFAT needs to be implemented to further validate the claims made in simulation and analyse the affect of self-evolving nature of hFAT for recognising metadata and userdata cluster requests. Furthermore, solid state storage devices have limited number of read/write cycles. However, regular backups can be made by hFAT driver automatically to avoid data loss.

Nevertheless, the idea behind hFAT is valuable and can be extended to other file systems. The strong point of this technique is that it does not require any design or source modification of file systems. The hFAT file system implementation in Linux can be investigated by developing a clean interface for driver stacking. Furthermore, the self-evolving feature of hFAT module can be optimised and more generalised.

References

[Agrawal et al. 2007] Agrawal, N., Bolosky, W. J., Douceur, J. R., and Lorch, J. R. (2007). A five-year study of file-system metadata. *Transactions on Storage*, 3(3):338 – 346.

[Alei et al. 2007] Alei, L., Kejia, L., Xiaoyong, L., and Haibing, G. (2007). Fatty: A reliable fat file system. In *Proceedings of the 10th Euromicro Conference on Digital System Design Architectures, Methods and Tools*, DSD 2007, pages 390–395. IEEE Computer Society.

[Baker et al.1992] Baker, M., Asami, S., Deprit, E., Ouseterhout, J., and Seltzer, M. (1992). Non-volatile memory for fast, reliable file systems. In *Proceedings of the fifth international conference on Architectural support for programming languages and operating systems*, ASPLOS-V, pages 10–22, New York, NY, USA. ACM.

[Bellis] Bellis, M. History of the ms-dos operating systems, ibm & microsoft.

[Fisher et al. 2012] Fisher, N., He, Z., and McCarthy, M. (2012). A hybrid filesystem for hard disk drives in tandem with flash memory. *Computing*, 94:21–68.

[Hamm and Greene 2004] Hamm, S. and Greene, J. (2004). The man who could have been bill gates. [Online; accessed August-2010].

[Heybruck] Heybruck, W. F. An introduction to fat 16/fat 32 file systems. [Online; accessed August-2010].

[Kirps 2008] Kirps, J. (2008). A short history of the windows fat file system. [Online; accessed August-2010].

[Kwon et al.2005] Kwon, M., Bae, S., Jung, S., Seo, D., and Kim, C. (2005). Kfat: Log-based transactional fat filesystem for embedded mobile systems. In *Proceedings of 2005 US-Korea Conference*, ICTS-142.

[Matthews et al. 2008] Matthews, J., Trika, S., Hensgen, D., Coulson, R., and Grimsrud, K. (2008). Intel turbo memory: Nonvolatile disk caches in the storage hierarchy of mainstream computer systems. *Transactions on Storage*, 4:4:1–4:24.

[Microsofta] Microsoft. Fat32 file system specification. [Online; accessed August-2010].

[Microsoft b] Microsoft. Transaction-safe fat file system. [Online; accessed August-2011].

[Miller et al.2001] Miller, E. L., Brandt, S. A., and Long, D. D. E. (2001). Hermes: High-performance reliable mram-enabled storage. In *Proceedings of the Eighth Workshop on Hot Topics in Operating Systems*, pages 95–, Washington, DC, USA. IEEE Computer Society.

[Soundararajan et al. 2010] Soundararajan, G., Prabhakaran, V., Balakrishnan, M., and Wobber, T. (2010). Extending ssd lifetimes with disk-based write caches. In *Proceedings of the 8th USENIX conference on File and storage technologies*, FAST'10, pages 8–8, Berkeley, CA, USA. USENIX Association.

[Tomov] Tomov, A. A brief introduction to fat (file allocation table) formats. [Online; accessed August-2010].

[Wang et al. 2006] Wang, A.-I. A., Kuenning, G., Reiher, P., and Popek, G. (2006). The conquest file system: Better performance through a disk/persistent-ram hybrid design. *Transactions on Storage*, 2:309–348.

INDEX

A

access, x, 12, 26, 32, 35, 36, 37, 47, 74, 80, 93, 94, 95, 96, 100, 106, 110, 132, 143, 157, 189, 238, 247, 285, 290, 291, 294, 295, 296, 297, 298
actuators, vii, 1, 8, 226
ad hoc network, 3, 29, 41, 42
adaptations, 164
ADC, 238
African-American, 150
agglutination, 277
aggregation, 26, 27, 28, 42, 247
aging process, 183
aging society, 200
algorithm, x, 3, 5, 6, 7, 22, 23, 30, 80, 81, 95, 107, 111, 119, 125, 139, 147, 199, 201, 205, 206, 208, 209, 211, 212, 213, 215, 222, 228, 286, 288, 294
annealing, 280
architects, 154, 156
architecture design, 163
Artificial Neural Networks, 99
assessment, 16, 20, 43, 142, 147, 148, 149, 150, 151, 166, 173, 184, 227
assessment tools, 16
asymmetry, 28, 29, 280
atmosphere, 78
atomic clocks, 77
attachment, 186
attacker, 22, 25, 27, 31, 32, 33, 34, 35, 37
Austria, 180
authentication, 28, 29, 35, 36, 37
authenticity, 28
automation, 155
autonomy, 46

B

background noise, 189
bandwidth, 46, 226, 229, 247, 248
banking, 15
base, viii, 3, 14, 24, 25, 26, 28, 29, 33, 34, 37, 38, 45, 46, 51, 52, 59, 69, 81, 156, 157, 196, 243, 251, 252, 257, 258, 260, 262, 264, 265
batteries, 20, 47, 50, 235, 239, 247
Beijing, 136, 138
bending, 33, 273
benefits, vii, 1, 15, 25, 142, 176, 188, 255, 296
bias, 78, 144
bile, 82
biodiversity, 155, 178
biological samples, 157
birds, 6, 7
birth rate, 183
black hole, 33
Bluetooth, 236
Boltzmann constant, 200
brain, 184, 185, 187
brain functions, 185
Brazil, 70
breakdown, 280
building blocks, 157, 162, 163
business model, 163, 174

C

C++, 207, 215
CAD, x, 251, 269, 273
capillary, 253, 254, 255, 256, 257, 258, 266
carbon emissions, 15
Caribbean, 179
case study, ix, 153, 154, 157
casting, 280
categorization, 154
category a, 176
central nervous system (CNS), 185
CG character, ix, x, 199, 200, 201, 202, 211, 212, 213, 214, 215, 216, 217, 218, 220, 221, 222, 223
challenges, viii, x, 19, 20, 21, 73, 135, 216, 225, 226, 227, 235, 247, 286
children, 28, 29
China, 136, 138, 141
circulation, 185, 255, 256
classification, x, 100, 103, 179, 225
clients, 155
clone, 287
clustering, 135, 139, 234

clusters, 233, 286, 287, 288, 289, 290, 291, 292, 293, 297, 298
coding, 143, 146
cognition, 150, 185, 189
cognitive style, 143, 146
collaboration, 12, 145, 147
college students, 150
collisions, 32, 229, 248
Colombia, 153, 155, 157, 178, 179
color, 139, 186, 188, 200, 281
commercial, 2, 20, 47, 50, 252, 258, 273, 279
communication, viii, ix, 2, 7, 11, 13, 17, 20, 21, 23, 24, 26, 32, 34, 35, 41, 45, 46, 48, 62, 69, 73, 74, 155, 156, 173, 181, 199, 200, 211, 212, 217, 221, 222, 226, 235, 239, 249
communication overhead, 26
communication systems, 73
communication technologies, 200
community(ies), 10, 148, 177
compatibility, 286
competition, 131, 145, 235
complexity, 184, 286, 291
compliance, 16
computation, 5, 20, 22, 23, 29, 73, 117, 130, 274
computational fluid dynamics, 269
computer, vii, viii, ix, x, 11, 12, 13, 14, 15, 16, 37, 39, 48, 135, 141, 142, 143, 145, 146, 147, 148, 149, 150, 151, 180, 184, 199, 200, 204, 207, 208, 212, 215, 216, 222, 251, 252, 254, 269, 282, 287, 299
computer software, 252
computer systems, 184, 200, 299
computer technology, 269
computer-aided design, x, 251
computing, vii, viii, 2, 11, 13, 14, 15, 16, 18, 20, 43, 46, 73, 74, 136, 143, 148, 149, 151, 184, 258, 266
conception, 167, 176
condensation, 253, 254, 255, 256, 258, 262
conductivity, 253, 254, 265, 266, 267, 280
confidentiality, viii, 19, 21, 22, 26, 29, 38
configuration, 35, 52, 69, 96, 122, 136, 159
connectivity, vii, 1, 3, 8, 25, 29, 51, 74, 131
conservation, vii, 1, 13, 46, 70, 186, 262
consolidation, 154
construction, viii, 3, 73, 116, 132, 138, 163, 174
consumption, x, 12, 15, 46, 50, 58, 62, 69, 225, 226, 235, 236, 237, 238, 239, 240, 252
contamination, 187
convergence, 126, 129, 258
cooling, x, 15, 251, 252, 253, 254, 255, 258, 265, 269, 276
copper, 253, 254, 265, 273, 274, 275, 277, 278, 280, 282
cornea, 188
corruption, 291
cost, 2, 7, 12, 14, 15, 20, 23, 46, 76, 81, 122, 131, 139, 155, 238, 239, 248, 252, 253, 265, 269, 276, 279
covering, 177
CPU, x, 207, 208, 215, 236, 237, 238, 251, 252, 257, 282, 295
CRLB, viii, 73, 86, 87, 88, 89, 90, 91, 92, 95, 96, 98, 99, 107, 112
cryptography, 22, 23, 25, 26, 27, 37
crystallization, 167
cultural heritage, 46
current limit, viii, 73
curriculum, 142, 146, 148, 149
curriculum development, 146, 148
cycles, 280, 298

D

data center, viii, 11, 12, 13, 14, 15, 16, 17
data collection, 8, 26, 27, 247
data communication, 236
data processing, 2, 15, 20, 32
data set, 103, 108, 114
data structure, 132, 290
database, 110, 113, 167, 190, 191, 267
decay, 85, 86
declarative knowledge, 143
deduction, 269
defects, 184
deficiencies, 169, 170, 176, 184
Delta, 105
Department of Defense, 77
Department of Energy, 12
deployments, 52
desynchronization, 34
detection, vii, 1, 4, 6, 7, 20, 27, 28, 32, 33, 42
detection system, 27
developed countries, 183
deviation, 28, 57, 107, 295
diet, 6
differential equations, 75
diffraction, 84
diffusion, 242, 243, 244, 248, 249
digital cameras, 286
digital divide, 143, 148
directional antennas, 83
diseases, 189
distortions, 33
distribution, ix, 2, 5, 8, 24, 26, 52, 53, 64, 66, 68, 86, 90, 94, 95, 103, 104, 158, 199, 232, 234, 279, 295
diversification, 150
diversity, 29, 154, 180
DNA, 155, 157, 165, 169, 170, 172, 174, 176, 178
DOI, 9, 10, 249

E

ecology, 6, 7
economics, 181
education, 145, 148
educators, 142

election, 229, 240, 248
electric circuits, 277
electricity, 12, 15
electronic circuits, 228
encryption, 22, 23, 26
energy, vii, viii, x, 1, 5, 6, 7, 11, 12, 13, 14, 15, 16, 17, 20, 22, 23, 25, 26, 31, 32, 34, 41, 47, 58, 62, 69, 80, 225, 226, 227, 228, 229, 230, 235, 236, 237, 238, 239, 240, 246, 247, 248, 249, 253, 262, 282
energy consumption, vii, viii, 11, 12, 13, 14, 15, 16, 20, 226, 227, 228, 235, 236, 237, 239, 240, 247, 248
energy efficiency, 5, 12
energy expenditure, 7, 15
energy supply, 47
engineering, ix, 7, 141, 143, 151, 153, 154, 155, 157, 179, 180, 181, 223, 291
England, 136, 180
environment, viii, ix, 2, 6, 10, 11, 13, 14, 15, 16, 19, 20, 21, 23, 25, 30, 32, 36, 38, 43, 46, 52, 74, 84, 85, 89, 91, 93, 98, 108, 112, 132, 135, 141, 143, 144, 145, 146, 147, 148, 156, 171, 177, 181, 226, 228, 229, 231, 247, 256
environmental change, 229
environmental conditions, 46, 80
environmental degradation, 46
environmental effects, 15
environmental impact, 15
environmental protection, 253
Environmental Protection Agency (EPA), viii, 11, 12, 13, 14, 15, 16, 17
environmental sustainability, 16
equipment, vii, 1, 15, 275
European Commission, 46, 70
evaporation, 252, 253, 254, 255, 256, 258
evolution, 75, 76, 171, 180
execution, 23, 129, 130, 147, 169, 174, 176, 295
experimental condition, 279

F

Facebook, 12
facial expression, ix, 199, 200, 216, 217, 221, 223
facilitated communication, 178
faster delivery, 247, 248
FAT file system, xi, 285, 286, 287, 288, 289, 291, 297, 298, 299
feedback inhibition, 187
filters, 126, 243
fingerprints, 84
Finland, 137
fire detection, vii, 1, 2
fixation, 186, 190
flexibility, 46, 117, 184, 188
fluid, 253, 254, 255, 256, 257, 258, 265, 267, 269
food, 6, 7
force, 255, 272
Ford, 149
forest fire, vii, 1, 2, 4
formula, x, 85, 93, 94, 104, 115, 118, 251, 253, 254, 266, 267, 268
France, 136
fusion, 26, 28, 117

G

Galileo, 70
gender differences, ix, 141, 142, 143, 145
gender gap, 143
genetics, 155, 178
genre, 184
geolocation, 135
geometry, 77, 89, 92
Germany, 70, 222
gestures, 189, 196
Google, 141
GPS, 2, 74, 76, 77, 78, 79, 131, 132, 134, 136, 137, 139, 232, 234
gravitational force, 256
gravity, 255, 274
green IT, vii, viii, 11, 13, 15, 16
greening, viii, 11, 13, 15, 16
grouping, 25
growth, vii, 11, 12, 177
guidance, 176, 178, 283
guidelines, 148, 155, 157, 163, 165, 176, 185, 198

H

Hawaii, 249
health, ix, 20, 183, 184, 235
health care, 184
health services, ix, 183, 184
heat capacity, x, 251, 252, 253, 255, 256, 257, 258, 262, 265
heat removal, x, 251
heat transfer, x, 251, 252, 253, 256, 262, 269, 273
height, 7, 188, 262, 267, 276
high school, 142
higher education, 151
histogram, 85, 86, 126
history, vii, 11, 12, 16, 167, 299
Hong Kong, 41, 135, 141, 148, 149
Hops, 230, 246
host, 15, 27, 28, 34, 277
House, 134, 180
housing, 273
human, ix, x, 7, 62, 80, 145, 184, 185, 199, 200, 202, 204, 211, 212, 213, 221, 222, 223
human behavior, 185
human body, 184
Hungary, 179
hybrid, vii, x, xi, 48, 110, 116, 285, 286, 288, 291, 297, 299

I

ICC, 9
icon, 265, 269
IDSs, 28
illumination, 253, 254, 280, 282
image, vii, ix, 10, 132, 136, 139, 151, 186, 187, 190, 199, 200, 201, 203, 204, 205, 207, 208, 212, 213, 215, 216, 221, 222, 223
images, 186, 196, 200, 201, 213, 216
impairments, ix, 183, 188
improvements, 12, 155, 164, 269
independence, 190
indexing, 139
India, 285
individual characteristics, 186
individual differences, 143, 149
individualization, 148, 149
individuals, viii, 19, 20, 144, 148, 184, 185
industry(ies), vii, ix, 8, 17, 23, 46, 131, 141, 142, 153, 266, 269, 282
inertia, 187
inertial sensors, viii, 73, 76, 117, 122
information processing, 2, 144, 145
information seeking, 149
information technology, 149, 180
infrastructure, 15, 36, 74, 79, 136
initial state, 121
initiation, 247, 255
injury, 189
INS, 137, 139
insulation, 269
integration, 76, 117, 122, 126, 132, 139, 163, 172, 174, 178
integrity, viii, 19, 21, 26, 27, 38, 46, 77
interdependence, 163, 174, 178
interface, 20, 48, 74, 148, 168, 184, 189, 190, 196, 207, 215, 222, 252, 255, 256, 286, 293, 294, 298
internet, vii, viii, 9, 11, 12, 13, 14, 15, 16, 17, 42, 134, 141, 215
intervals, 128
intrusion detection, vii, 1, 27, 28, 42
Israel, 138
Italy, 136, 149, 249

J

Japan, 199, 200, 223
Java, 171, 207, 215
Jordan, 283

K

Kalman Filtering, ix, 73, 117, 120
Korea, 299

L

labeling, 16
laminar, 251
landscape, ix, 73
languages, ix, 153, 154, 155, 156, 177, 178, 181
laptop, 21, 93, 110, 125, 288
latency, xi, 27, 33, 247, 285, 286, 289, 290, 291, 294, 296, 297, 298
Latin America, 179
lead, 7, 15, 27, 122, 148, 255, 293
leakage, 236
learners, 144, 145, 146, 151
learning, ix, 105, 141, 142, 143, 144, 145, 146, 147, 148, 149, 150, 151, 185, 187, 192, 193, 196
learning difficulties, 144
learning process, 142
learning styles, ix, 141, 143, 144, 145, 146, 147, 148, 149, 150, 151
LED, x, 251, 253, 254, 277, 278, 279, 280, 281, 282
lens, 188
lesions, 184
life expectancy, ix, 183
life experiences, 185
lifetime, vii, viii, 1, 6, 8, 45, 46, 54, 58, 59, 62, 69, 254, 277, 282
light, 131, 189, 253, 277
light emitting diode, 253
line graph, 211
linear model, 105
linear systems, 117
living environment, 6
localization, viii, ix, 3, 73, 74, 122, 131, 132, 135, 136, 138
location information, 2, 3, 8, 25, 26, 30, 36, 37, 41
logging, 132
longevity, x, 225, 226, 228, 229, 235, 239, 240, 247
luminescence, 253

M

MAC protocols, 32
machine learning, 103
machinery, 254
management, viii, 11, 13, 15, 16, 22, 23, 24, 25, 26, 27, 37, 40, 74, 154, 155, 157, 176, 178, 179, 181, 235, 239, 240, 243, 246
manufacturing, 13, 15, 265, 269, 279, 280
mapping, 227, 292
marginalization, 103
marketing, 145, 253
Mars, 234, 248
Maryland, 249, 250
mass, 253, 255, 256, 274
materials, x, 144, 189, 251, 253, 255, 257, 264, 265, 268, 271, 278, 282, 283
matrix, 75, 76, 87, 106, 107, 117, 118, 120, 129

matter, 5, 8, 148, 150, 228, 291
MBTI, 146, 150
measurements, 33, 46, 54, 74, 78, 79, 82, 83, 84, 85, 86, 87, 88, 90, 91, 93, 103, 107, 117, 118, 121, 122, 125, 126, 134, 200, 222, 237, 238, 269
medicine, 226, 247
membership, 151, 205, 206, 208, 212
memory, vii, ix, 5, 20, 22, 23, 25, 34, 50, 183, 184, 185, 186, 187, 190, 196, 197, 207, 208, 215, 226, 228, 247, 288, 291, 298, 299
memory loss, 184
memory processes, 184, 186
mental health, ix, 183, 184
mental impairment, ix, 183
mental model, 144, 145, 151
messages, viii, 21, 27, 29, 32, 33, 34, 35, 45, 46, 48, 49, 54, 55, 56, 57, 58, 62, 69, 147, 189, 230, 242
meta-analysis, 151
metals, x, 251
meter, 89, 126
methodology, viii, 16, 20, 38, 45, 46, 62, 69, 74, 114, 137, 154, 155, 156, 157, 158, 162, 163, 165, 167, 169, 173, 176, 178, 179
Mexico, 183
Microsoft, 12, 207, 215, 260, 268, 285, 286, 287, 288, 299
military, vii, 1, 2, 8, 20, 226, 232, 235, 240, 247
Ministry of Education, 70
mobile communication, 134
mobile computing, vii, viii, 73, 74, 184
mobile device, vii, ix, 73, 79, 80, 81, 131, 184, 185, 188, 189, 190, 191, 196
mobile phone, 7
mobile robots, 3
model specification, 179
modelling, ix, 141, 148, 153, 179, 180
models, ix, x, 13, 50, 85, 86, 103, 107, 108, 110, 117, 121, 127, 137, 141, 143, 144, 145, 150, 151, 154, 173, 174, 178, 179, 235, 238, 239, 248, 251, 254, 273, 282
modules, x, 37, 212, 221, 251, 252, 258, 269, 273, 274, 276, 282
motivation, 145, 154, 173
motor impairments, ix, 183
motor skills, 184
multidimensional, 99, 139

N

naming, 290
navigation system, 74, 117
neighbor list, 34
Netherlands, 149
networking, 13, 17, 49, 200
neural networks, 105, 110, 223, 240
neurologist, 185
neurons, 99
New Zealand, 151
next generation, 131
nickel, 275, 282
nodes, 2, 4, 5, 7, 13, 20, 22, 23, 24, 25, 26, 27, 28, 29, 30, 31, 32, 33, 34, 35, 36, 37, 38, 46, 51, 59, 74, 80, 87, 88, 89, 92, 100, 109, 225, 226, 227, 228, 229, 230, 231, 232, 233, 235, 239, 240, 246, 247, 248
nonlinear systems, 76, 119
numerical analysis, 269

O

obstacles, 93, 94
oil, 275
online learning, 151
operating system, 47, 49, 50, 51, 285, 286, 287, 295, 298
operations, xi, 23, 37, 239, 282, 285, 286, 291, 294, 296, 297, 298
opportunities, viii, 13, 19, 21, 37, 235
optimization, 2, 7, 23, 155, 240, 276
orbit, 77, 232
organism, 7

P

Pakistan, 135
parallel, ix, 153, 251, 283
participants, 146, 155, 157, 161, 170, 173, 176
Particle Filtering, ix, 73, 76, 117, 121, 137
partition, 287, 295
path planning, 3
pathways, 262
pattern recognition, 84
PCBs, 280
pedagogy, 148
peer assessment, 142
personality, 143, 146, 149, 150, 180, 221
personality type, 146, 149, 180
pervasive computing, 39
physical properties, 274
physics, 265
physiology, 151
pictogram, 188, 196
pitch, 278, 281
plasticity, ix, 183, 184, 185
plastics, x, 251, 273
platform, viii, 45, 46, 47, 59, 69, 74, 77, 81, 122, 123, 131, 171, 177, 190, 196, 236, 237
policy, 27, 37
portability, 132
Portugal, 149
predictability, 101
probability, 4, 5, 24, 28, 86, 103, 104, 105, 106, 118, 121, 125, 126, 135, 230, 232, 233, 234, 248, 252, 289
probability density function, 104, 105, 126

probability distribution, 103, 106, 125, 135
problem-solving, 145, 151, 154
procedural knowledge, 143
process control, 156
programming, vii, ix, 141, 142, 143, 144, 145, 146, 147, 148, 149, 150, 151, 154, 156, 171, 180, 207, 215, 298
programming languages, 154, 156, 298
project, ix, 70, 153, 155, 157, 158, 161, 163, 164, 165, 166, 167, 168, 170, 171, 172, 173, 174, 175, 176, 177, 178
propagation, viii, 73, 77, 84, 93, 95, 100, 103, 106, 110, 114, 115, 229, 231, 241, 242, 243, 247, 269
proposition, 142
protection, 21, 22, 24, 30, 35, 38, 74
prototype, 158, 163, 168, 169, 174, 276
pumps, 15
pure water, 254

Q

quality of life, 184
quality of service (QoS), 9, 12, 14, 38, 229, 247, 248
quantization, 139
queuing theory, 229

R

race, 143, 184, 294
radar, 20
radio, viii, 2, 31, 34, 37, 45, 50, 58, 69, 70, 73, 77, 79, 80, 86, 87, 88, 89, 90, 93, 103, 106, 110, 111, 112, 113, 114, 116, 131, 132, 135, 226, 236, 237
radius, 77, 81, 123, 124, 256
random walk, 37
reactions, 221
reading, xi, 125, 180, 184, 186, 269, 285, 294, 296, 298
reality, 2, 6, 26, 34, 132, 145, 215
recall, 188, 191
reception, 31, 229, 231, 232, 236, 237
recognition, 110, 200, 222, 223
recommendations, x, 15, 188, 189, 225, 226
recycling, 16
redundancy, 5, 29
regression model, 103, 105
rehabilitation, 185
reliability, 4, 15, 235, 248, 282, 288
renewable energy, 16
repetitions, 191
replication, 15
reproduction, 186, 187, 196
requirements, vii, 1, 2, 20, 46, 83, 139, 163, 167, 181, 188
resistance, 252, 267, 274, 275
resolution, 89, 136, 188, 207, 215
resource allocation, 14, 74
resource management, 155
resources, viii, 7, 11, 12, 13, 14, 16, 34, 38, 46, 130, 142, 143, 176
response, 6, 25, 51, 222, 226, 255
response time, 255
restrictions, 162, 166, 169
reusability, 46
risk(s), 15, 6, 16, 24, 35, 43, 146, 162, 166, 169, 183, 230, 233, 234, 248
root, 26, 28, 48, 51, 126, 292
routes, 27, 49, 51, 240, 246
rubber, 278
rules, 74, 163, 196, 201, 204, 205, 206, 208, 212, 213, 215

S

samplings, 213
Sarajevo, 139
scaling, 33, 89, 90, 92
school, 141, 142, 147, 148, 149
science, vii, ix, 10, 75, 141, 143, 145, 146, 149, 151
scope, 13, 16, 173, 175, 176, 286
search space, 6
secondary students, 150
secure communication, 36
security, vii, viii, 19, 20, 21, 22, 23, 25, 26, 27, 28, 29, 30, 35, 37, 38, 39, 43, 46, 74, 235
security services, 23
self-efficacy, 144, 145
self-regulation, 185
senses, 31
sensing, vii, viii, 1, 2, 5, 6, 19, 20, 23, 30, 43, 146
sensor nodes, 2, 4, 5, 6, 7, 21, 23, 24, 27, 28, 29, 37, 232, 240
sensors, vii, viii, ix, 1, 3, 4, 5, 8, 20, 28, 33, 34, 36, 42, 46, 73, 74, 76, 77, 80, 117, 122, 131, 132, 184, 226, 228, 229, 232, 234, 235, 237, 239, 240, 247
sensory data, 20, 26, 29
Serbia, 139
servers, 12, 13, 15
services, ix, 12, 15, 30, 36, 43, 117, 155, 161, 183, 184
shape, ix, 6, 21, 73, 184, 205, 252
short-term memory, 189
showing, 96, 124, 157, 186, 265, 269, 295
signals, 2, 46, 77, 78, 79, 86, 99, 117, 135, 136, 231
signs, 189
silicon, 275
silver, 275, 278
simulation, 89, 90, 142, 232, 265, 269, 274, 276, 277, 279, 282, 286, 293, 294, 295, 298
Singapore, 135, 137
social environment, 185
social network, 12
social security, 184
software, vii, ix, 15, 47, 49, 50, 74, 132, 141, 143, 153, 154, 155, 156, 157, 158, 163, 166, 167, 171,

172, 173, 174, 176, 177, 178, 179, 180, 181, 184, 185, 188, 239, 252, 258, 269, 273, 277, 279
solid state, x, xi, 285, 286, 288, 291, 292, 294, 296, 297, 298
solution, 5, 17, 22, 28, 29, 32, 34, 35, 76, 96, 98, 99, 117, 119, 121, 124, 125, 133, 135, 143, 154, 155, 165, 170, 177, 178, 184, 196, 226, 258, 276, 291
Spain, 45, 135, 153, 157
specialists, ix, 183, 184
specifications, 36, 196
speed of light, 87
stabilization, 173
stakeholders, 147
standard deviation, 57, 58, 103, 106, 107, 125, 126, 213
state(s), vii, viii, 1, 7, 19, 21, 31, 34, 37, 73, 74, 75, 76, 77, 117, 118, 121, 125, 185, 246, 253, 255, 274, 275, 282, 286, 287
statistics, 295
STEM, ix, 141, 143
storage, x, xi, 13, 15, 33, 285, 286, 288, 290, 291, 292, 294, 296, 297, 298, 299
strategy use, 37
stress, 255
structure, 3, 24, 25, 30, 154, 155, 159, 167, 185, 189, 228, 239, 253, 254, 255, 256, 258, 266, 267, 273, 282, 287
structuring, 157, 162, 178
style, 145, 146, 148, 149, 150, 151, 188
Sun, 8, 9, 17
surface area, 252
surface tension, 255, 256
surveillance, vii, 1, 2, 6, 7, 8, 21, 30, 38
Sweden, 138
Sybil, 33, 42
symmetry, 278, 281
synchronization, 82, 83
synchronize, ix, 199, 200, 212, 222

T

Taiwan, 251, 274, 283, 284
target, 2, 7, 21, 30, 81, 82, 83, 212
task allocation, 14
task difficulty, 145
taxonomy, viii, 19, 21, 24, 40, 145
teachers, 142, 147
teams, 180
techniques, ix, x, 2, 3, 23, 24, 26, 32, 36, 38, 73, 74, 76, 80, 84, 89, 93, 99, 110, 117, 122, 179, 189, 251, 253, 282, 286
technological advances, 131
technologies, viii, 12, 46, 73, 184, 221
technology, viii, ix, 2, 46, 73, 74, 75, 77, 131, 132, 135, 139, 141, 142, 143, 146, 179, 183, 196, 232, 235
temperature, x, 80, 200, 251, 252, 253, 254, 255, 256, 257, 262, 269, 274, 275, 277, 279, 280, 282
testing, 23, 96, 102, 107, 124, 142, 143, 184, 185, 190, 191, 196, 252, 269, 274, 275
thermal resistance, 252, 254, 256, 258, 260, 262, 265, 269, 274, 276, 277, 278, 279
thermodynamic cycle, 255
threats, 142
throws, 215
timbre, 189
topology, vii, viii, 13, 23, 29, 33, 45, 46, 48, 50, 62, 69
total energy, 235, 237, 239
toxicity, 265
tracks, ix, 73, 186
trade-off, 20
training, 101, 103, 105, 106, 108, 109, 110, 114, 179
trajectory, 96, 98, 99, 102, 107, 124, 125, 132, 133
transducer, 20
transfer pricing, 13
transformation, 201, 211
transmission, 20, 21, 27, 29, 31, 34, 226, 227, 229, 230, 231, 232, 234, 236, 237, 238, 246, 247, 248
transport, 34, 46, 255
treatment, 184, 280
tree routing topology, vii
triangulation, 3, 4
turbulent flows, 251
Turkey, 225, 283

U

UK, 149, 151, 249
United Nations, 183
United States (USA), 42, 43, 77, 135, 136, 138, 149, 150, 151, 197, 249, 250, 298, 299
universities, 142, 157
urban, 81, 82, 134, 232, 234
urban areas, 81, 232

V

vacuum, 253, 254, 255, 265
vapor, x, 251, 253, 254, 255, 256, 265, 266, 267, 268, 269, 271, 273, 274, 276, 277, 278, 279, 280, 282
variables, ix, 103, 141, 144, 147, 148, 246, 266, 267, 280
variations, 6, 99, 101, 106, 135, 142, 143, 161, 223
vector, 75, 77, 86, 87, 100, 103, 201, 203, 213
vehicles, 147
velocity, 77, 78, 122, 123, 269, 272, 279
video games, 143
viscosity, 255, 265
visualization, 33, 142, 145, 147, 151, 174
vocabulary, ix, 153, 154, 156, 157, 172, 173, 177

W

Washington, 134, 299
waste, 32, 34, 228
water, 234, 248, 256
weakness, 24
web, 12, 167, 174
web service, 167
welding, 264, 271, 280
windows, 147, 265, 268, 299
wireless connectivity, 79, 80
wireless networks, 22, 42, 49, 74, 77, 83, 226, 228, 235
wireless sensor networks (WSN), vii, viii, 1, 2, 6, 8, 19, 20, 21, 22, 23, 24, 26, 27, 28, 29, 30, 31, 33, 35, 38, 41, 42, 45, 46, 47, 51, 52, 56, 57, 58, 59, 61, 62, 64, 66, 68, 69, 70, 80, 225, 226, 227, 232, 235, 236
wires, 46
workforce, 180
working memory, 189
workload, 161, 288, 289, 290, 291, 293, 296

X

XML, 37, 132